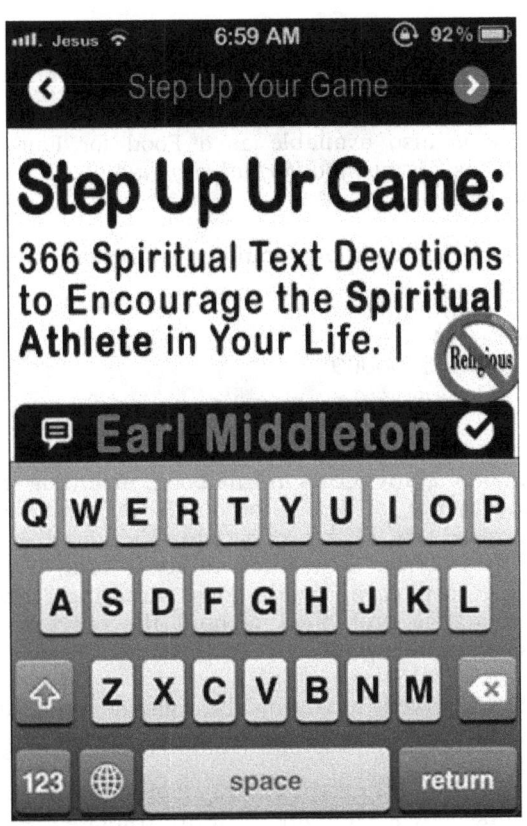

*Step Up Your Game: 366 Spiritual Text Messages to Encourage the Spiritual Athlete in Your Life*
© 2013 by Food for Faith Publications

This title is also available as a Food for Faith Audio product. Visit *http://foodforfaith.org/audiobooks* for more information.

Requests for information should be addressed to:

Food for Faith Publications
P.O. Box 88445
Los Angeles, CA 90009
*www.foodforfaith.org*

This book is the proprietary work of Food for Faith Publications. Many terms in this book, including the title, are trademarks of Food for Faith Publications. Any unauthorized use of this copyrighted material or use of any of these terms in relation to goods and/or services (including seminars, workshops, training programs, classes, etc.) is prohibited without the express written permission of the owner.

All rights reserved, including the right to reproduce this book or portions thereof in any form whatsoever.

FOOD FOR FAITH and the portrayal of an open bible on a plate flanked by a knife and fork are trademarks of Food for Faith Publications.

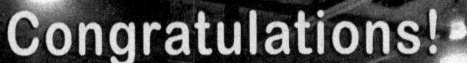

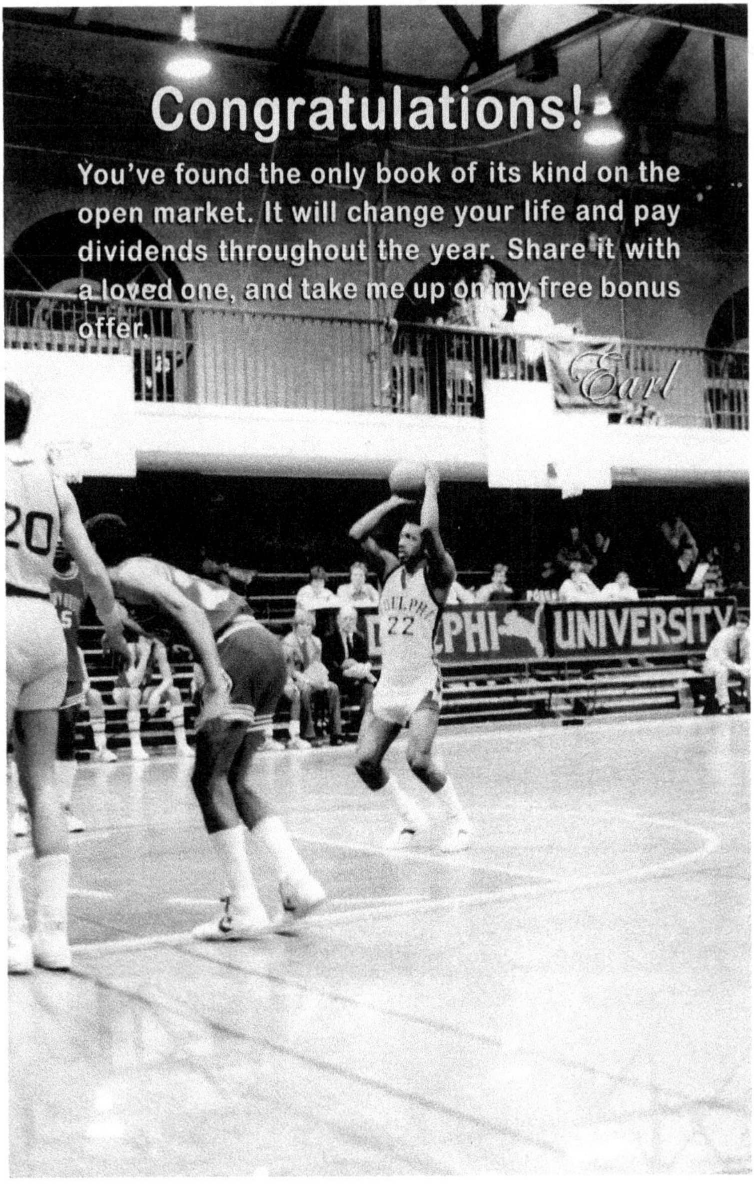
Congratulations!
You've found the only book of its kind on the open market. It will change your life and pay dividends throughout the year. Share it with a loved one, and take me up on my free bonus offer.
Earl
UNIVERSITY
22
20

# ACKNOWLEDGMENTS

Shout out to my internet communities and the three in one. *ons.*


*For the Westchester Rec Paper Clips, and their parents.*


*Lifting a text out of its context leaves you with nothing but a con!*
~ A. Louis Patterson

# Introduction

**The world is changing**, along with the way we communicate in it. In short bursts rather than long tomes. The day of Pentecost has arrived and little did we suspect that it would be in the form of SMS technology and smart phones. Today the world's 6 billion people stay connected by exchanging more than 9 **trillion** text messages per day! The imagined community has truly become a global village.

Jesus told his disciples to go into all the world, every sphere of it, and publish the good news to every person. One way to fulfill that great commission is to invade the SMS world with spiritually centering messages that will stand the test of time. This book is intended to help you do that.

It's structured like a devotional, except it's meant to be shared. A shared devotional if you will. There is **one spiritual-not-religious devotion created for each day of the year.** Type it into your SMS program (or copy and paste if you are reading an e-book version on your tablet or cell phone) and send it to all the athletes you would like to inspire with good news on that day. You'll be **developing your own spiritual sensitivity,** and helping the people in your life you care most about to step up their inner game & live more authentically.

**Bonus**

If you'd like to **receive your own *Step Up Your Game* text message devotion from me at 6:59 each morning** just send an e-mail to my e-mail address found at the end of this book. **Include "Help me step up my inner game" in the subject line and your cell phone number and time zone in the body.** You will receive from me personally, each morning at 6:59 your time, a fresh *Step Up Your Game* text message devotion, different than the one found in this book for that day. That's a two for one offer! For as long as you want them.

**Become part of a growing global community** of spiritual, not religious athletes who are connecting with their higher selves and locating the kingdom within.

And don't worry, **I will never share your information with anyone else** nor send you unsolicited text message ads.

Find my e-mail address at the end of this book, send me your cell phone number and time zone, and begin receiving your free *Step Up Your Game* spiritual text message devotion designed specifically for athletes, directly on your phone each morning!

# January 1

## Step Up Your Game

Athletics, like parenthood, preaching, & protective policing, is a divine calling. You were called to be an athlete and blessed to succeed in your sport.

— Earl Middleton

# January 2

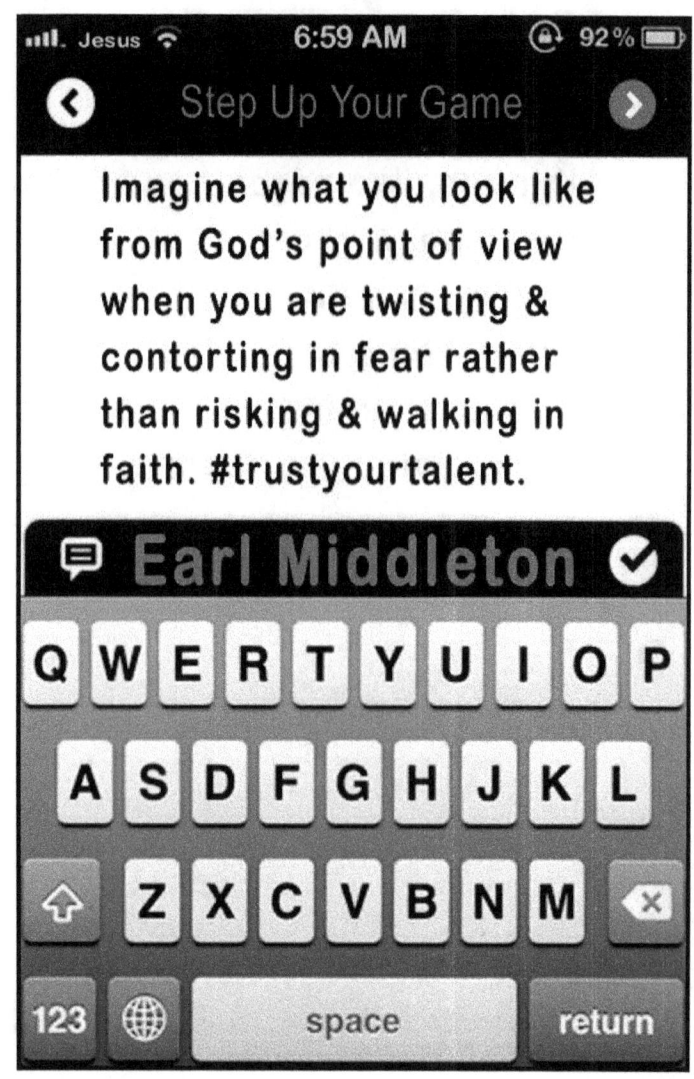

**Step Up Your Game**

Imagine what you look like from God's point of view when you are twisting & contorting in fear rather than risking & walking in faith. #trustyourtalent.

# January 3

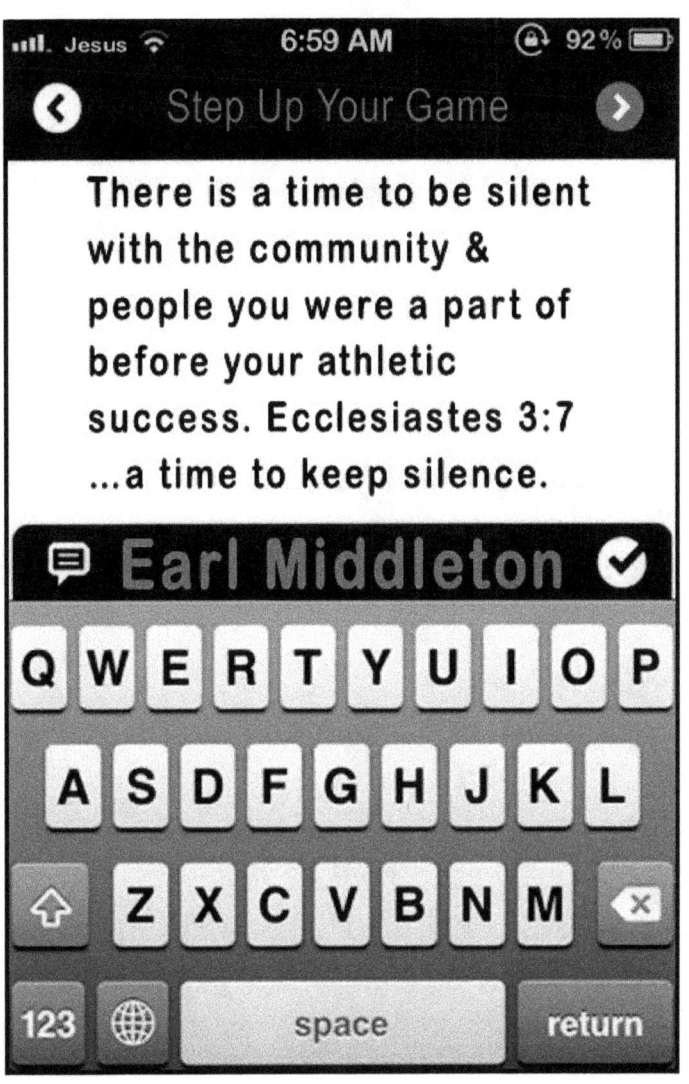

# January 4

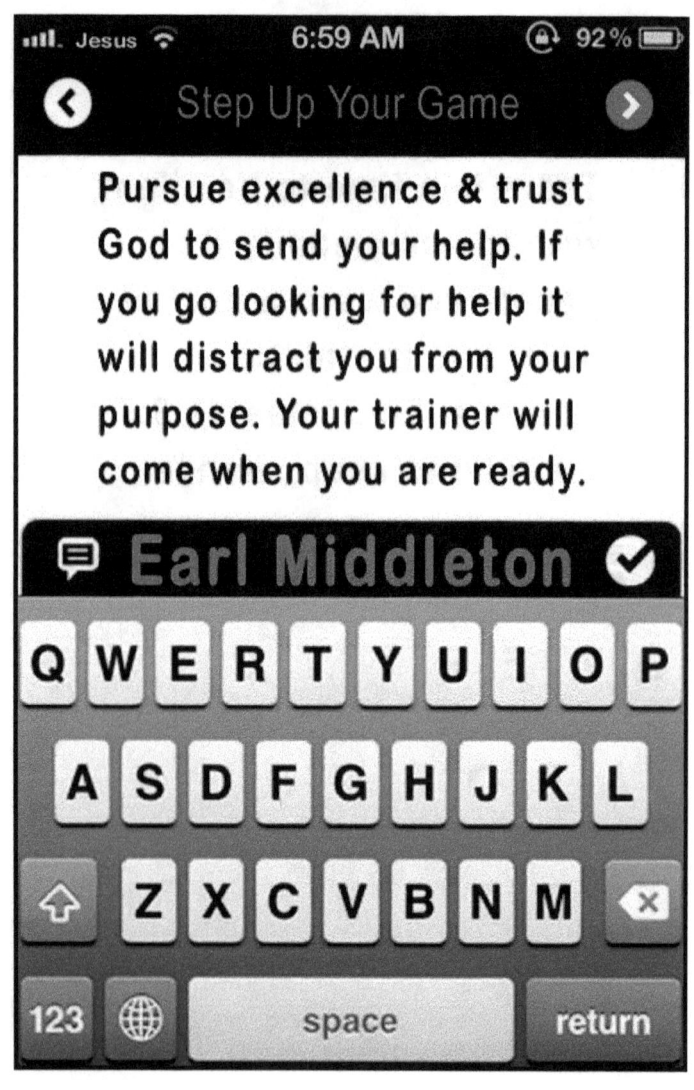

**Step Up Your Game**

Pursue excellence & trust God to send your help. If you go looking for help it will distract you from your purpose. Your trainer will come when you are ready.

Earl Middleton

# January 5

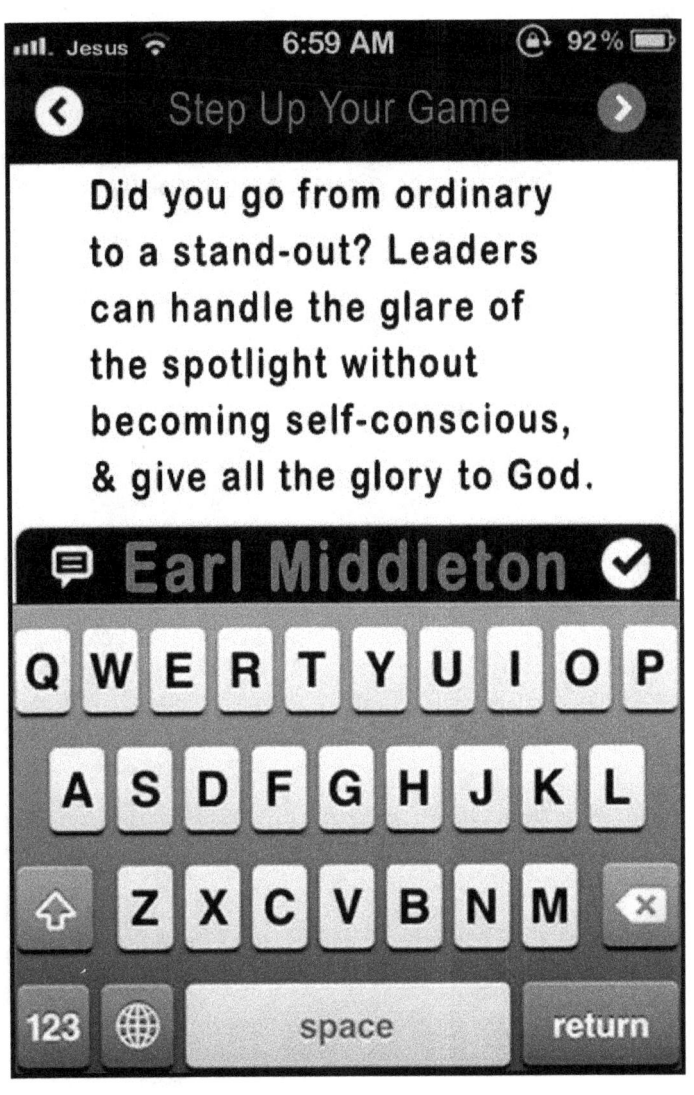

## Step Up Your Game

Did you go from ordinary to a stand-out? Leaders can handle the glare of the spotlight without becoming self-conscious, & give all the glory to God.

— Earl Middleton

# January 6

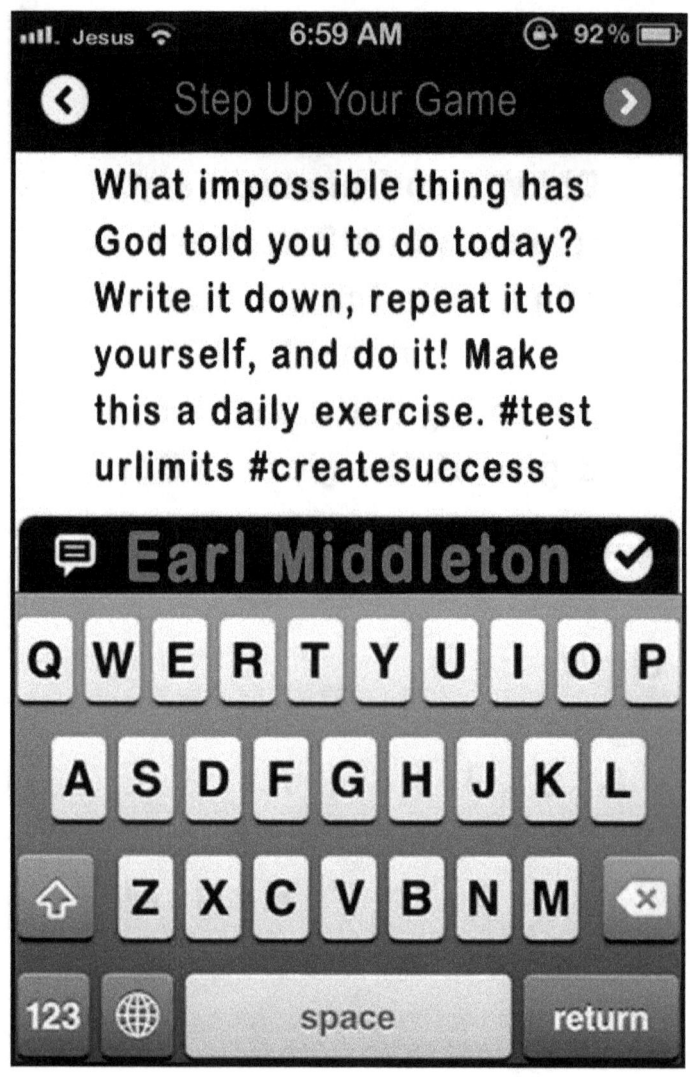

**Step Up Your Game**

What impossible thing has God told you to do today? Write it down, repeat it to yourself, and do it! Make this a daily exercise. #testurlimits #createsuccess

Earl Middleton

# January 7

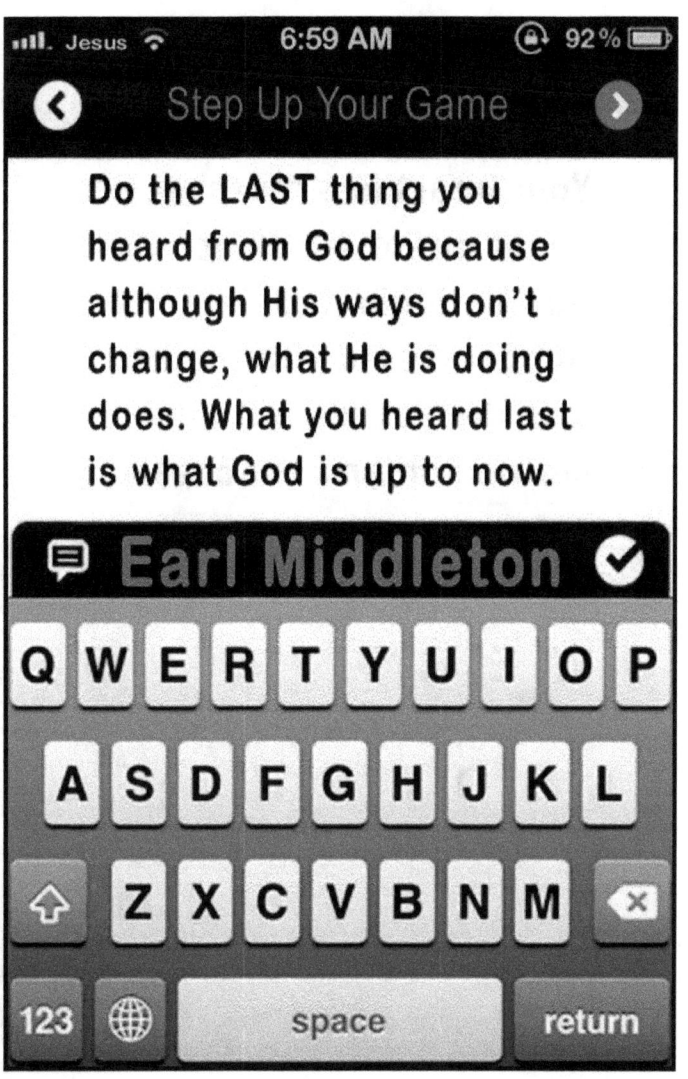

Do the LAST thing you heard from God because although His ways don't change, what He is doing does. What you heard last is what God is up to now.

— Earl Middleton

# January 8

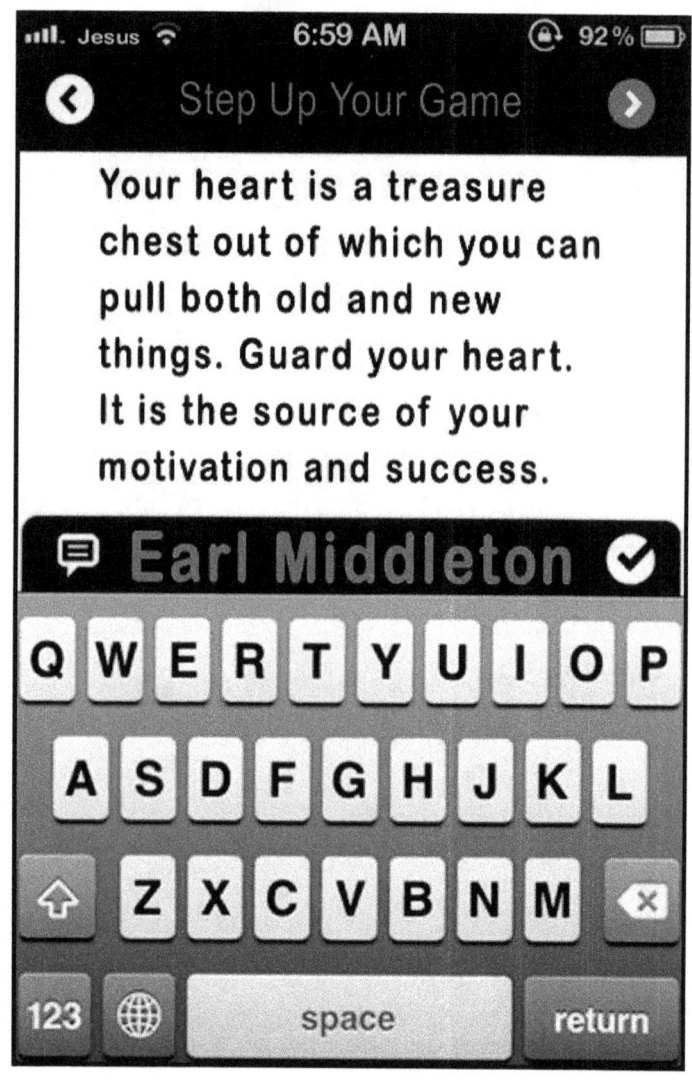

Your heart is a treasure chest out of which you can pull both old and new things. Guard your heart. It is the source of your motivation and success.

— Earl Middleton

# January 9

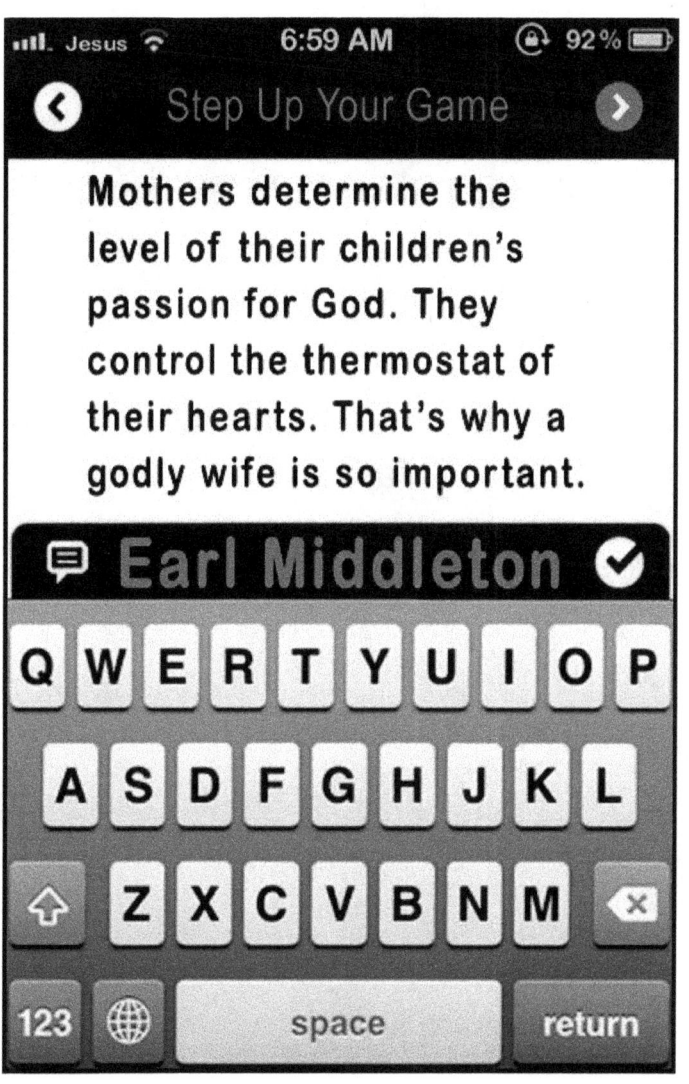

# January 10

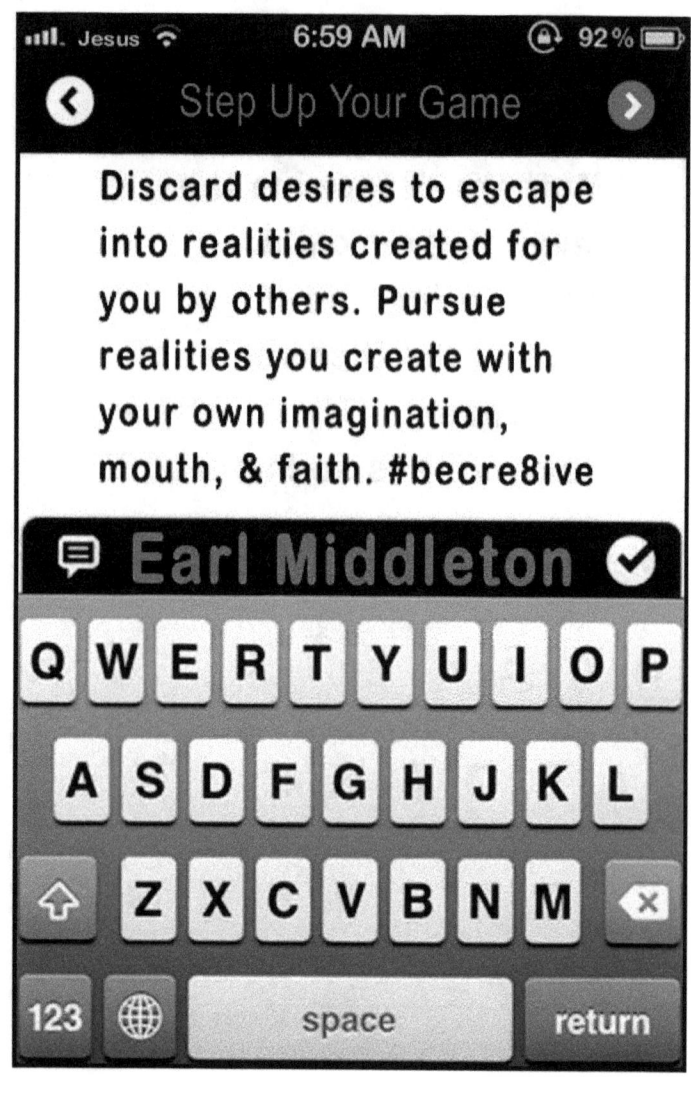

**Step Up Your Game**

Discard desires to escape into realities created for you by others. Pursue realities you create with your own imagination, mouth, & faith. #becre8ive

# January 11

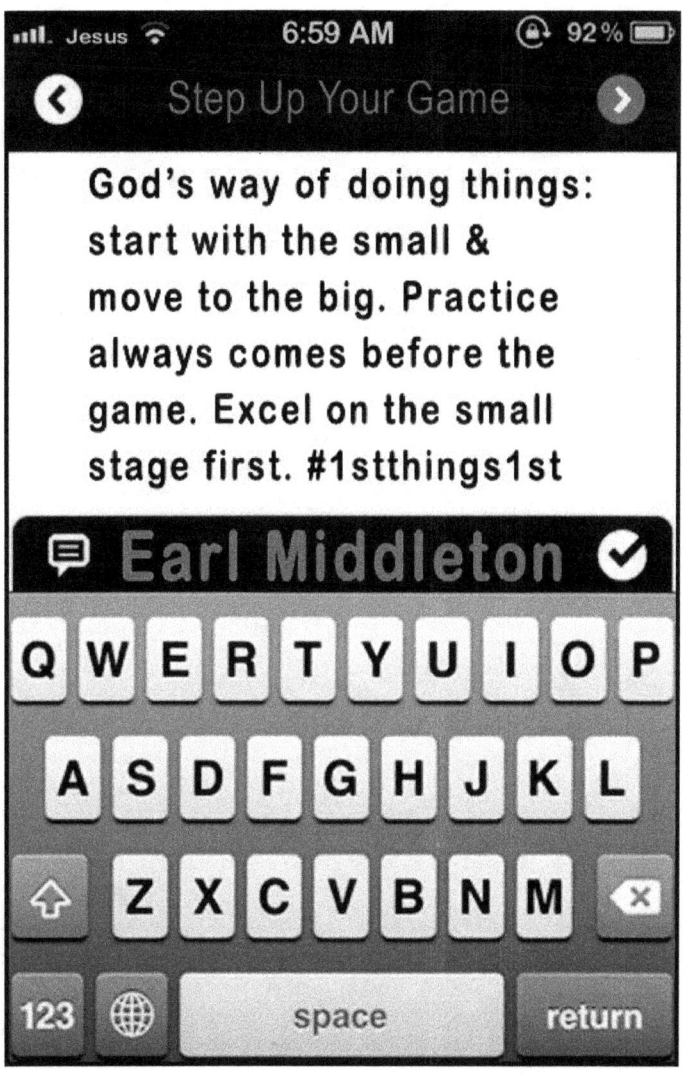

**Step Up Your Game**

God's way of doing things: start with the small & move to the big. Practice always comes before the game. Excel on the small stage first. #1stthings1st

Earl Middleton

# January 12

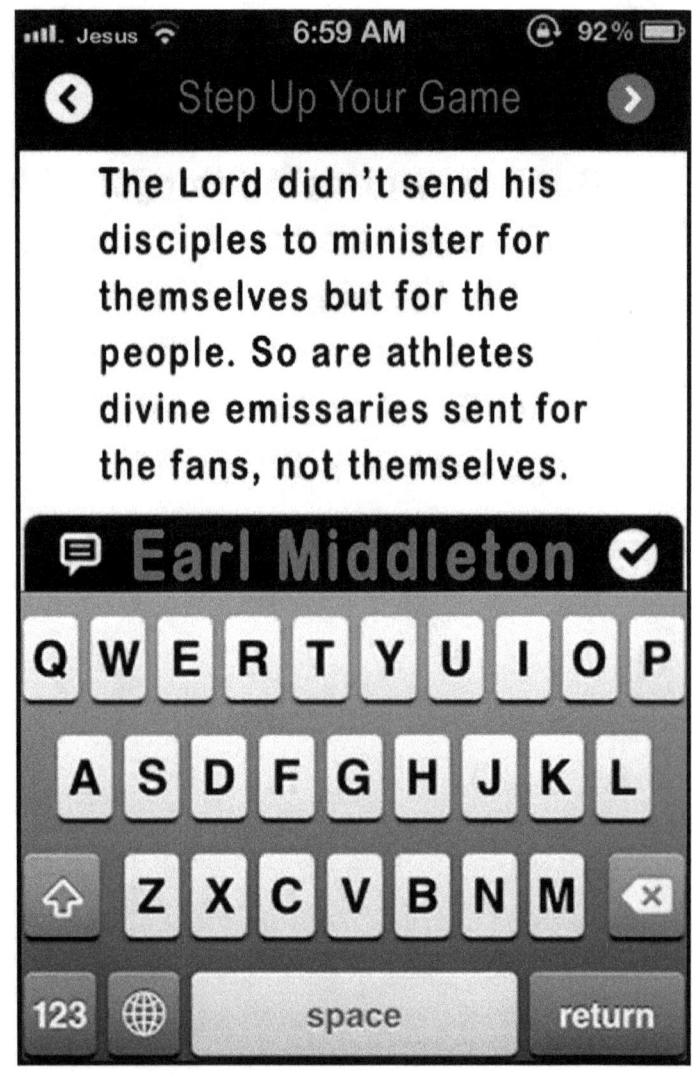

# January 13

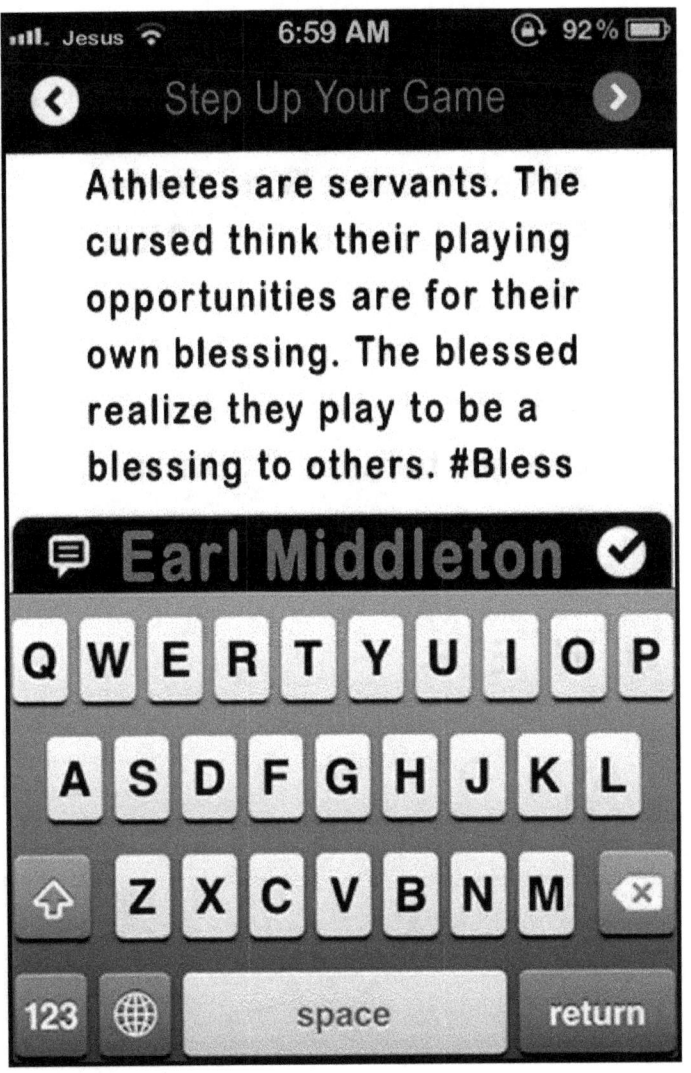

# January 14

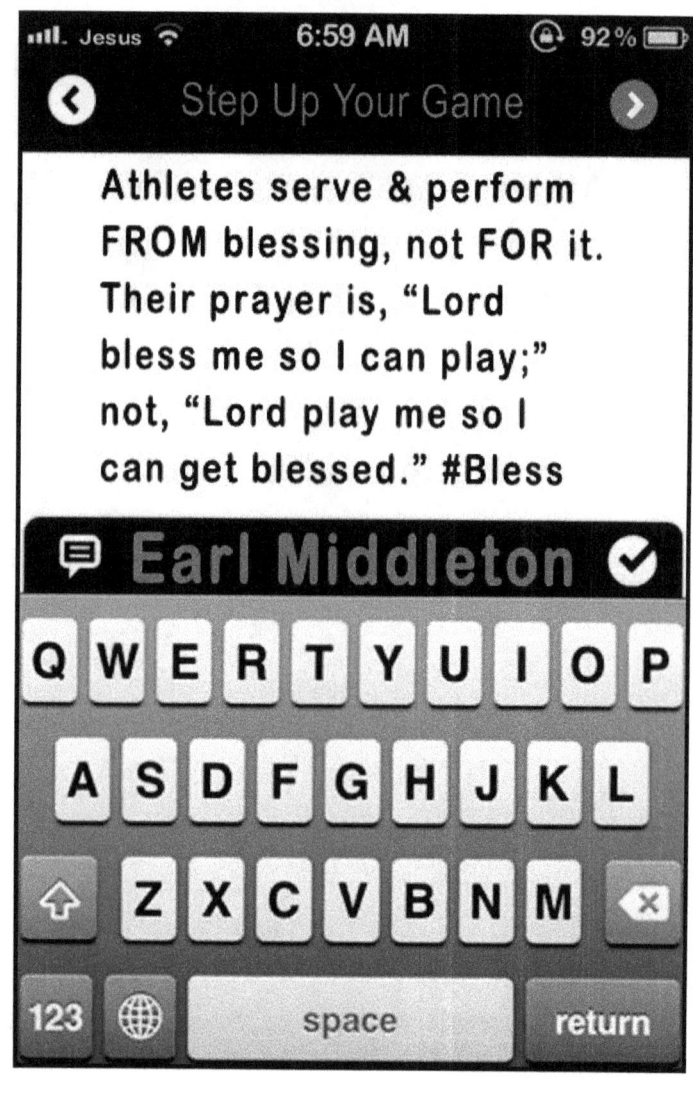

**Step Up Your Game**

Athletes serve & perform FROM blessing, not FOR it. Their prayer is, "Lord bless me so I can play;" not, "Lord play me so I can get blessed." #Bless

— Earl Middleton

# January 15

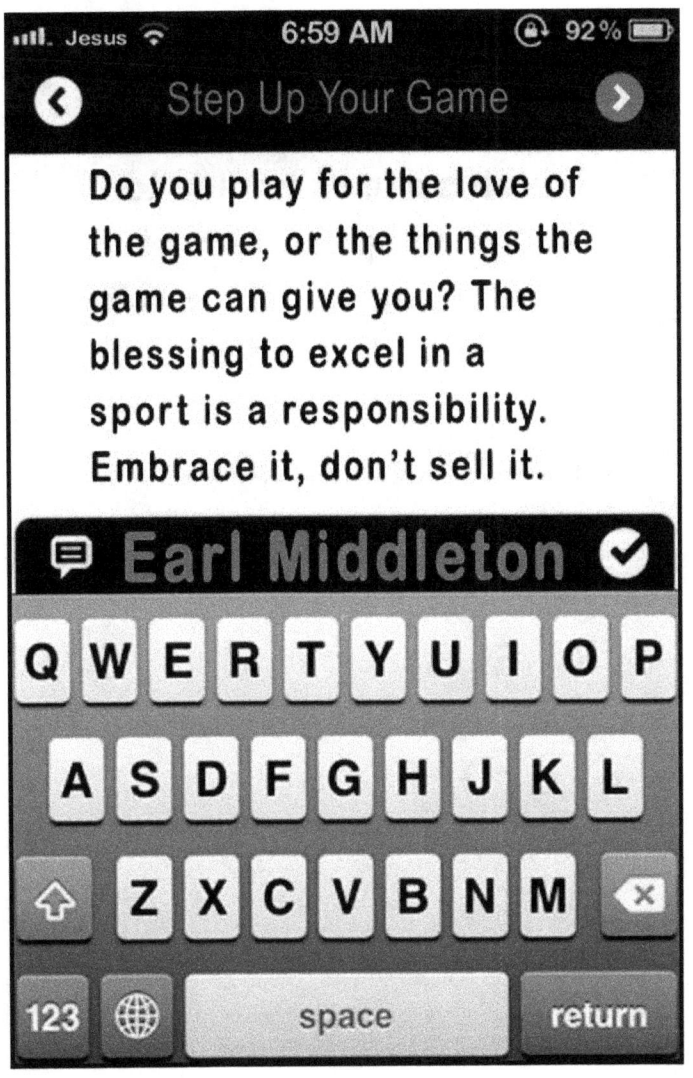

## Step Up Your Game

Do you play for the love of the game, or the things the game can give you? The blessing to excel in a sport is a responsibility. Embrace it, don't sell it.

— Earl Middleton

# January 16

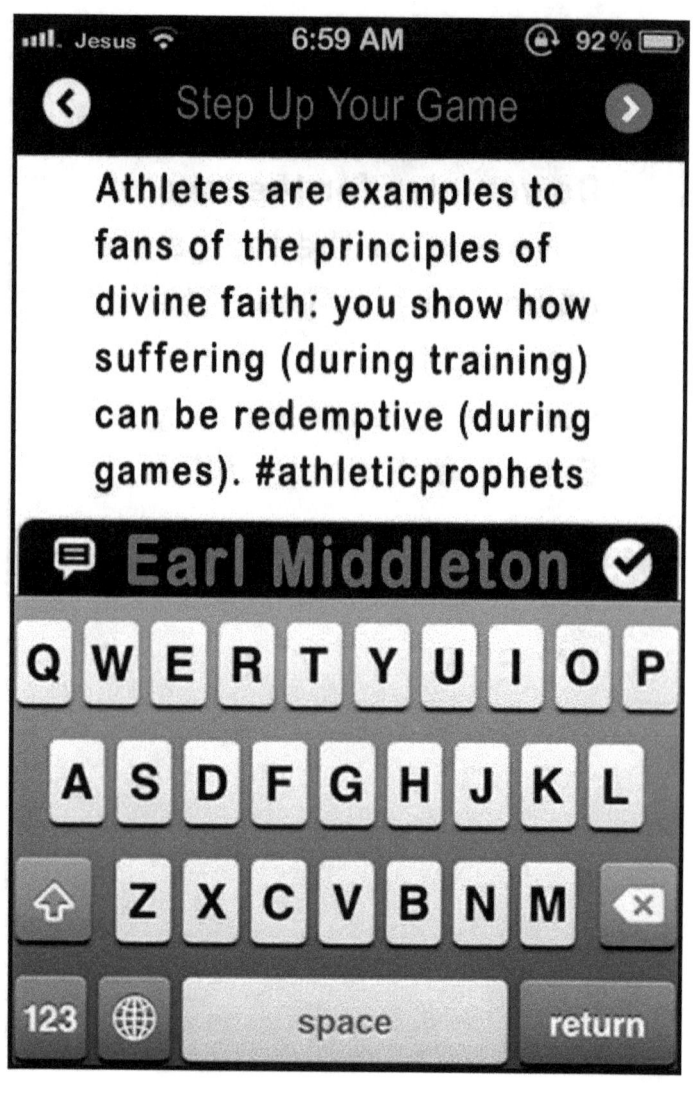

> Athletes are examples to fans of the principles of divine faith: you show how suffering (during training) can be redemptive (during games). #athleticprophets
>
> — Earl Middleton

# January 17

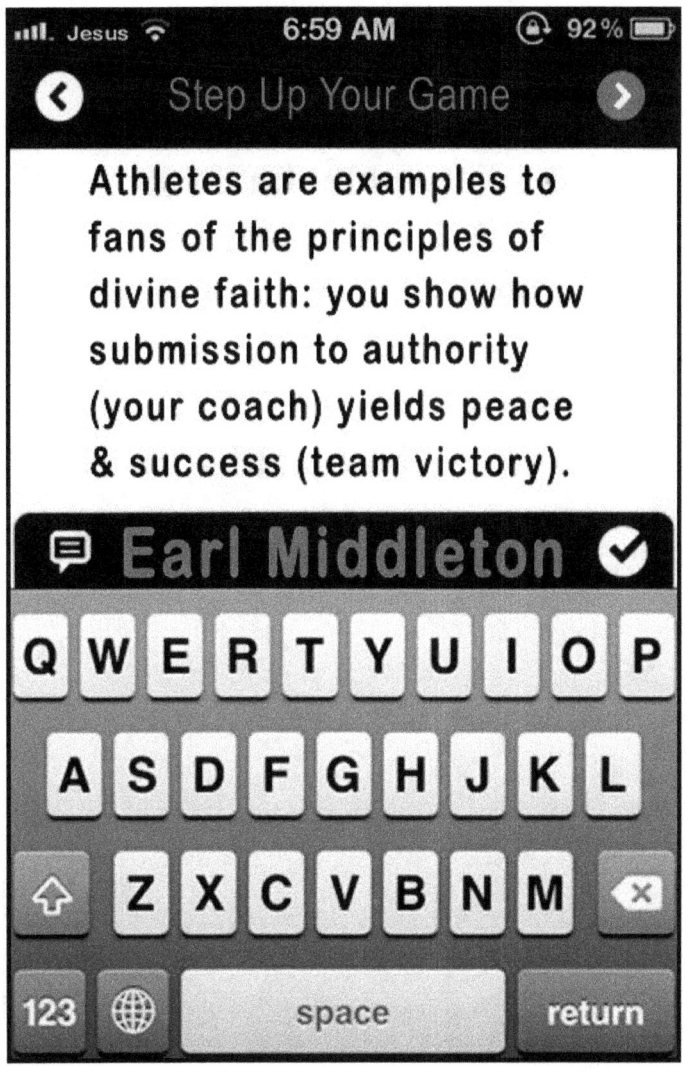

Athletes are examples to fans of the principles of divine faith: you show how submission to authority (your coach) yields peace & success (team victory).

— Earl Middleton

# January 18

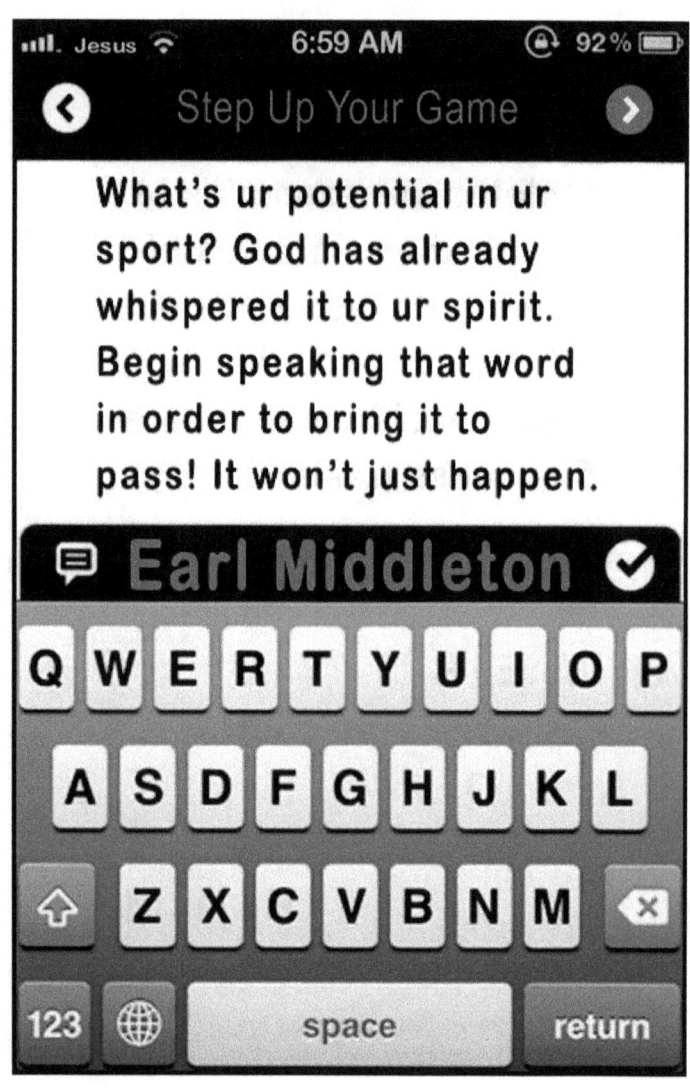

**Step Up Your Game**

What's ur potential in ur sport? God has already whispered it to ur spirit. Begin speaking that word in order to bring it to pass! It won't just happen.

Earl Middleton

# January 19

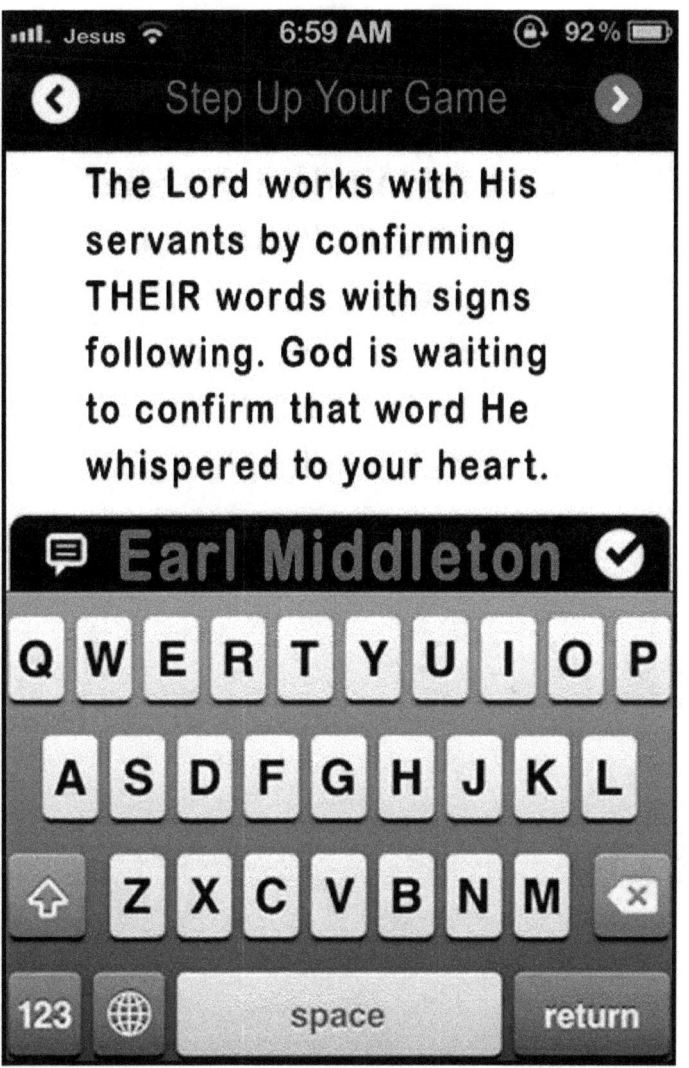

# January 20

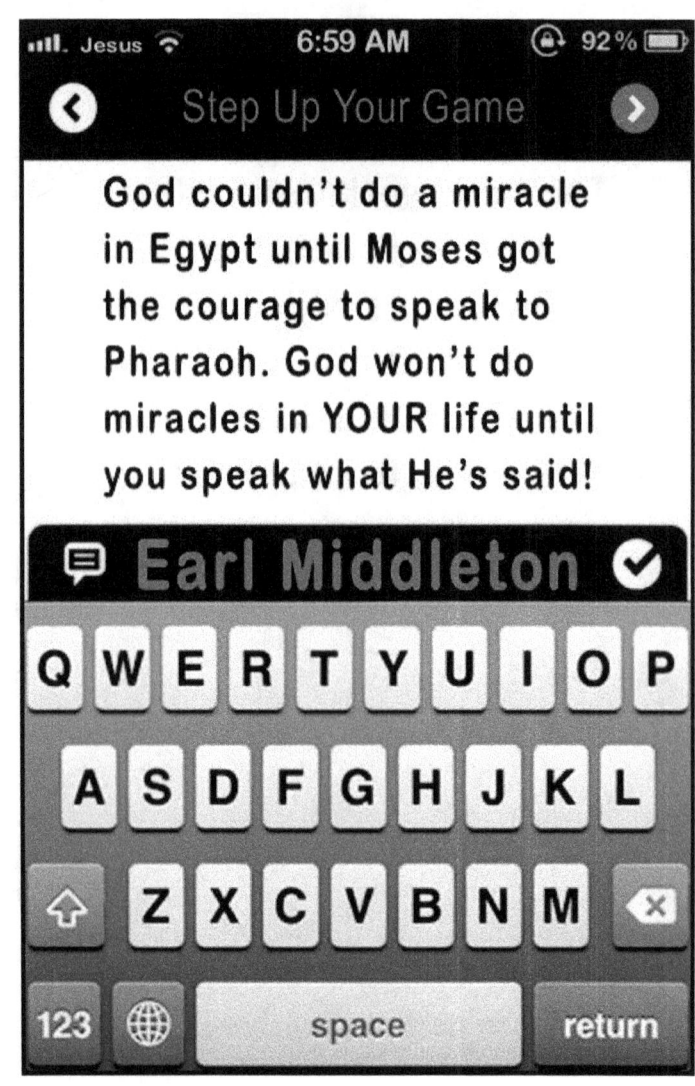

God couldn't do a miracle in Egypt until Moses got the courage to speak to Pharaoh. God won't do miracles in YOUR life until you speak what He's said!

# January 21

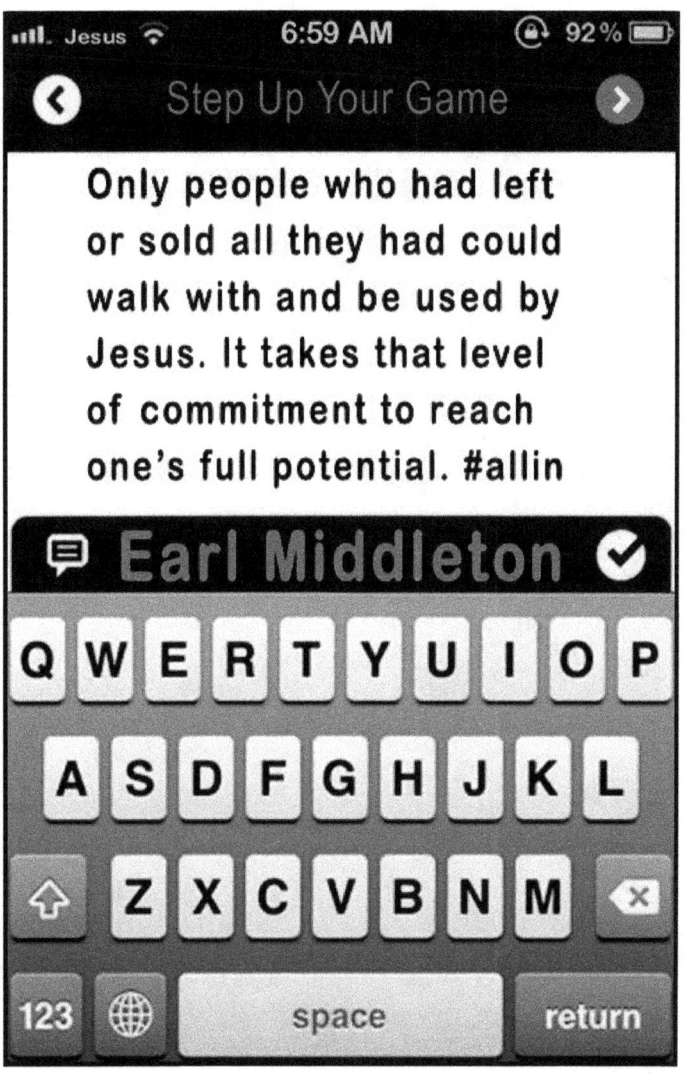

**Step Up Your Game**

Only people who had left or sold all they had could walk with and be used by Jesus. It takes that level of commitment to reach one's full potential. #allin

Earl Middleton

# January 22

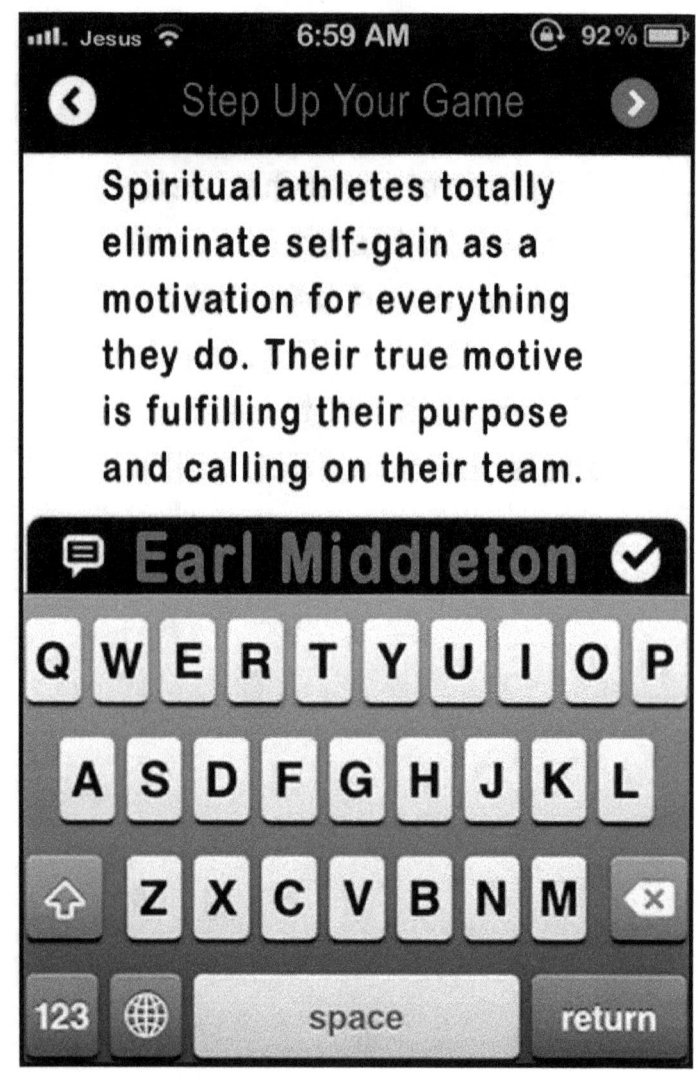

## Step Up Your Game

Spiritual athletes totally eliminate self-gain as a motivation for everything they do. Their true motive is fulfilling their purpose and calling on their team.

— Earl Middleton

# January 23

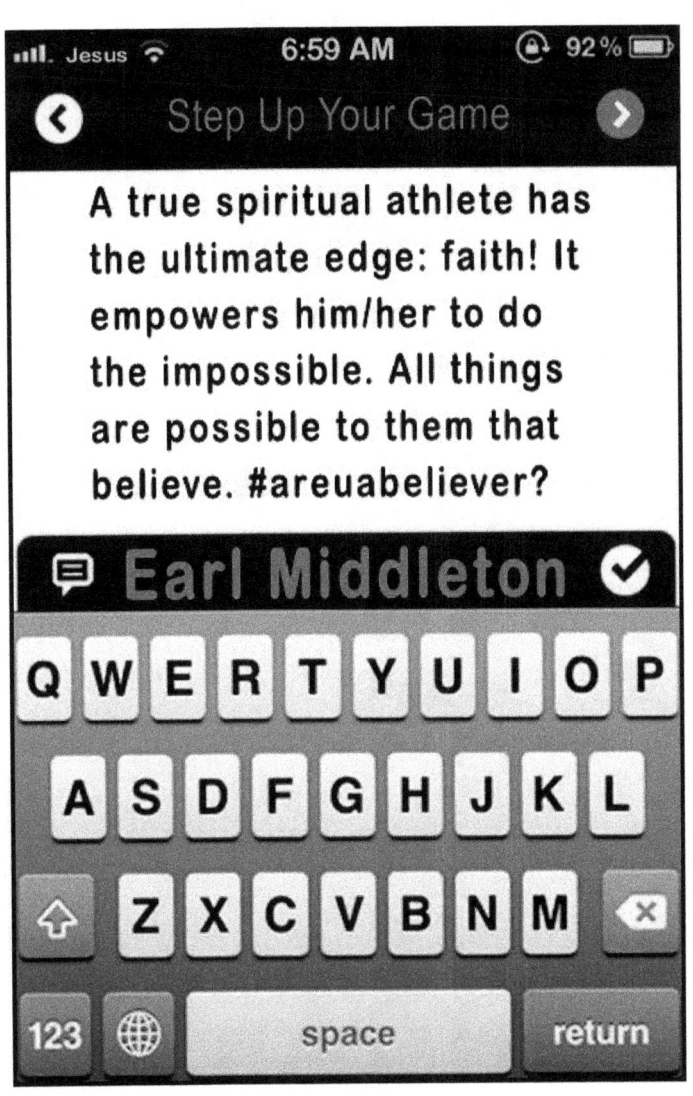

**Step Up Your Game**

A true spiritual athlete has the ultimate edge: faith! It empowers him/her to do the impossible. All things are possible to them that believe. #areuabeliever?

# January 24

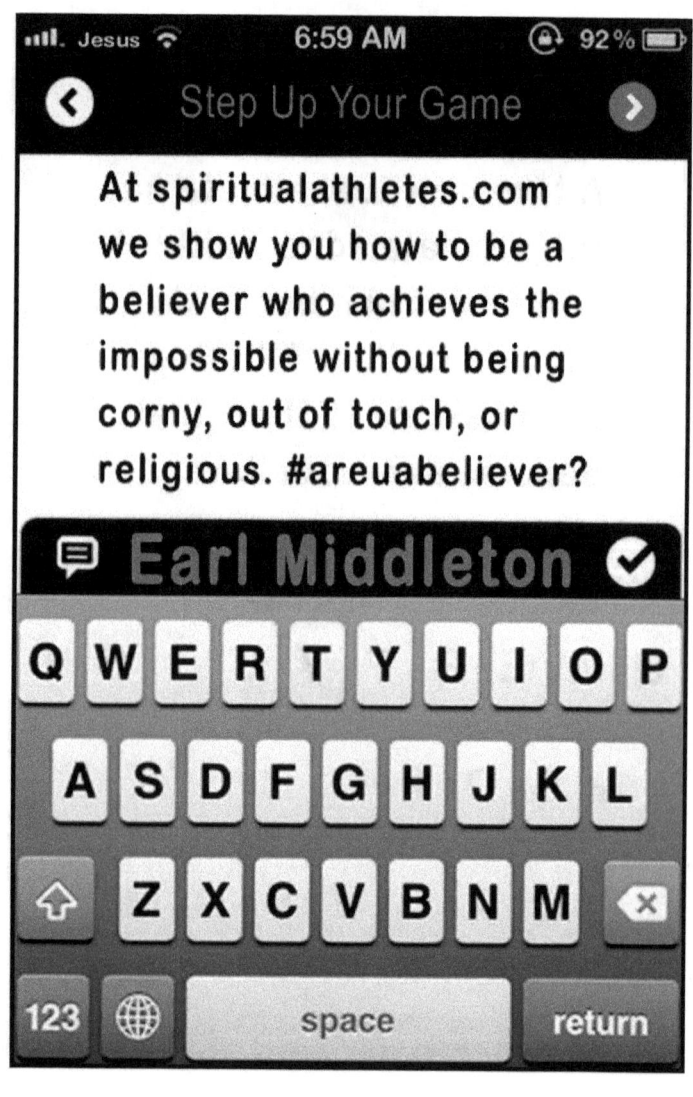

# January 25

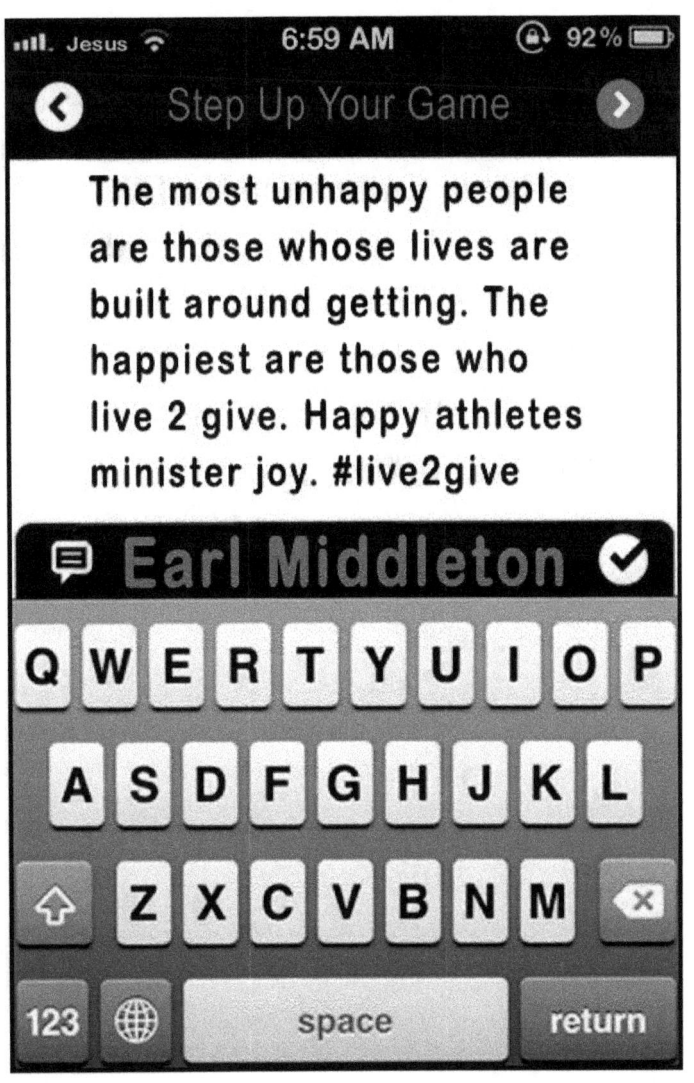

> The most unhappy people are those whose lives are built around getting. The happiest are those who live 2 give. Happy athletes minister joy. #live2give
>
> — Earl Middleton

# January 26

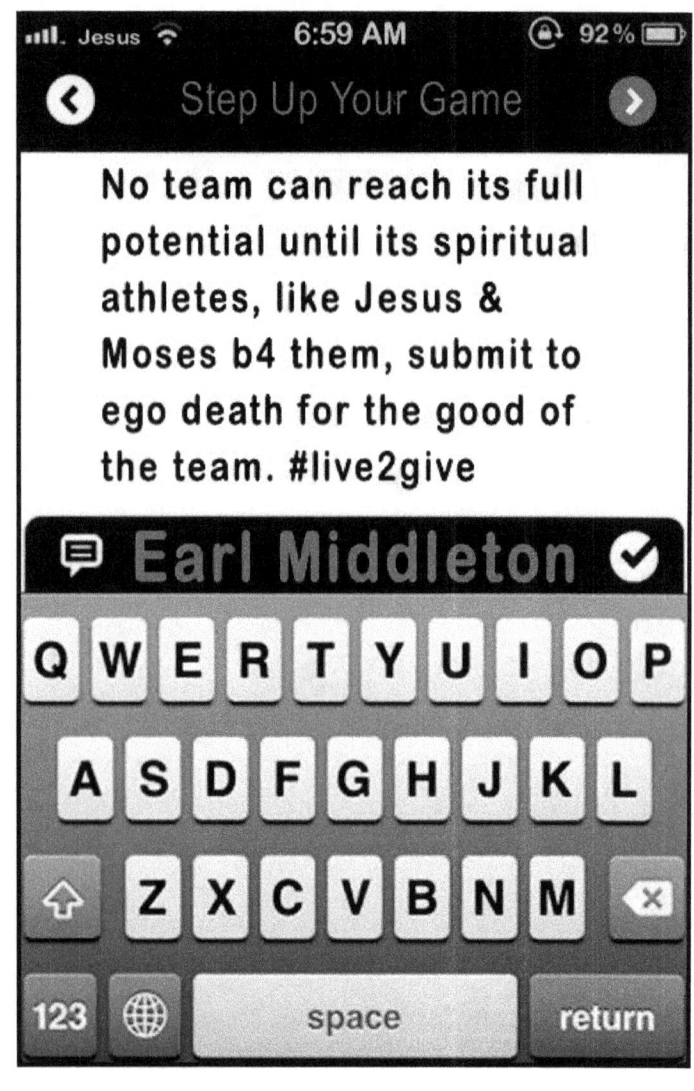

**Step Up Your Game**

No team can reach its full potential until its spiritual athletes, like Jesus & Moses b4 them, submit to ego death for the good of the team. #live2give

# January 27

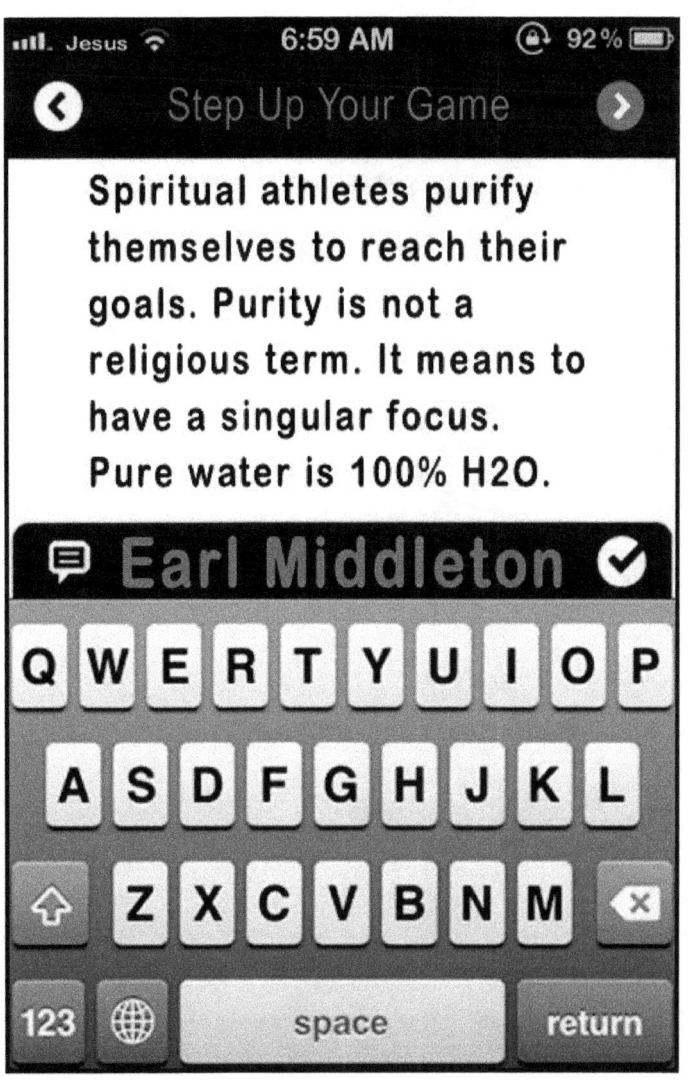

**Step Up Your Game**

Spiritual athletes purify themselves to reach their goals. Purity is not a religious term. It means to have a singular focus. Pure water is 100% H2O.

# January 28

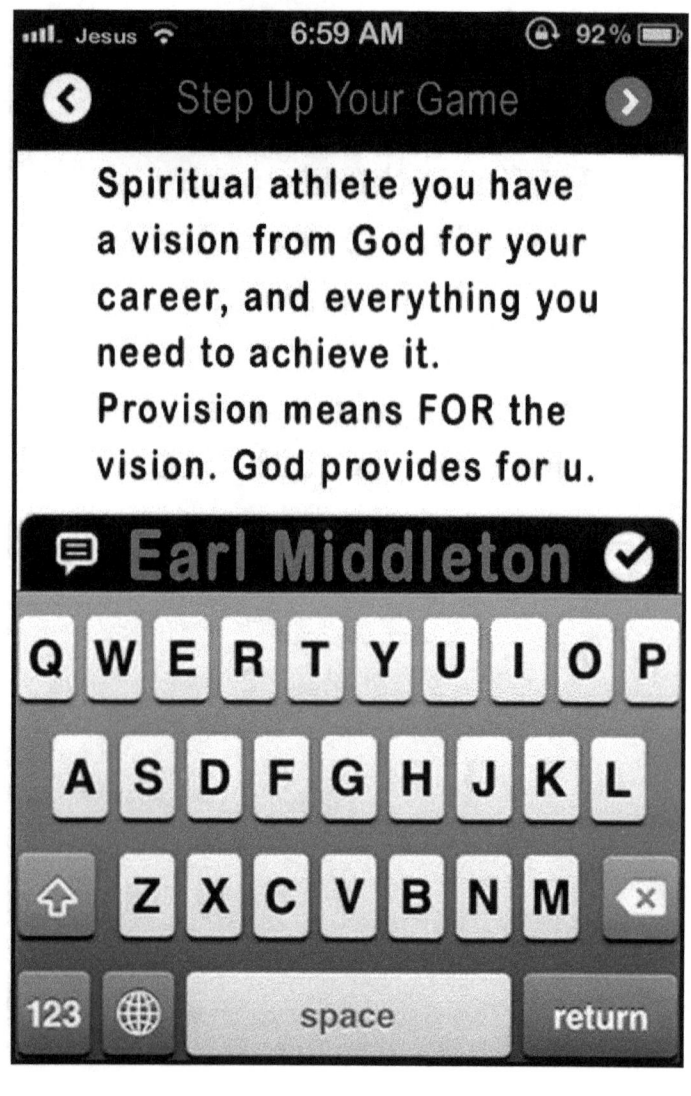

**Step Up Your Game**

Spiritual athlete you have a vision from God for your career, and everything you need to achieve it. Provision means FOR the vision. God provides for u.

Earl Middleton

# January 29

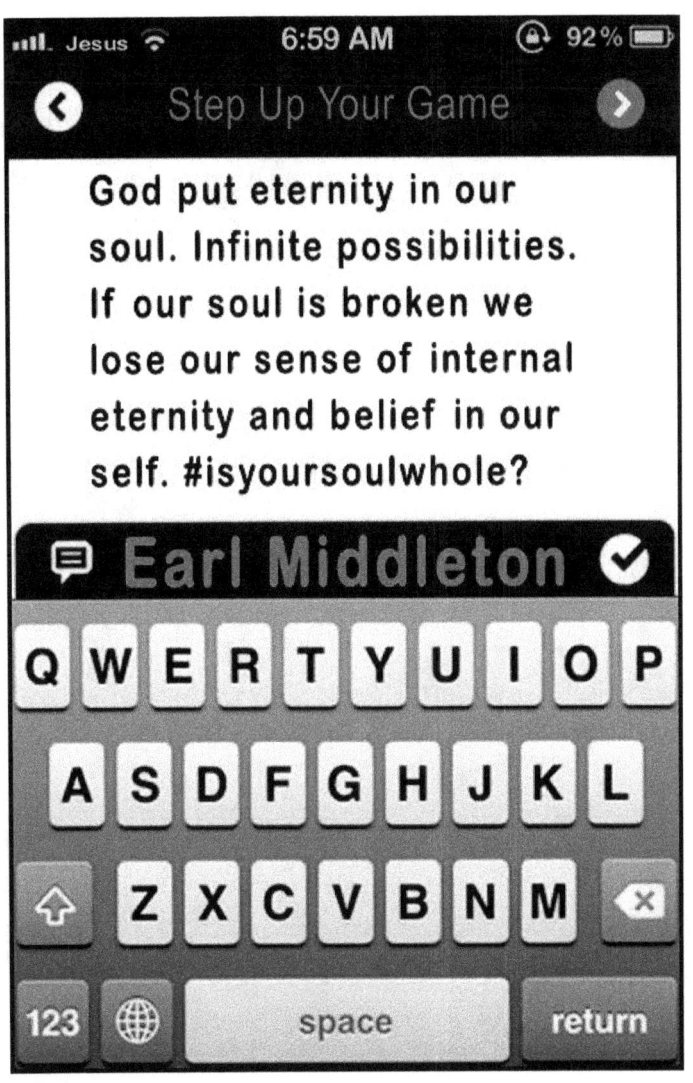

# January 30

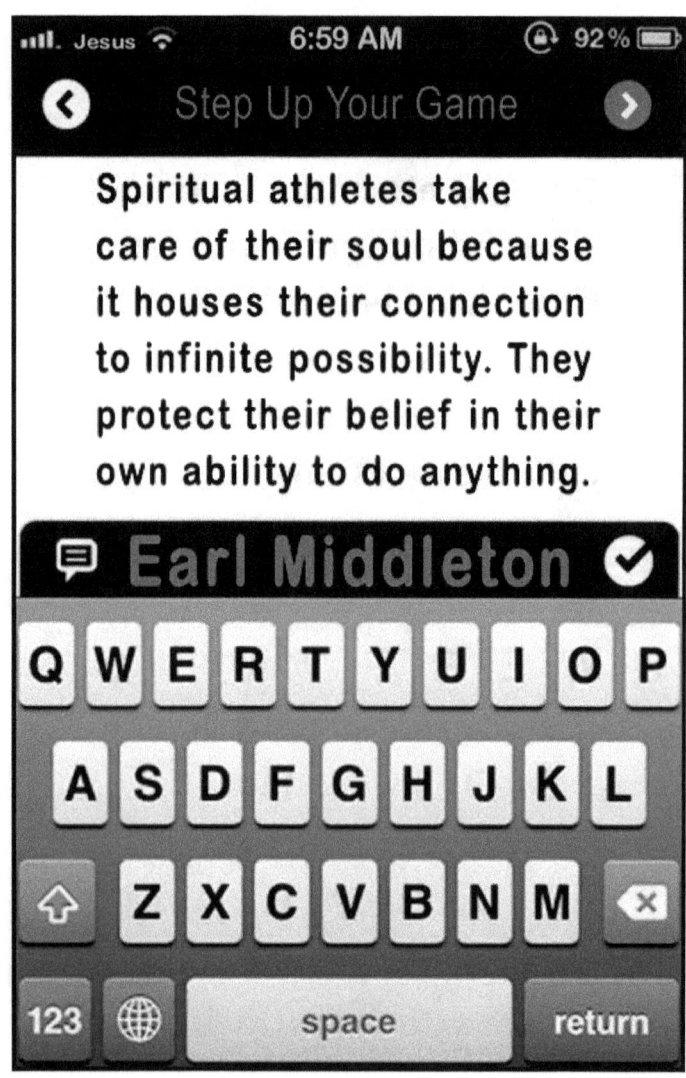

**Step Up Your Game**

Spiritual athletes take care of their soul because it houses their connection to infinite possibility. They protect their belief in their own ability to do anything.

Earl Middleton

# January 31

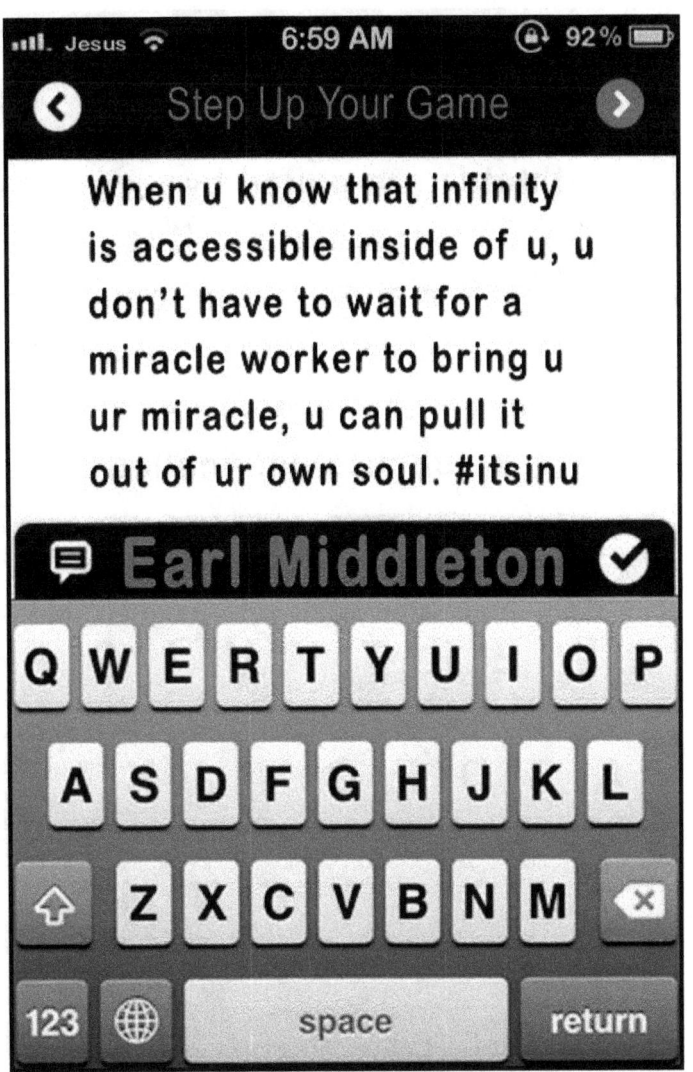

> When u know that infinity is accessible inside of u, u don't have to wait for a miracle worker to bring u ur miracle, u can pull it out of ur own soul. #itsinu

# February 1

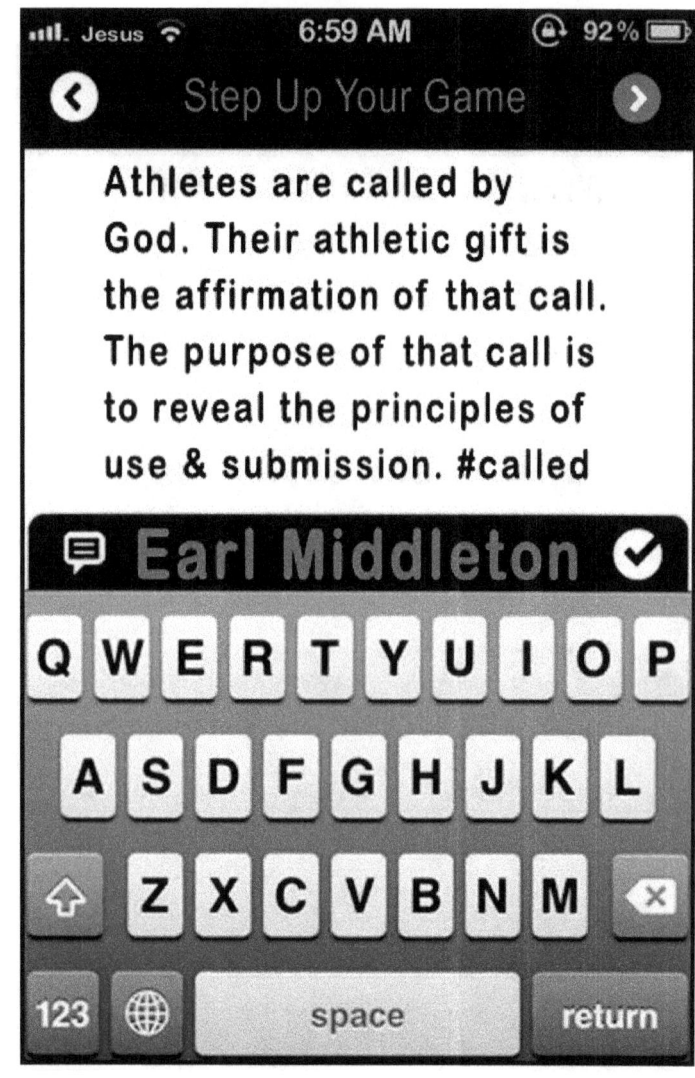

## Step Up Your Game

Athletes are called by God. Their athletic gift is the affirmation of that call. The purpose of that call is to reveal the principles of use & submission. #called

Earl Middleton

# February 2

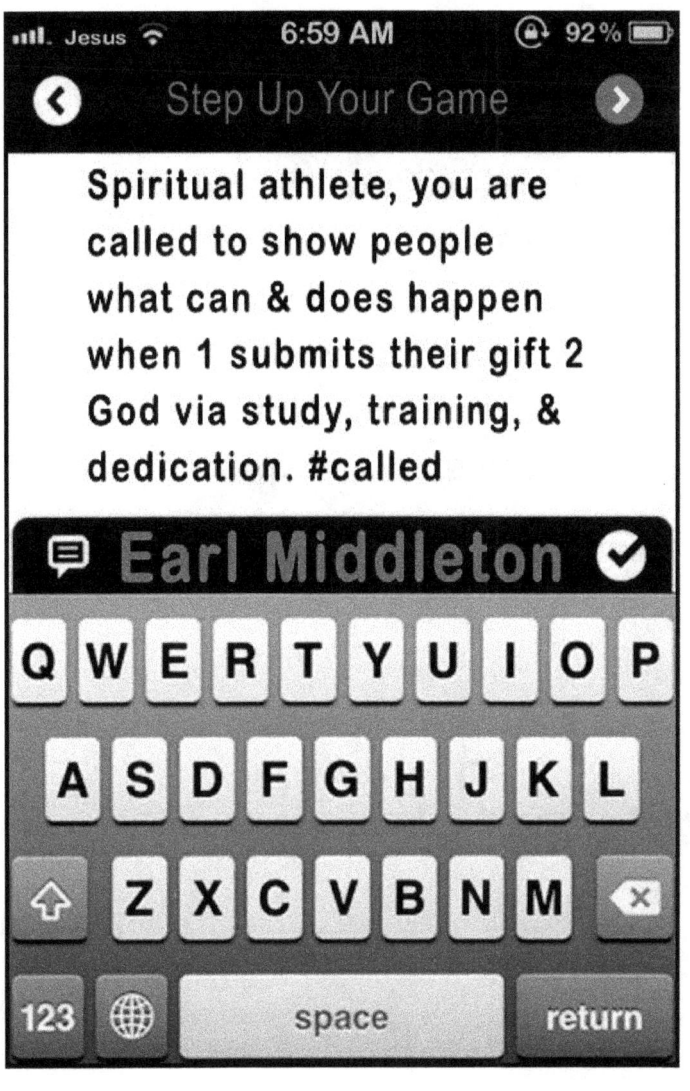

## Step Up Your Game

Spiritual athlete, you are called to show people what can & does happen when 1 submits their gift 2 God via study, training, & dedication. #called

# February 3

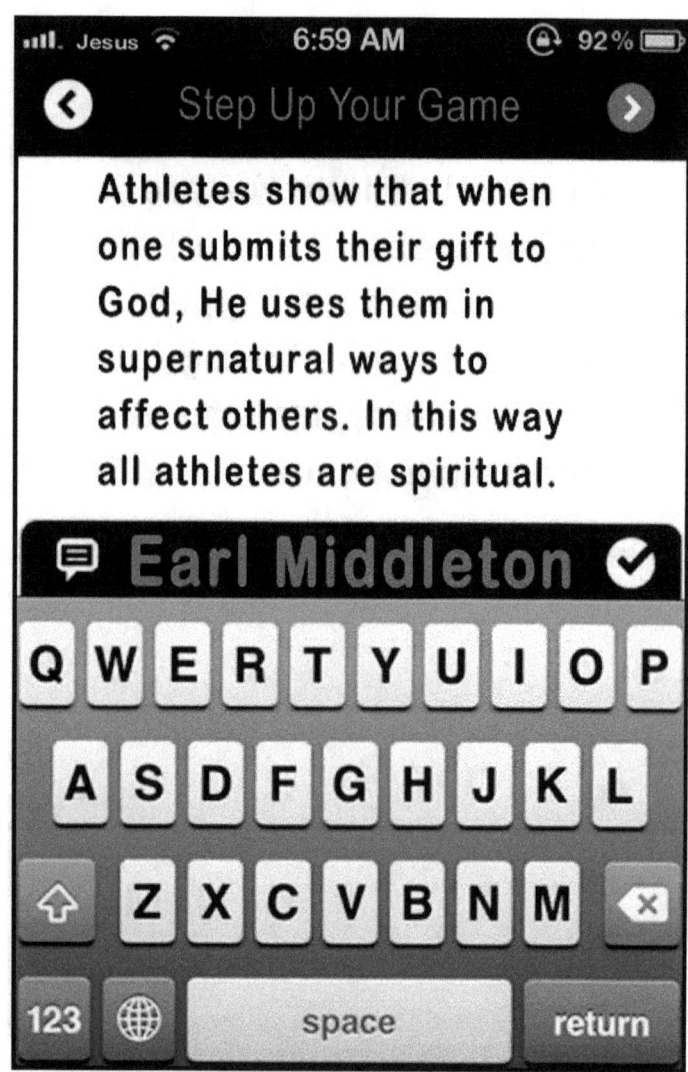

## Step Up Your Game

Athletes show that when one submits their gift to God, He uses them in supernatural ways to affect others. In this way all athletes are spiritual.

— Earl Middleton

# February 4

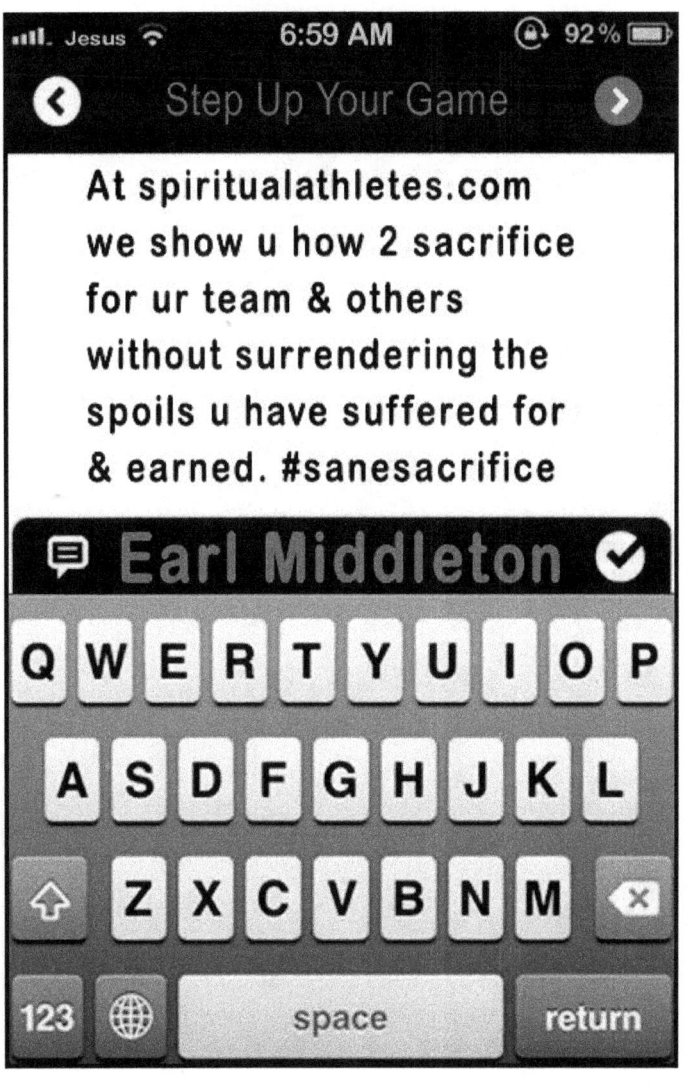

At spiritualathletes.com we show u how 2 sacrifice for ur team & others without surrendering the spoils u have suffered for & earned. #sanesacrifice

# February 5

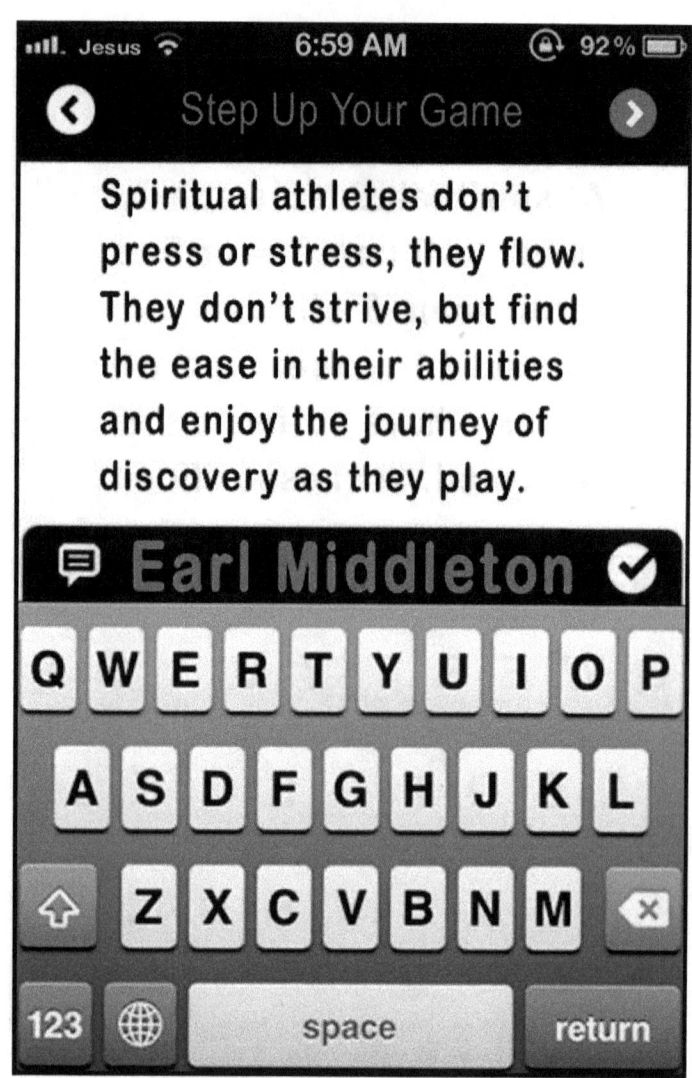

**Step Up Your Game**

Spiritual athletes don't press or stress, they flow. They don't strive, but find the ease in their abilities and enjoy the journey of discovery as they play.

— Earl Middleton

# February 6

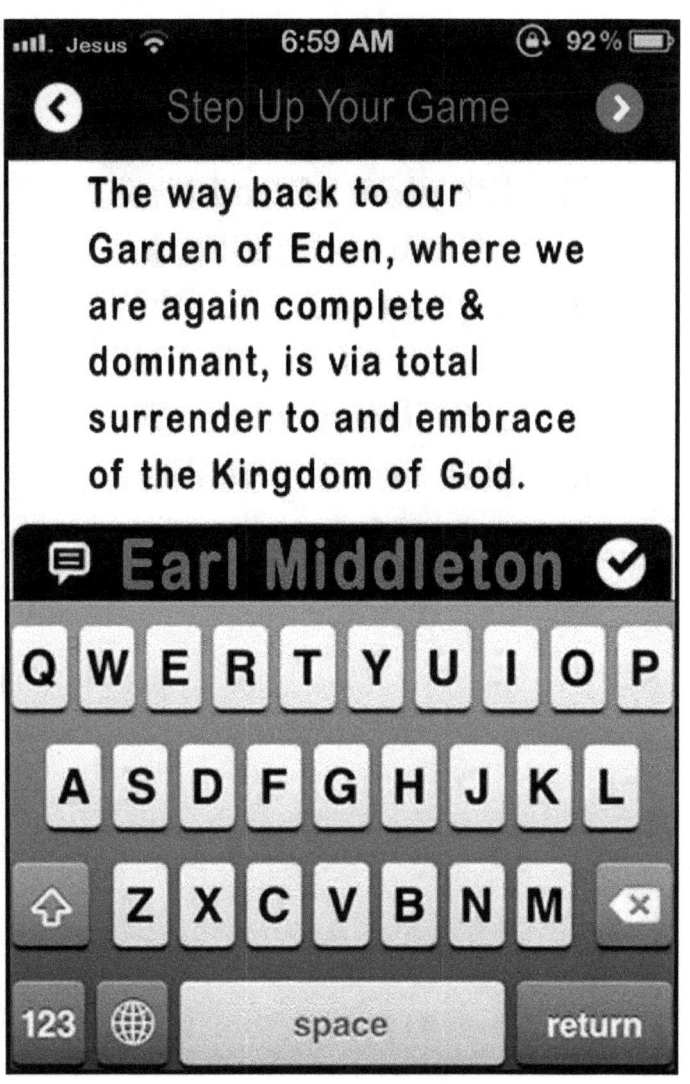

**Step Up Your Game**

The way back to our Garden of Eden, where we are again complete & dominant, is via total surrender to and embrace of the Kingdom of God.

Earl Middleton

# February 7

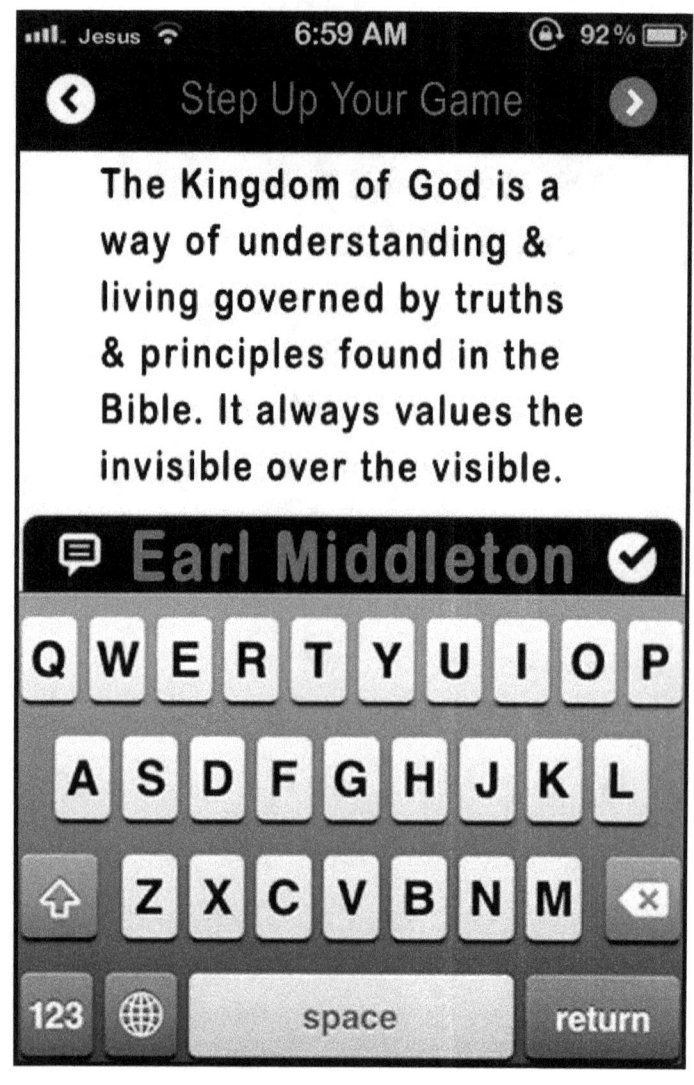

## Step Up Your Game

The Kingdom of God is a way of understanding & living governed by truths & principles found in the Bible. It always values the invisible over the visible.

— Earl Middleton

# February 8

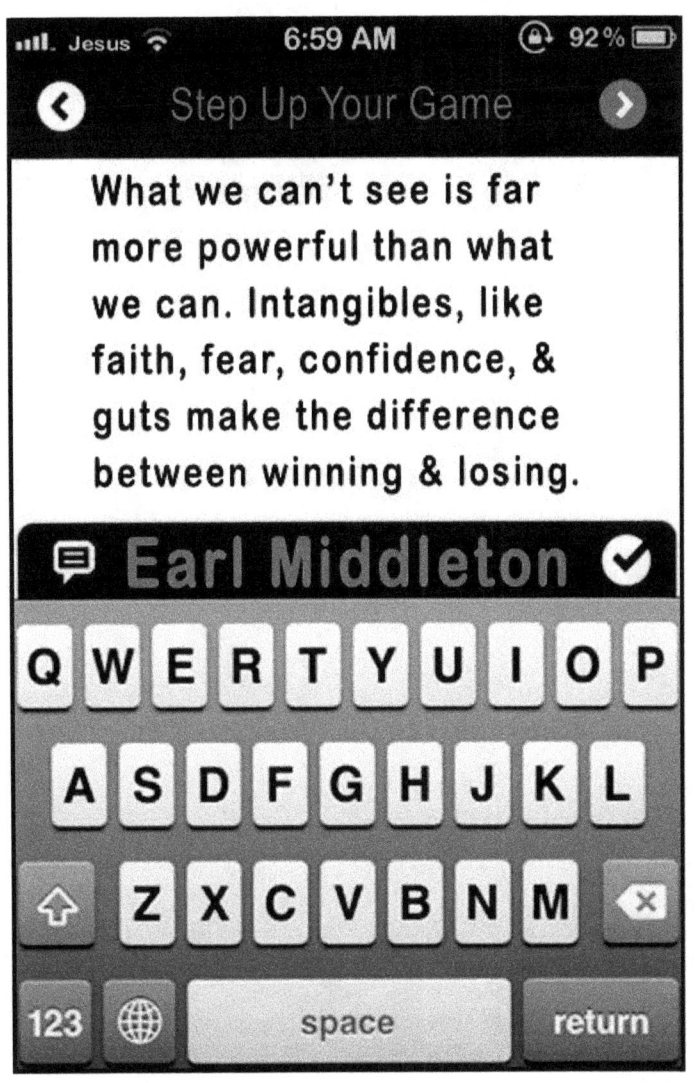

> What we can't see is far more powerful than what we can. Intangibles, like faith, fear, confidence, & guts make the difference between winning & losing.
>
> — Earl Middleton

# February 9

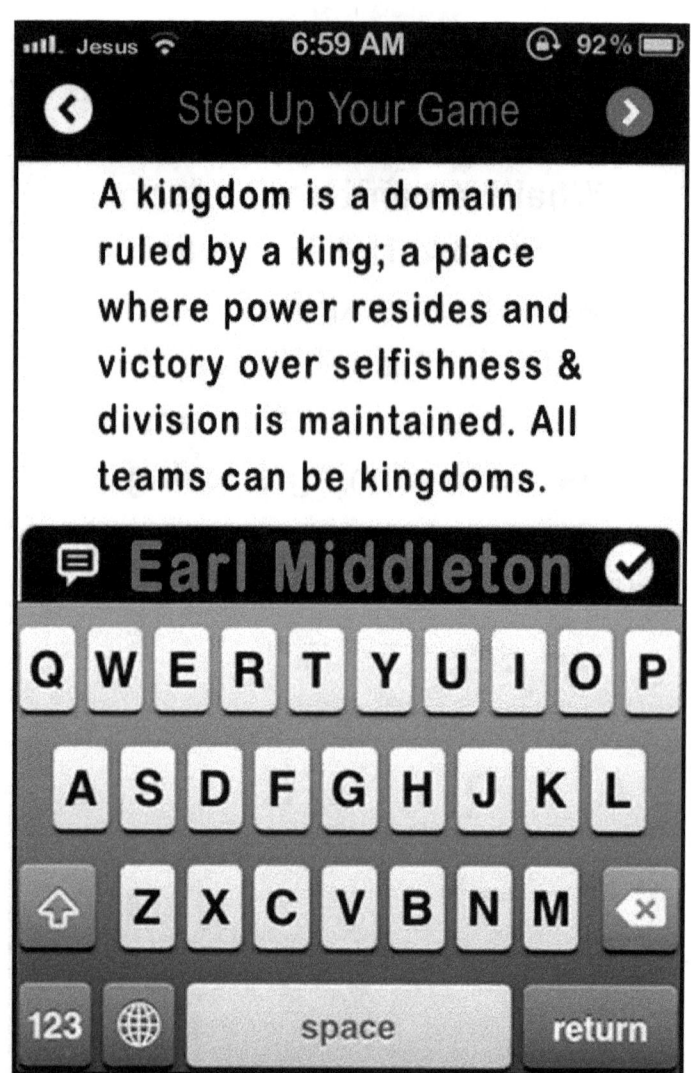

A kingdom is a domain ruled by a king; a place where power resides and victory over selfishness & division is maintained. All teams can be kingdoms.

— Earl Middleton

# February 10

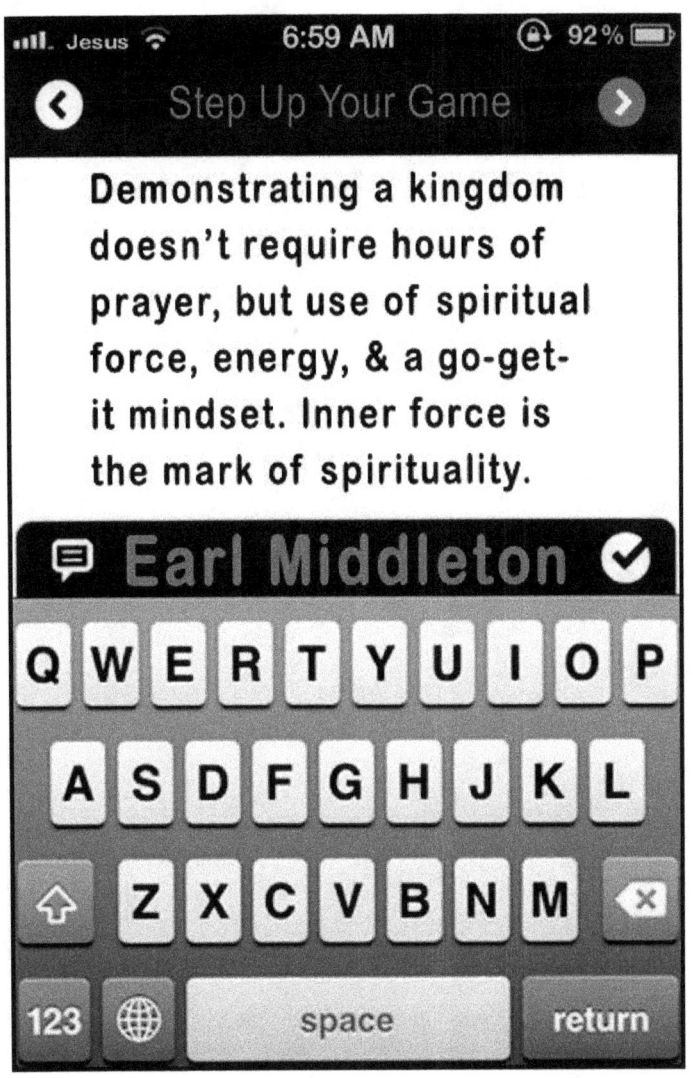

Demonstrating a kingdom doesn't require hours of prayer, but use of spiritual force, energy, & a go-get-it mindset. Inner force is the mark of spirituality.

— Earl Middleton

# February 11

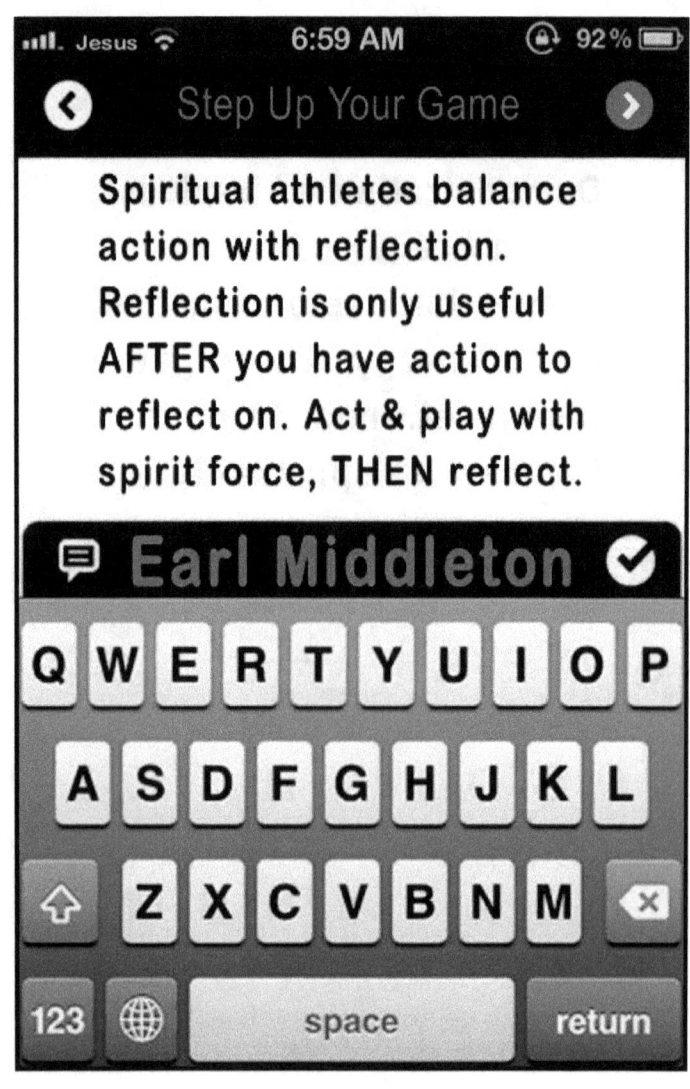

# February 12

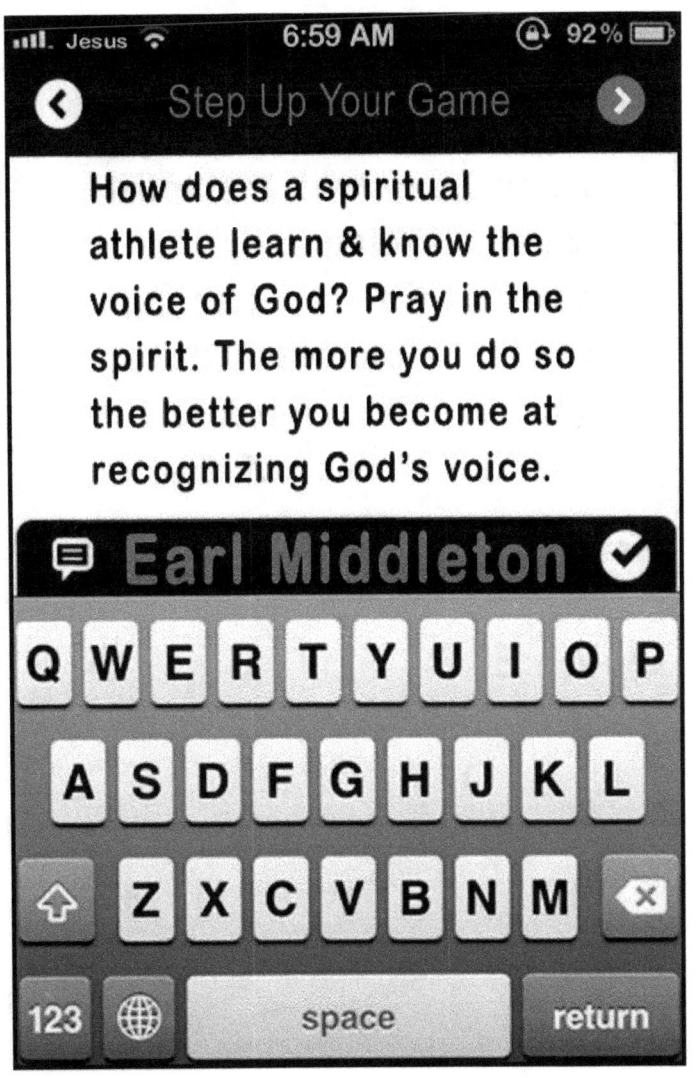

# February 13

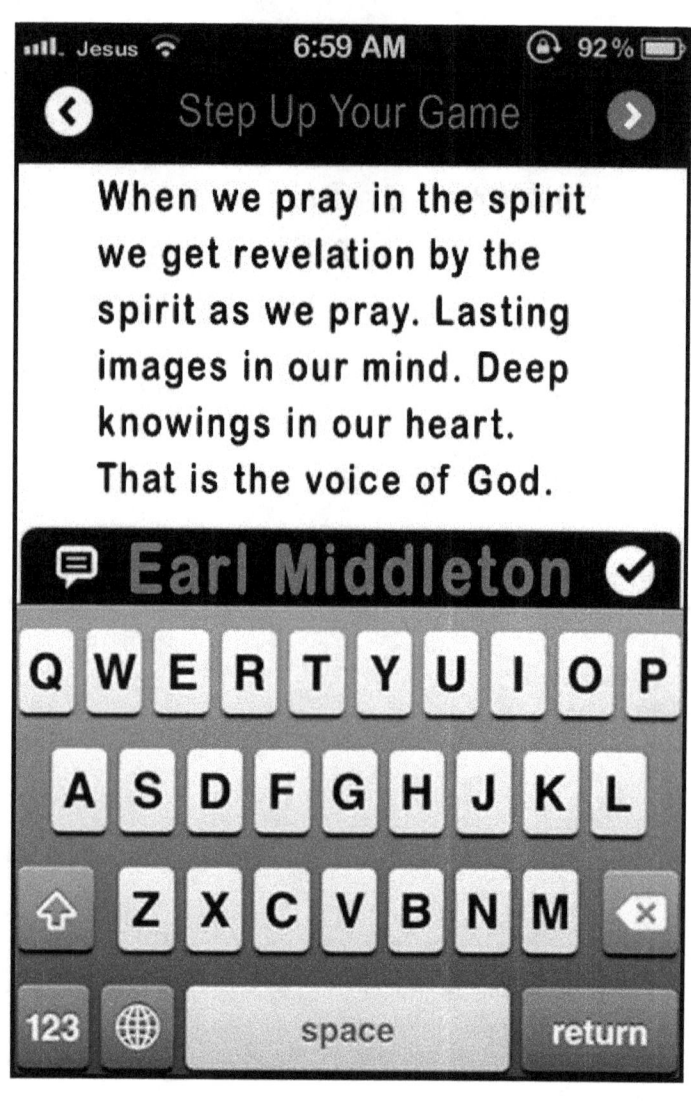

When we pray in the spirit we get revelation by the spirit as we pray. Lasting images in our mind. Deep knowings in our heart. That is the voice of God.

— Earl Middleton

# February 14

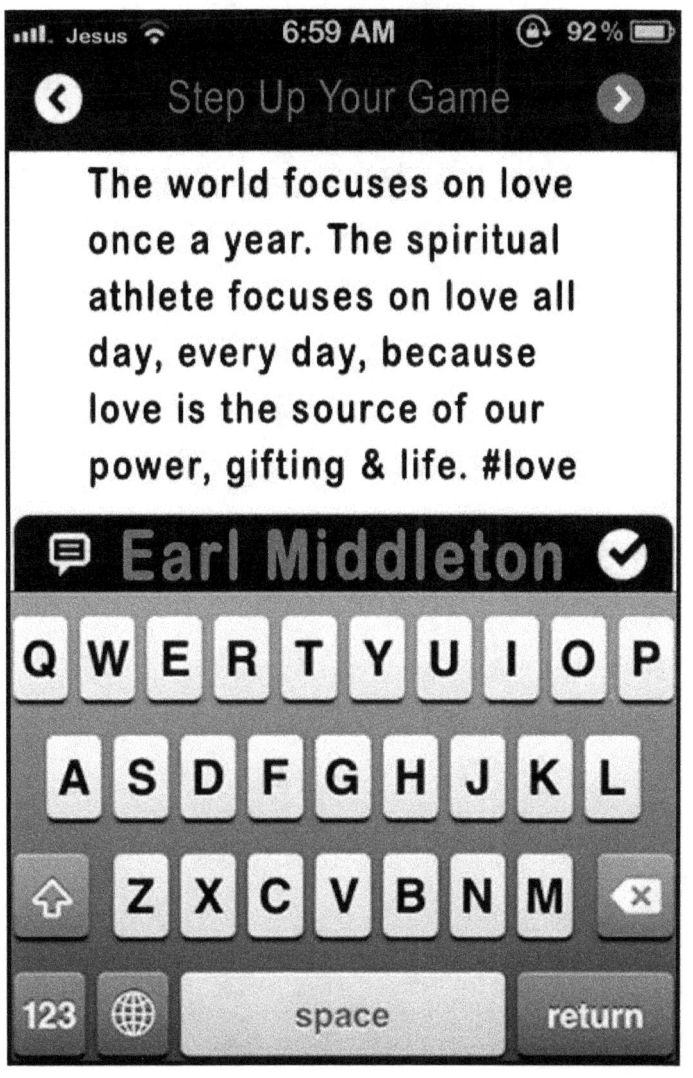

The world focuses on love once a year. The spiritual athlete focuses on love all day, every day, because love is the source of our power, gifting & life. #love

## February 15

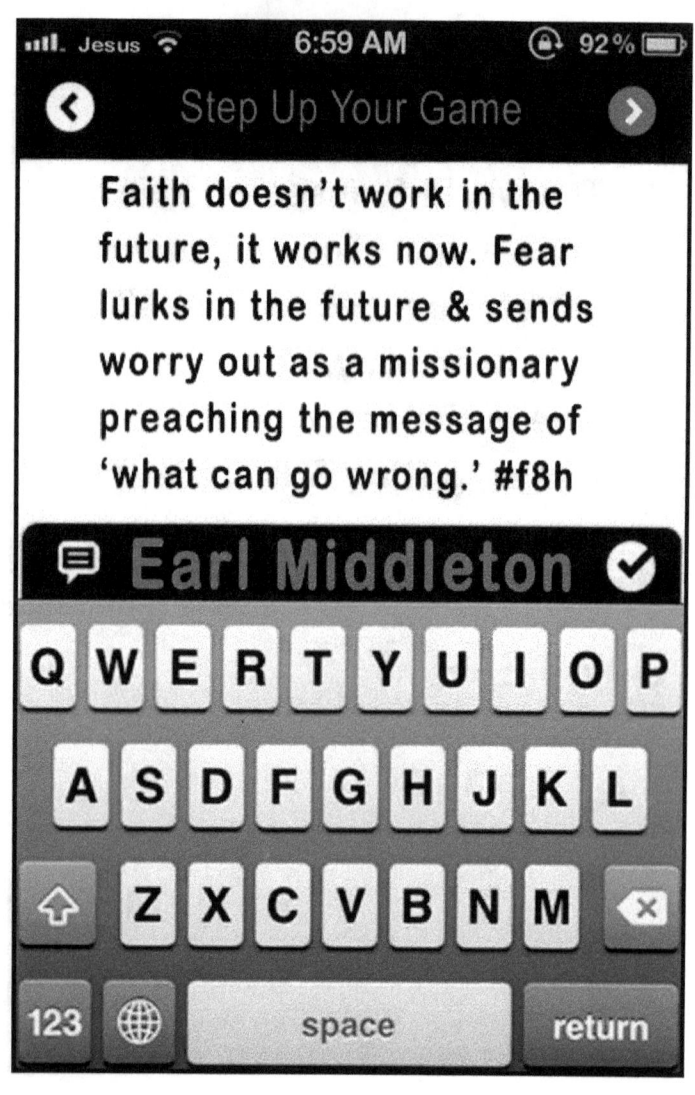

Faith doesn't work in the future, it works now. Fear lurks in the future & sends worry out as a missionary preaching the message of 'what can go wrong.' #f8h

— Earl Middleton

# February 16

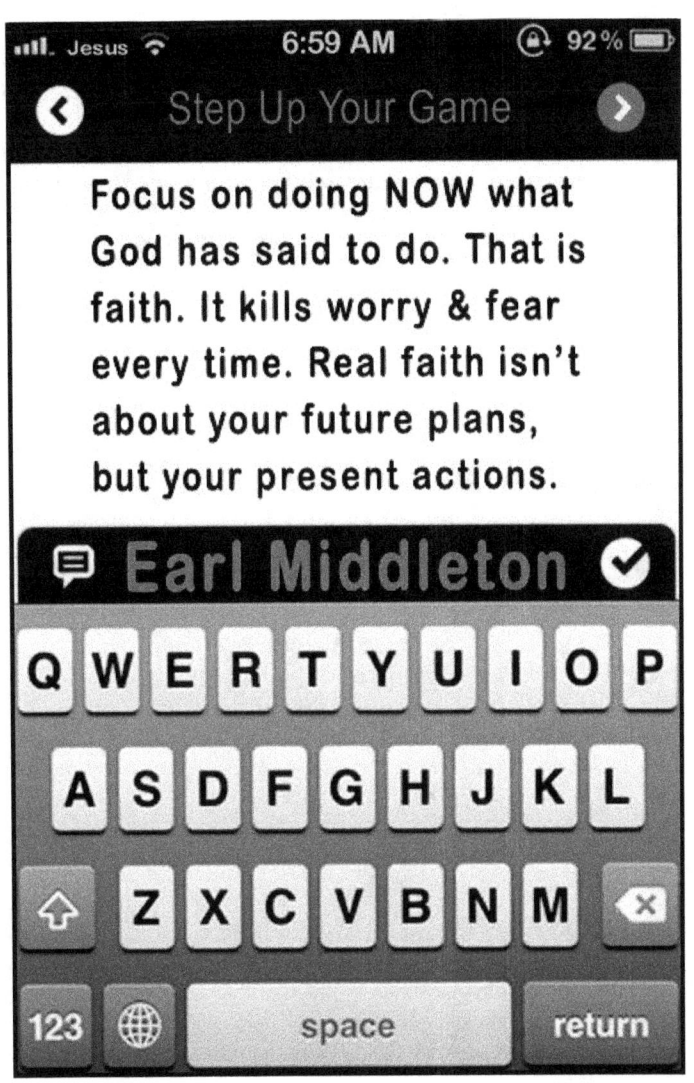

# February 17

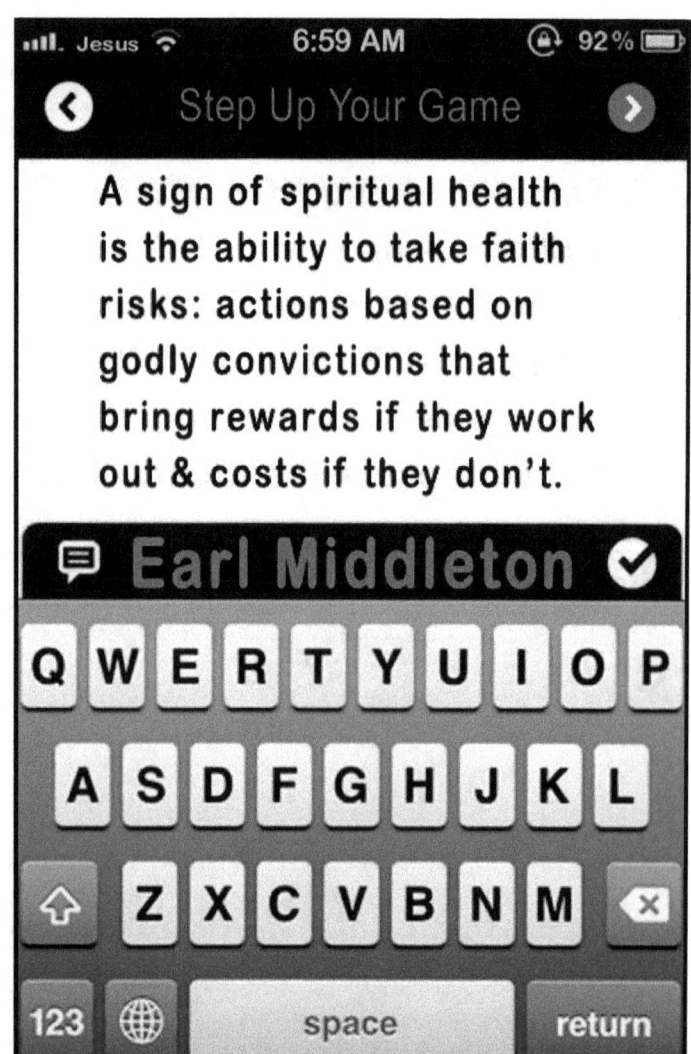

A sign of spiritual health is the ability to take faith risks: actions based on godly convictions that bring rewards if they work out & costs if they don't.

# February 18

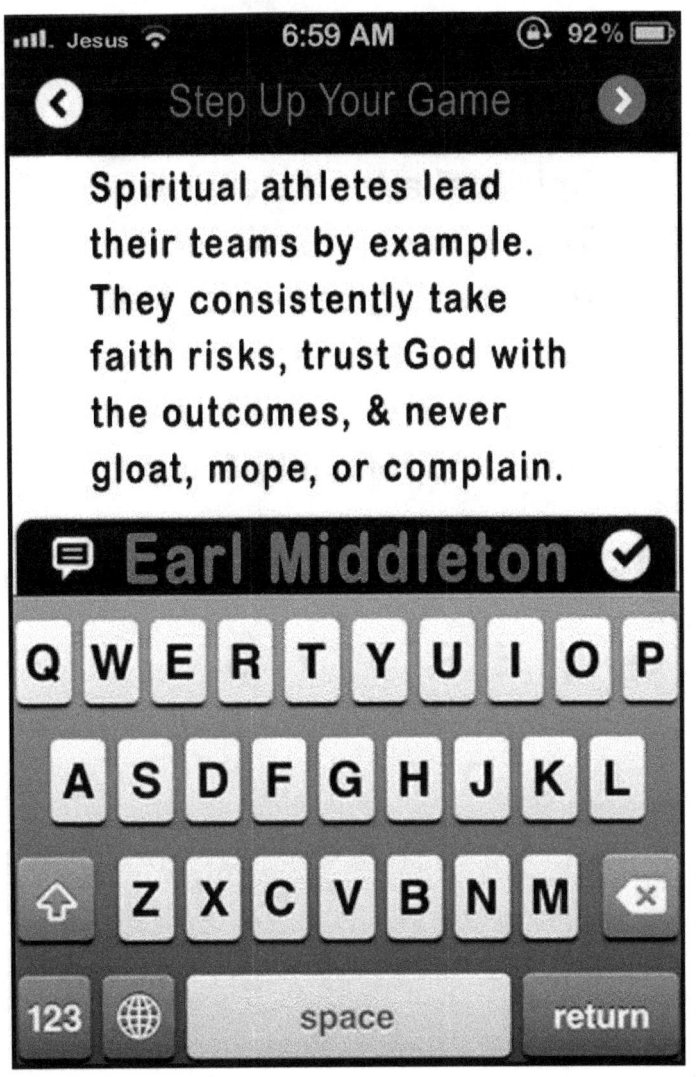

## Step Up Your Game

Spiritual athletes lead their teams by example. They consistently take faith risks, trust God with the outcomes, & never gloat, mope, or complain.

# February 19

## Step Up Your Game

Spiritual athletes overlive! They remain connected to the amazing because their faith risking keeps them in the place where challenge meets opportunity & wow!

— Earl Middleton

# February 20

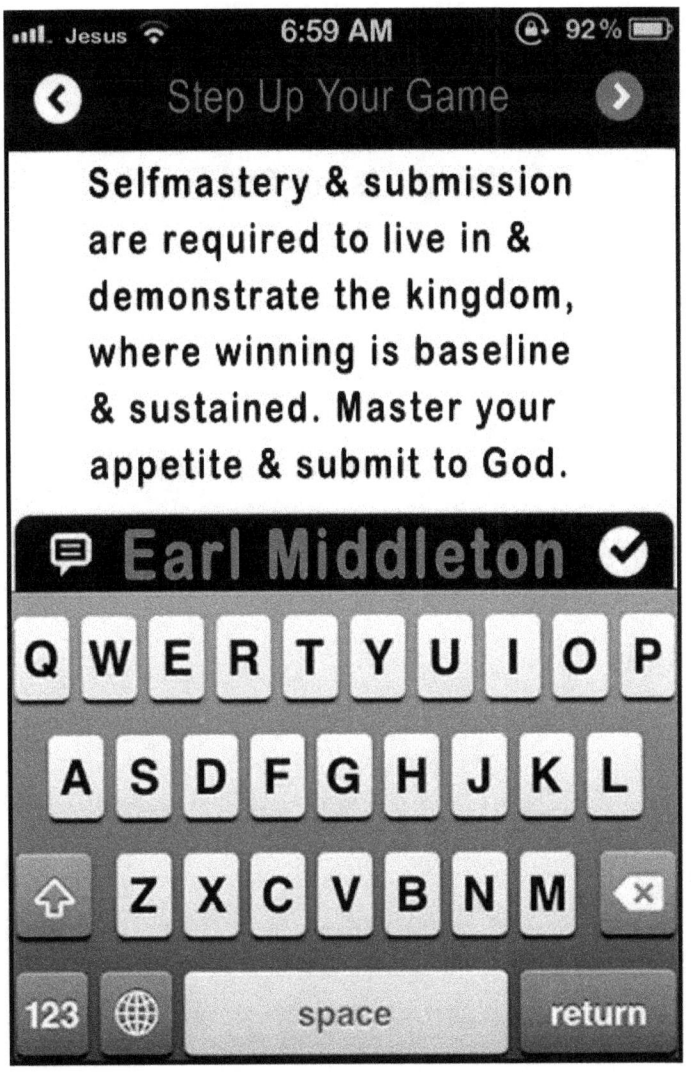

**Step Up Your Game**

Selfmastery & submission are required to live in & demonstrate the kingdom, where winning is baseline & sustained. Master your appetite & submit to God.

# February 21

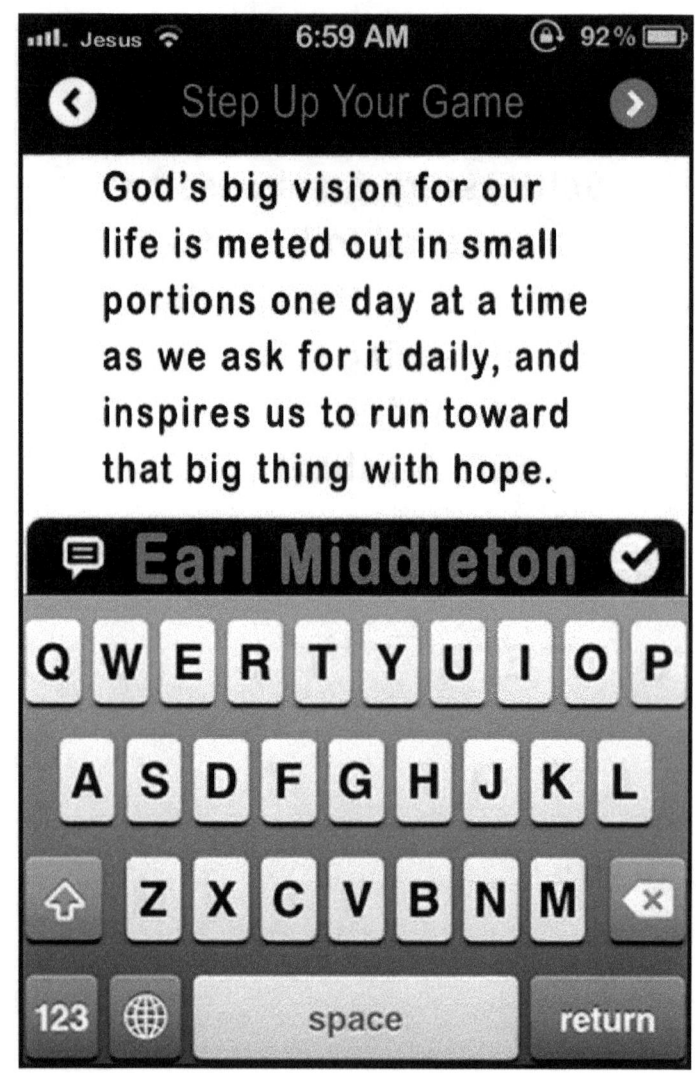

**Step Up Your Game**

God's big vision for our life is meted out in small portions one day at a time as we ask for it daily, and inspires us to run toward that big thing with hope.

Earl Middleton

# February 22

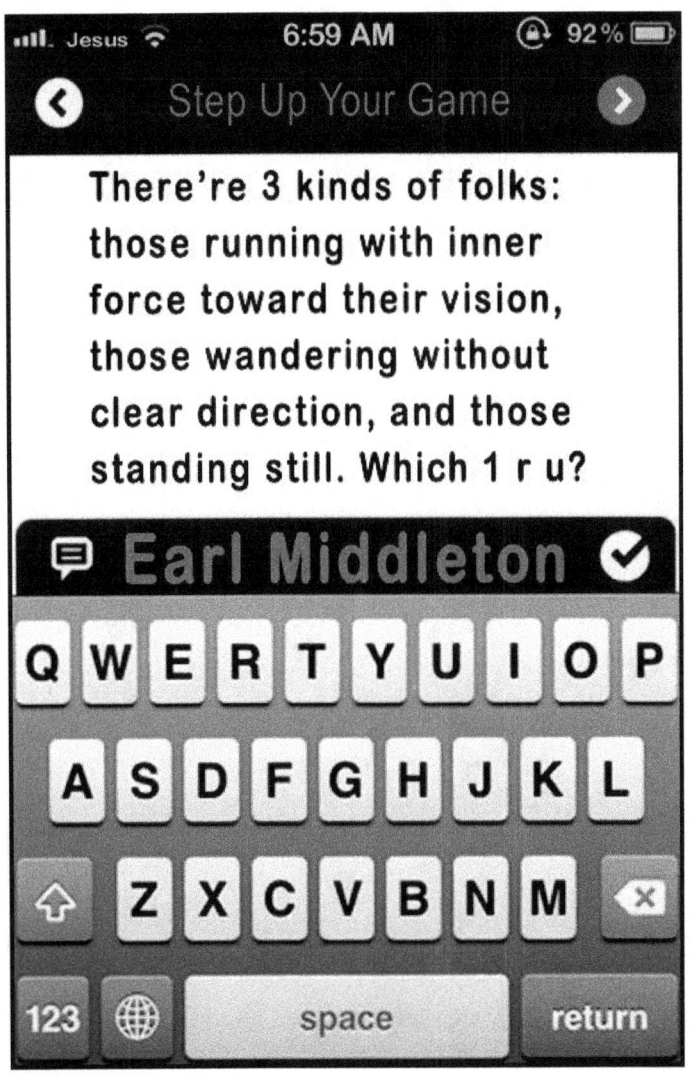

# February 23

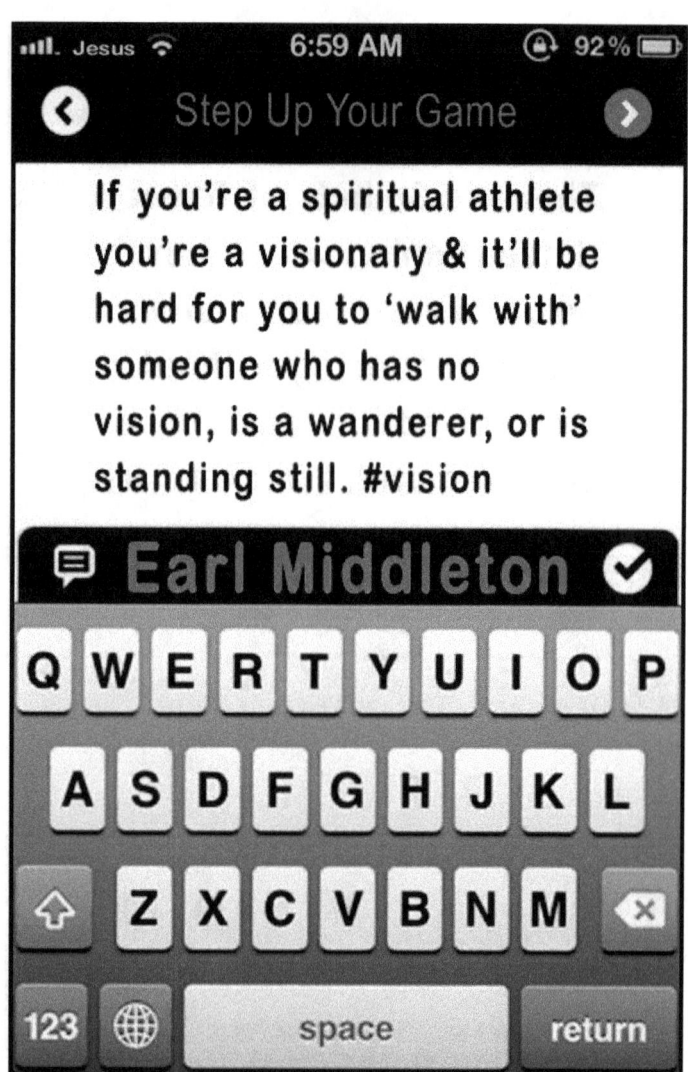

# February 24

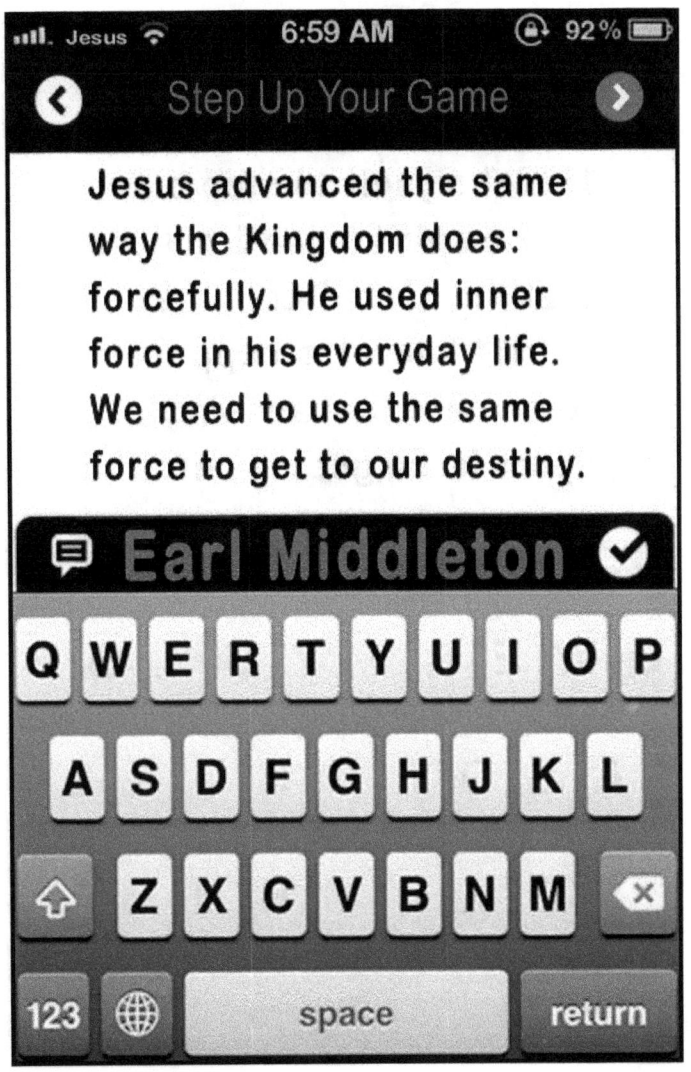

Jesus advanced the same way the Kingdom does: forcefully. He used inner force in his everyday life. We need to use the same force to get to our destiny.

# February 25

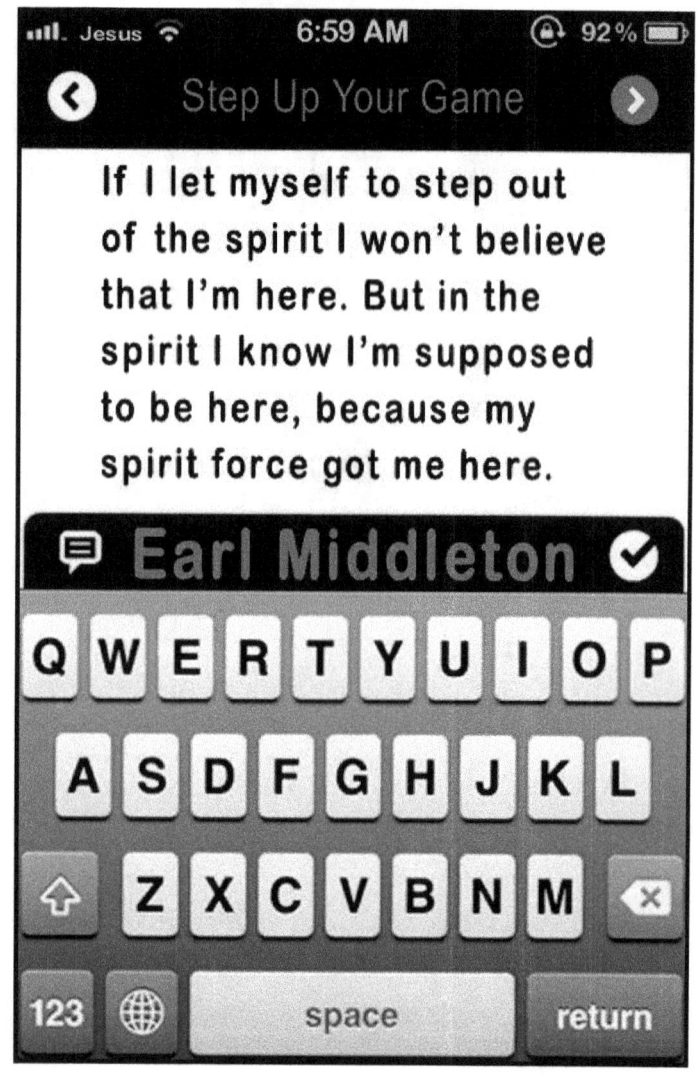

**Step Up Your Game**

If I let myself to step out of the spirit I won't believe that I'm here. But in the spirit I know I'm supposed to be here, because my spirit force got me here.

— Earl Middleton

# February 26

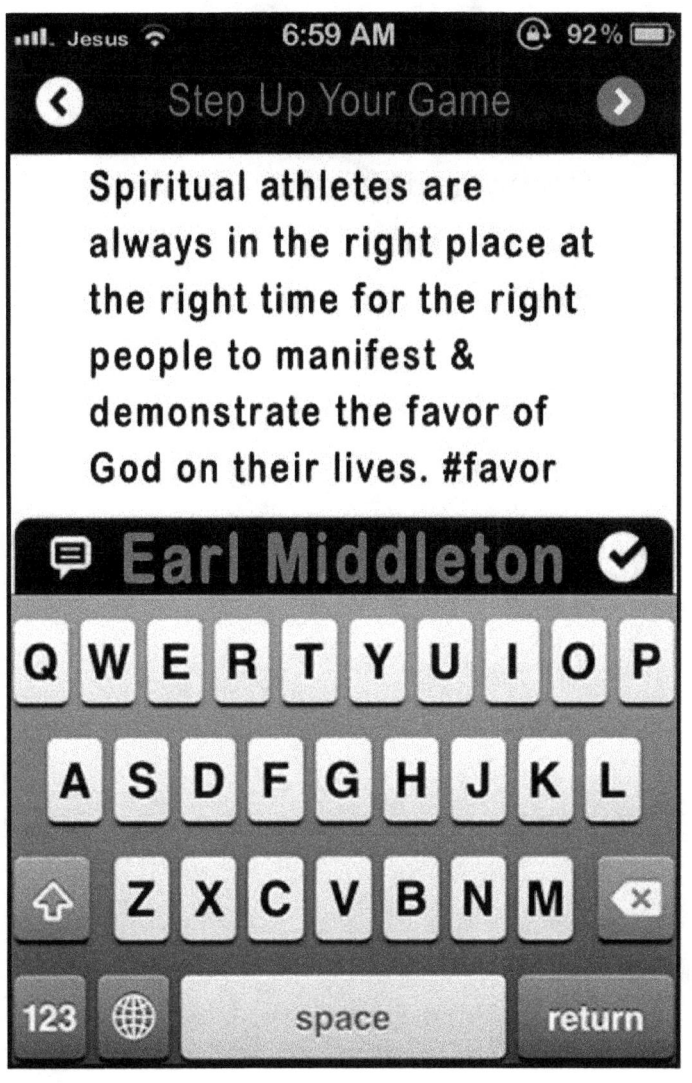

**Step Up Your Game**

Spiritual athletes are always in the right place at the right time for the right people to manifest & demonstrate the favor of God on their lives. #favor

# February 27

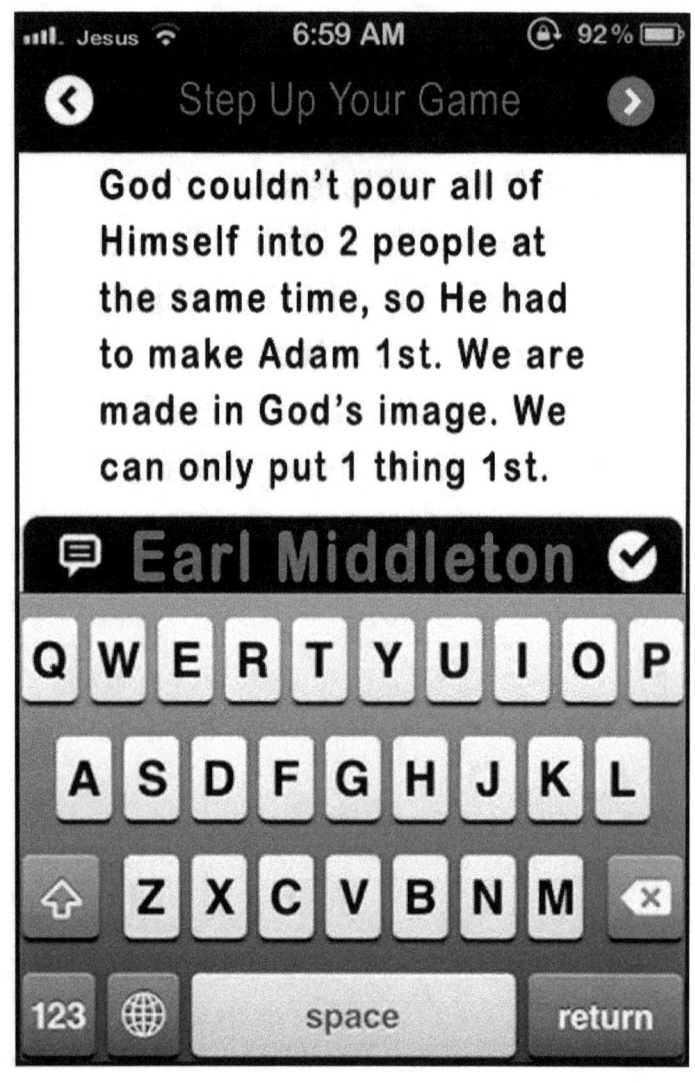

**Step Up Your Game**

God couldn't pour all of Himself into 2 people at the same time, so He had to make Adam 1st. We are made in God's image. We can only put 1 thing 1st.

— Earl Middleton

# February 28

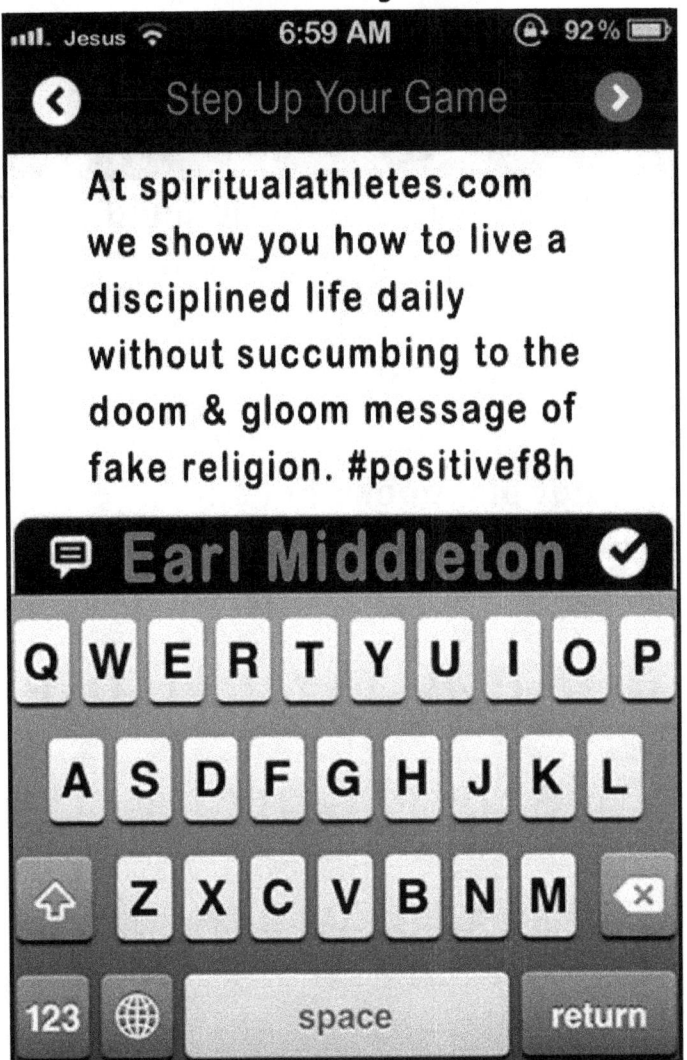

At spiritualathletes.com we show you how to live a disciplined life daily without succumbing to the doom & gloom message of fake religion. #positivef8h

# February 29

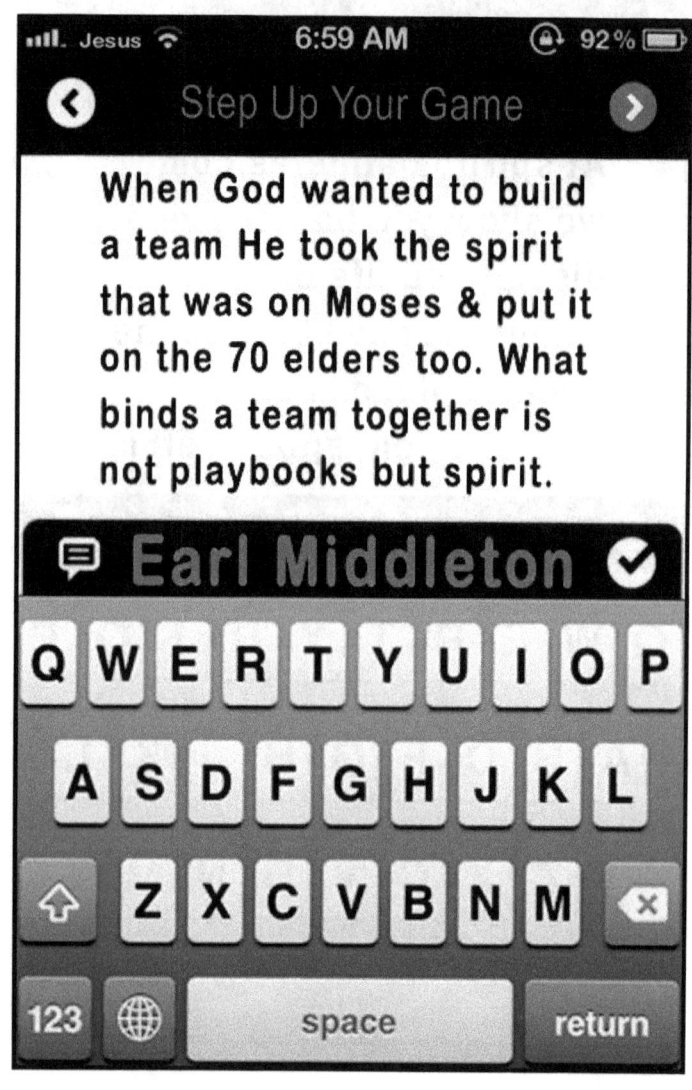

When God wanted to build a team He took the spirit that was on Moses & put it on the 70 elders too. What binds a team together is not playbooks but spirit.

— Earl Middleton

# March 1

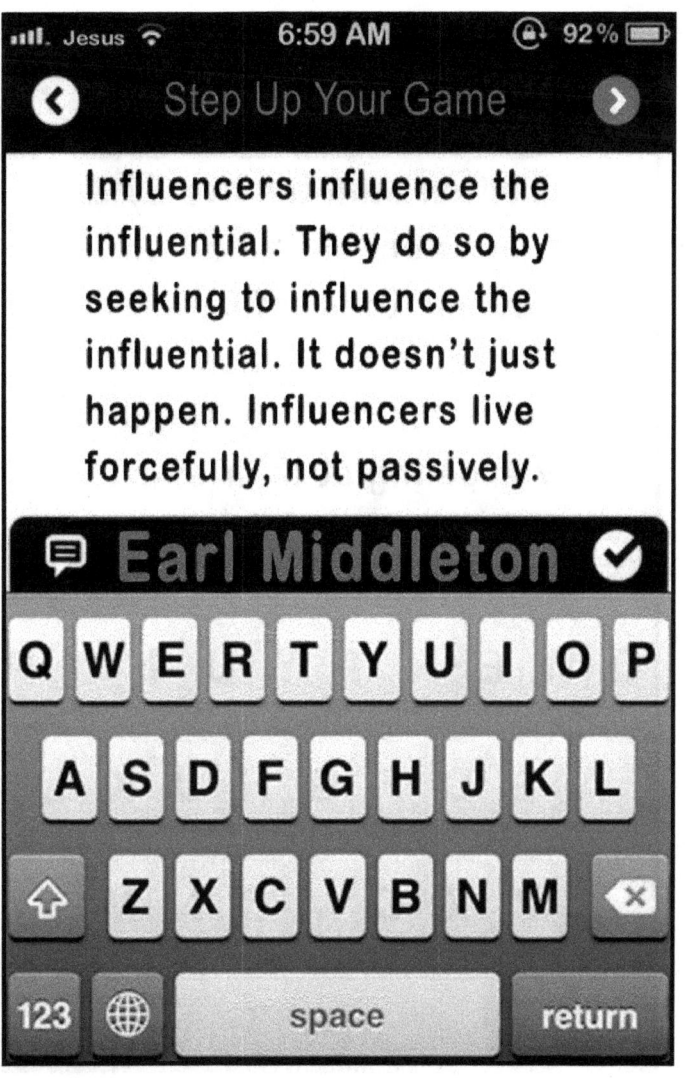

Influencers influence the influential. They do so by seeking to influence the influential. It doesn't just happen. Influencers live forcefully, not passively.

— Earl Middleton

# March 2

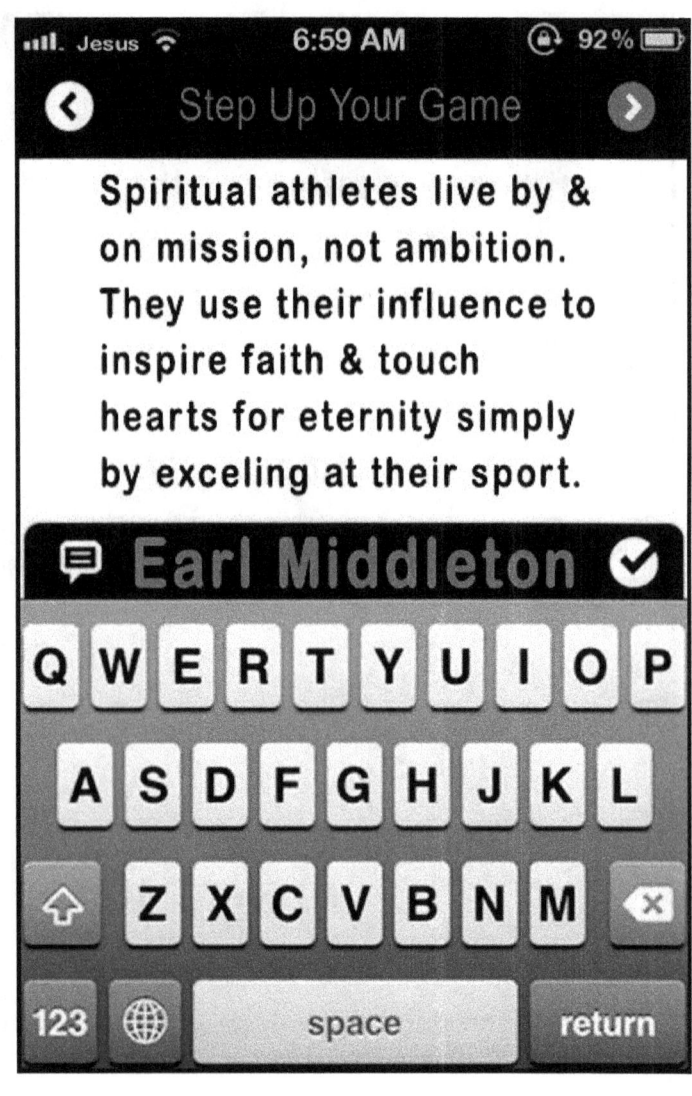

> Spiritual athletes live by & on mission, not ambition. They use their influence to inspire faith & touch hearts for eternity simply by exceling at their sport.
>
> — Earl Middleton

# March 3

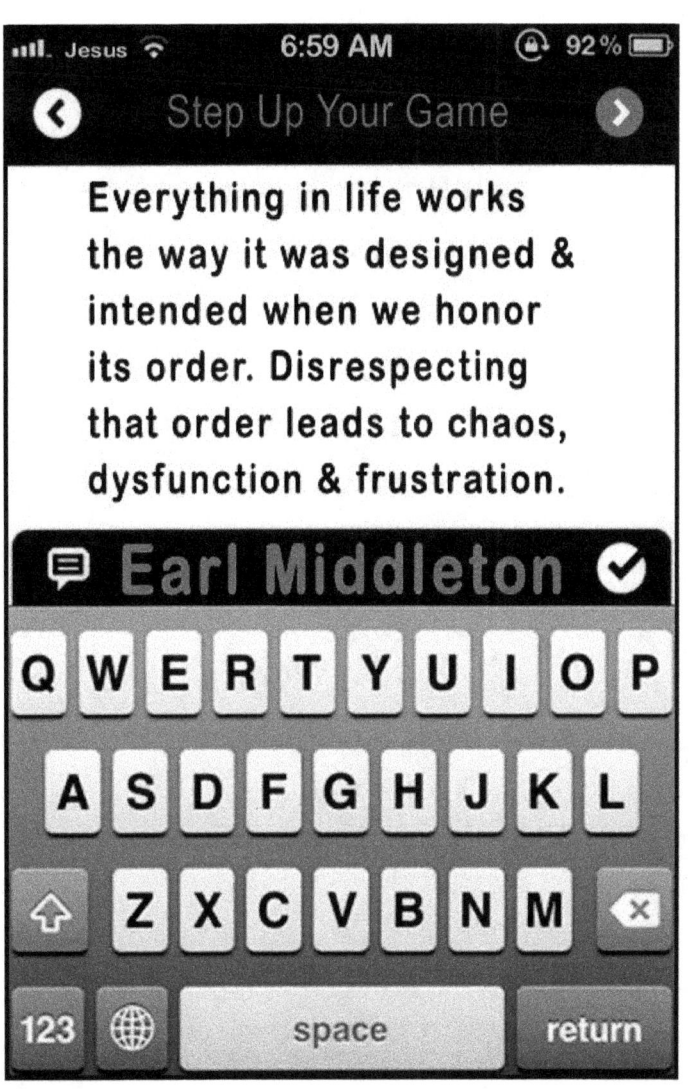

# March 4

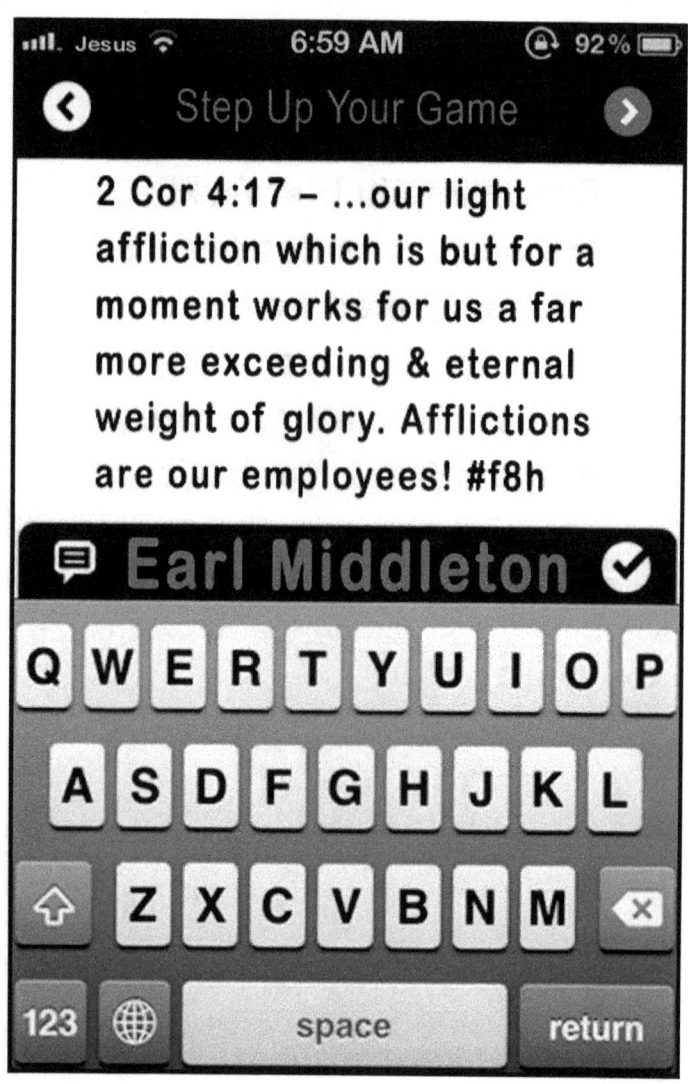

# March 5

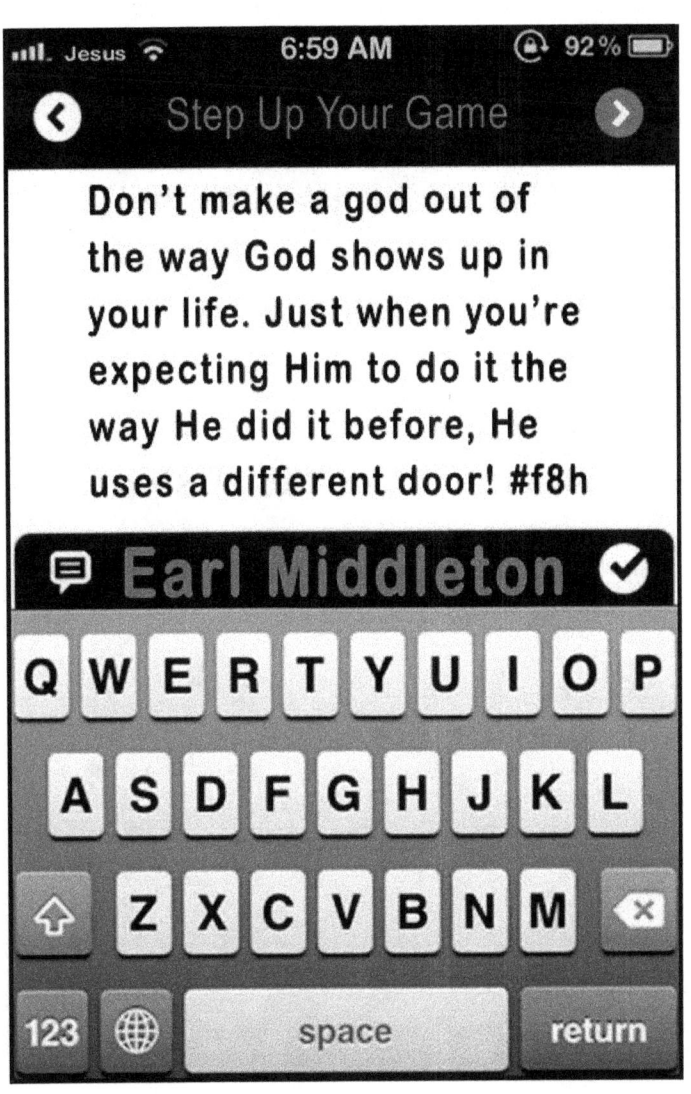

**Step Up Your Game**

Don't make a god out of the way God shows up in your life. Just when you're expecting Him to do it the way He did it before, He uses a different door! #f8h

# March 6

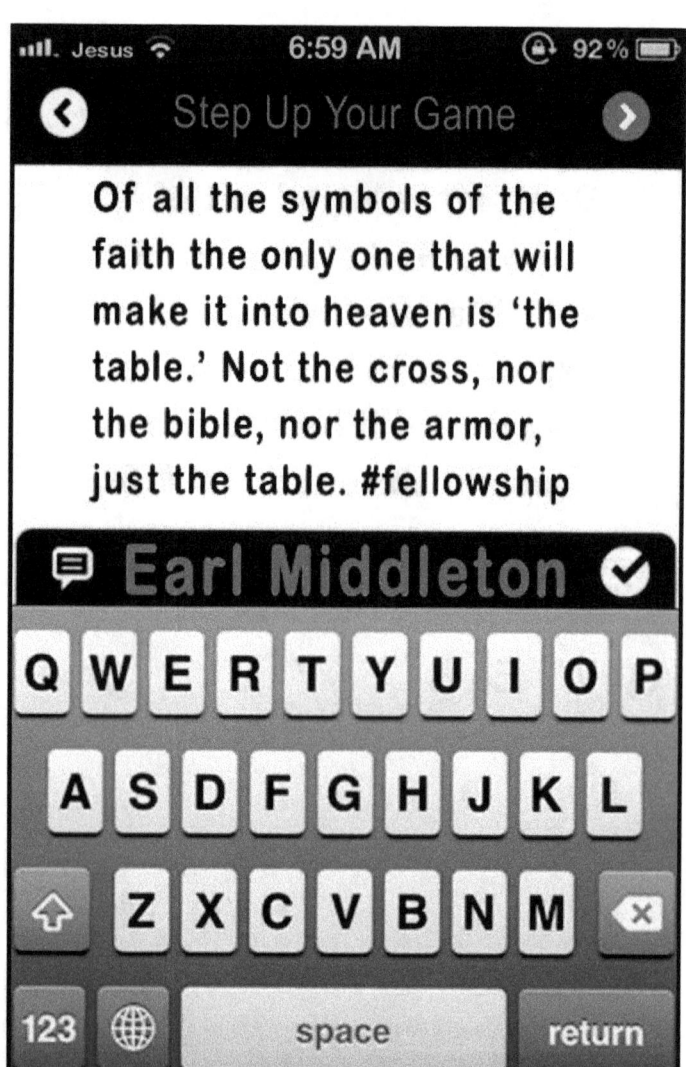

# March 7

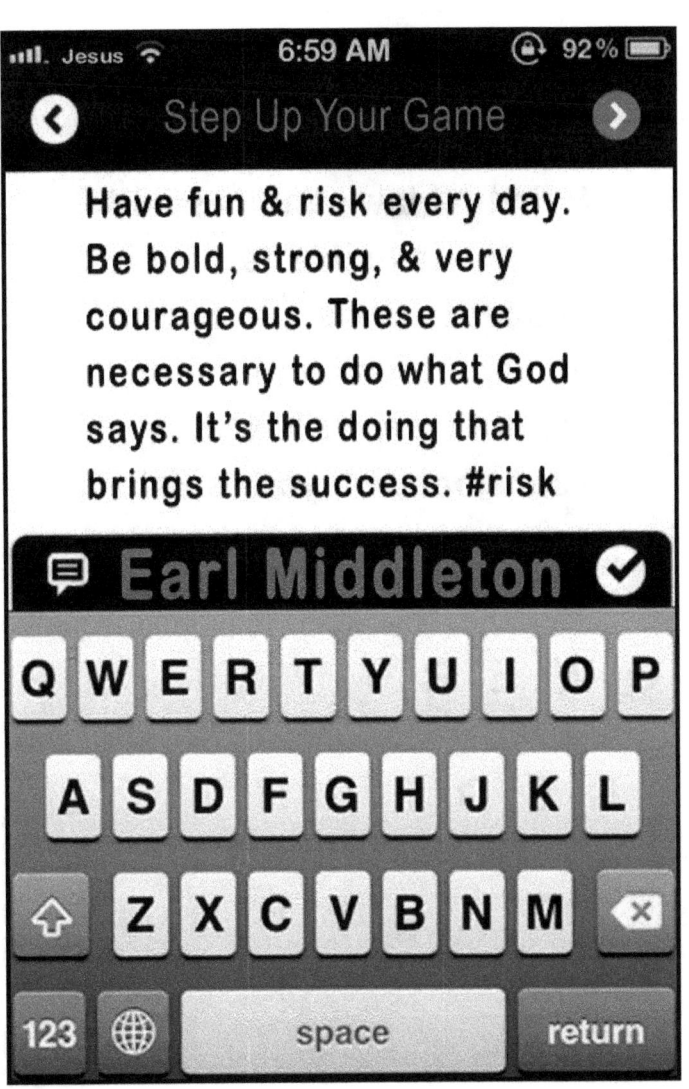

# March 8

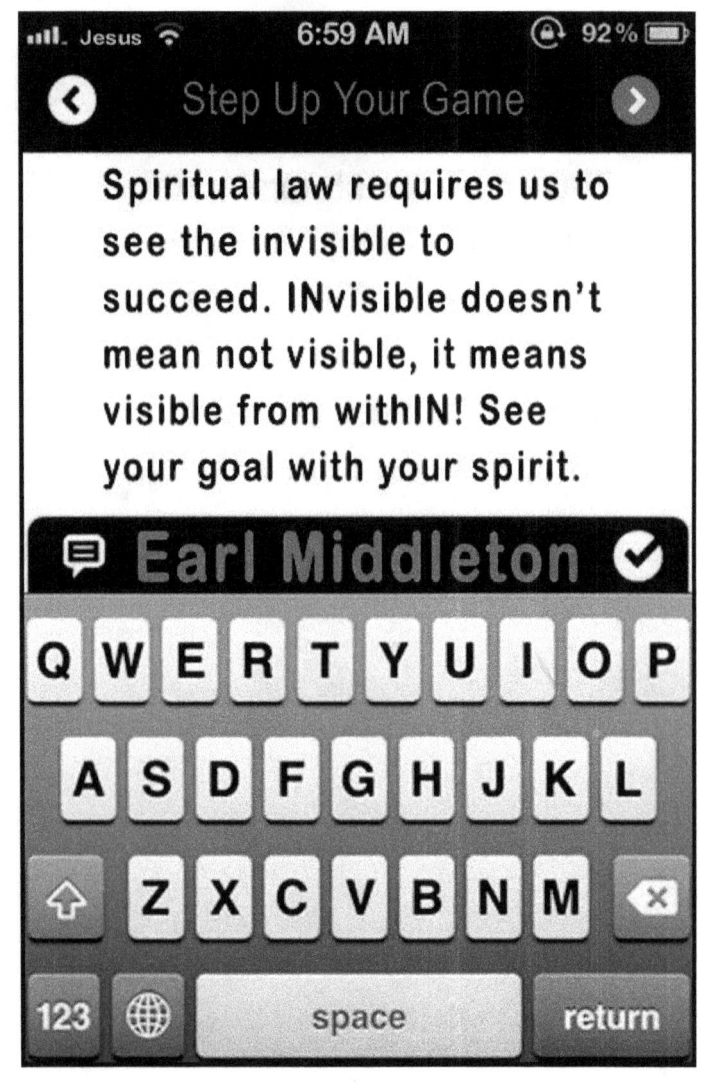

Spiritual law requires us to see the invisible to succeed. INvisible doesn't mean not visible, it means visible from withIN! See your goal with your spirit.

# March 9

**Step Up Your Game**

My body & spirit belong to God, so if they break He can fix them. My soul is mine, so if it breaks I must fix it. Spiritual athletes are soul care specialists.

Earl Middleton

# March 10

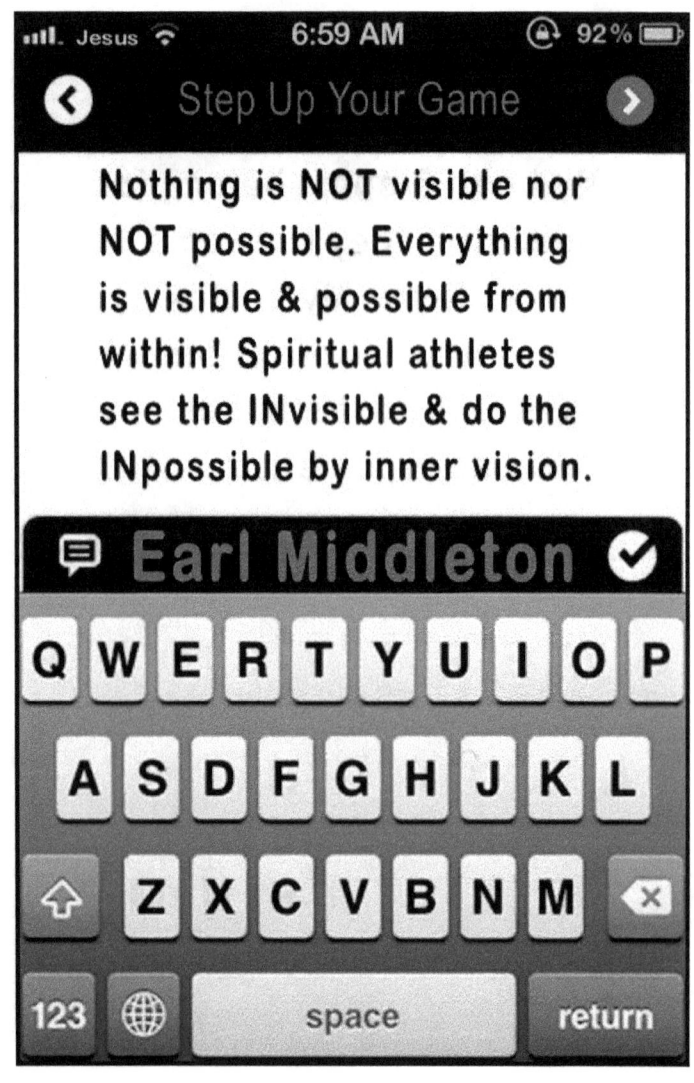

Nothing is NOT visible nor NOT possible. Everything is visible & possible from within! Spiritual athletes see the INvisible & do the INpossible by inner vision.

Earl Middleton

# March 11

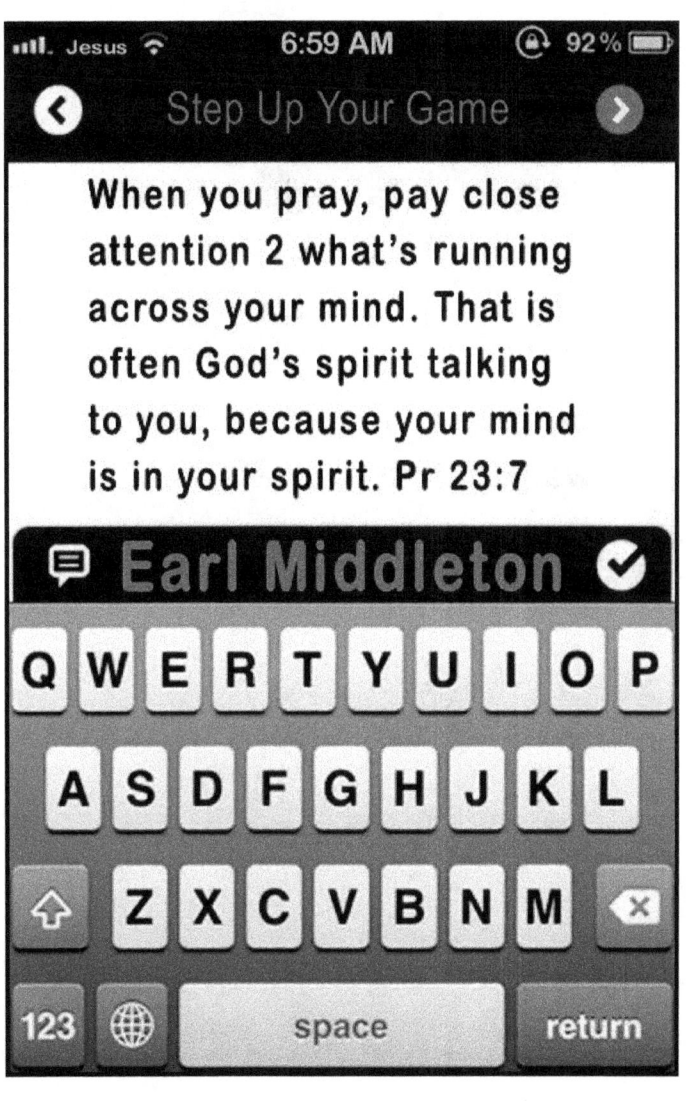

# March 12

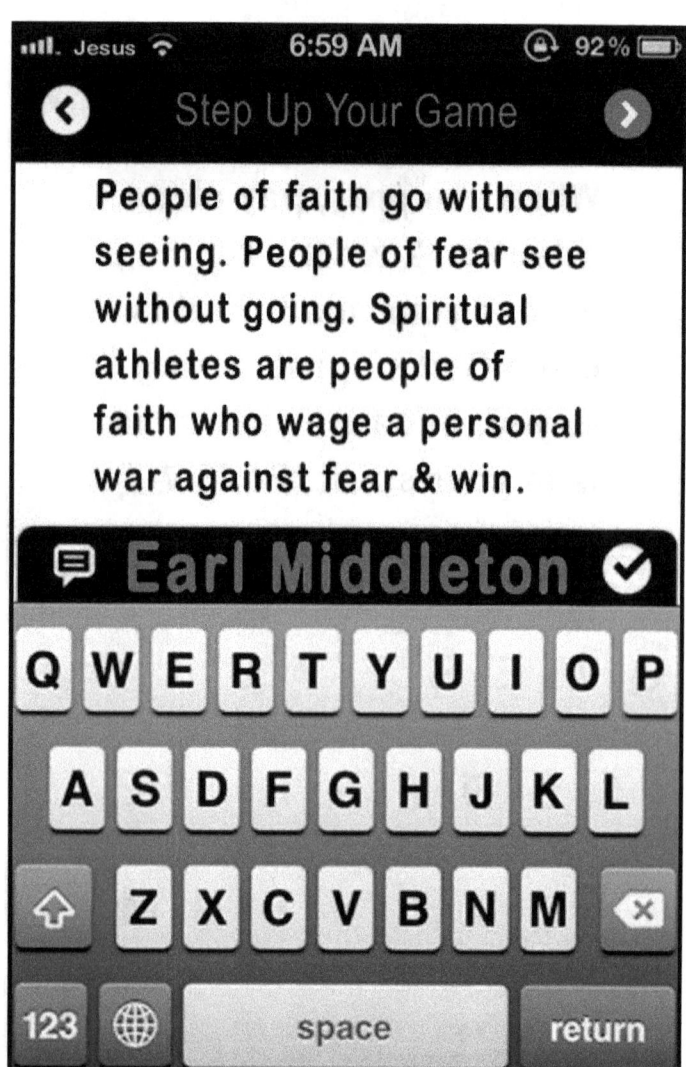

> People of faith go without seeing. People of fear see without going. Spiritual athletes are people of faith who wage a personal war against fear & win.

— Earl Middleton

# March 13

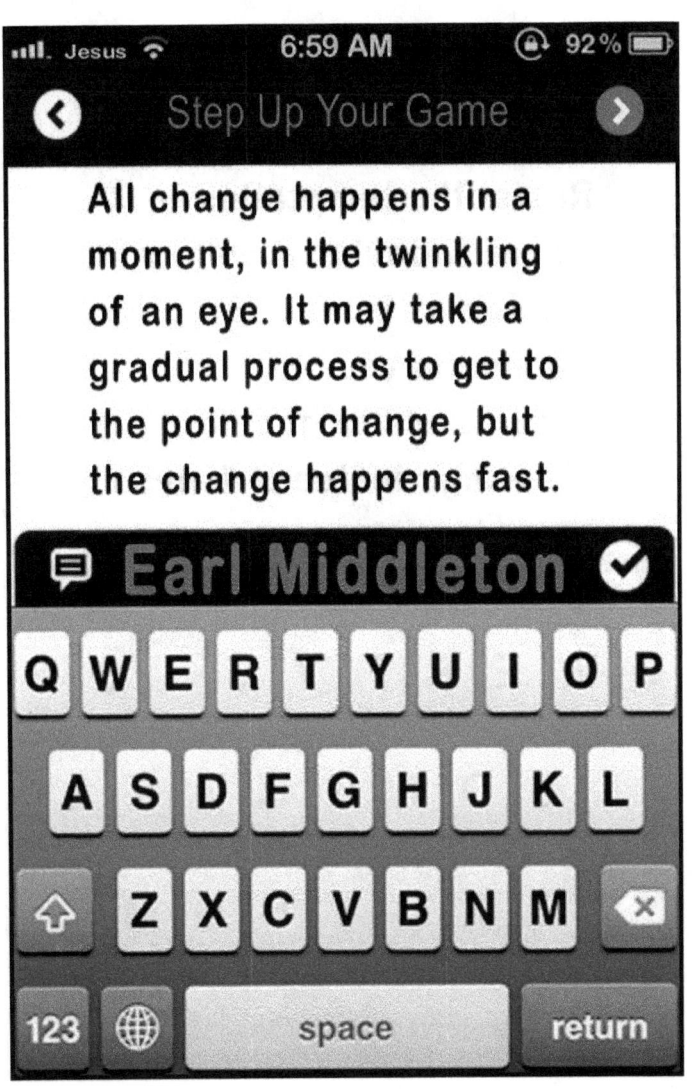

# March 14

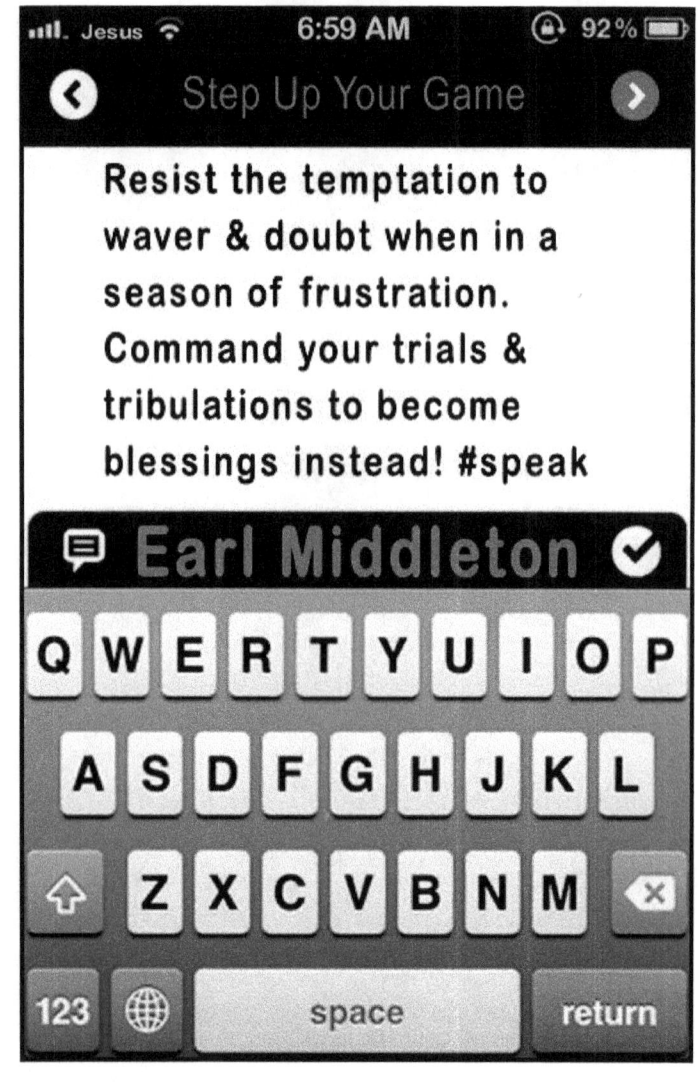

Resist the temptation to waver & doubt when in a season of frustration. Command your trials & tribulations to become blessings instead! #speak

# March 15

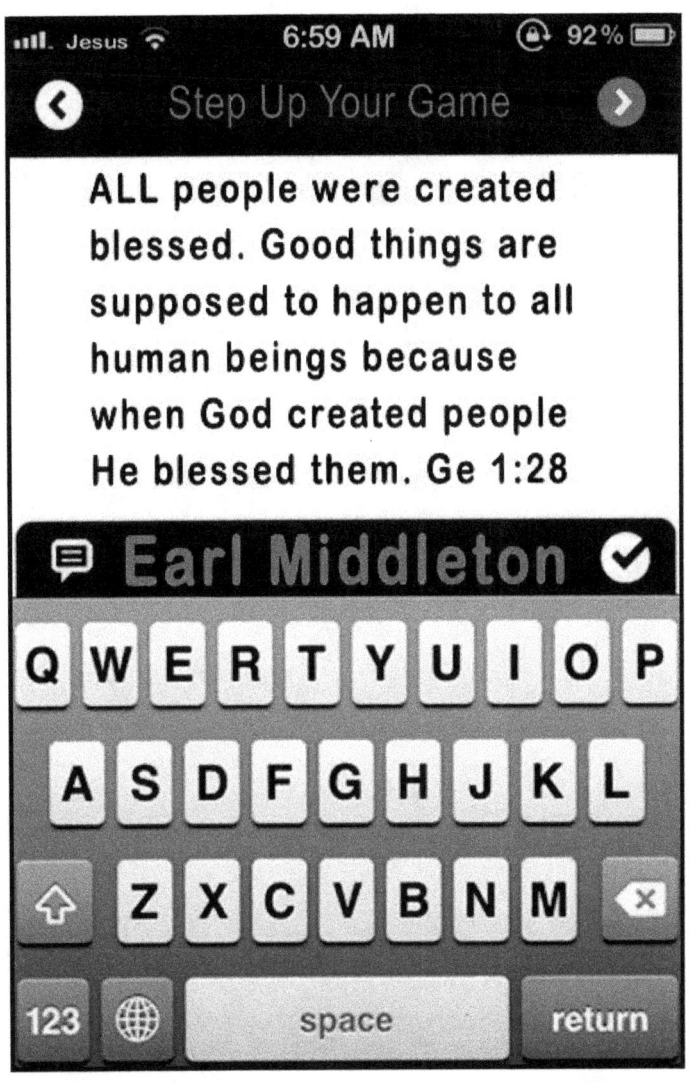

ALL people were created blessed. Good things are supposed to happen to all human beings because when God created people He blessed them. Ge 1:28

# March 16

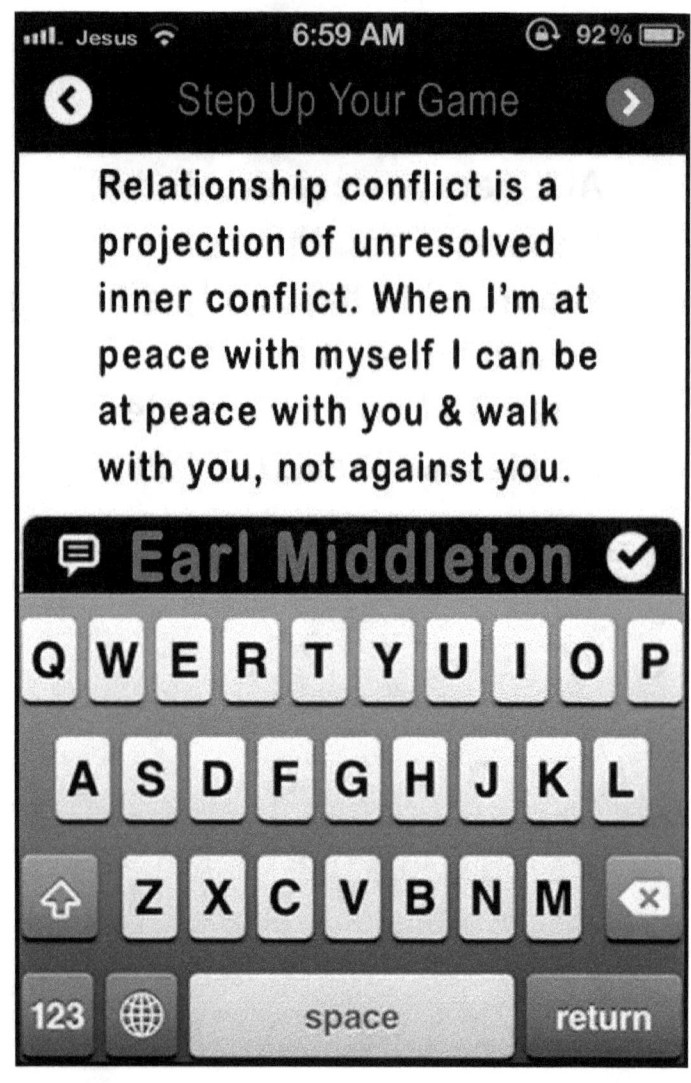

# March 17

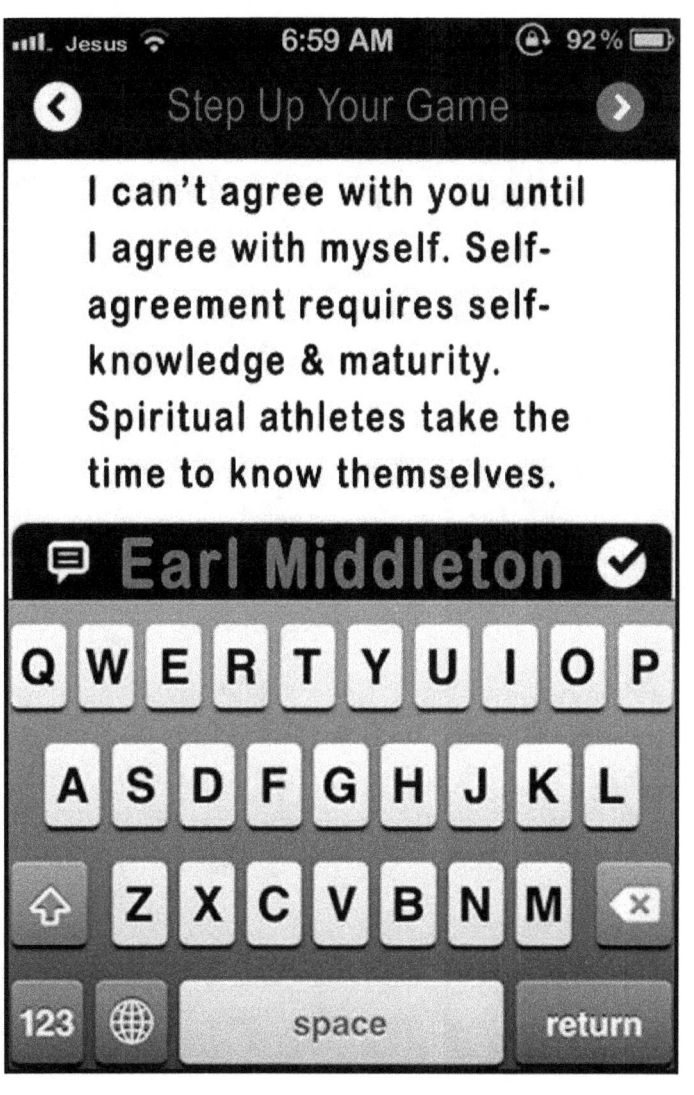

# March 18

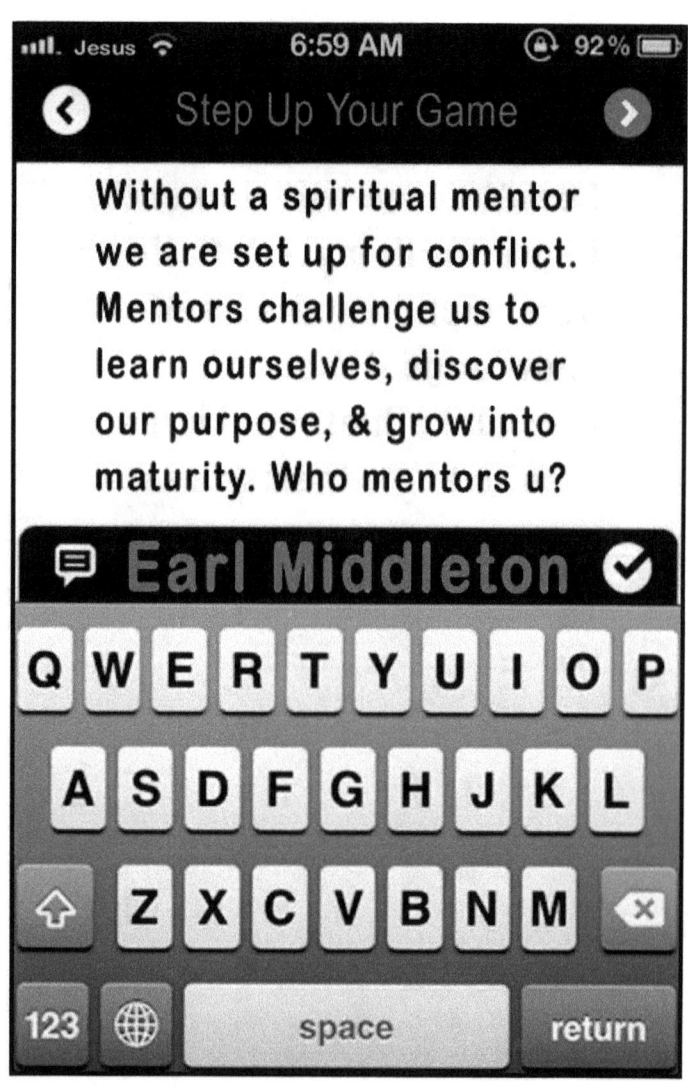

## Step Up Your Game

Without a spiritual mentor we are set up for conflict. Mentors challenge us to learn ourselves, discover our purpose, & grow into maturity. Who mentors u?

Earl Middleton

# March 19

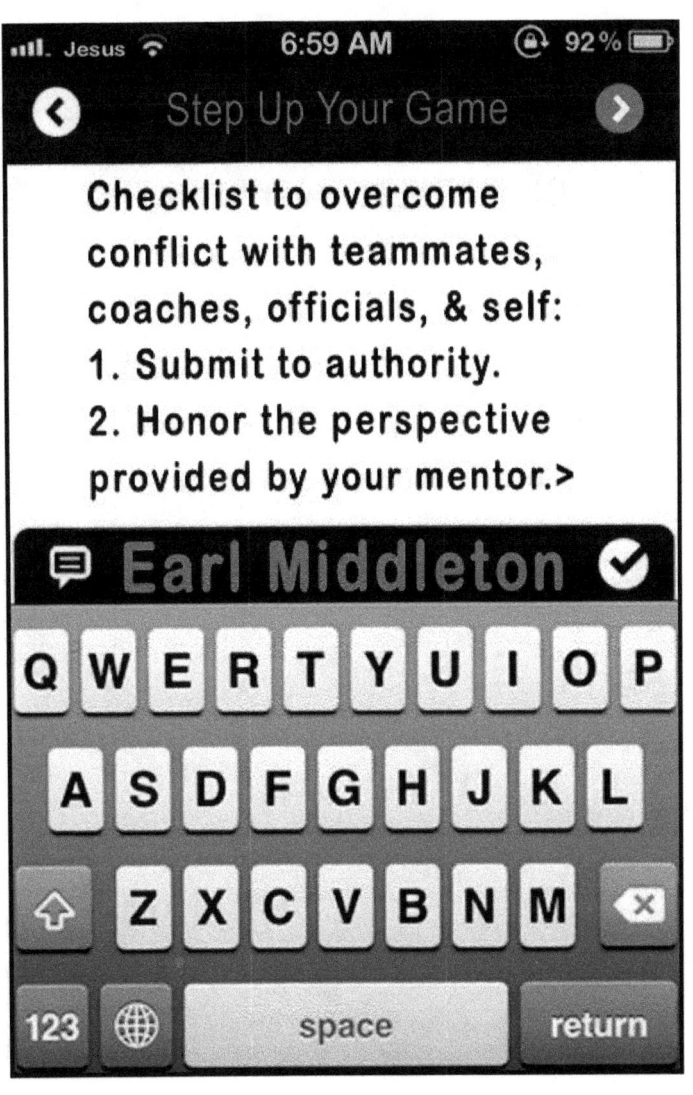

# March 20

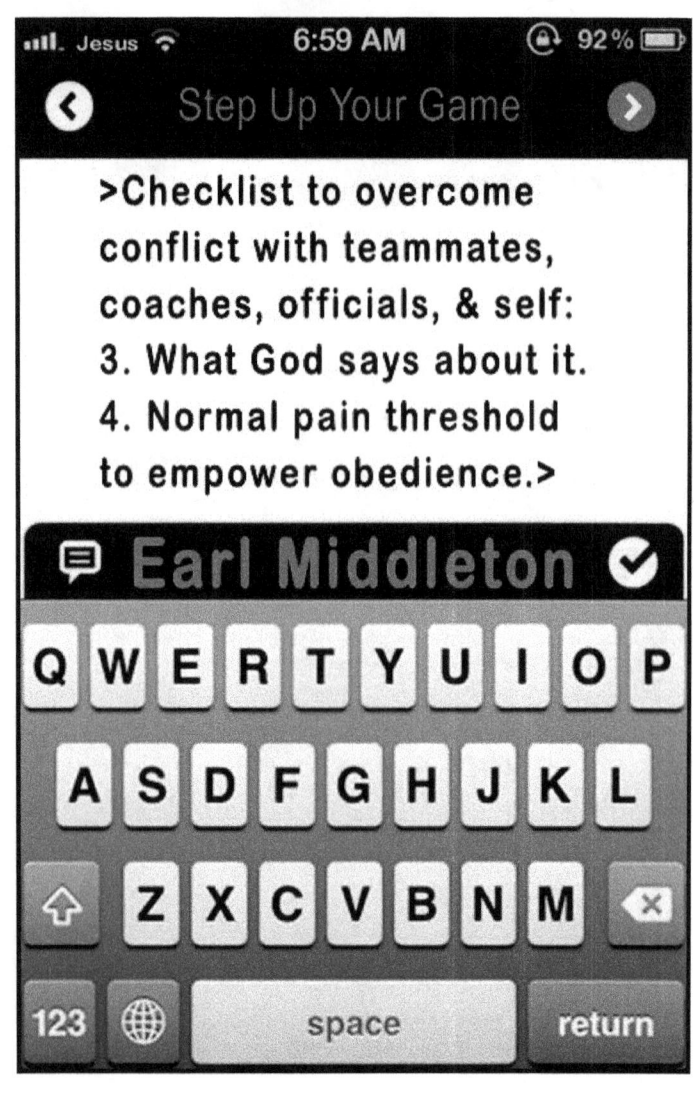

# March 21

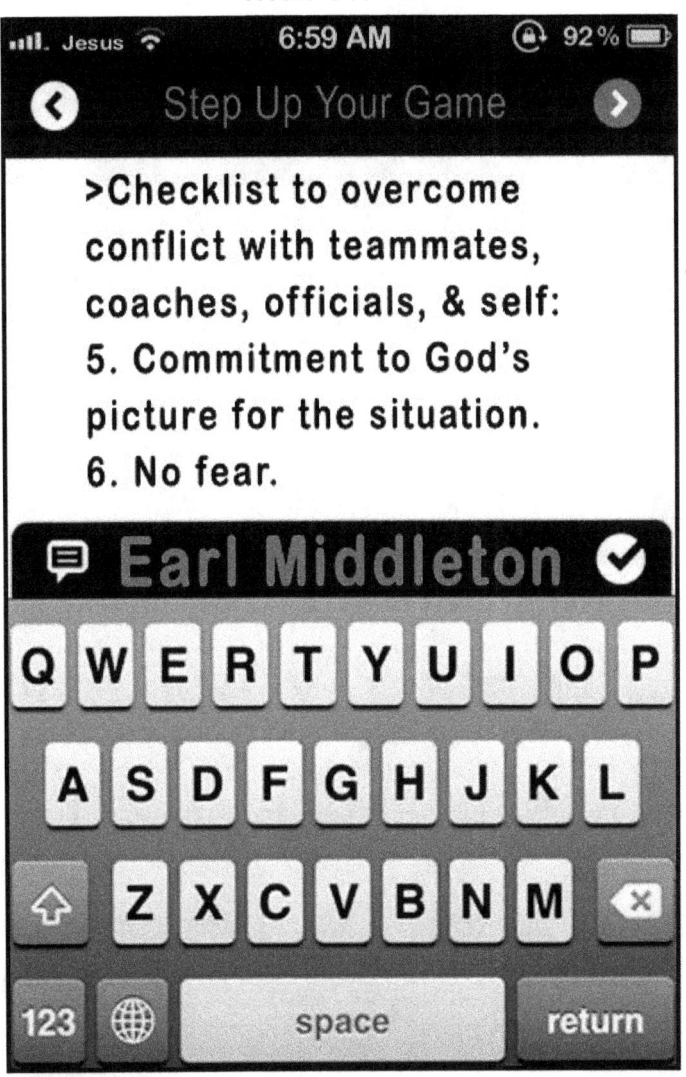

>Checklist to overcome conflict with teammates, coaches, officials, & self:
5. Commitment to God's picture for the situation.
6. No fear.

# March 22

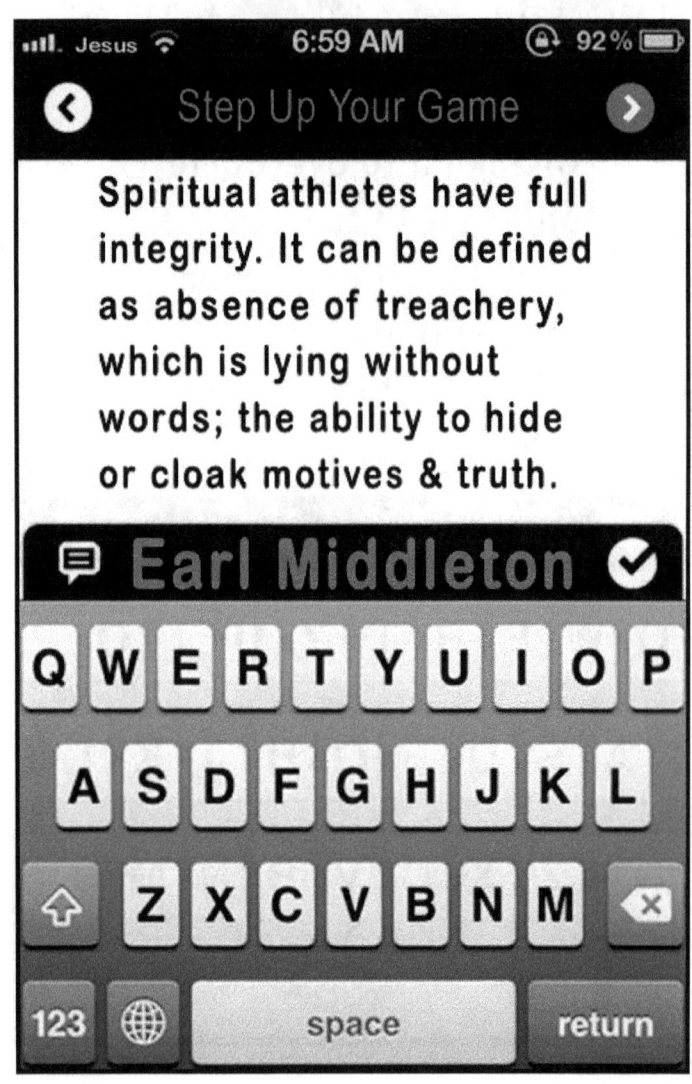

# March 23

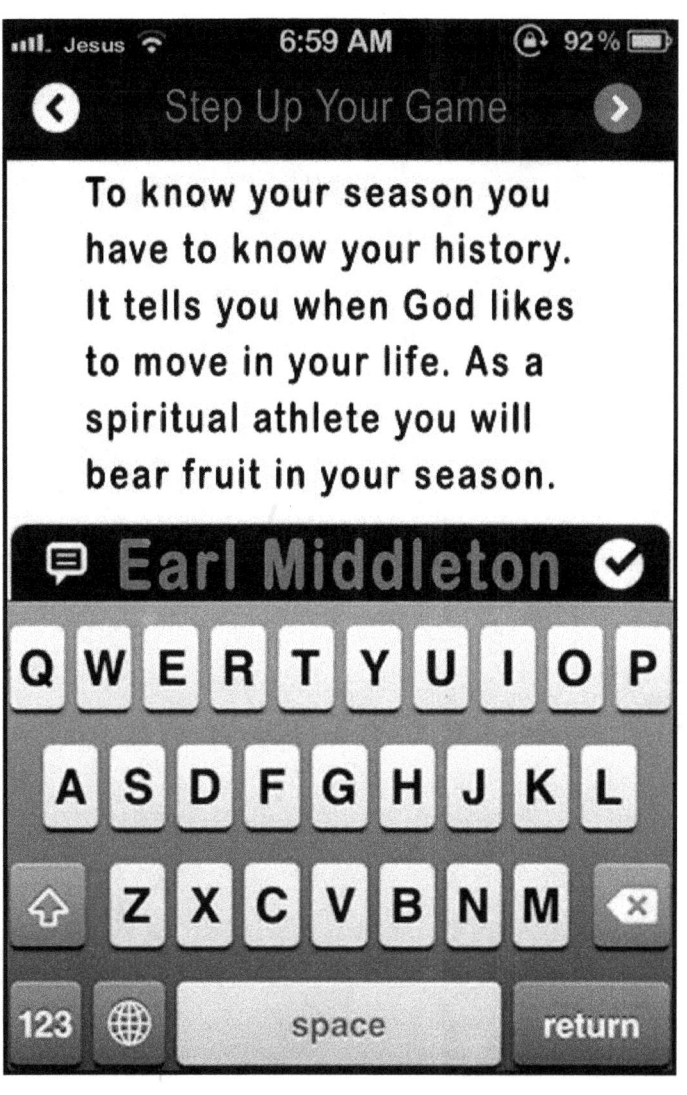

# March 24

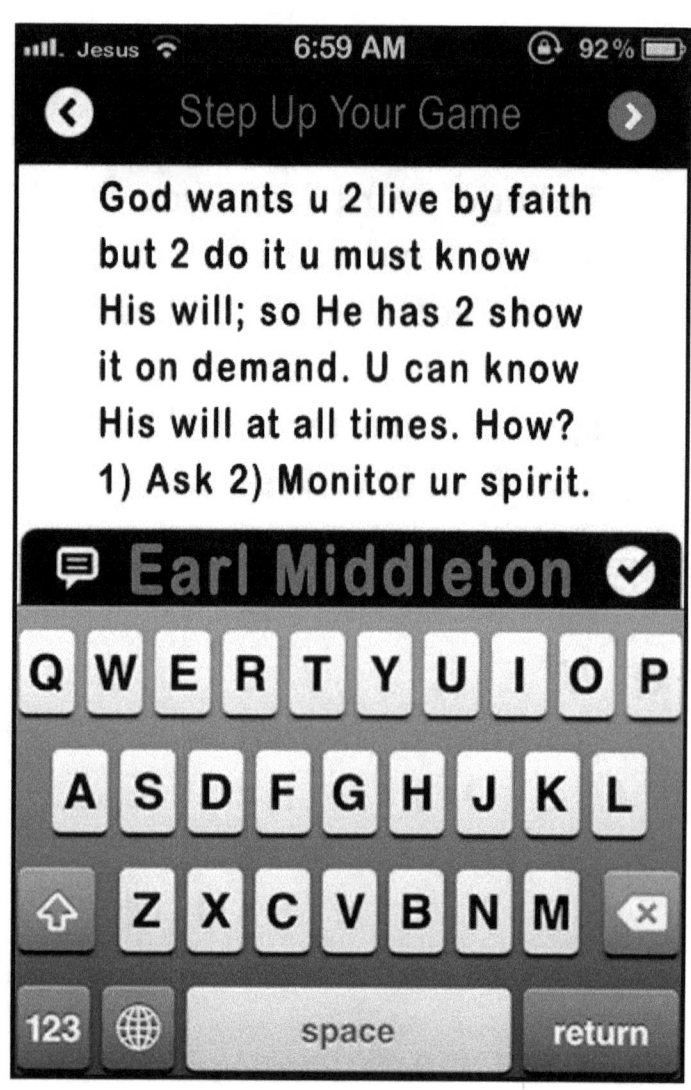

God wants u 2 live by faith but 2 do it u must know His will; so He has 2 show it on demand. U can know His will at all times. How? 1) Ask 2) Monitor ur spirit.

# March 25

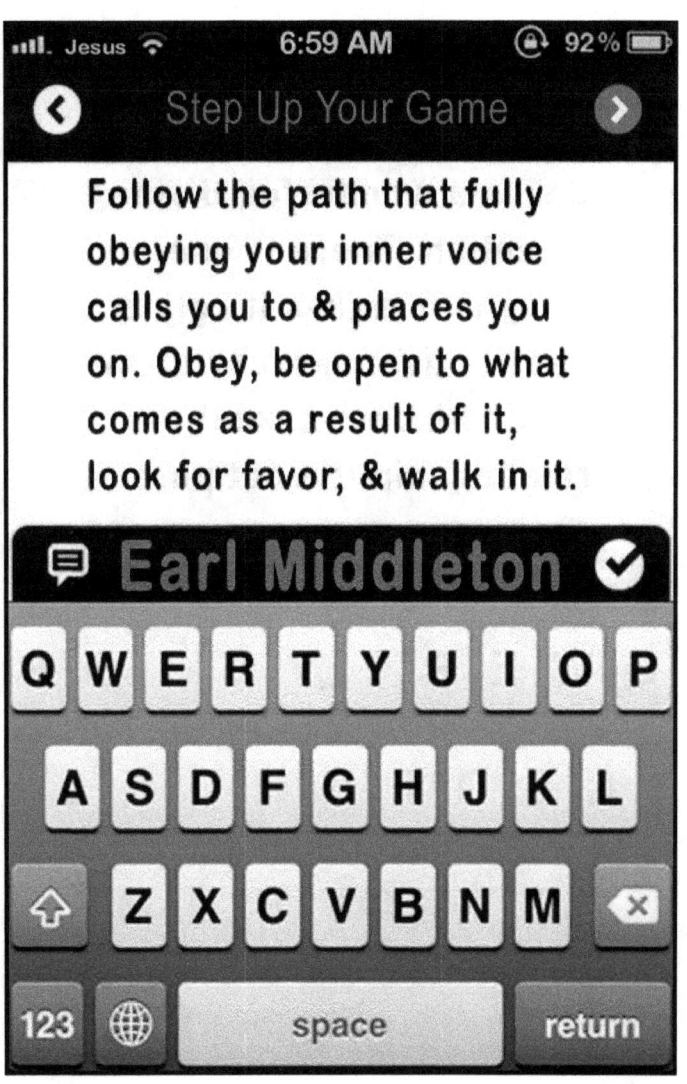

# March 26

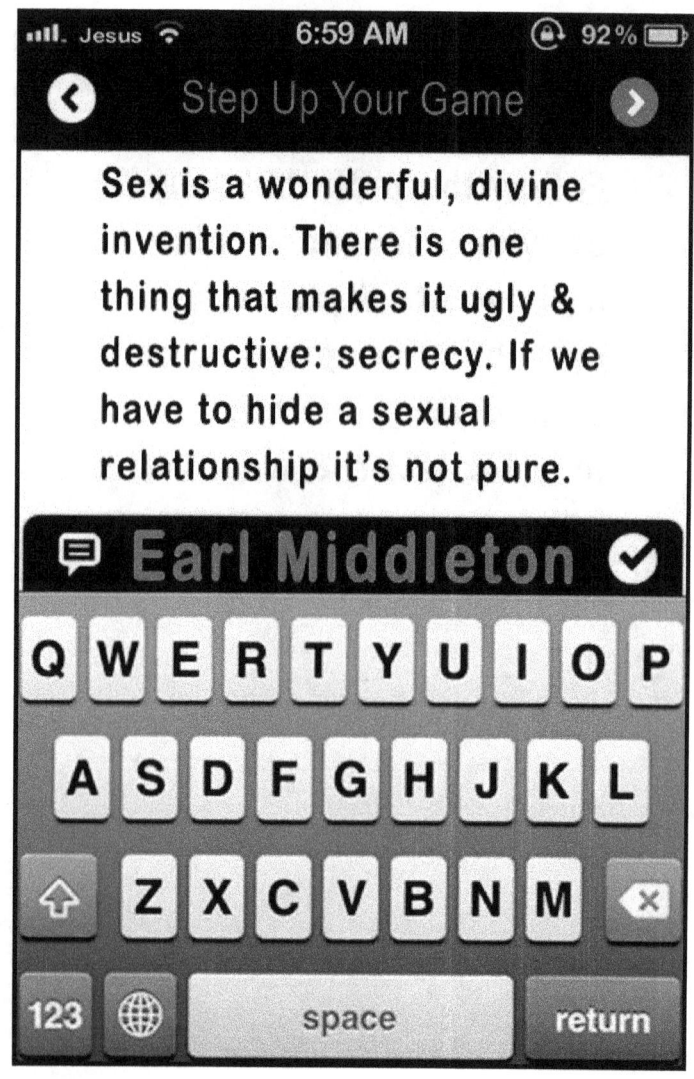

Sex is a wonderful, divine invention. There is one thing that makes it ugly & destructive: secrecy. If we have to hide a sexual relationship it's not pure.

— Earl Middleton

# March 27

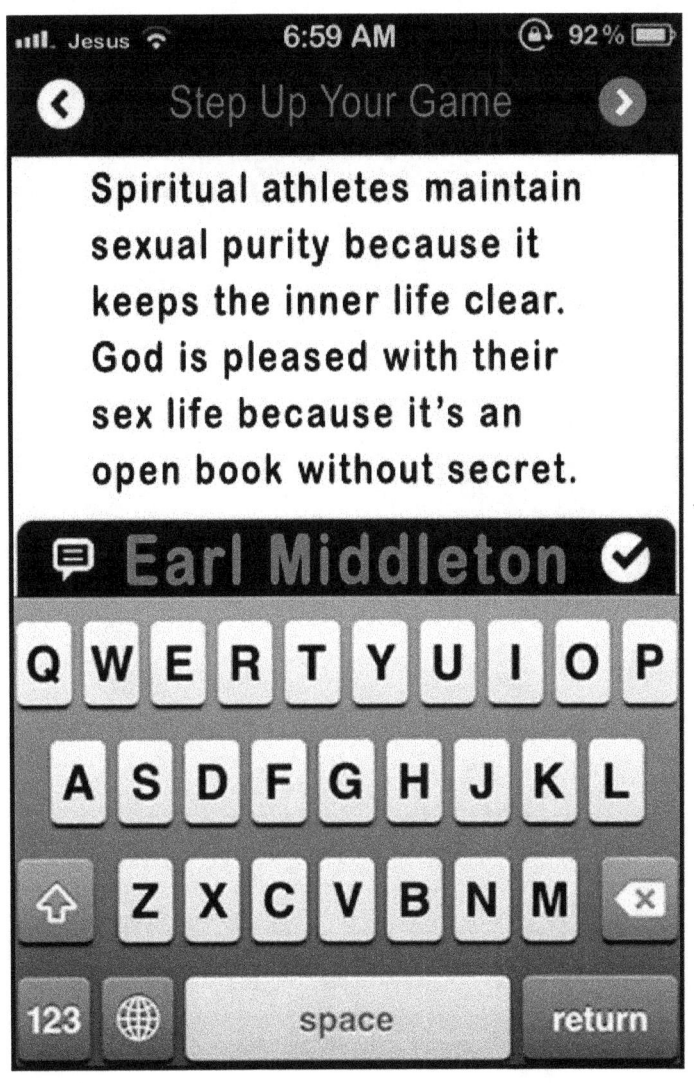

# March 28

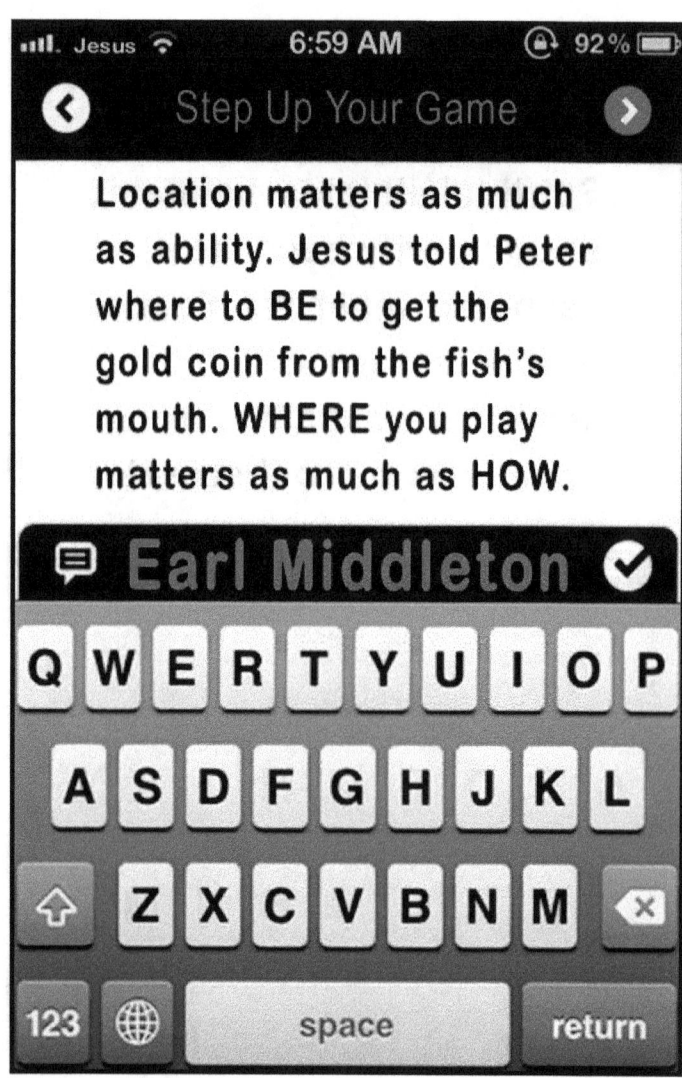

**Step Up Your Game**

Location matters as much as ability. Jesus told Peter where to BE to get the gold coin from the fish's mouth. WHERE you play matters as much as HOW.

Earl Middleton

# March 29

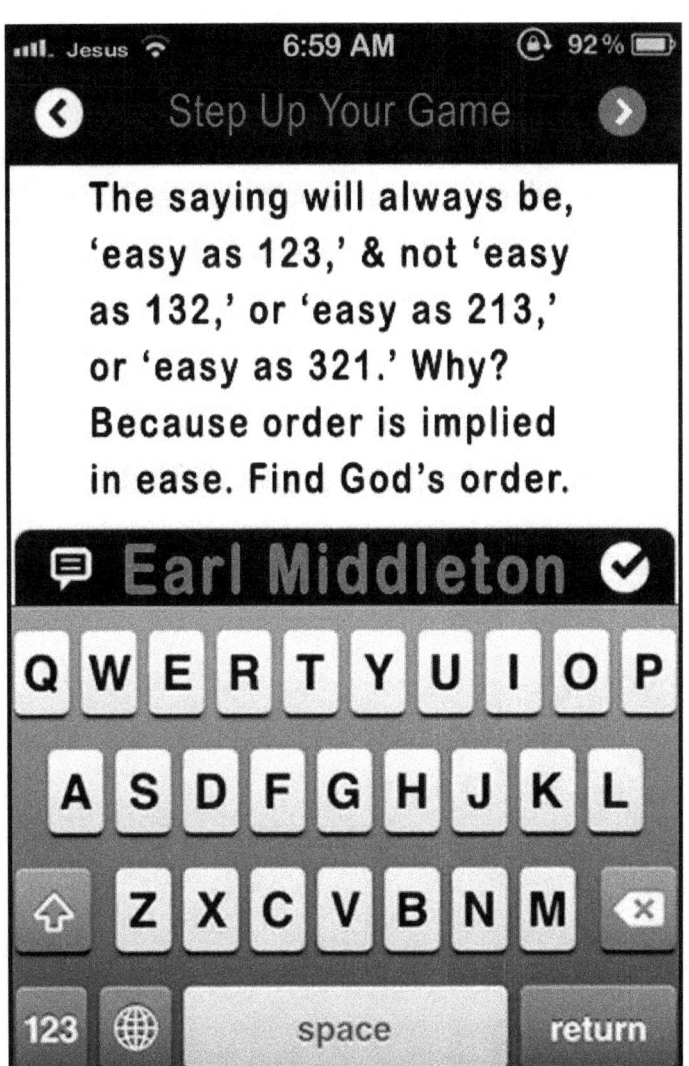

The saying will always be, 'easy as 123,' & not 'easy as 132,' or 'easy as 213,' or 'easy as 321.' Why? Because order is implied in ease. Find God's order.

Earl Middleton

# March 30

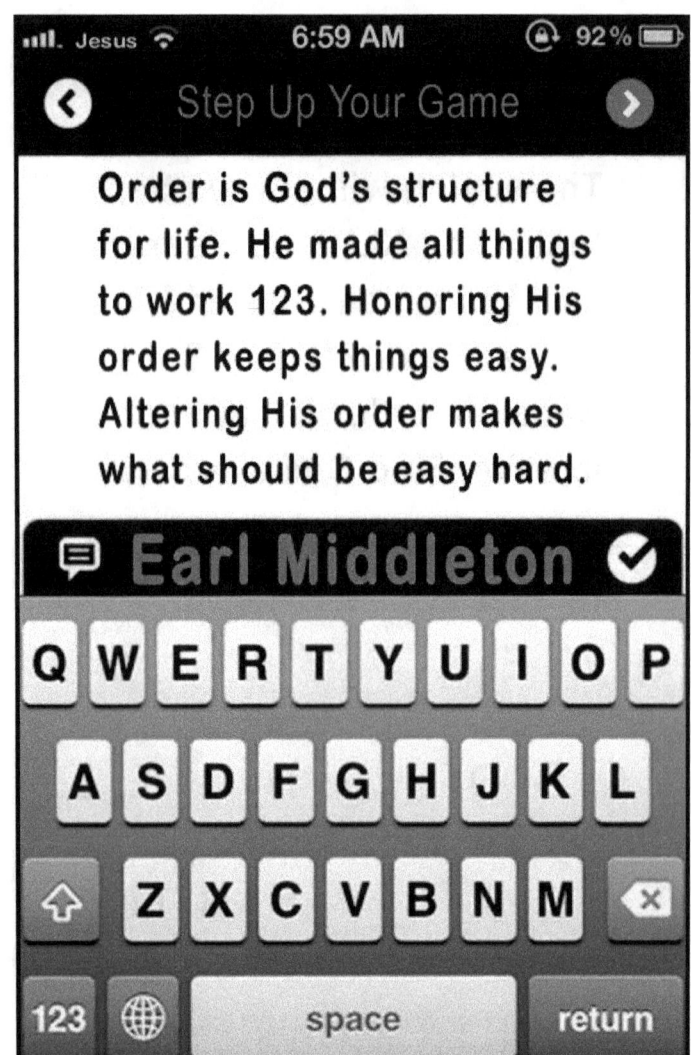

Order is God's structure for life. He made all things to work 123. Honoring His order keeps things easy. Altering His order makes what should be easy hard.

# March 31

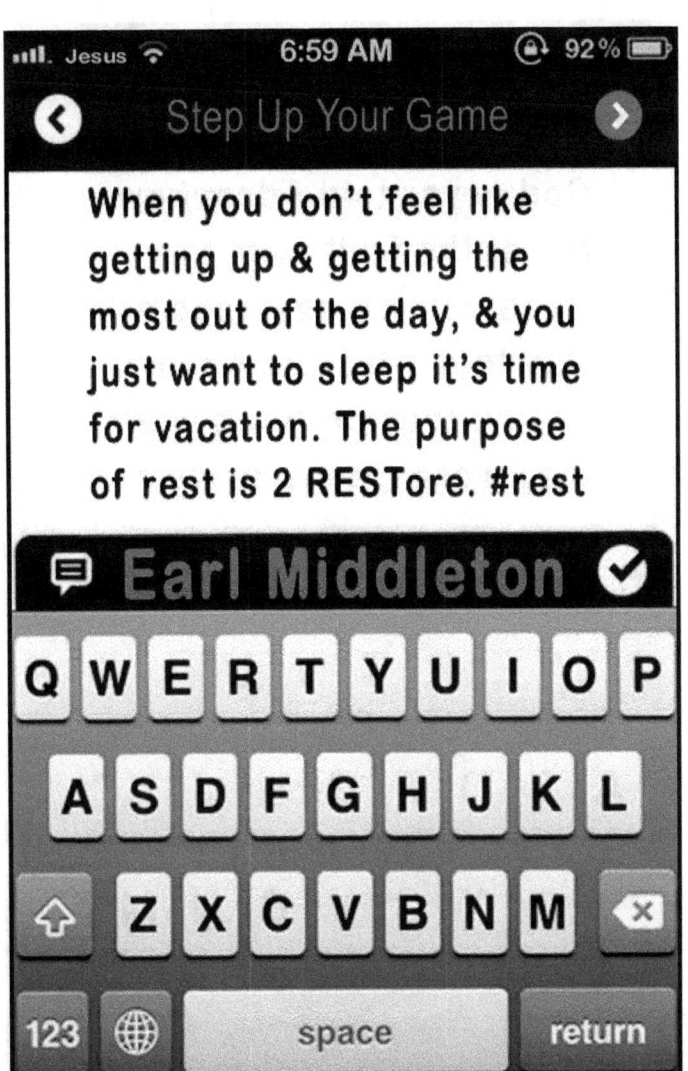

**Step Up Your Game**

When you don't feel like getting up & getting the most out of the day, & you just want to sleep it's time for vacation. The purpose of rest is 2 RESTore. #rest

# April 1

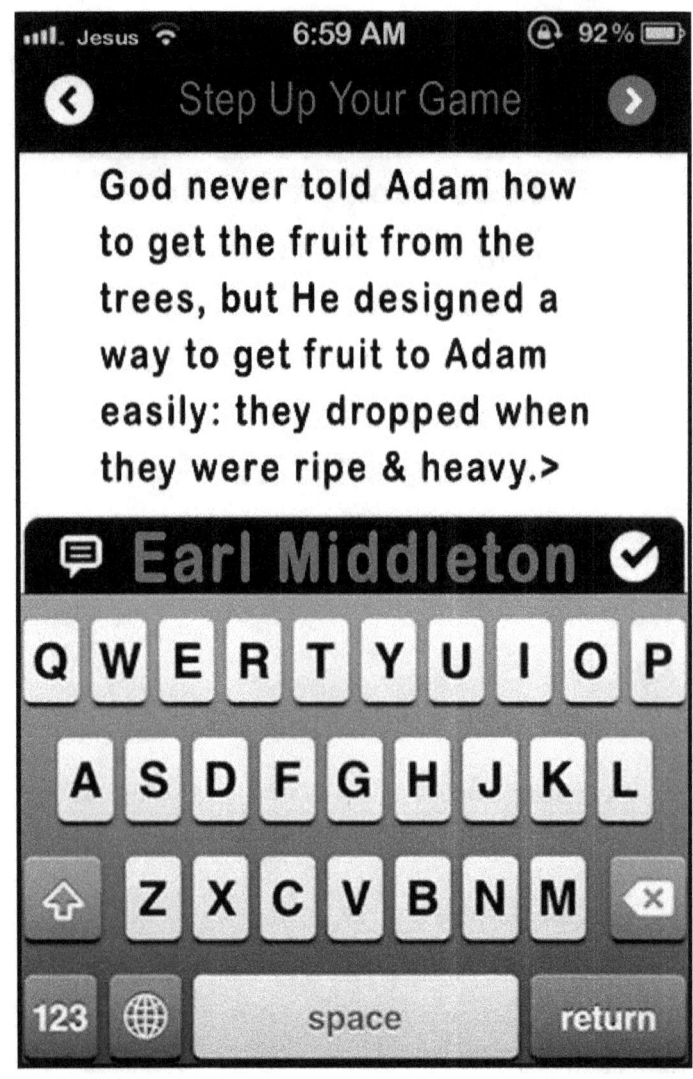

## Step Up Your Game

God never told Adam how to get the fruit from the trees, but He designed a way to get fruit to Adam easily: they dropped when they were ripe & heavy.>

Earl Middleton

# April 2

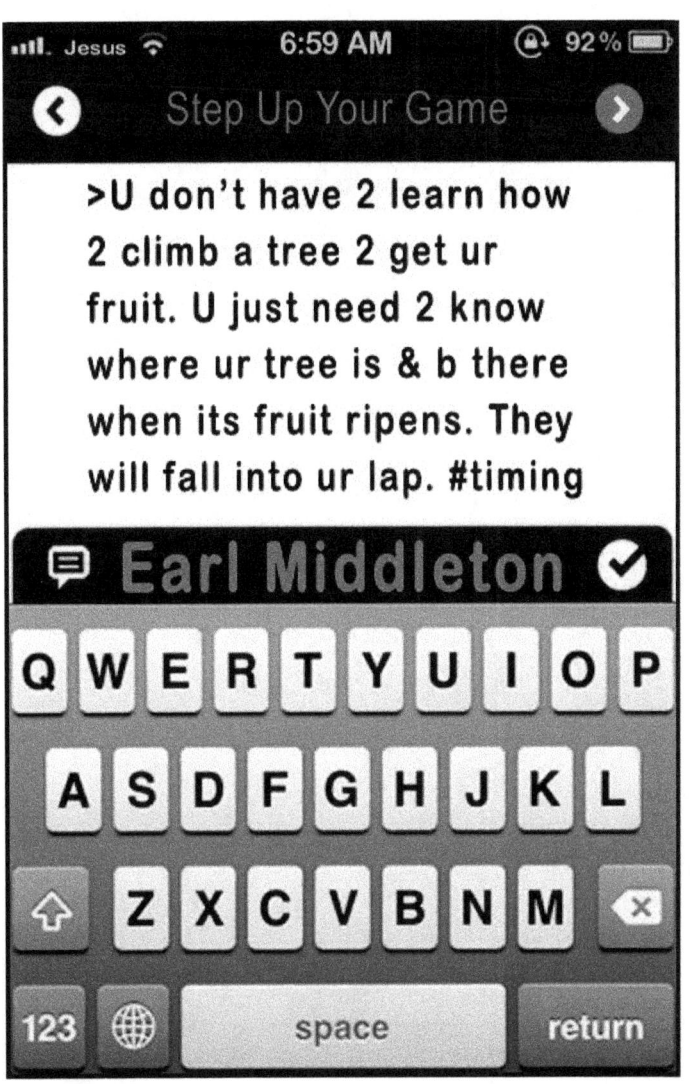

>U don't have 2 learn how 2 climb a tree 2 get ur fruit. U just need 2 know where ur tree is & b there when its fruit ripens. They will fall into ur lap. #timing

# April 3

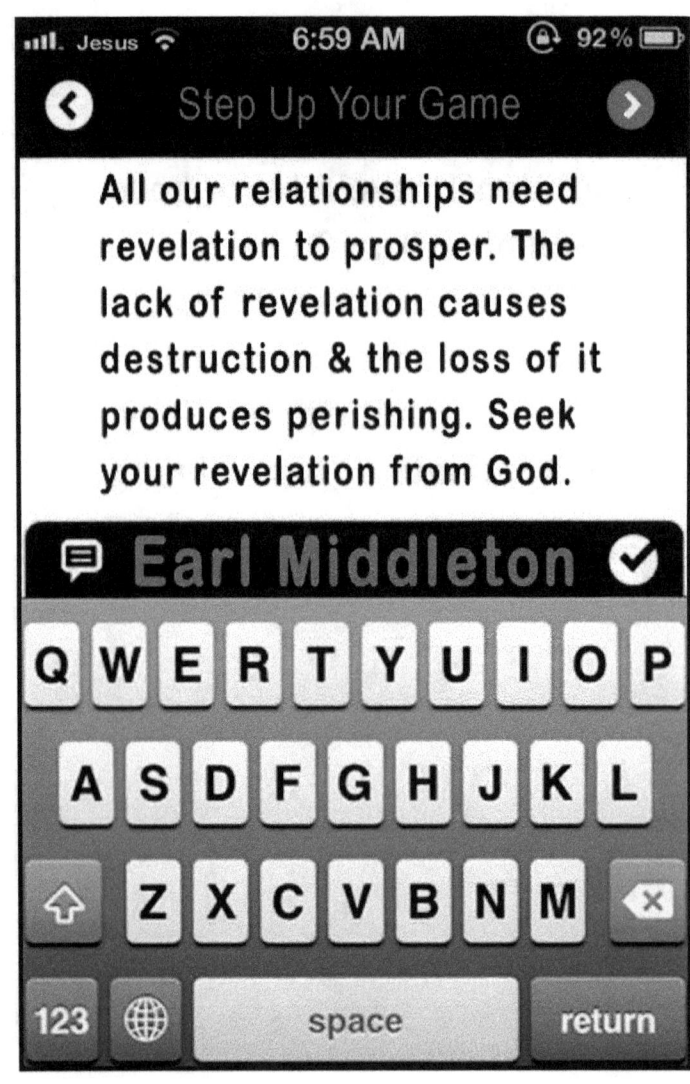

**Step Up Your Game**

All our relationships need revelation to prosper. The lack of revelation causes destruction & the loss of it produces perishing. Seek your revelation from God.

# April 4

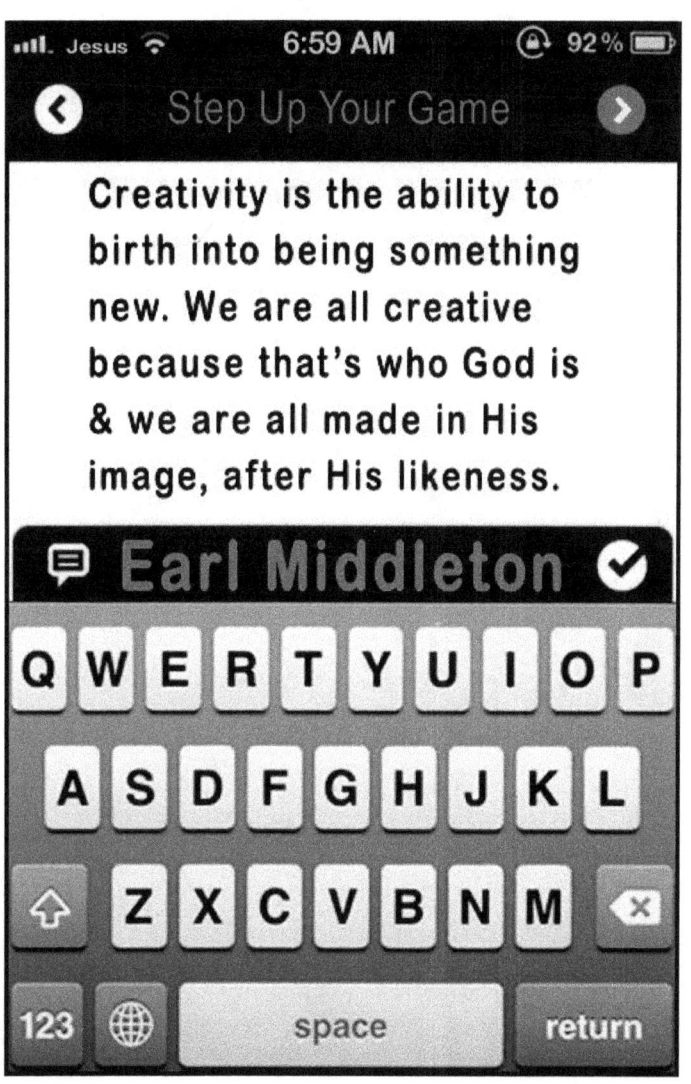

Creativity is the ability to birth into being something new. We are all creative because that's who God is & we are all made in His image, after His likeness.

— Earl Middleton

## April 5

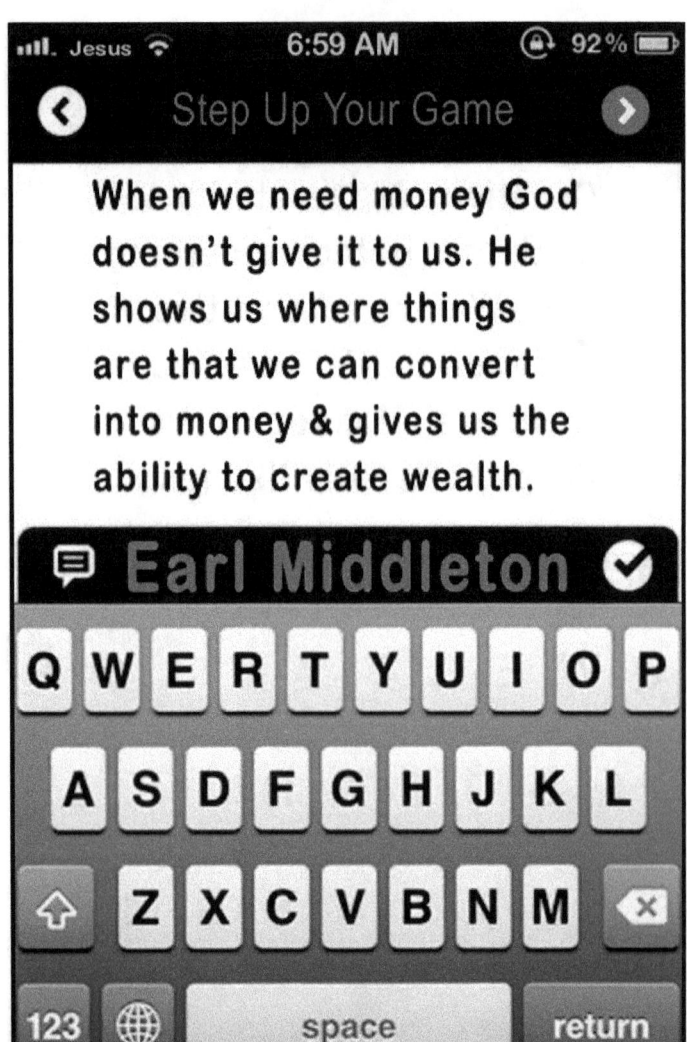

When we need money God doesn't give it to us. He shows us where things are that we can convert into money & gives us the ability to create wealth.

Earl Middleton

# April 6

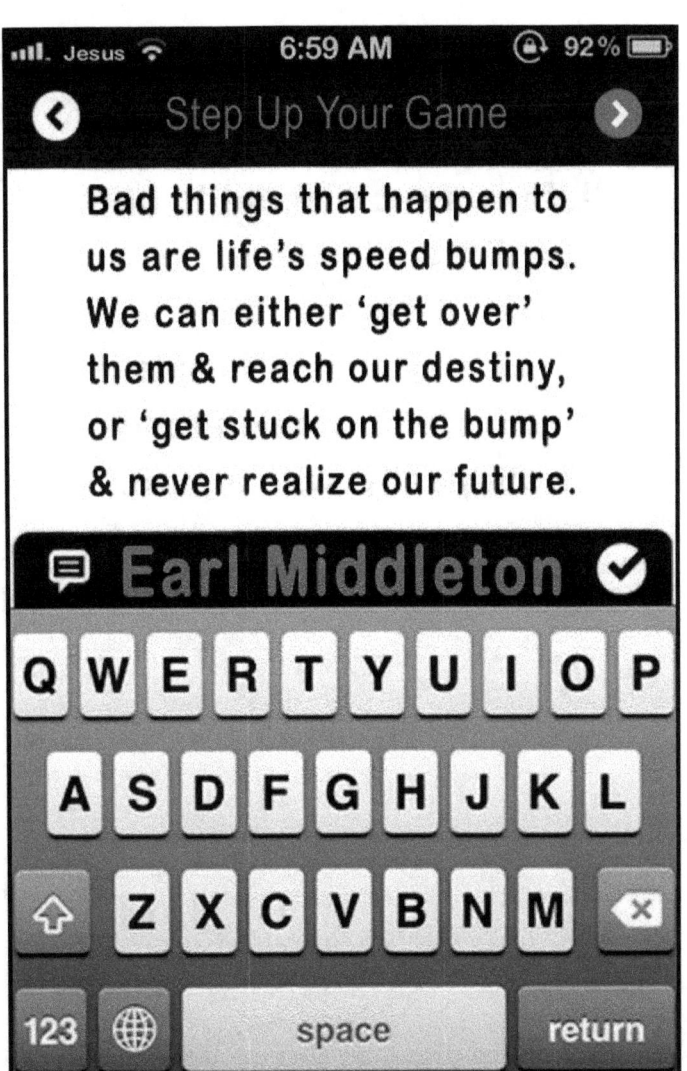

> Bad things that happen to us are life's speed bumps. We can either 'get over' them & reach our destiny, or 'get stuck on the bump' & never realize our future.
>
> — Earl Middleton

# April 7

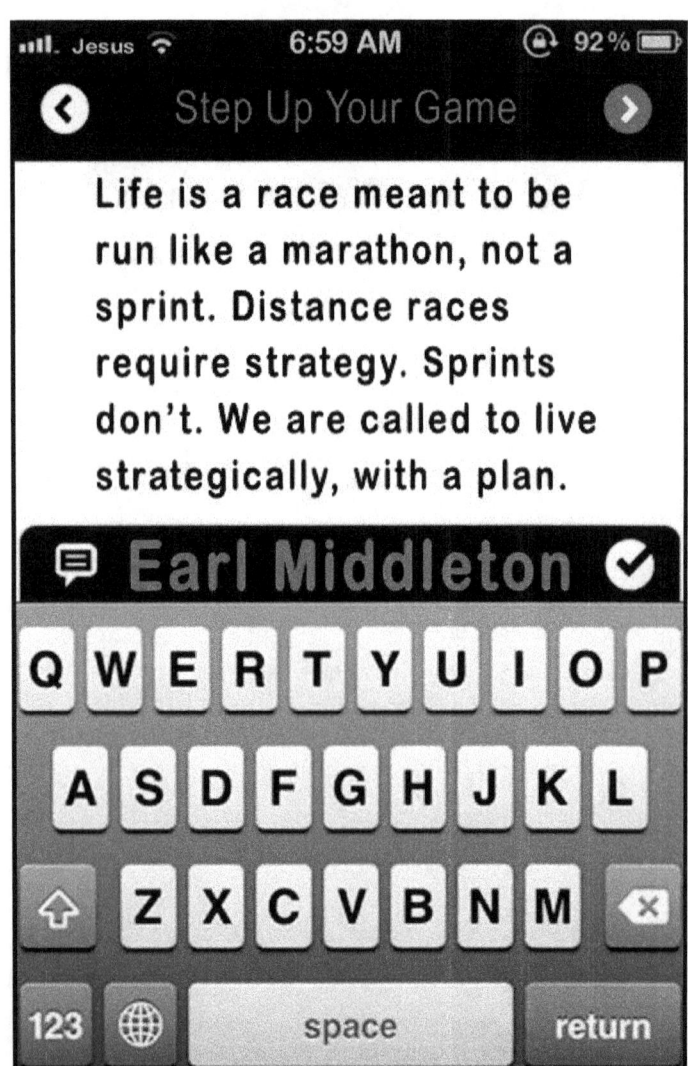

## Step Up Your Game

Life is a race meant to be run like a marathon, not a sprint. Distance races require strategy. Sprints don't. We are called to live strategically, with a plan.

— Earl Middleton

# April 8

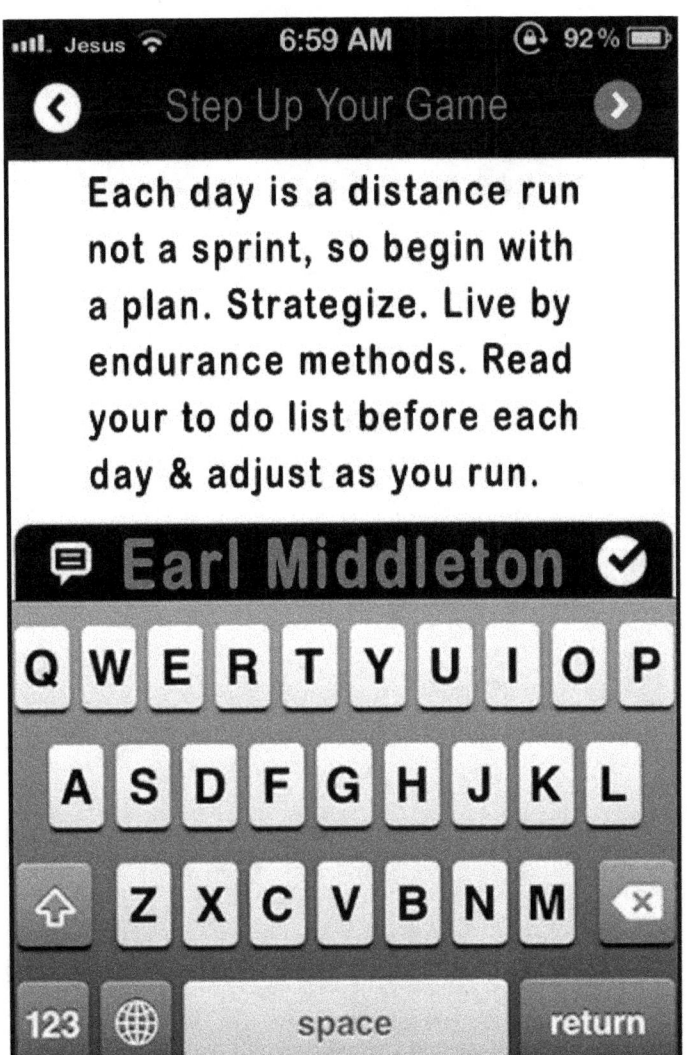

Each day is a distance run not a sprint, so begin with a plan. Strategize. Live by endurance methods. Read your to do list before each day & adjust as you run.

— Earl Middleton

# April 9

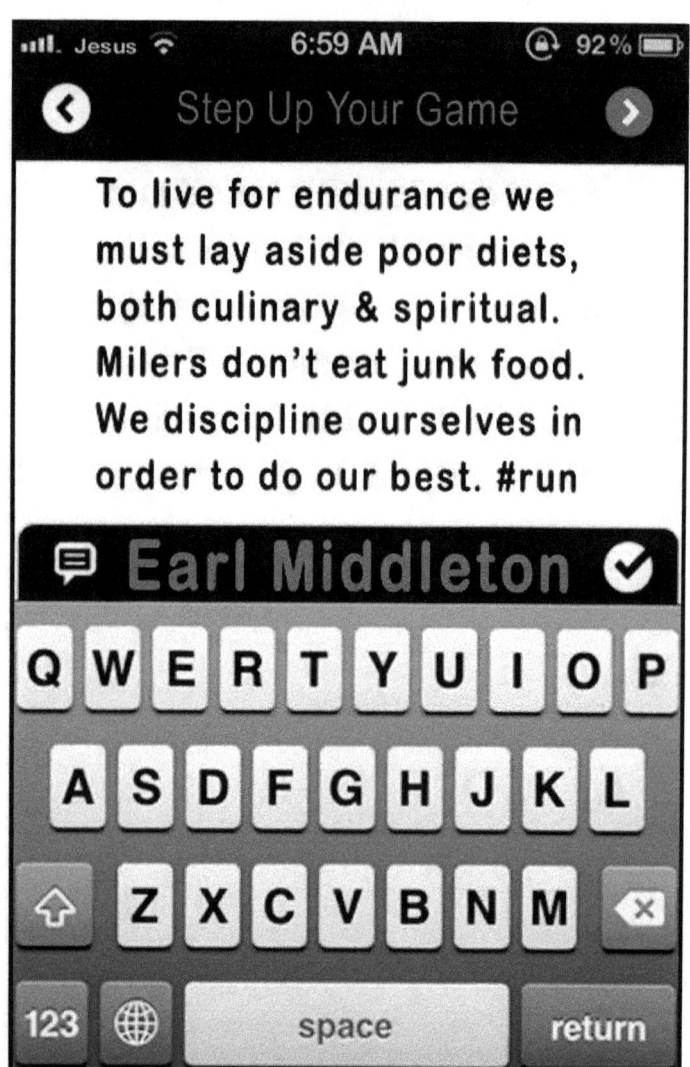

# April 10

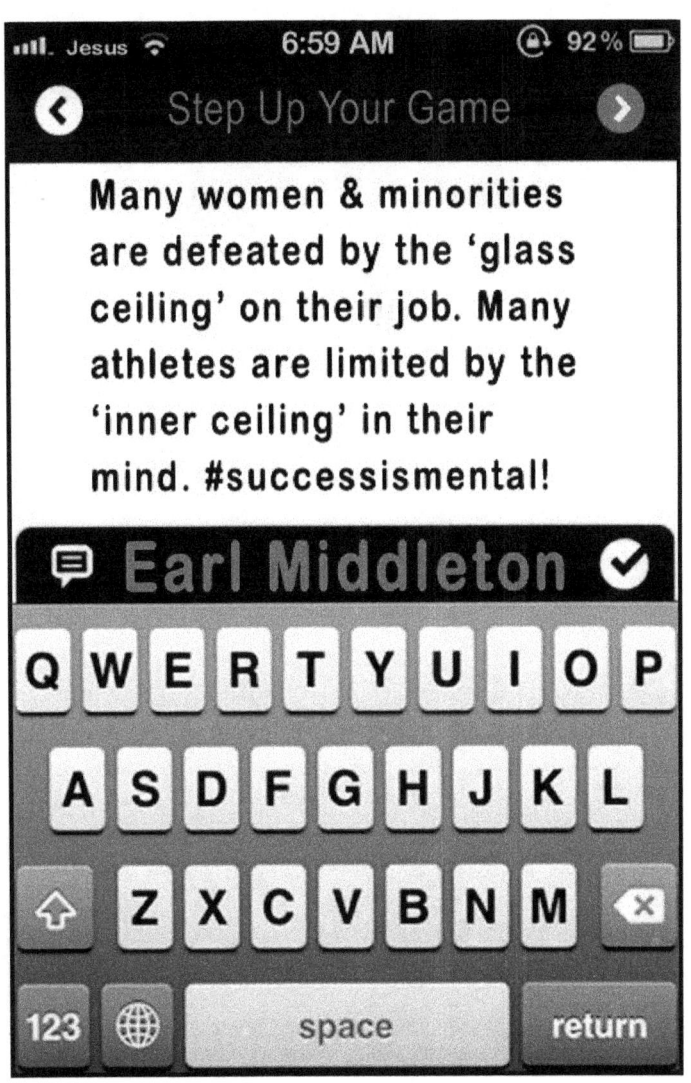

## Step Up Your Game

Many women & minorities are defeated by the 'glass ceiling' on their job. Many athletes are limited by the 'inner ceiling' in their mind. #successismental!

— Earl Middleton

# April 11

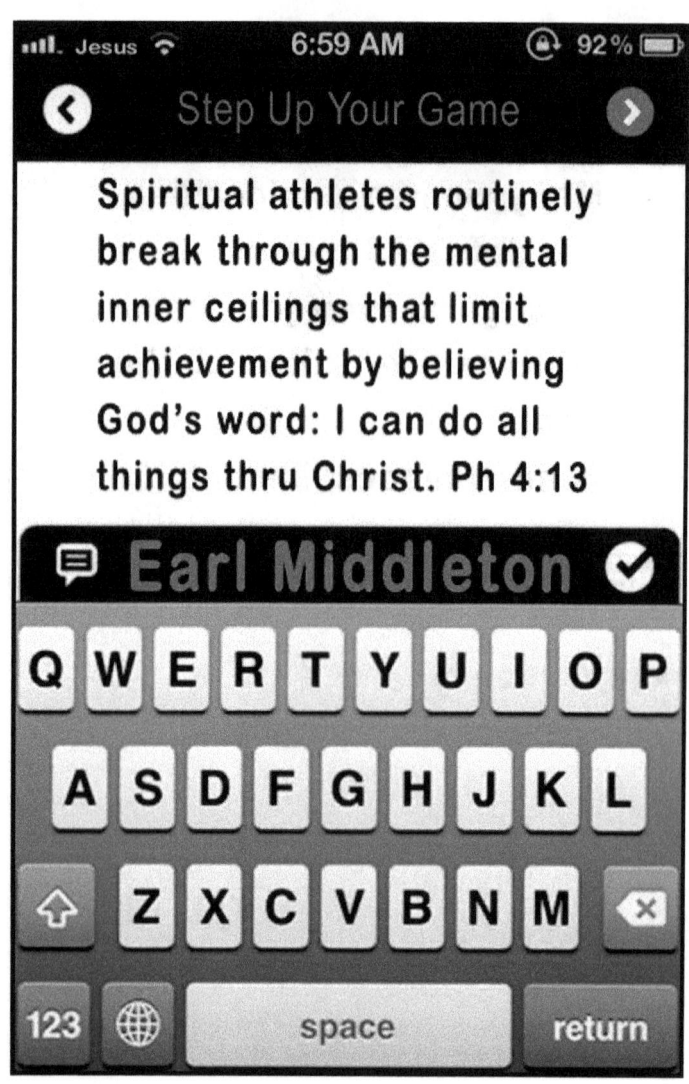

## Step Up Your Game

Spiritual athletes routinely break through the mental inner ceilings that limit achievement by believing God's word: I can do all things thru Christ. Ph 4:13

Earl Middleton

# April 12

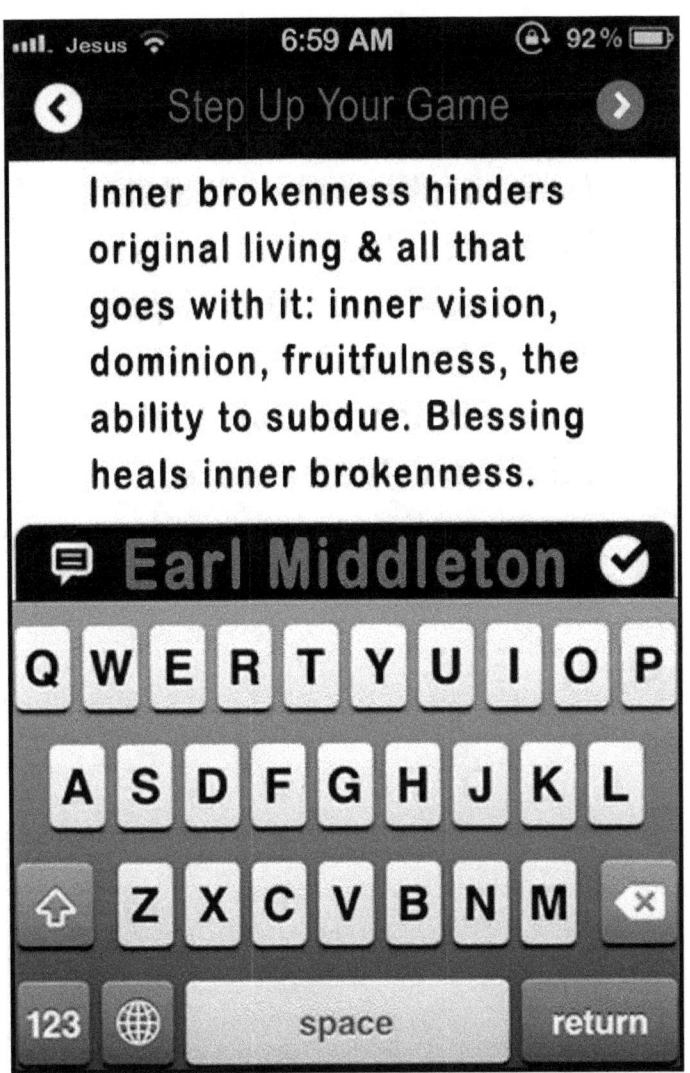

Inner brokenness hinders original living & all that goes with it: inner vision, dominion, fruitfulness, the ability to subdue. Blessing heals inner brokenness.

# April 13

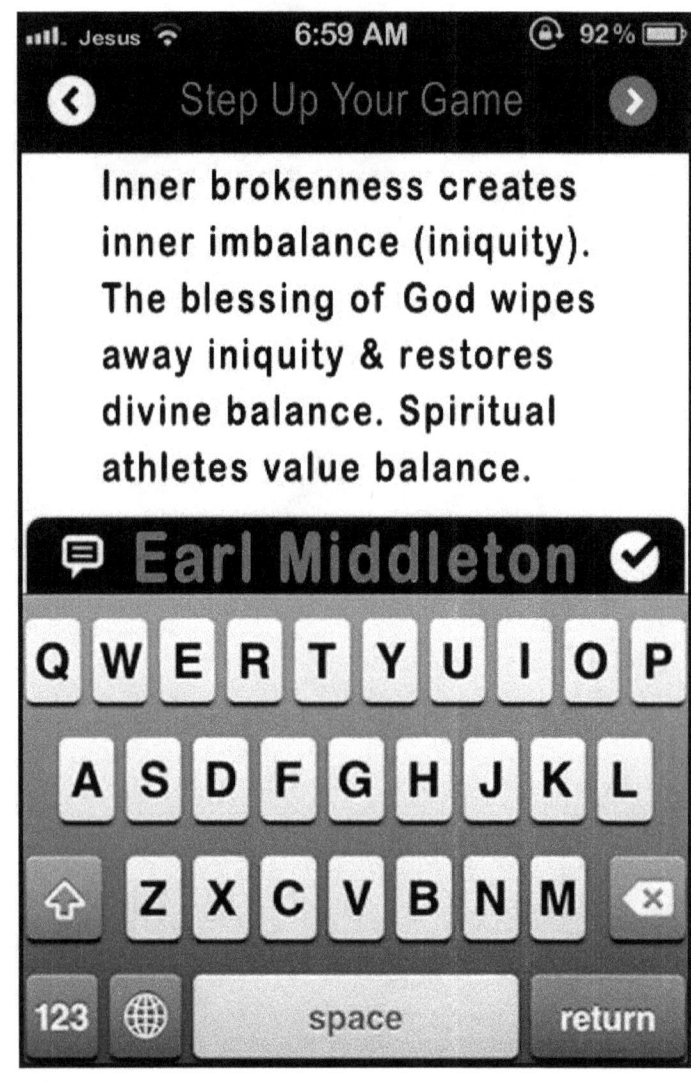

**Step Up Your Game**

Inner brokenness creates inner imbalance (iniquity). The blessing of God wipes away iniquity & restores divine balance. Spiritual athletes value balance.

Earl Middleton

# April 14

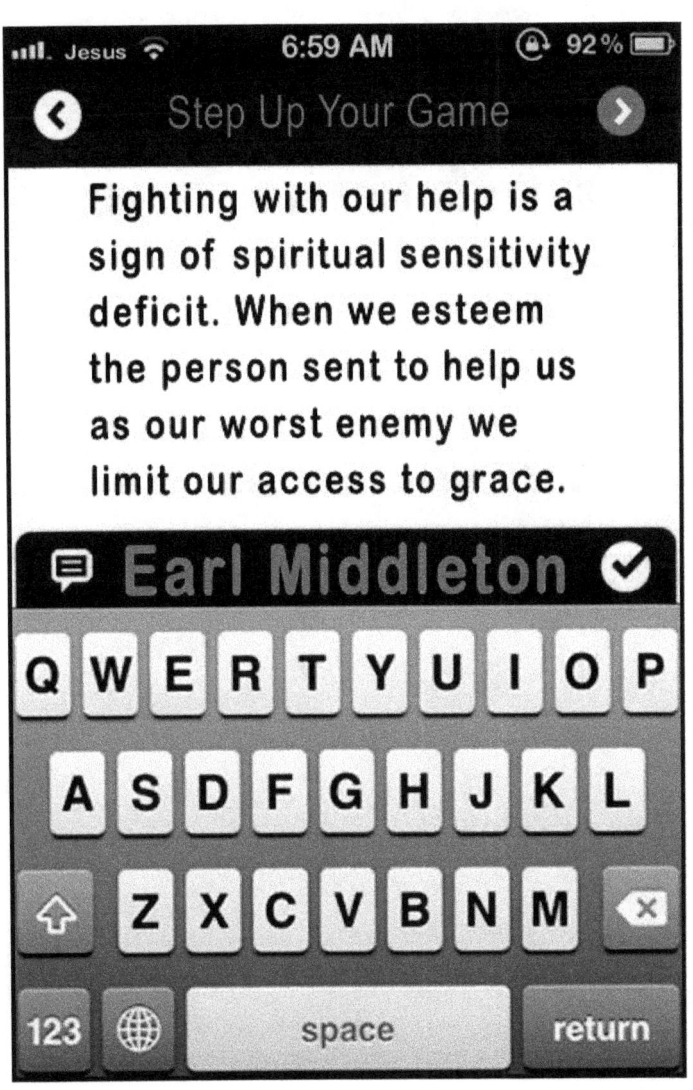

**Step Up Your Game**

Fighting with our help is a sign of spiritual sensitivity deficit. When we esteem the person sent to help us as our worst enemy we limit our access to grace.

Earl Middleton

# April 15

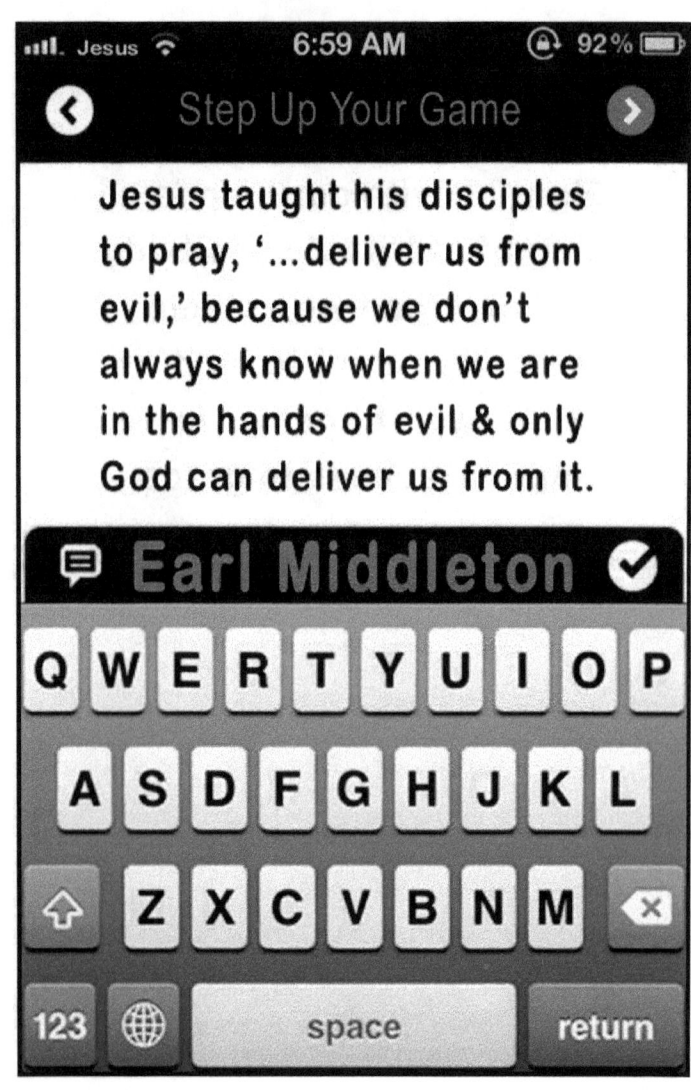

Jesus taught his disciples to pray, '...deliver us from evil,' because we don't always know when we are in the hands of evil & only God can deliver us from it.

# April 16

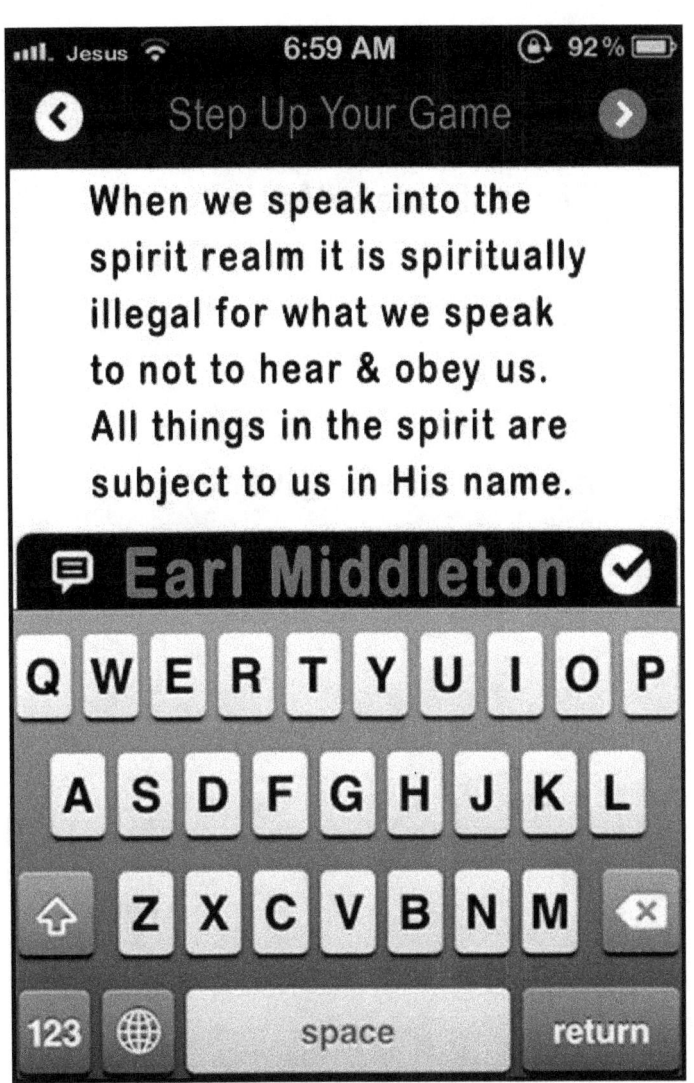

# April 17

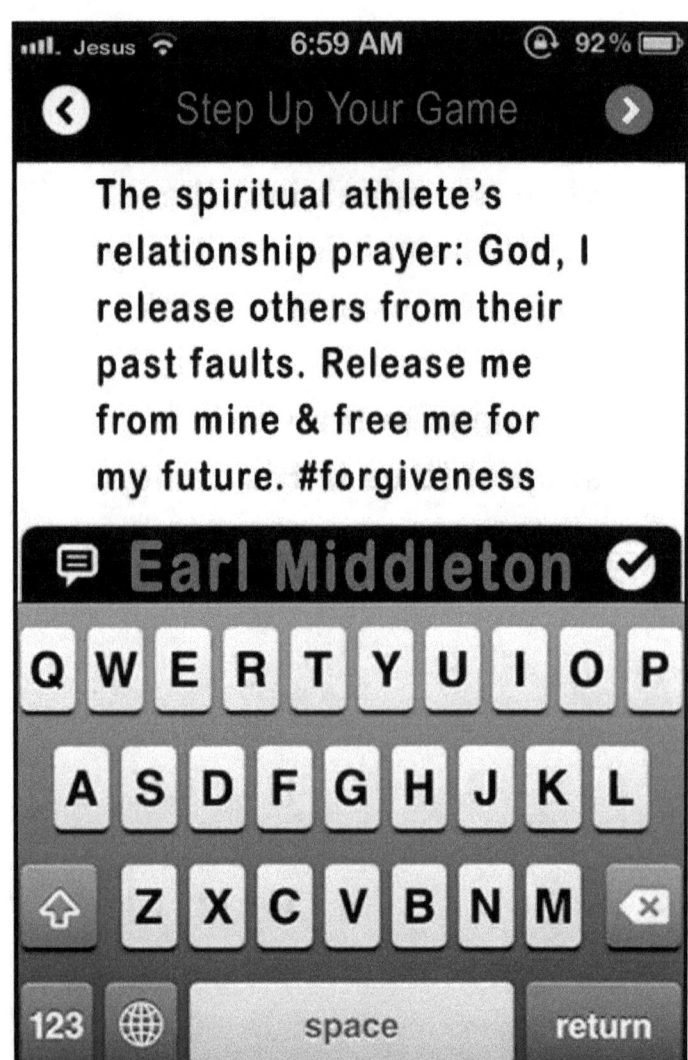

**Step Up Your Game**

The spiritual athlete's relationship prayer: God, I release others from their past faults. Release me from mine & free me for my future. #forgiveness

— Earl Middleton

# April 18

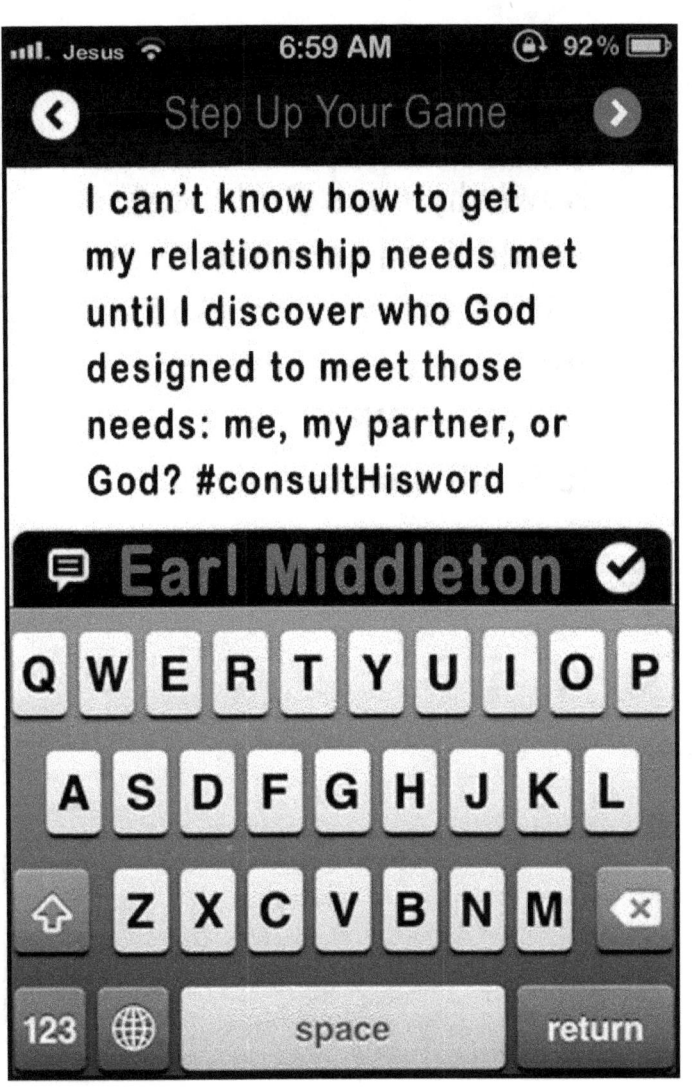

I can't know how to get my relationship needs met until I discover who God designed to meet those needs: me, my partner, or God? #consultHisword

# April 19

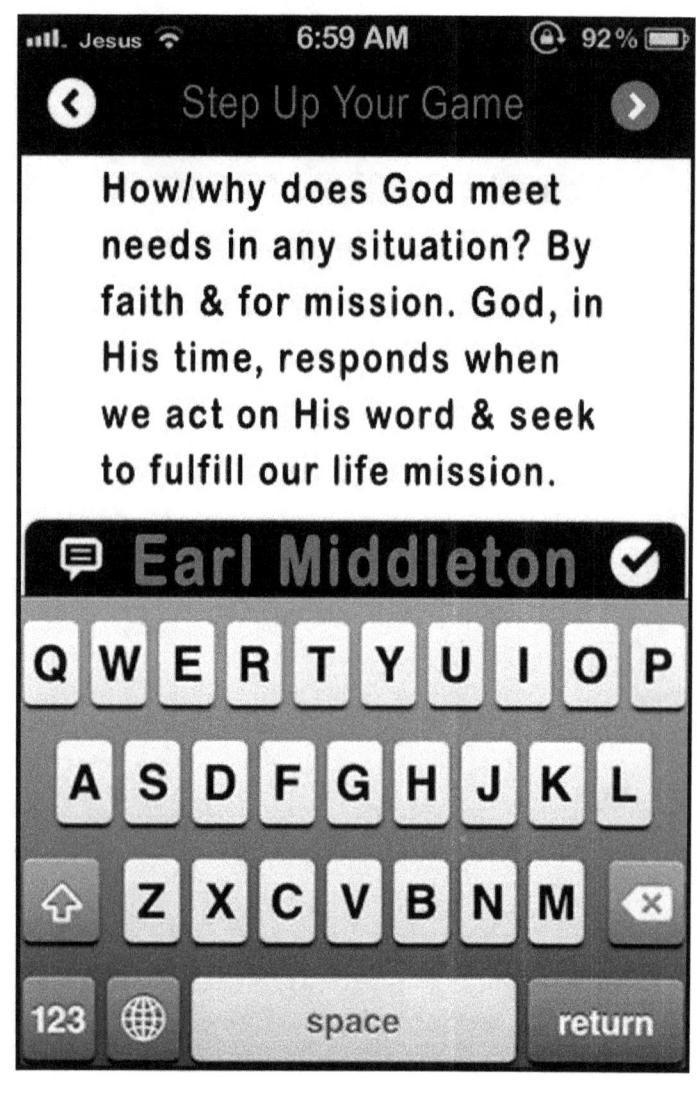

**Step Up Your Game**

How/why does God meet needs in any situation? By faith & for mission. God, in His time, responds when we act on His word & seek to fulfill our life mission.

— Earl Middleton

## April 20

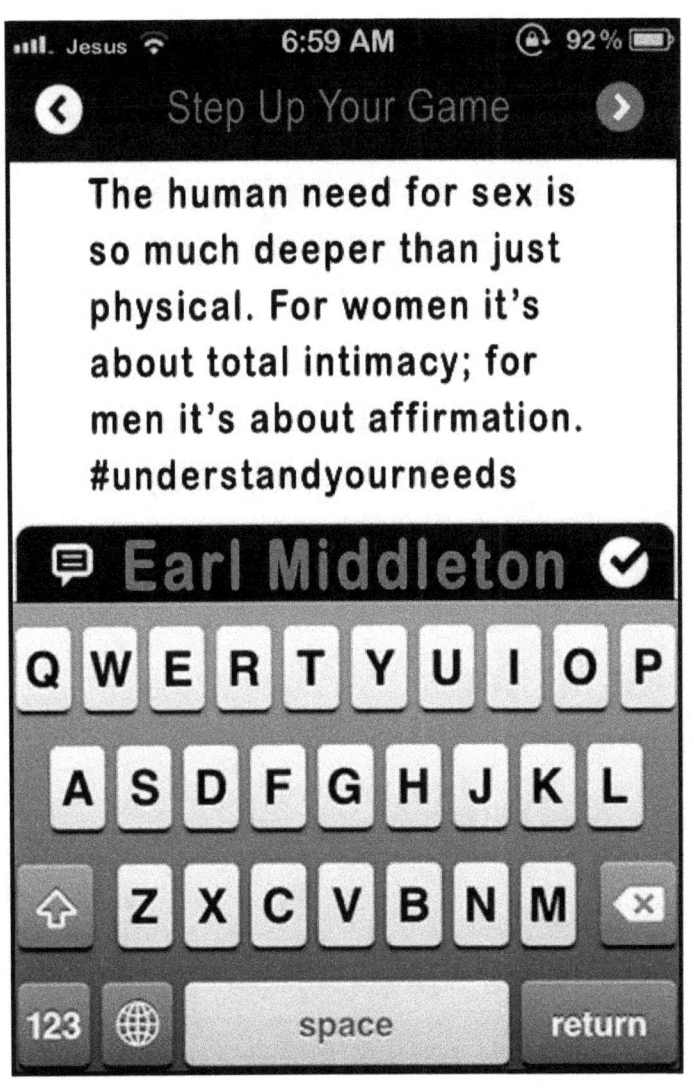

# April 21

## Step Up Your Game

Spiritual athletes seek to understand their need for intimacy or affirmation & trust God to meet it until a spouse becomes available & able. #theylookdeeper

— Earl Middleton

# April 22

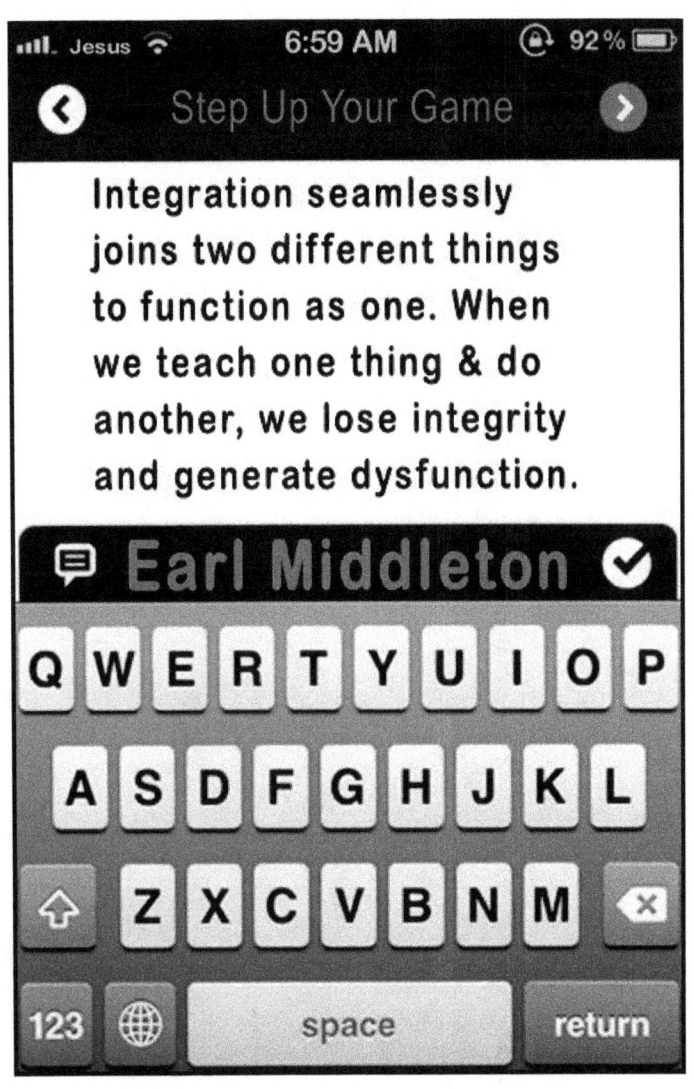

# April 23

**Step Up Your Game**

When God wants to move us He changes our views & relationships. Rebuke your natural desire to hold onto the past & allow your relationships to breathe.

Earl Middleton

# April 24

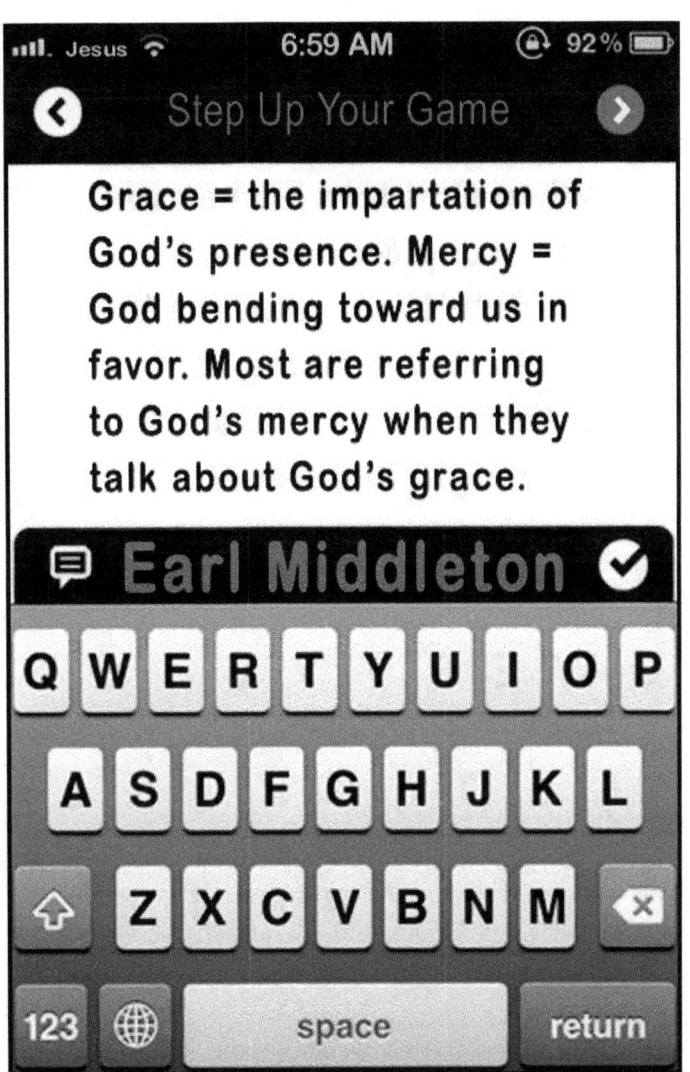

# April 25

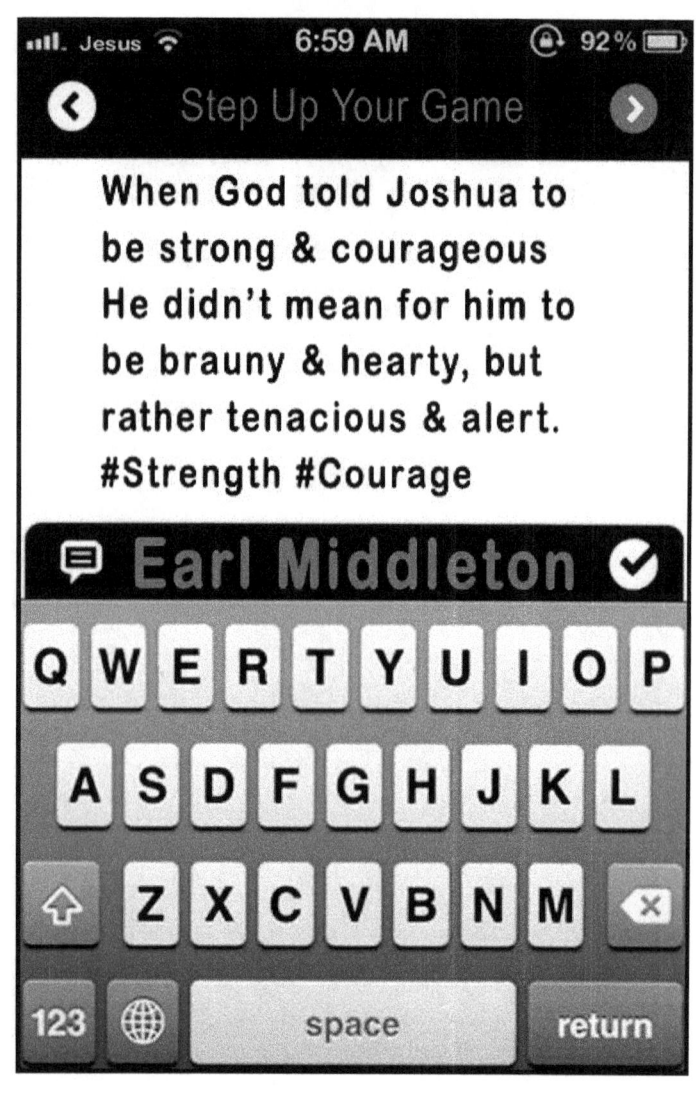

# April 26

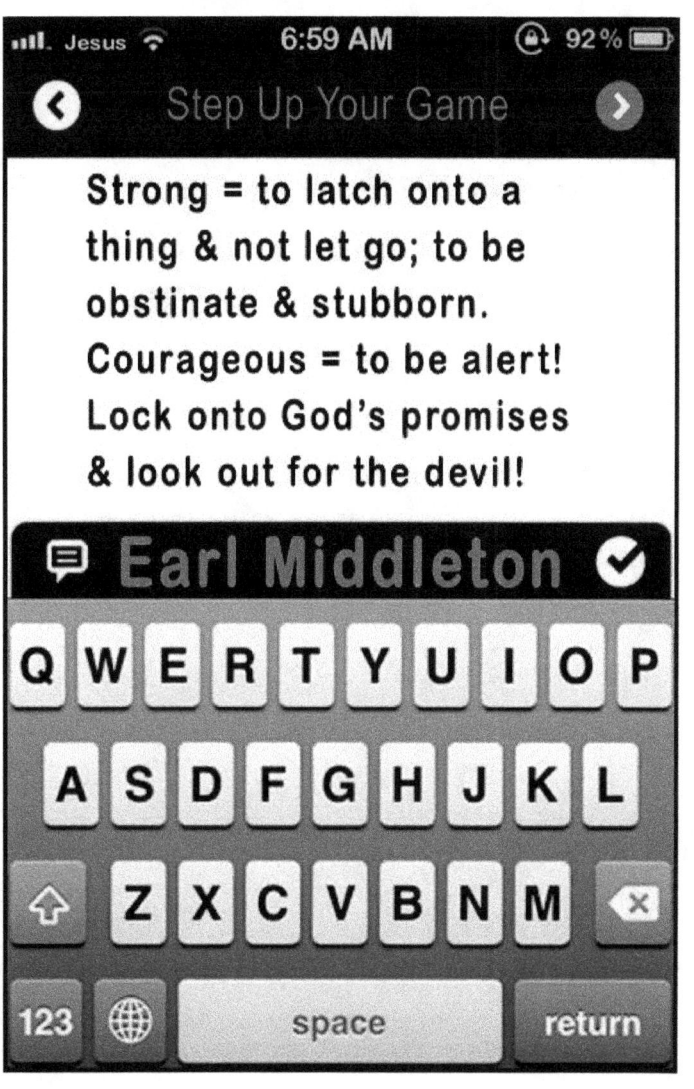

# April 27

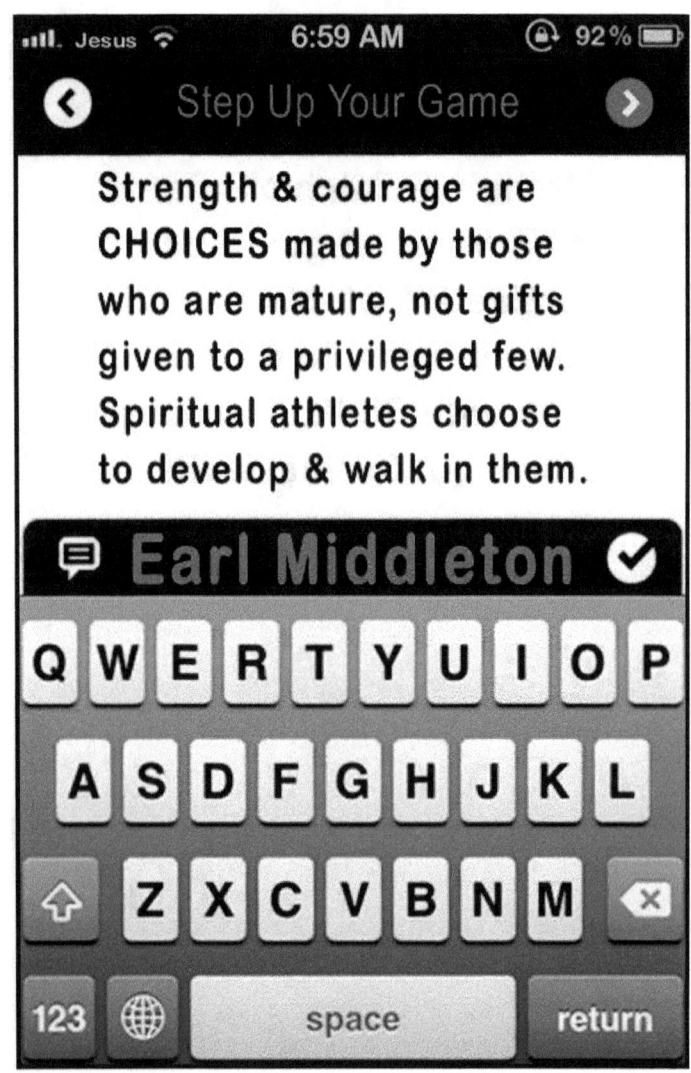

# April 28

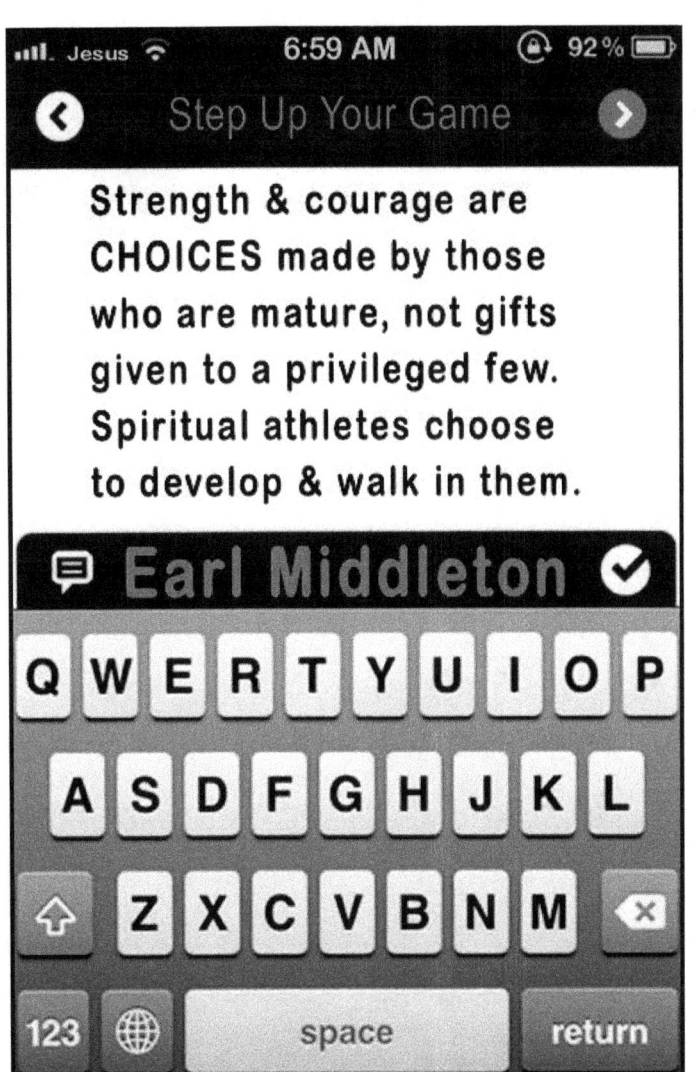

Strength & courage are CHOICES made by those who are mature, not gifts given to a privileged few. Spiritual athletes choose to develop & walk in them.

Earl Middleton

# April 29

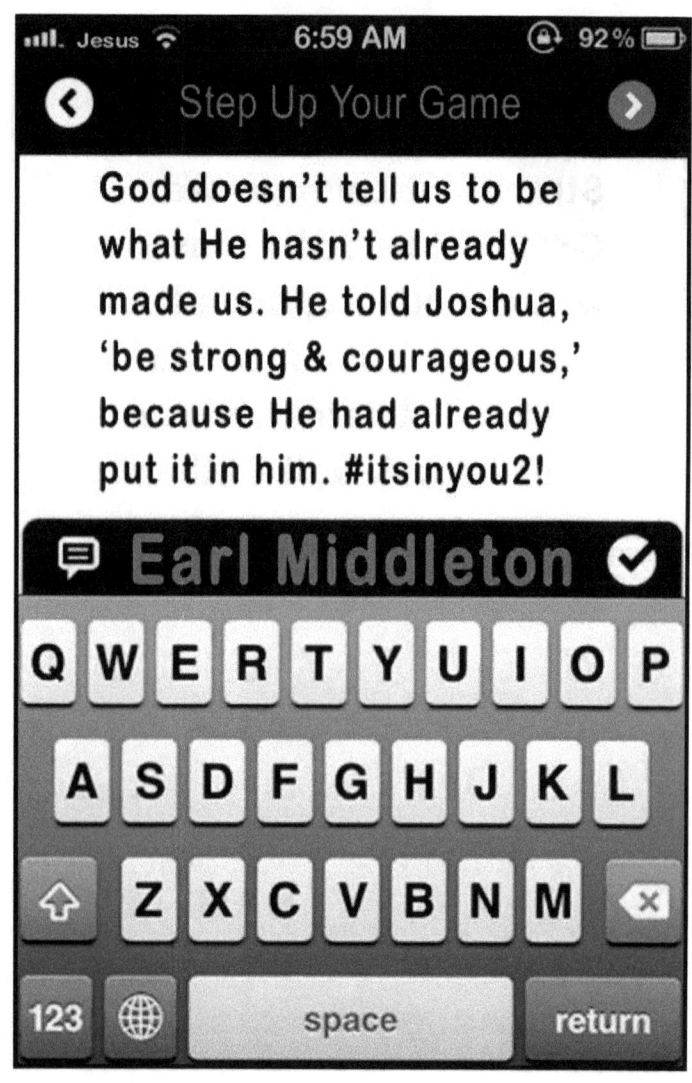

# April 30

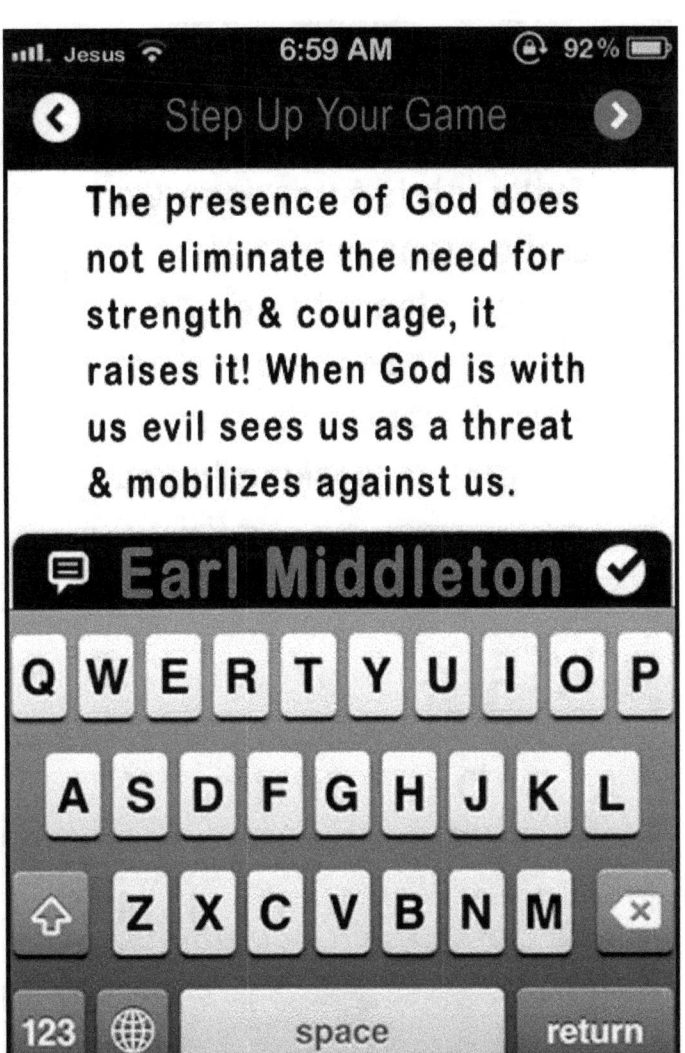

The presence of God does not eliminate the need for strength & courage, it raises it! When God is with us evil sees us as a threat & mobilizes against us.

Earl Middleton

# May 1

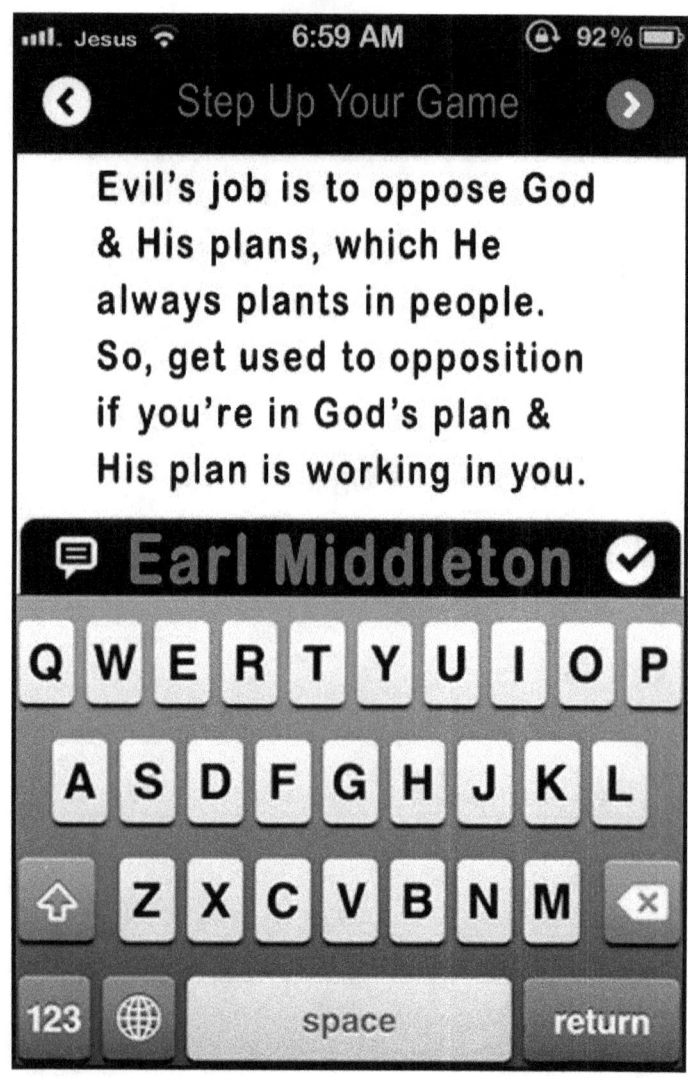

**Step Up Your Game**

Evil's job is to oppose God & His plans, which He always plants in people. So, get used to opposition if you're in God's plan & His plan is working in you.

Earl Middleton

# May 2

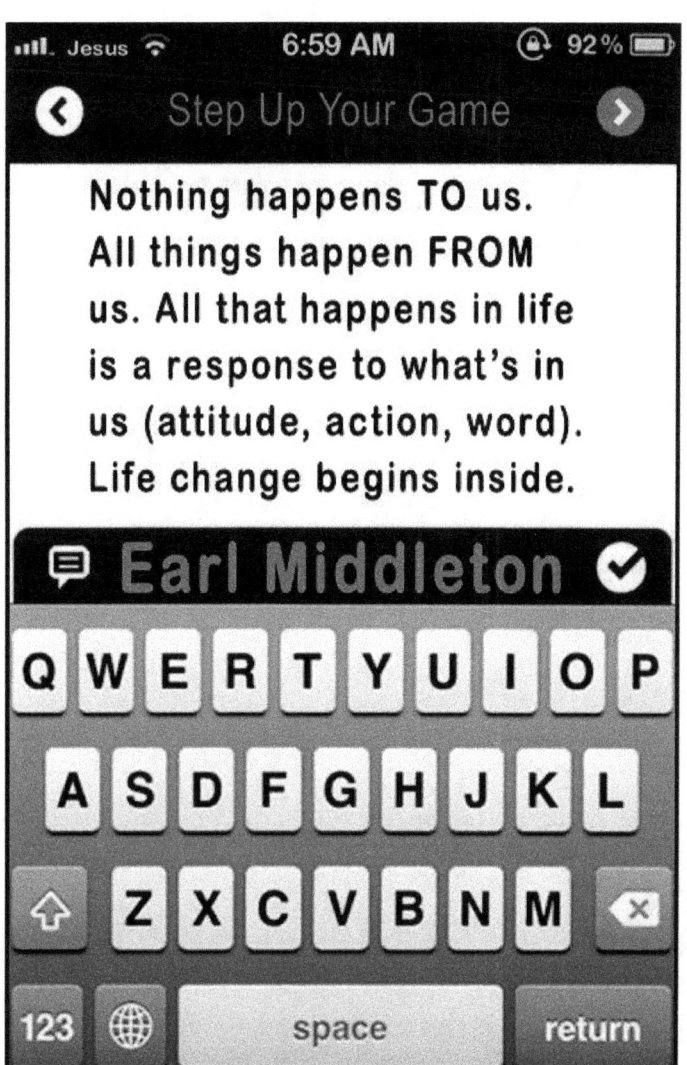

# May 3

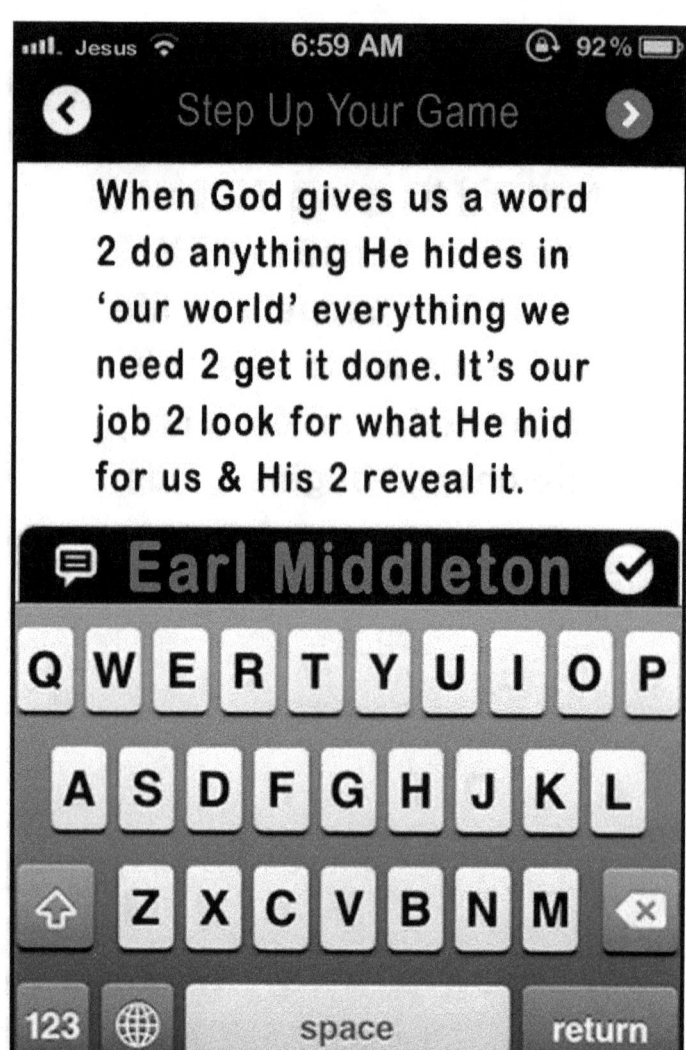

**Step Up Your Game**

When God gives us a word 2 do anything He hides in 'our world' everything we need 2 get it done. It's our job 2 look for what He hid for us & His 2 reveal it.

# May 4

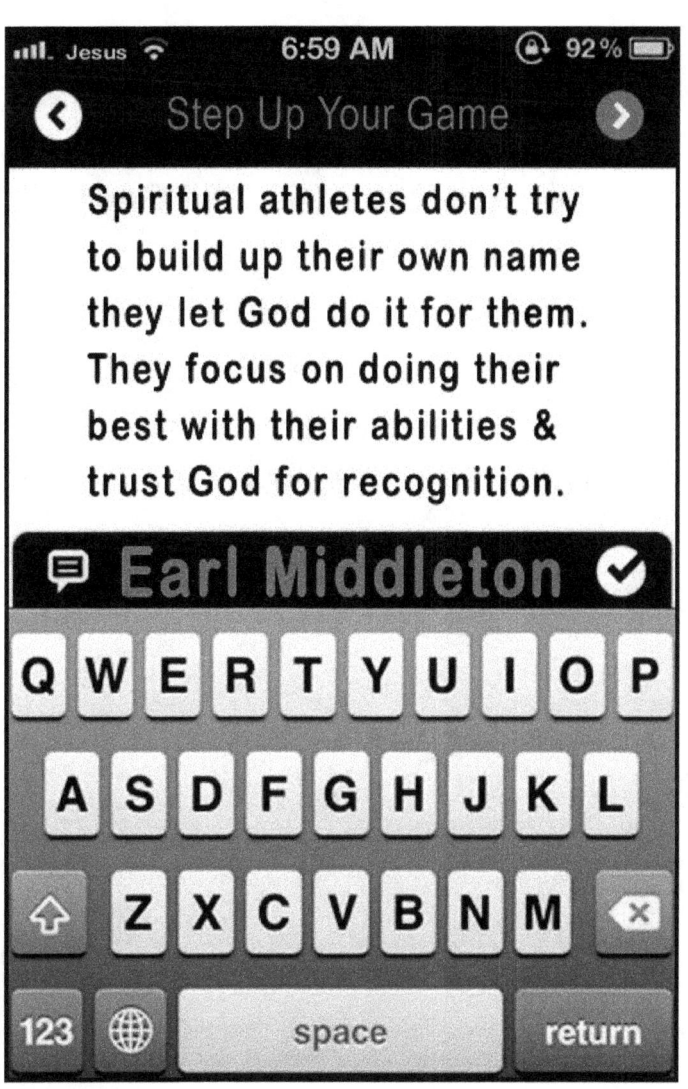

## Step Up Your Game

Spiritual athletes don't try to build up their own name they let God do it for them. They focus on doing their best with their abilities & trust God for recognition.

# May 5

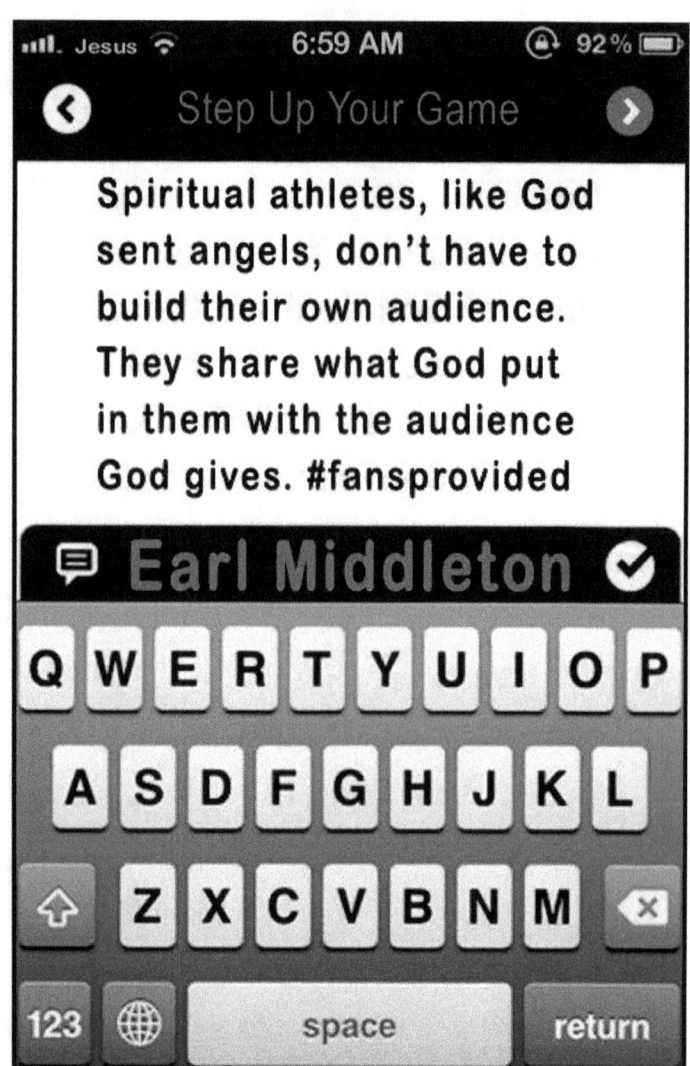

**Step Up Your Game**

Spiritual athletes, like God sent angels, don't have to build their own audience. They share what God put in them with the audience God gives. #fansprovided

Earl Middleton

# May 6

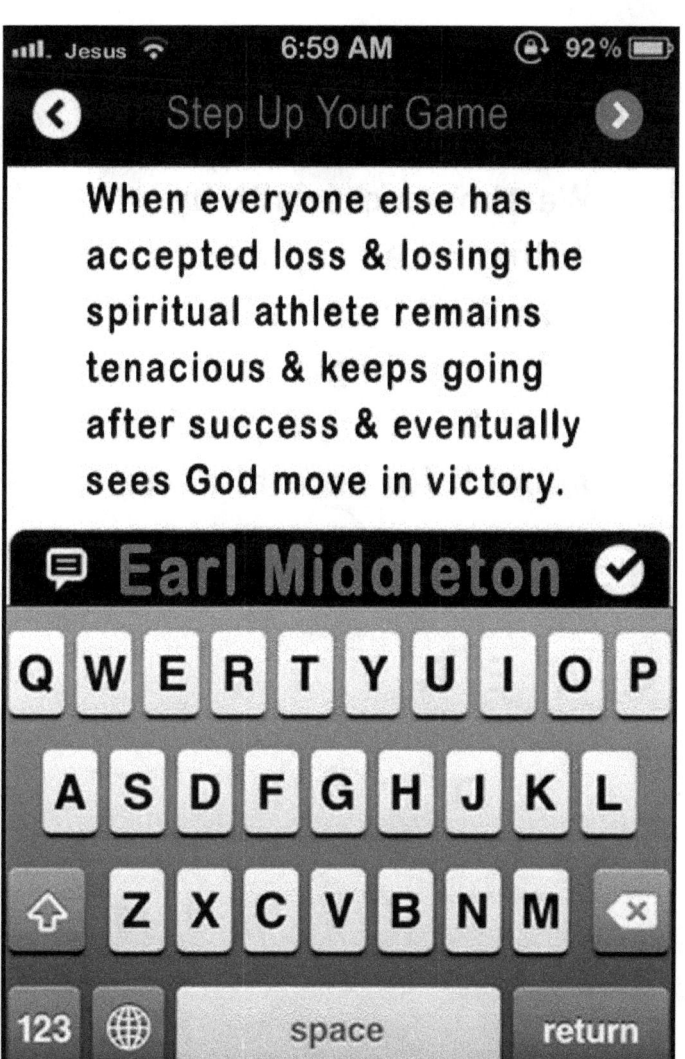

**Step Up Your Game**

When everyone else has accepted loss & losing the spiritual athlete remains tenacious & keeps going after success & eventually sees God move in victory.

— Earl Middleton

## May 7

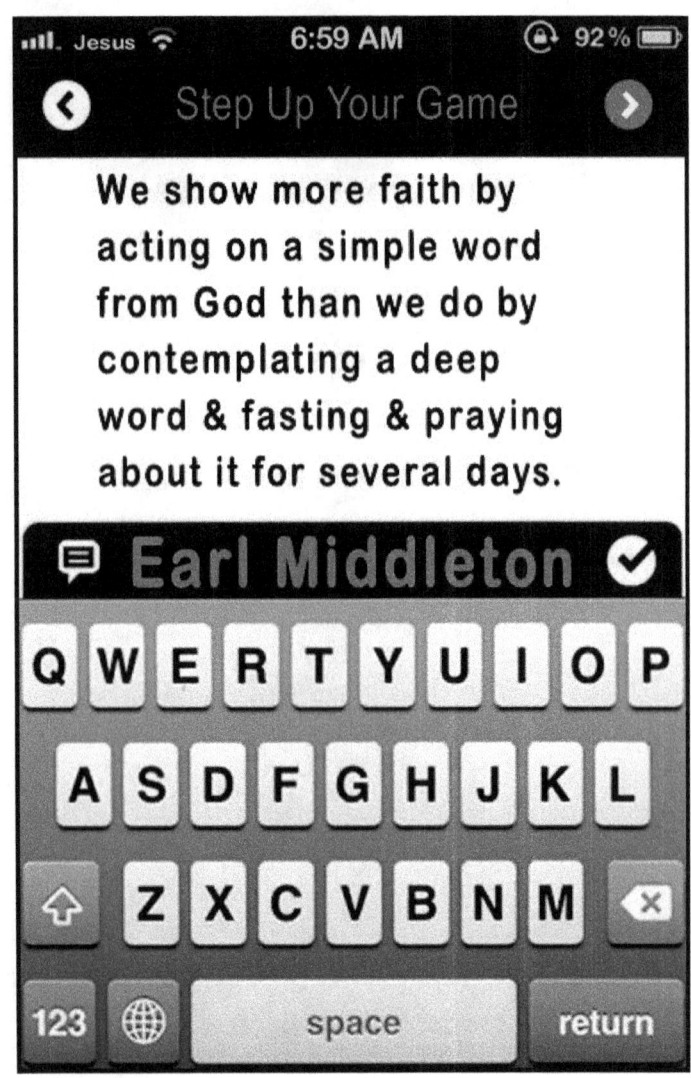

We show more faith by acting on a simple word from God than we do by contemplating a deep word & fasting & praying about it for several days.

— Earl Middleton

# May 8

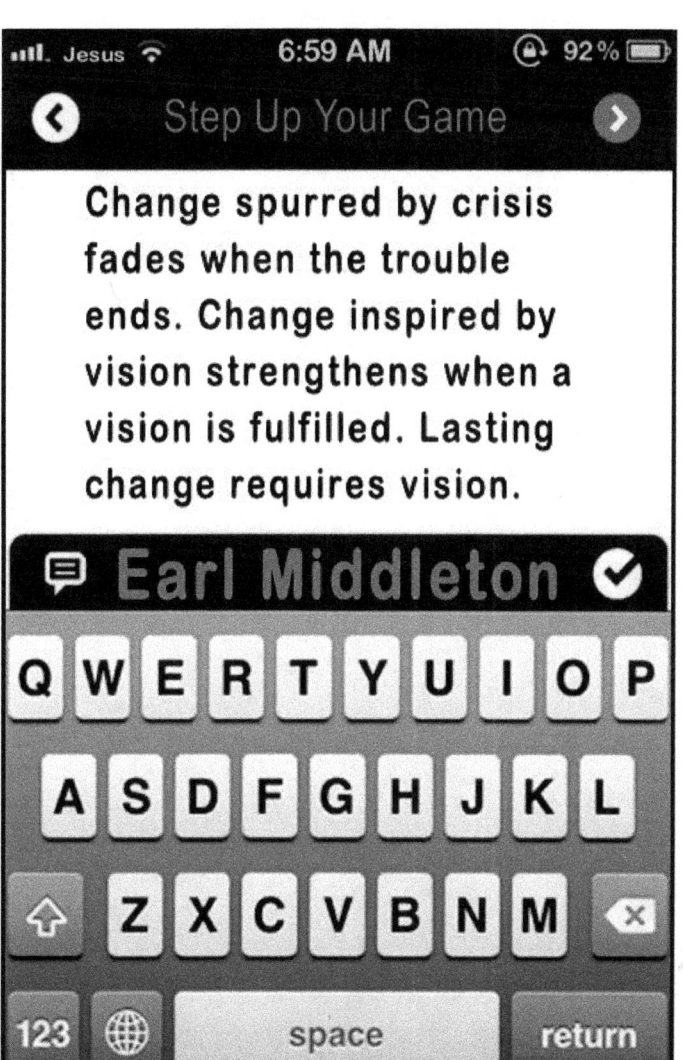

> Change spurred by crisis fades when the trouble ends. Change inspired by vision strengthens when a vision is fulfilled. Lasting change requires vision.
>
> — Earl Middleton

# May 9

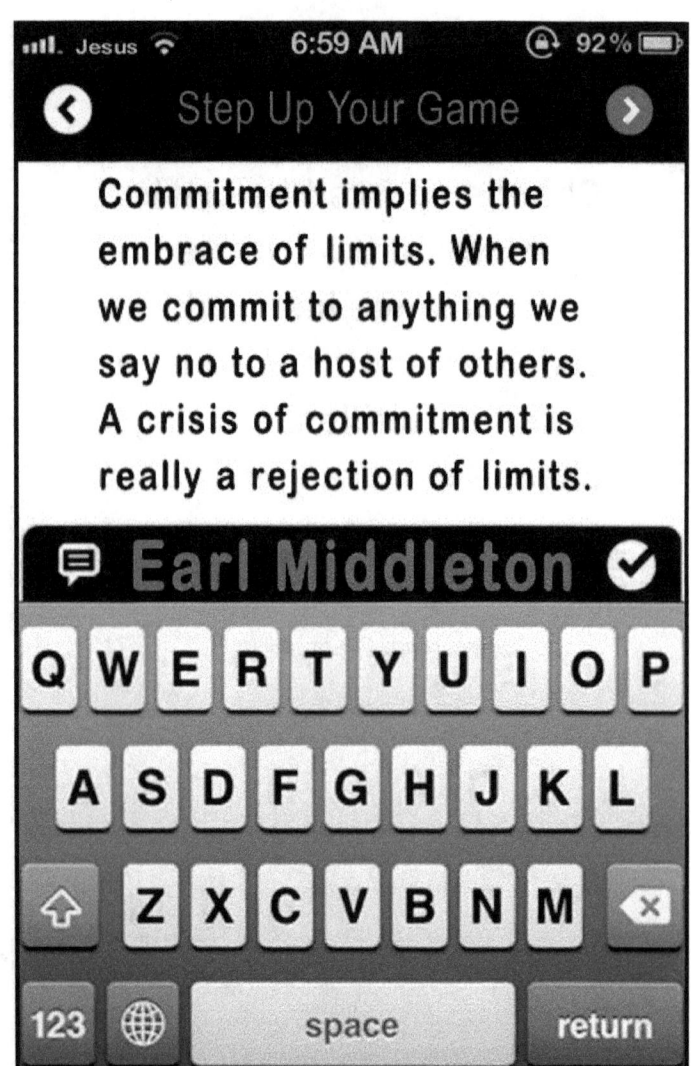

> Commitment implies the embrace of limits. When we commit to anything we say no to a host of others. A crisis of commitment is really a rejection of limits.
>
> — Earl Middleton

# May 10

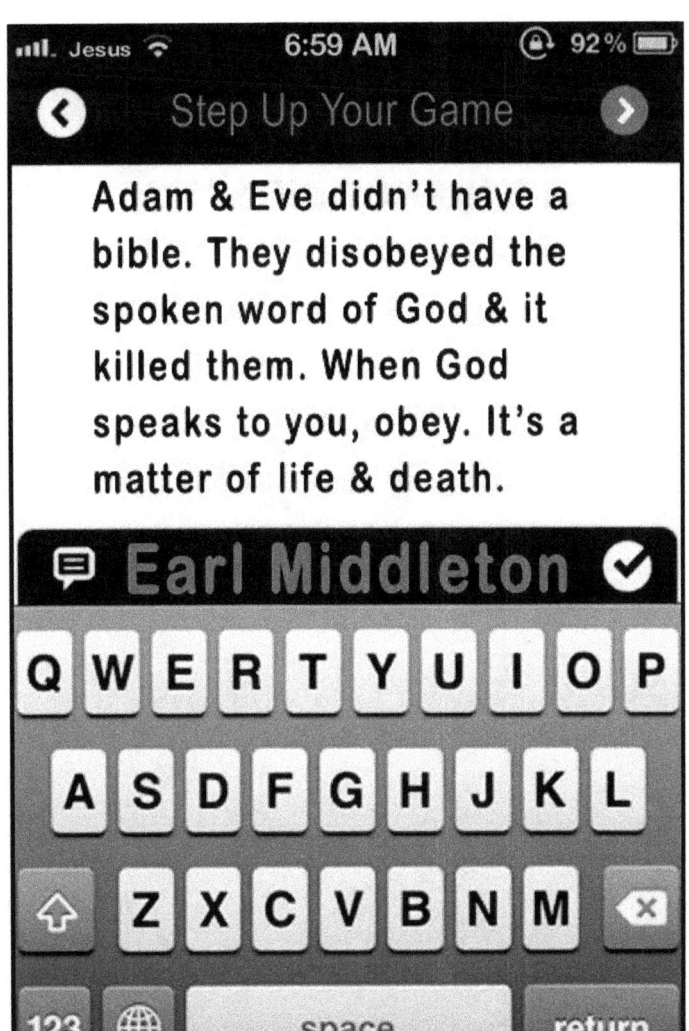

# May 11

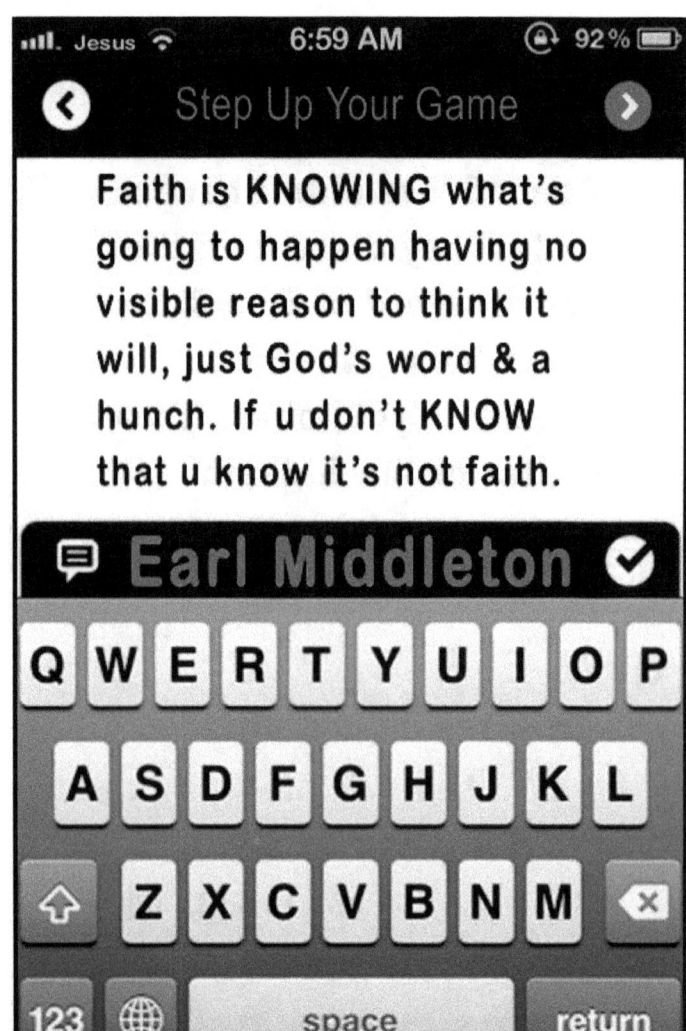

# May 12

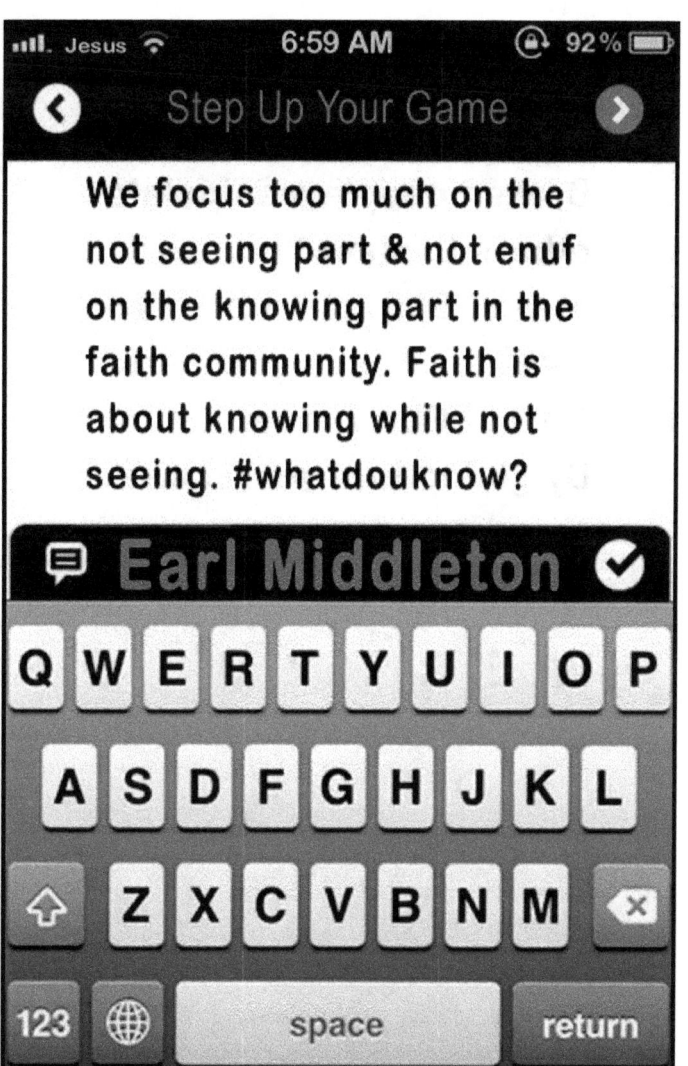

**May 13**

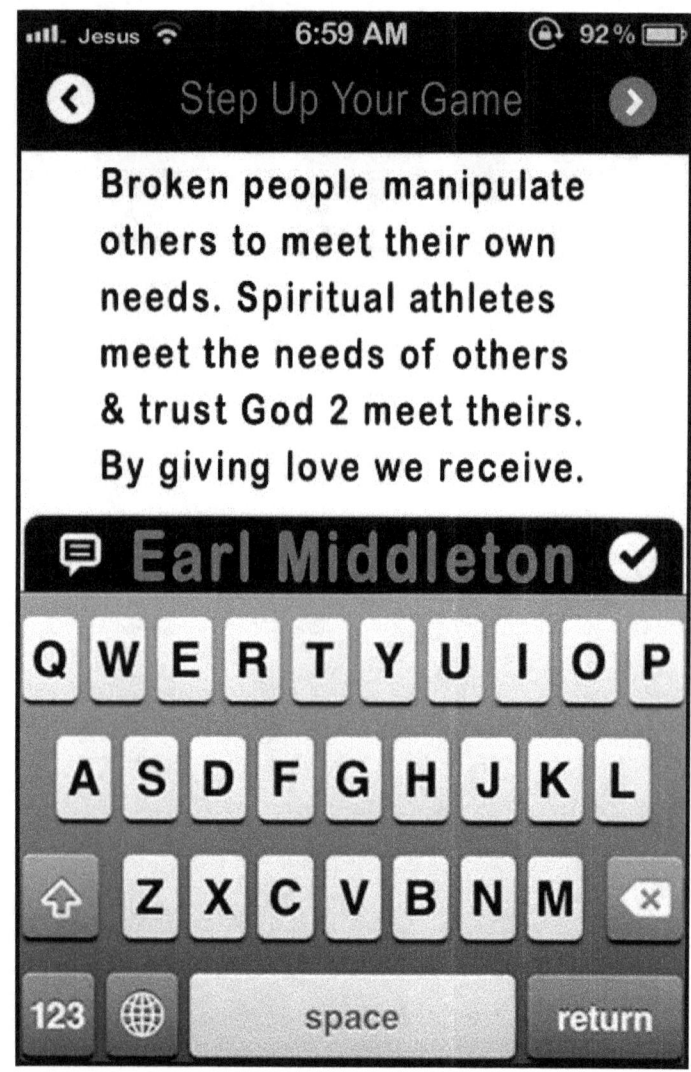

## May 14

**Step Up Your Game**

Vision is the 1st but not the only step in achievement. Holy Spirit energy is also needed to run toward the vision, & instruction to run effectively & in good form.

Earl Middleton

## May 15

**Step Up Your Game**

Acts 1:7 – there are some times & seasons in God's control, & there are some in our control. We control harvest time by the time we choose to sow seed.

Earl Middleton

## May 16

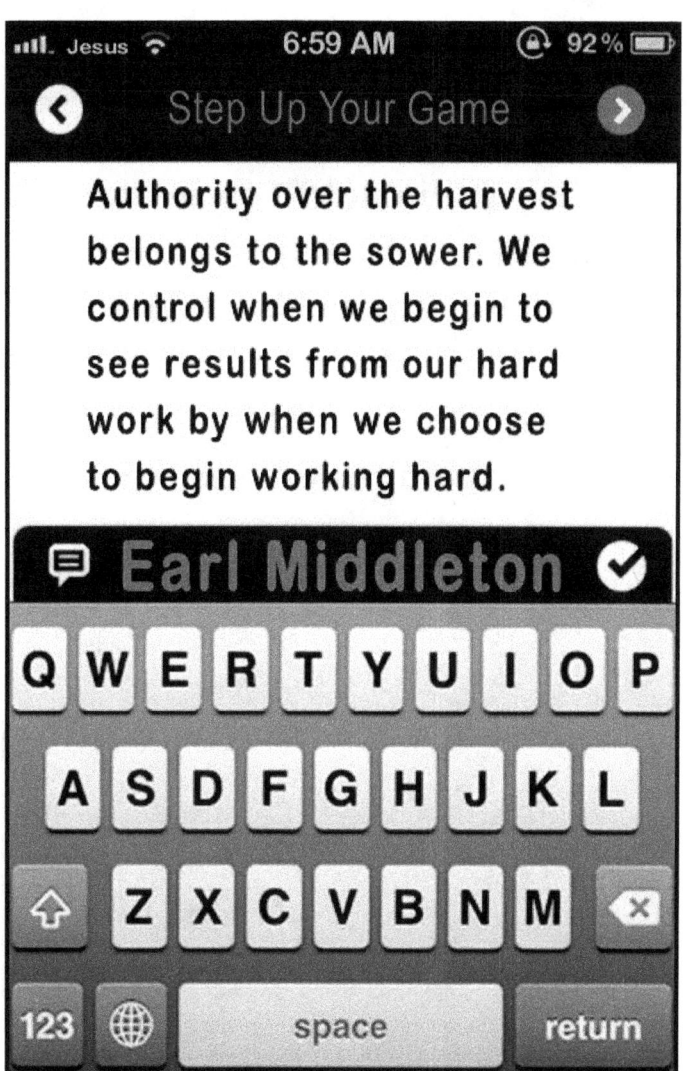

Authority over the harvest belongs to the sower. We control when we begin to see results from our hard work by when we choose to begin working hard.

— Earl Middleton

# May 17

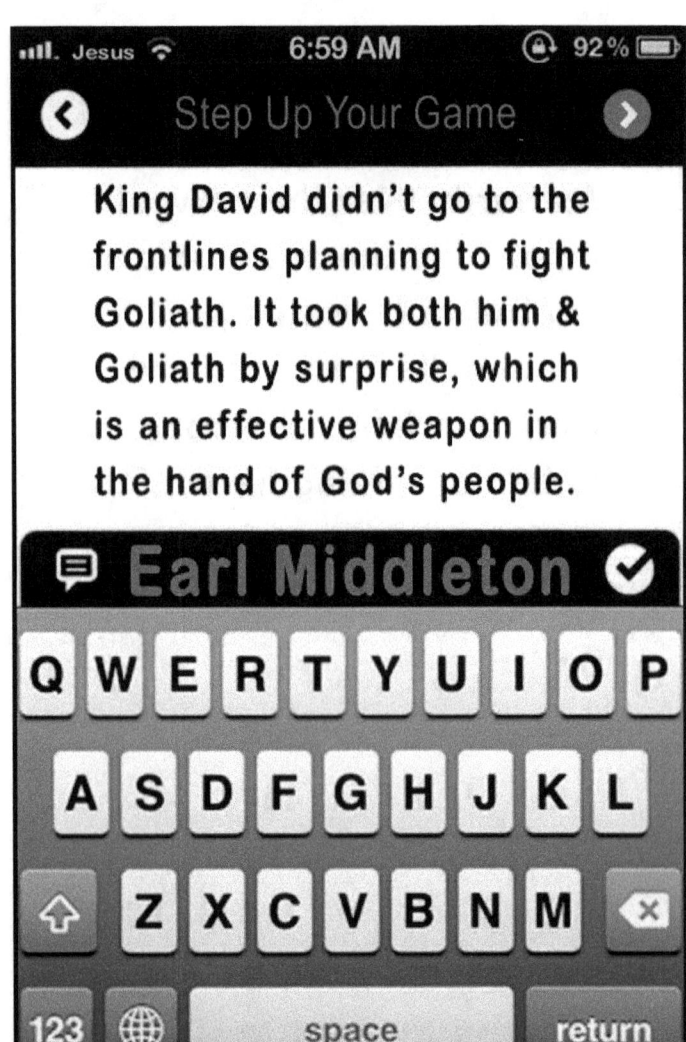

**Step Up Your Game**

King David didn't go to the frontlines planning to fight Goliath. It took both him & Goliath by surprise, which is an effective weapon in the hand of God's people.

Earl Middleton

# May 18

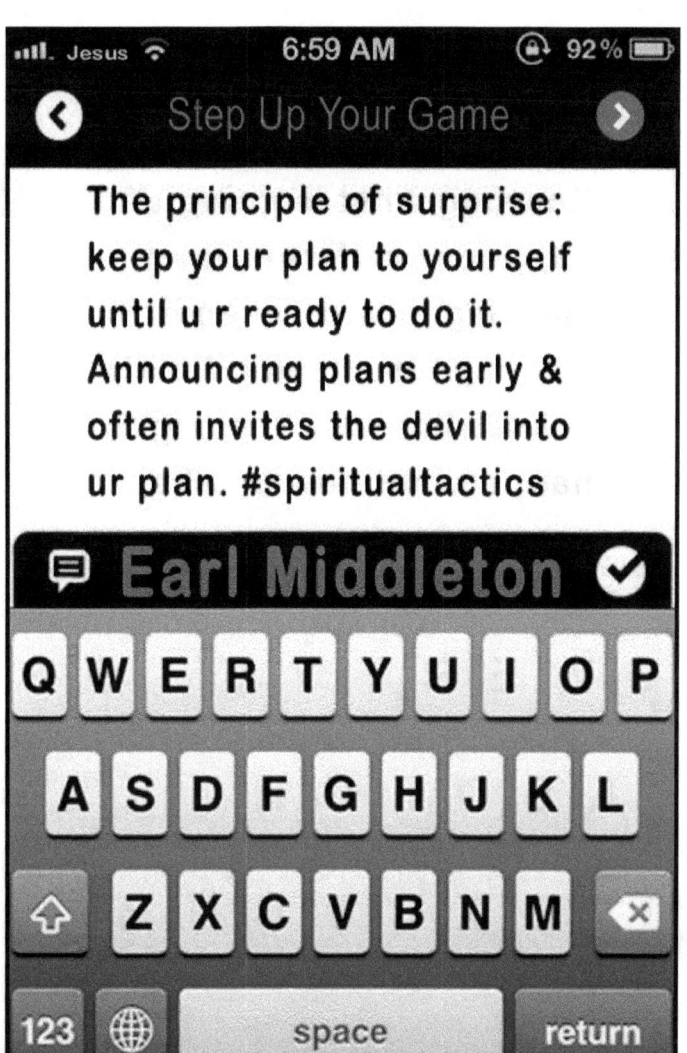

> The principle of surprise: keep your plan to yourself until u r ready to do it. Announcing plans early & often invites the devil into ur plan. #spiritualtactics

**May 19**

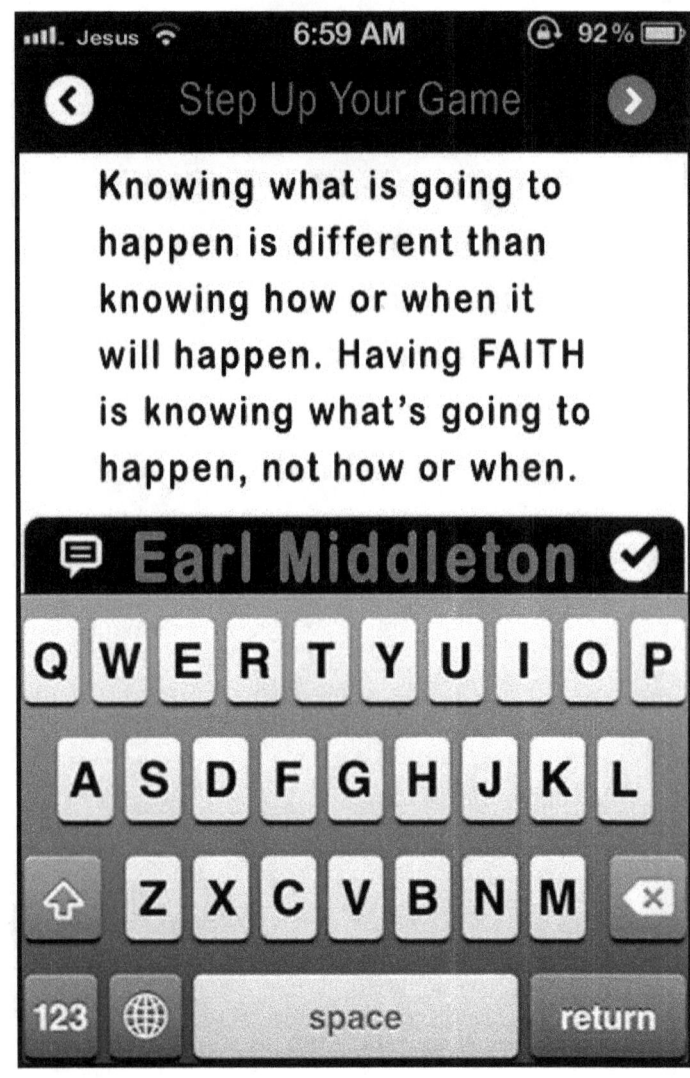

**May 20**

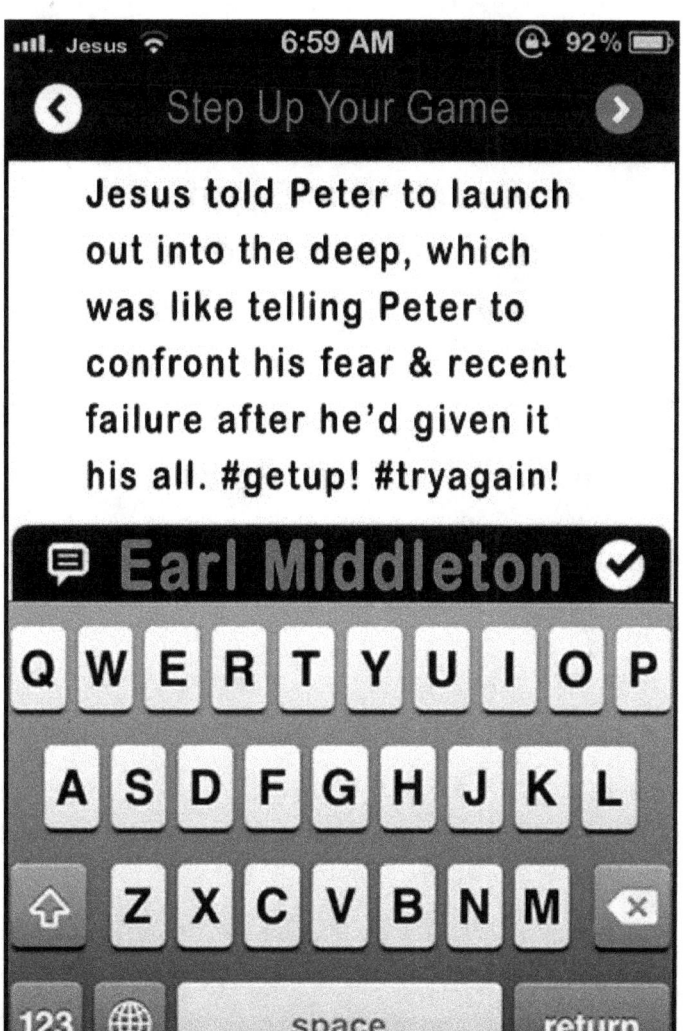

## May 21

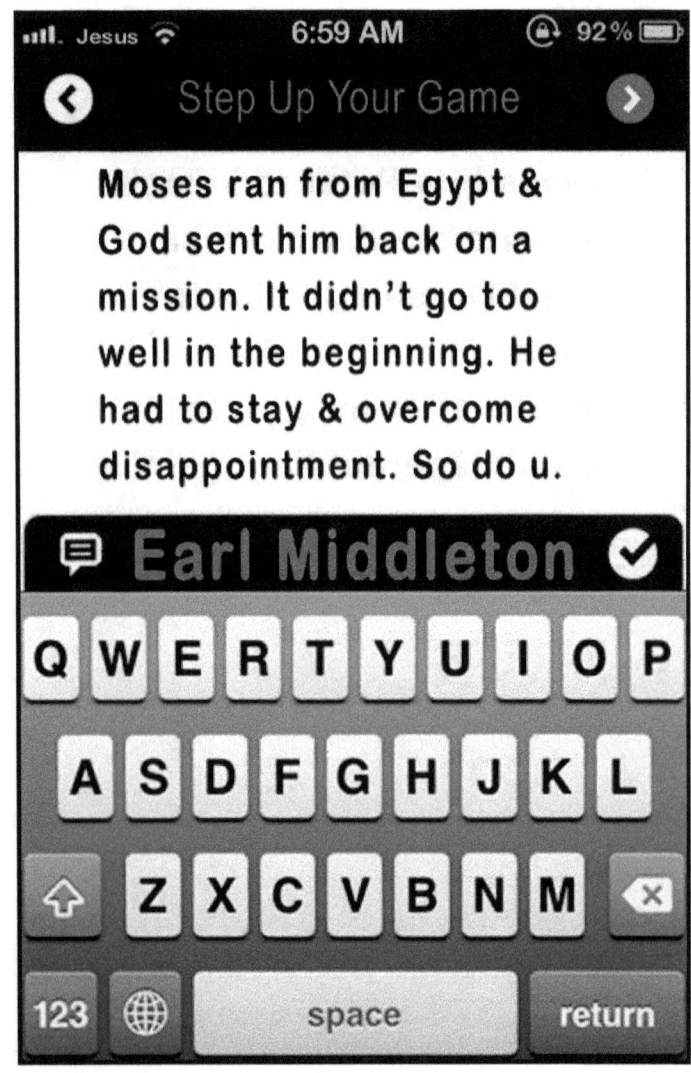

# May 22

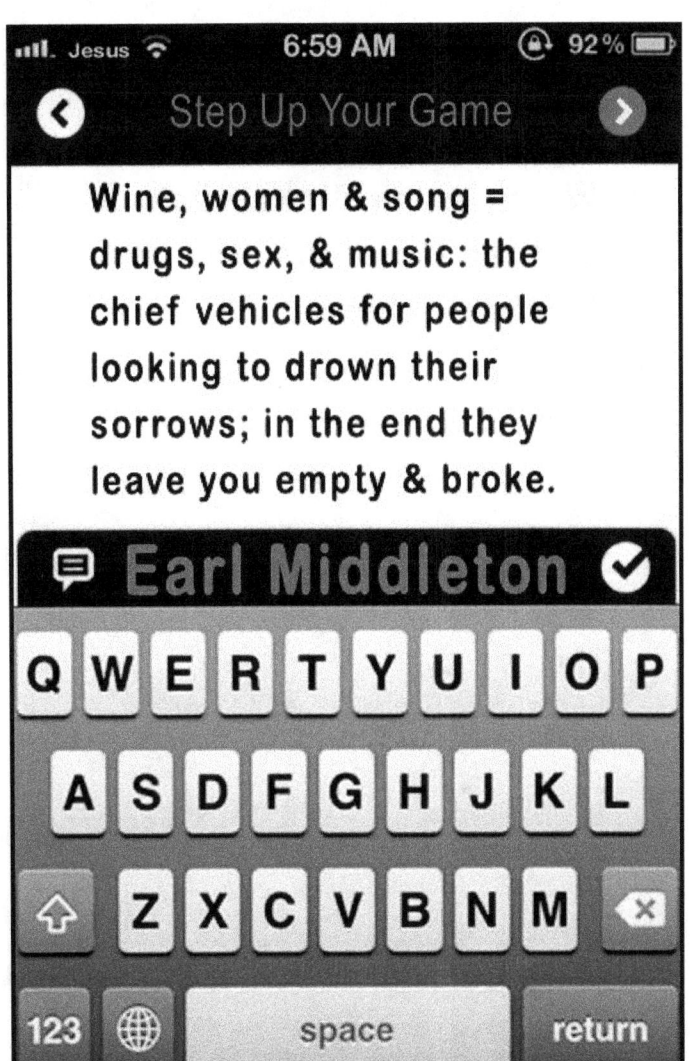

Wine, women & song = drugs, sex, & music: the chief vehicles for people looking to drown their sorrows; in the end they leave you empty & broke.

— Earl Middleton

# May 23

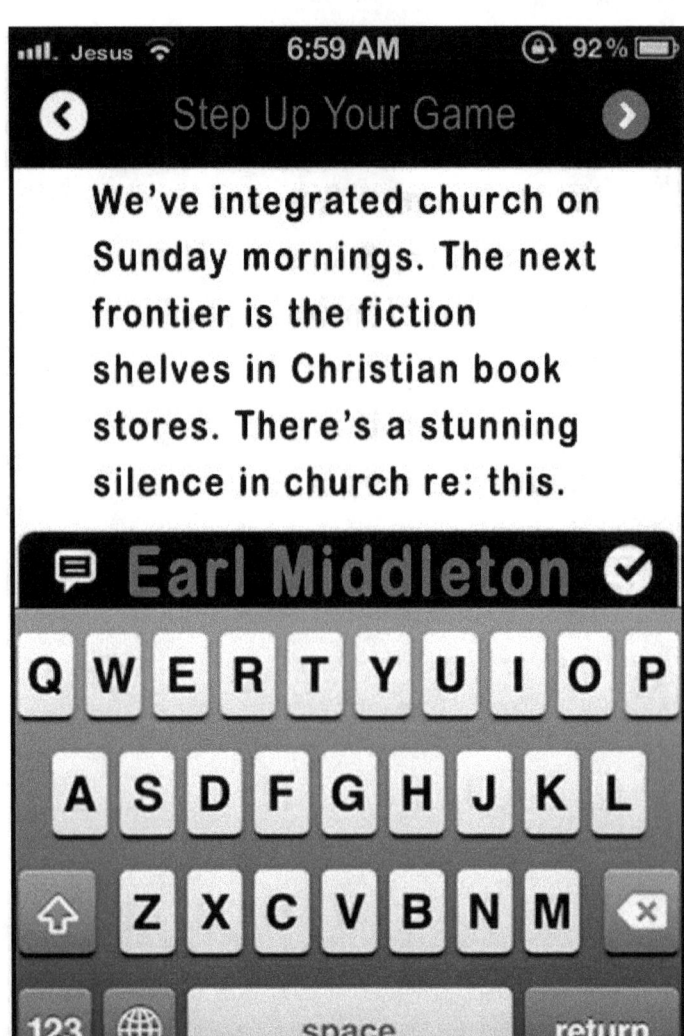

## Step Up Your Game

We've integrated church on Sunday mornings. The next frontier is the fiction shelves in Christian book stores. There's a stunning silence in church re: this.

— Earl Middleton

# May 24

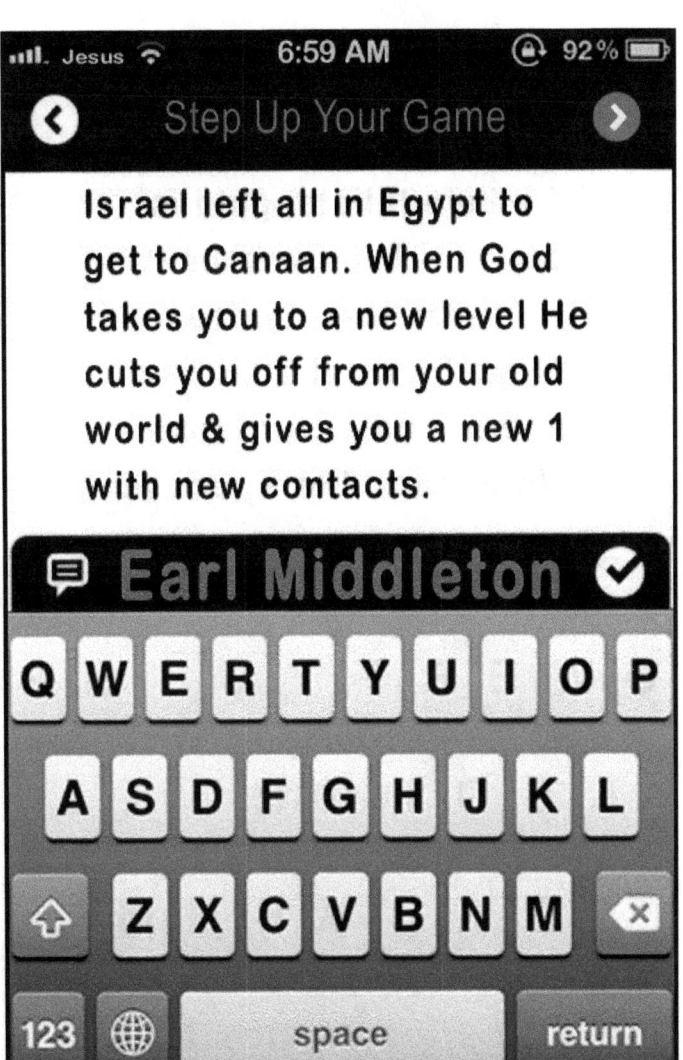

# May 25

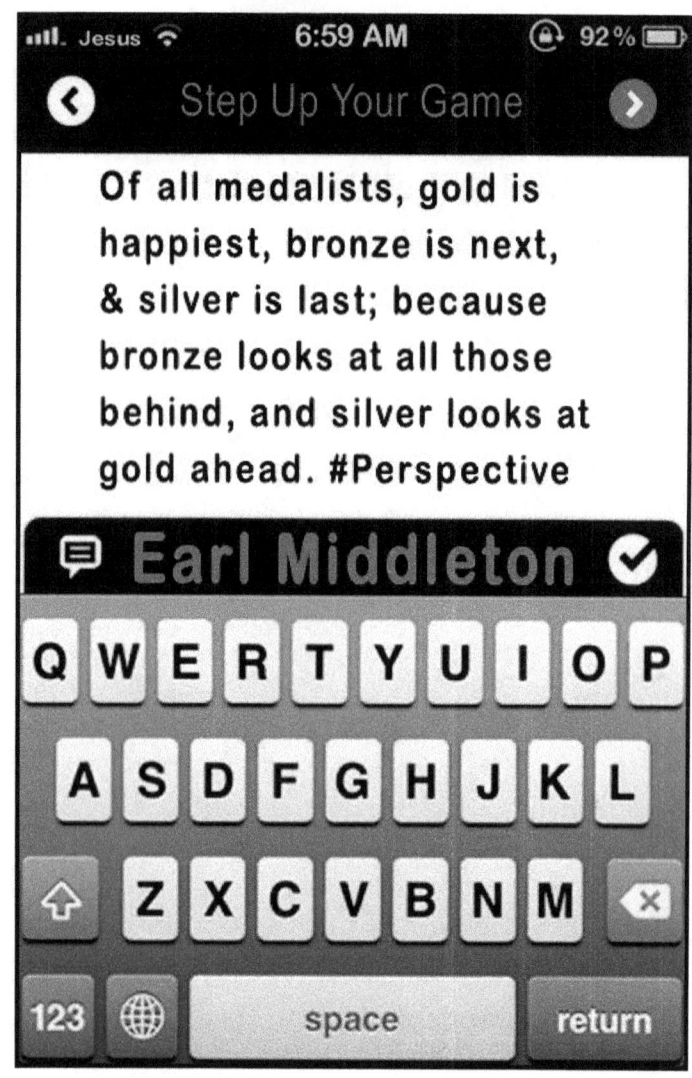

Of all medalists, gold is happiest, bronze is next, & silver is last; because bronze looks at all those behind, and silver looks at gold ahead. #Perspective

— Earl Middleton

## May 26

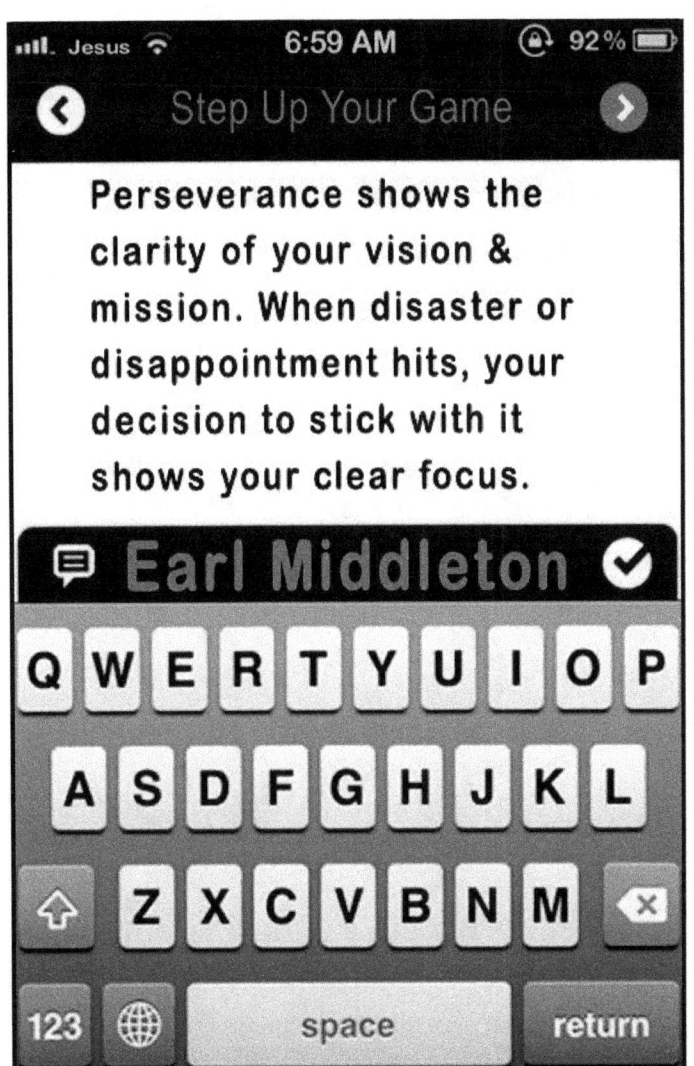

Perseverance shows the clarity of your vision & mission. When disaster or disappointment hits, your decision to stick with it shows your clear focus.

**May 27**

# May 28

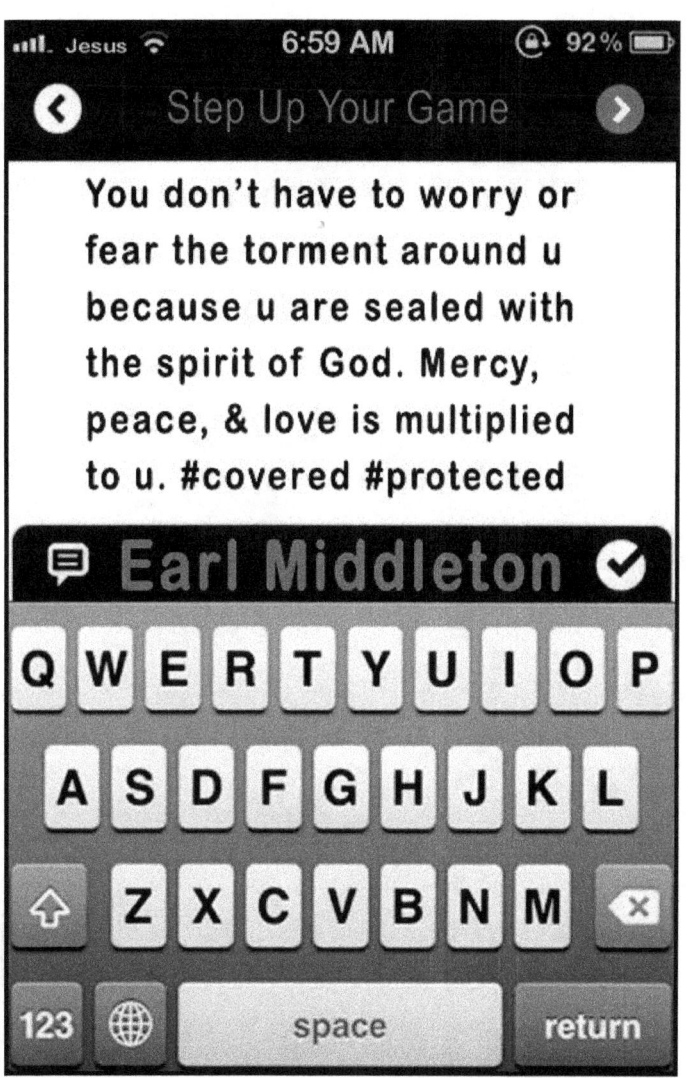

**Step Up Your Game**

You don't have to worry or fear the torment around u because u are sealed with the spirit of God. Mercy, peace, & love is multiplied to u. #covered #protected

# May 29

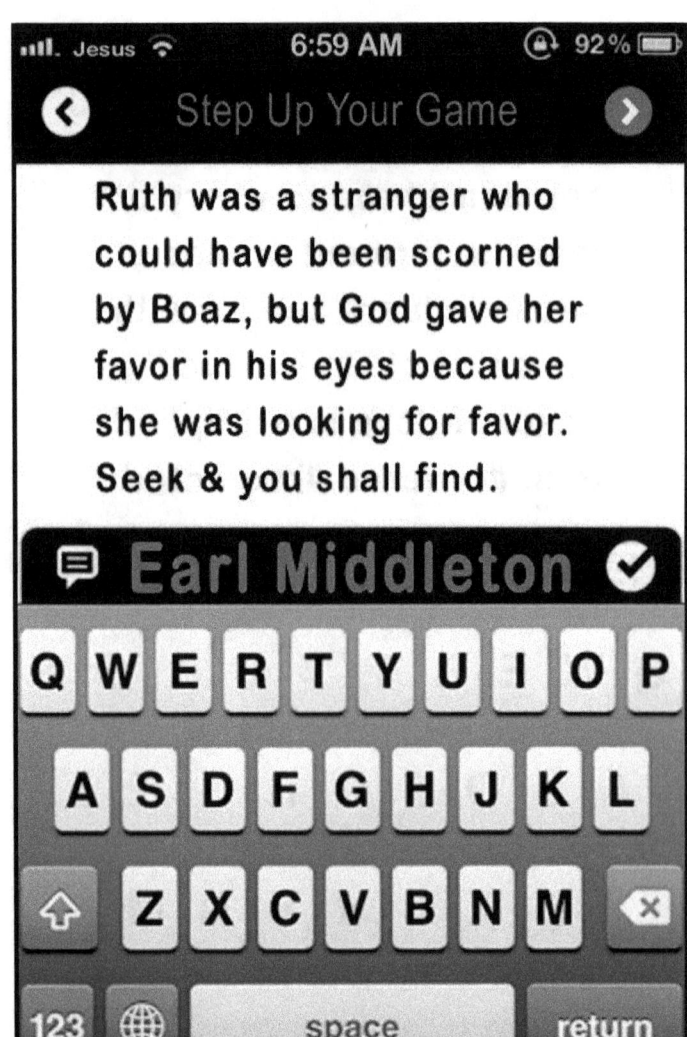

> Ruth was a stranger who could have been scorned by Boaz, but God gave her favor in his eyes because she was looking for favor. Seek & you shall find.

— Earl Middleton

# May 30

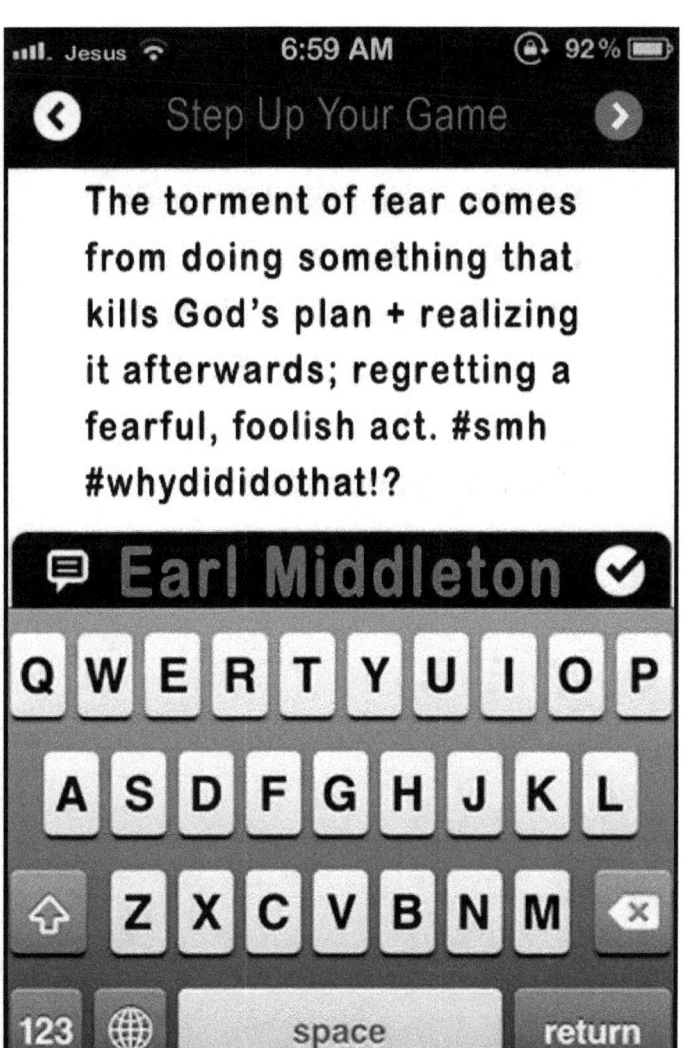

The torment of fear comes from doing something that kills God's plan + realizing it afterwards; regretting a fearful, foolish act. #smh #whydididothat!?

# May 31

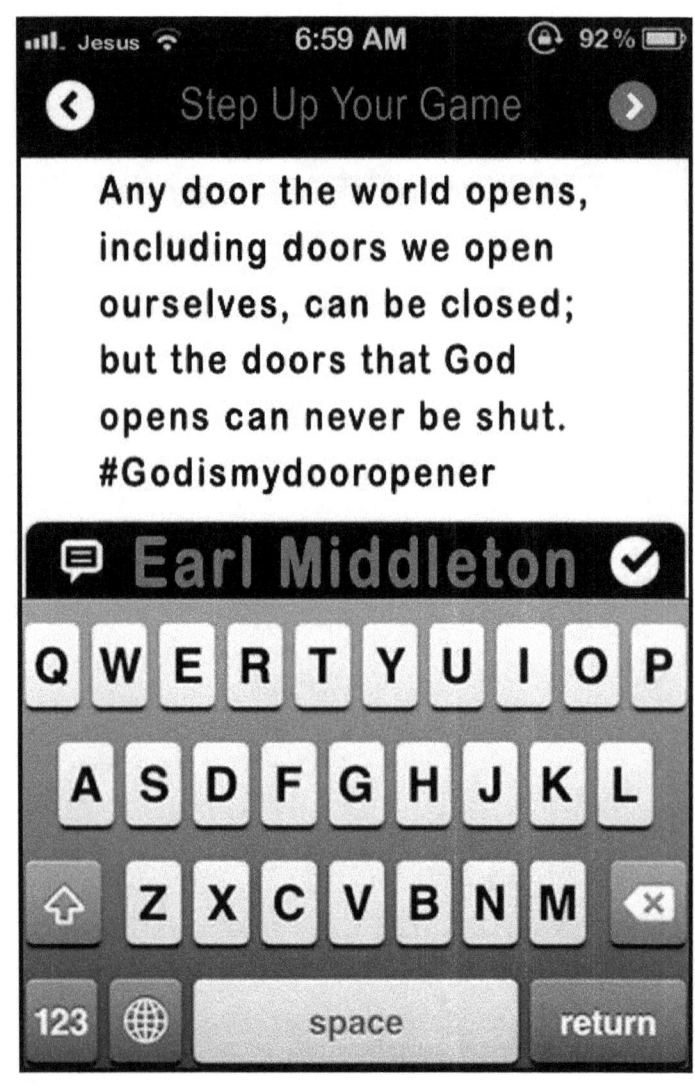

# June 1

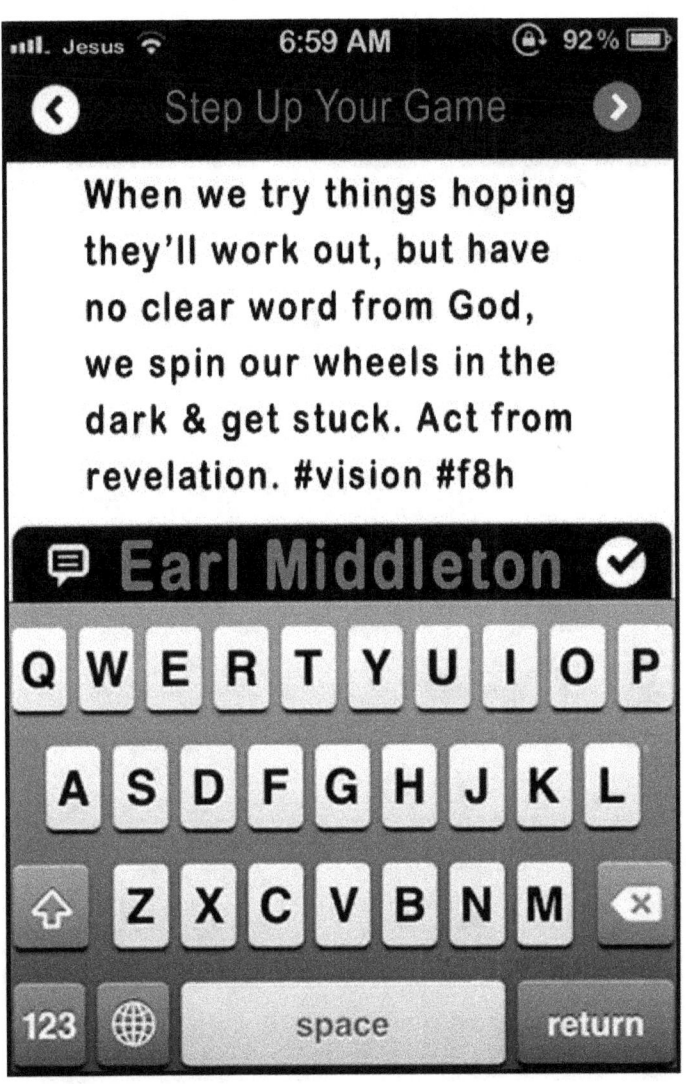

**Step Up Your Game**

When we try things hoping they'll work out, but have no clear word from God, we spin our wheels in the dark & get stuck. Act from revelation. #vision #f8h

Earl Middleton

# June 2

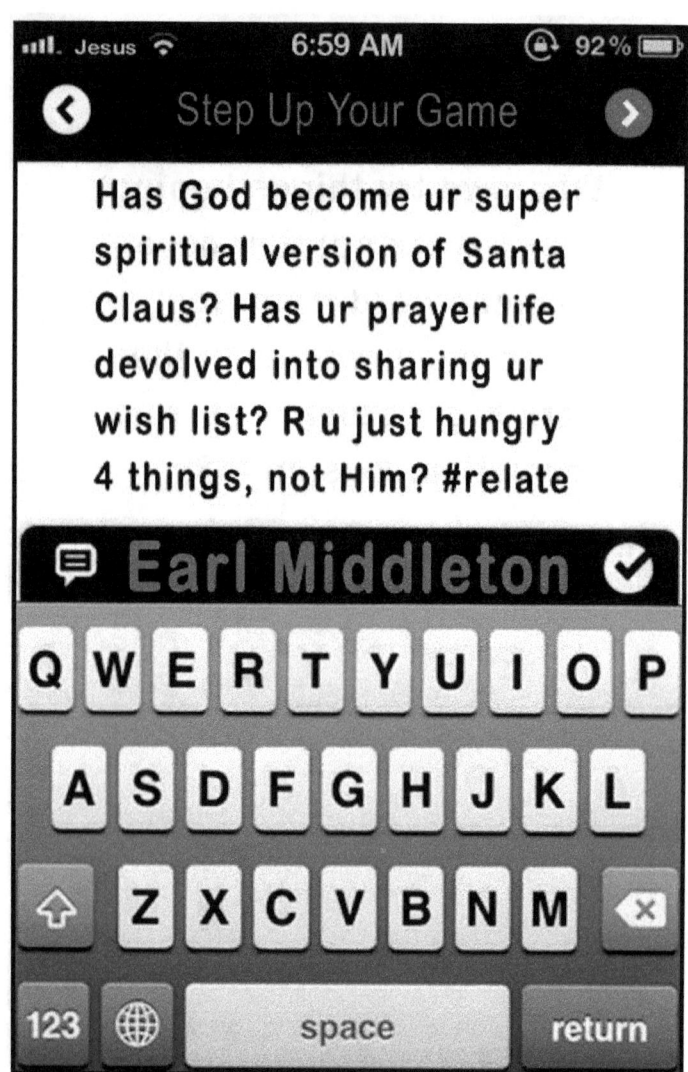

# June 3

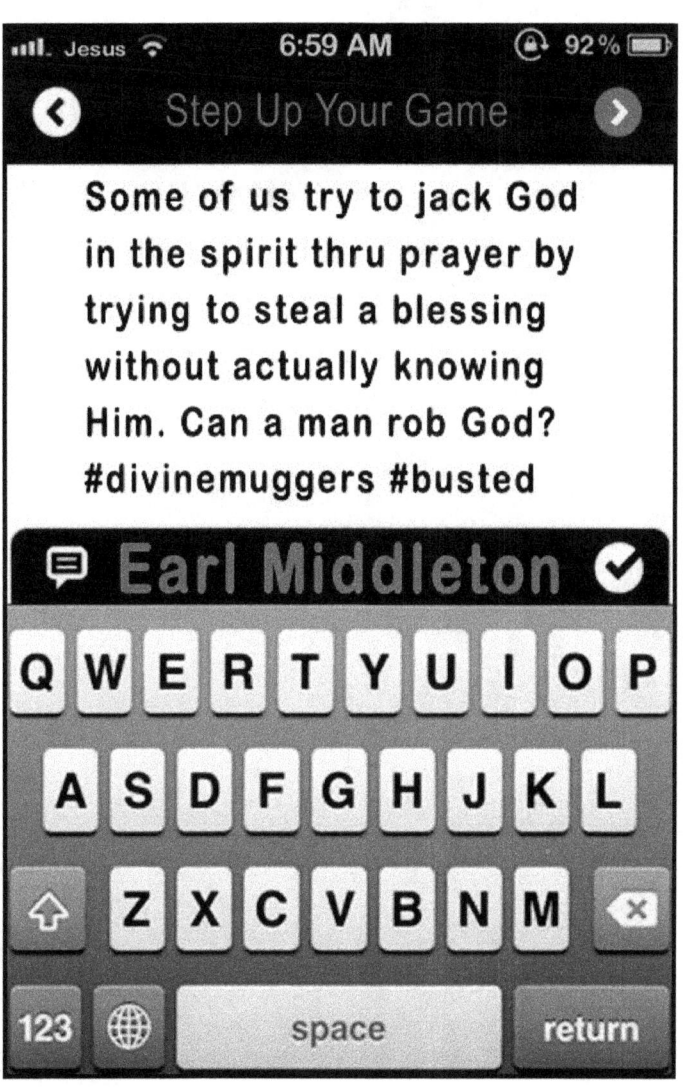

**Step Up Your Game**

Some of us try to jack God in the spirit thru prayer by trying to steal a blessing without actually knowing Him. Can a man rob God? #divinemuggers #busted

# June 4

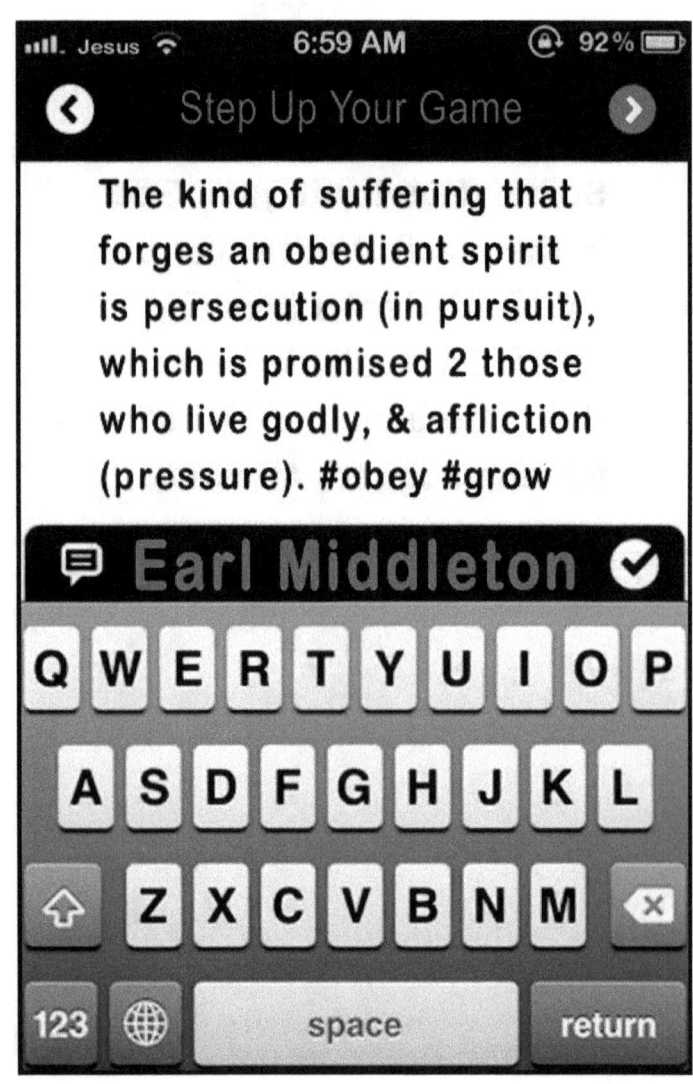

**Step Up Your Game**

The kind of suffering that forges an obedient spirit is persecution (in pursuit), which is promised 2 those who live godly, & affliction (pressure). #obey #grow

— Earl Middleton

# June 5

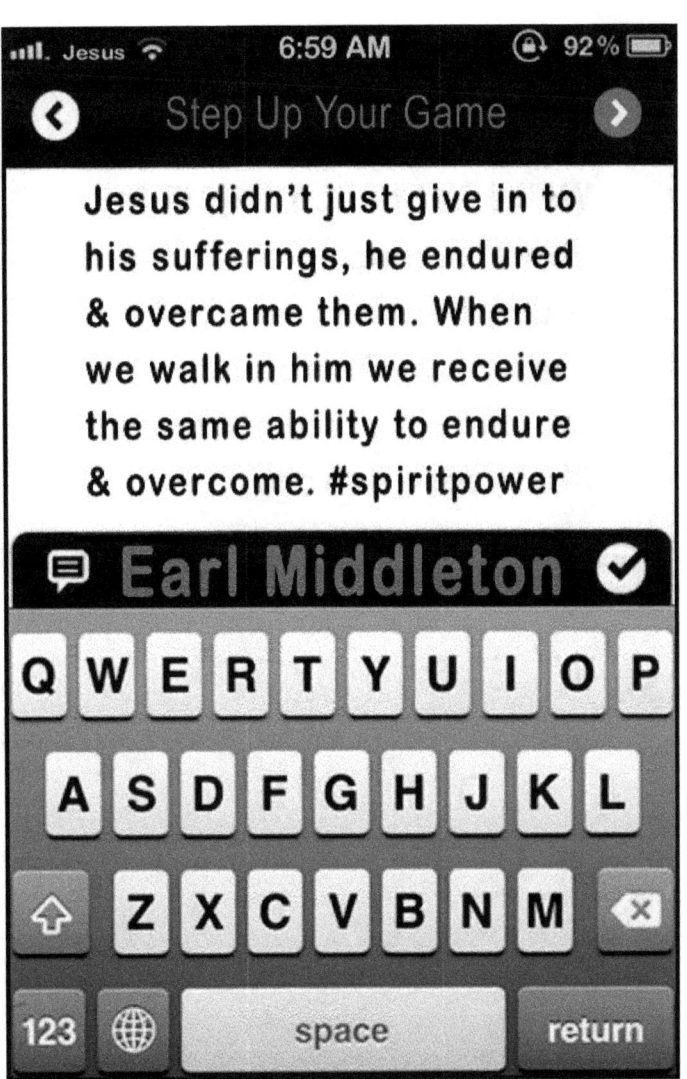

# June 6

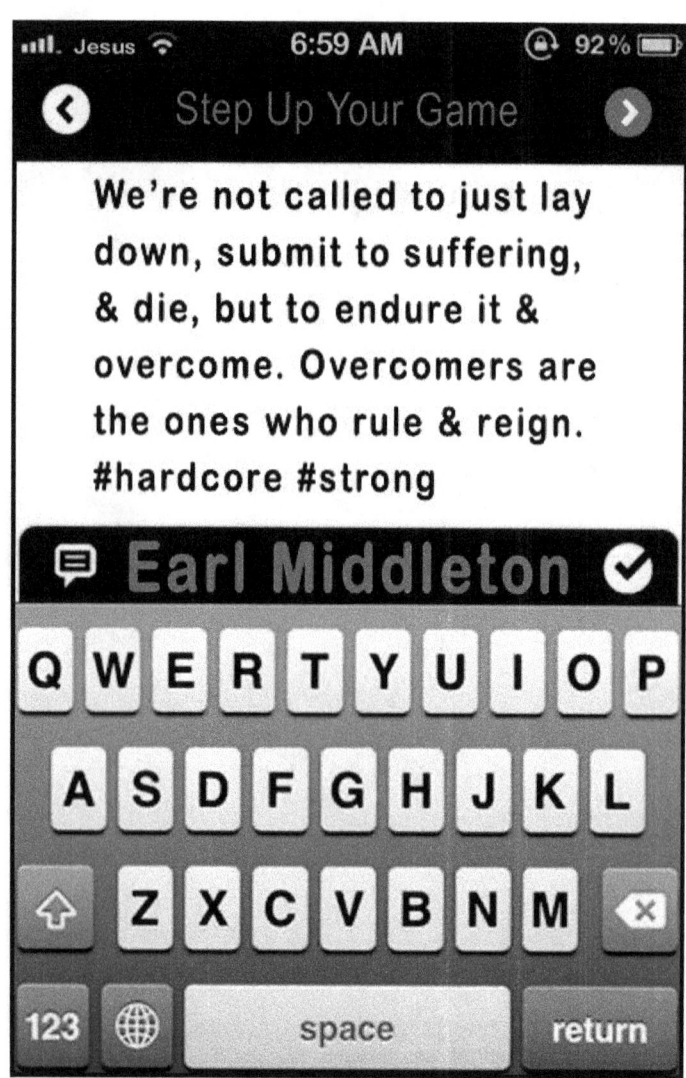

**Step Up Your Game**

We're not called to just lay down, submit to suffering, & die, but to endure it & overcome. Overcomers are the ones who rule & reign. #hardcore #strong

# June 7

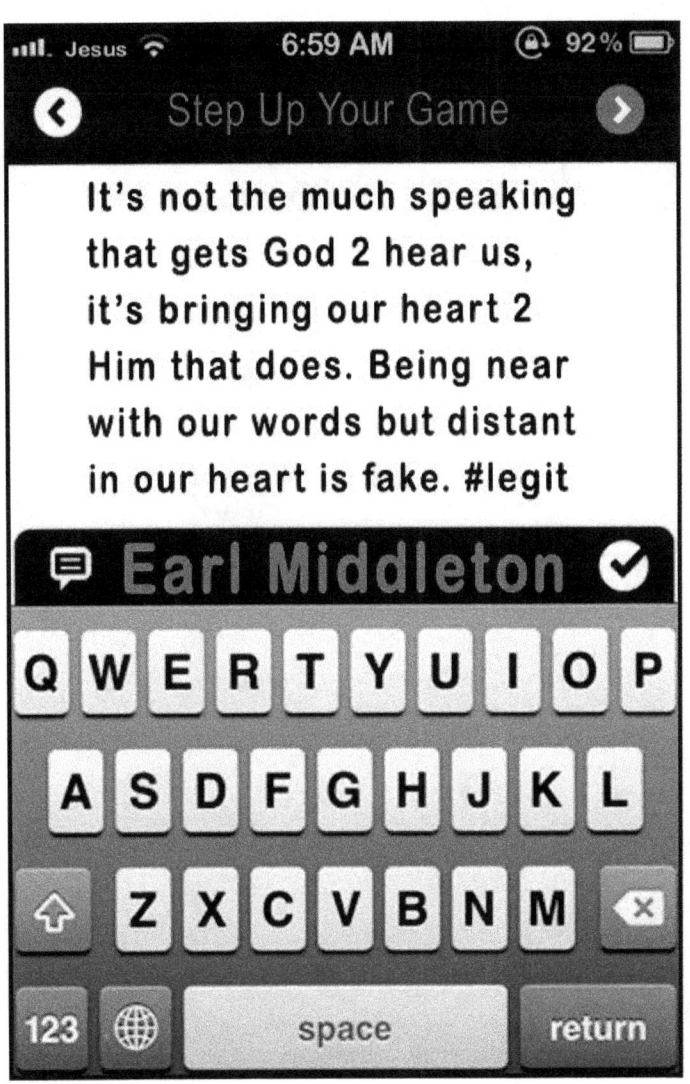

## June 8

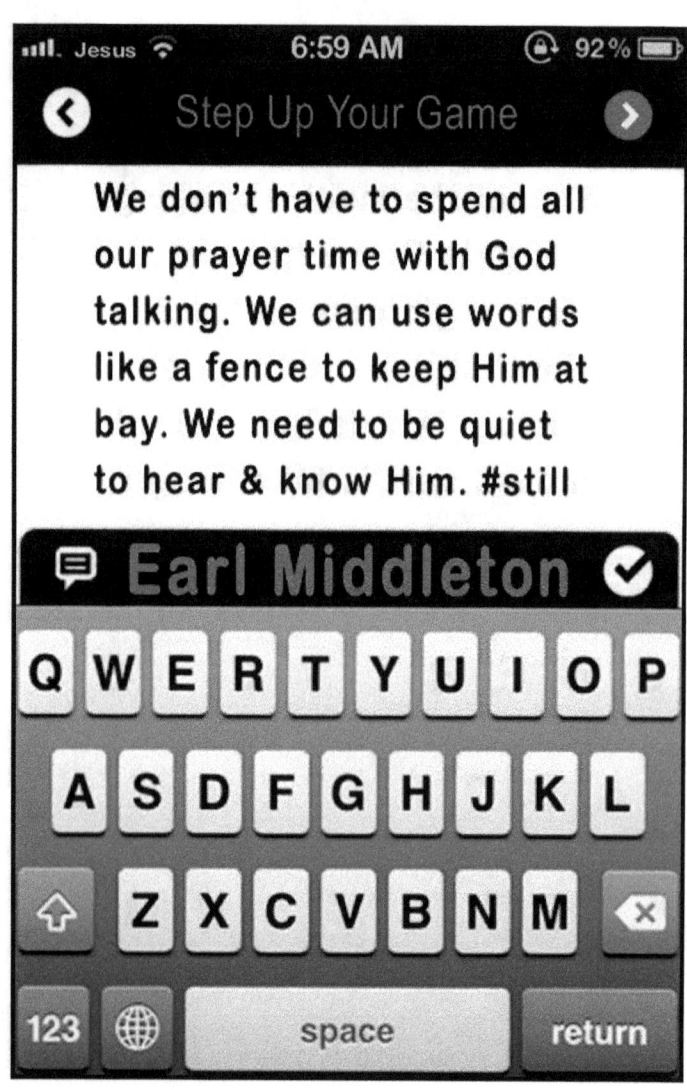

We don't have to spend all our prayer time with God talking. We can use words like a fence to keep Him at bay. We need to be quiet to hear & know Him. #still

# June 9

# June 10

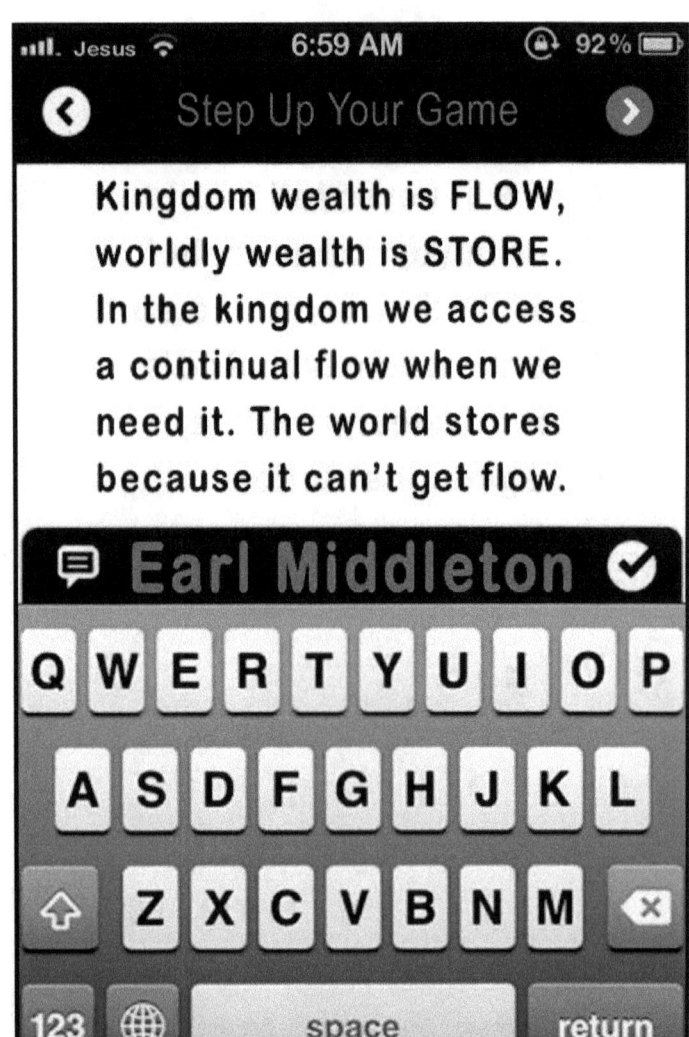

# June 11

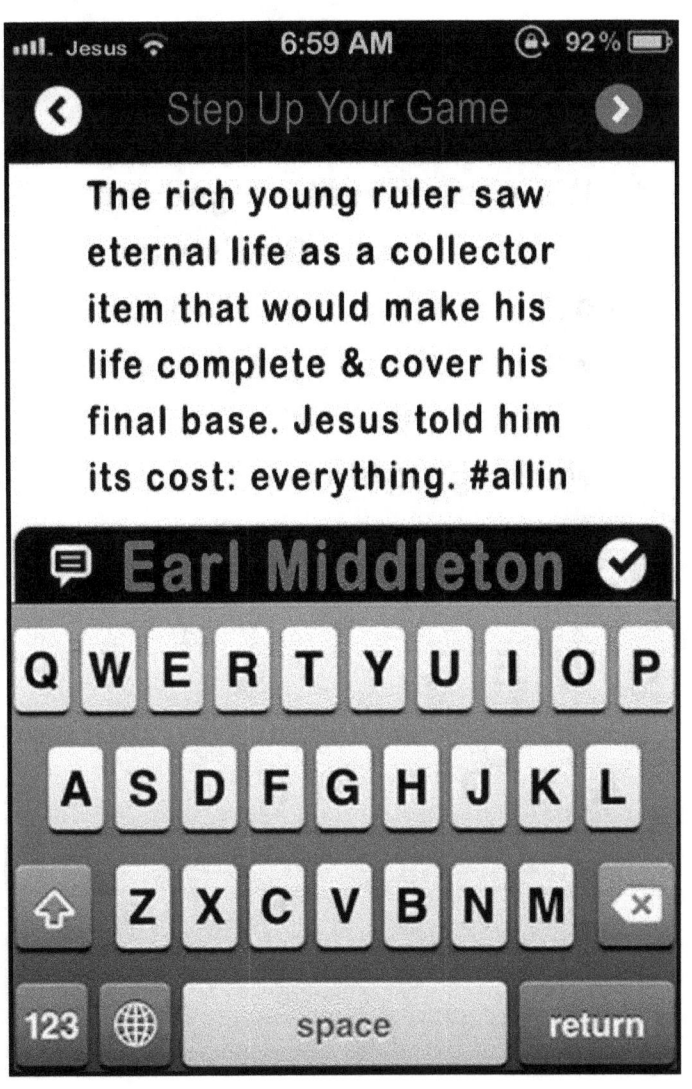

# June 12

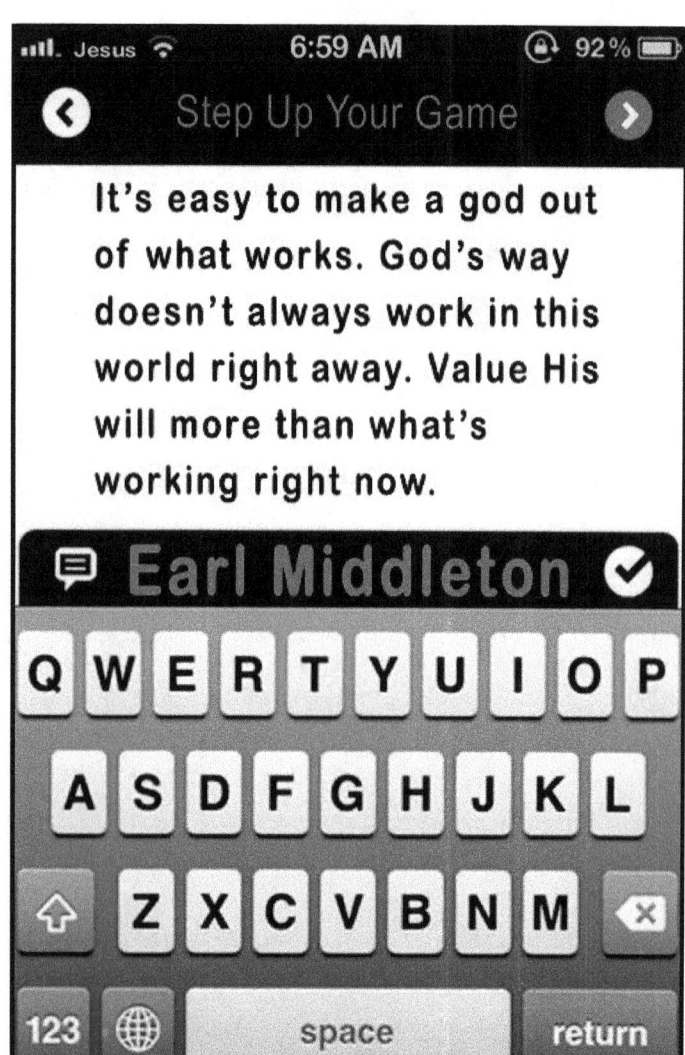

## Step Up Your Game

It's easy to make a god out of what works. God's way doesn't always work in this world right away. Value His will more than what's working right now.

— Earl Middleton

# June 13

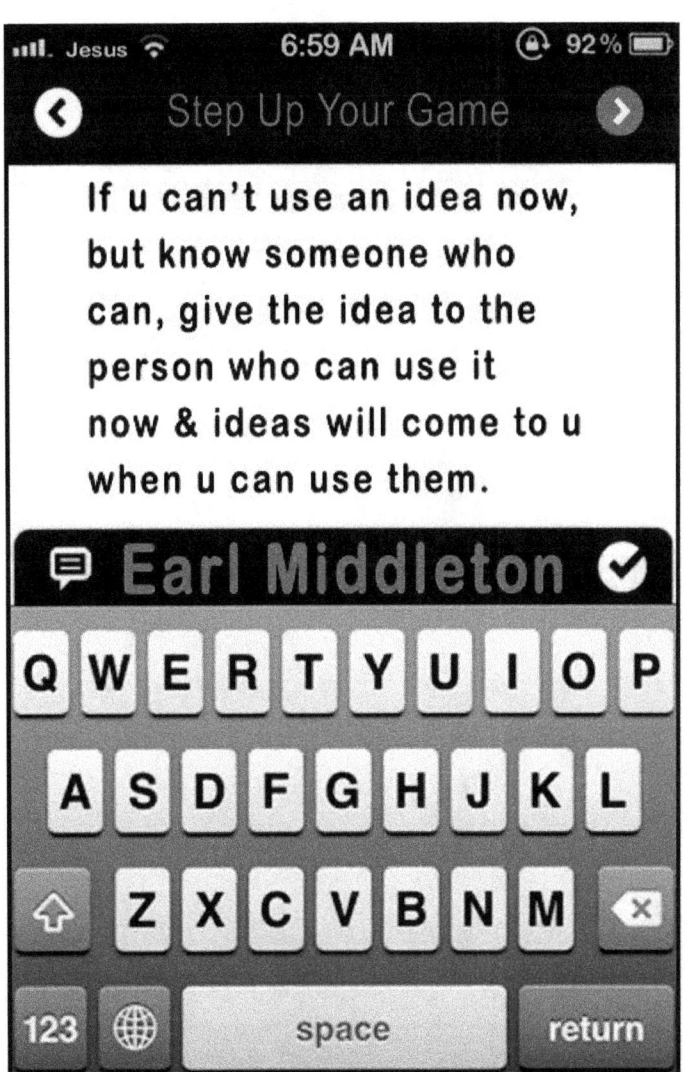

If u can't use an idea now, but know someone who can, give the idea to the person who can use it now & ideas will come to u when u can use them.

— Earl Middleton

# June 14

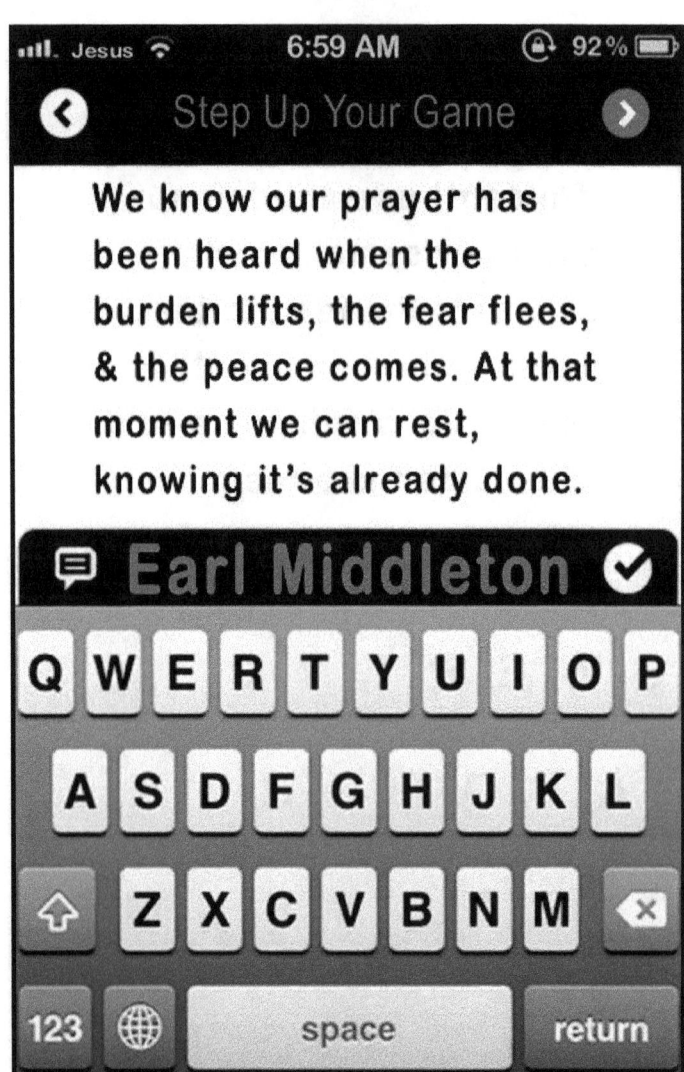

## Step Up Your Game

We know our prayer has been heard when the burden lifts, the fear flees, & the peace comes. At that moment we can rest, knowing it's already done.

Earl Middleton

# June 15

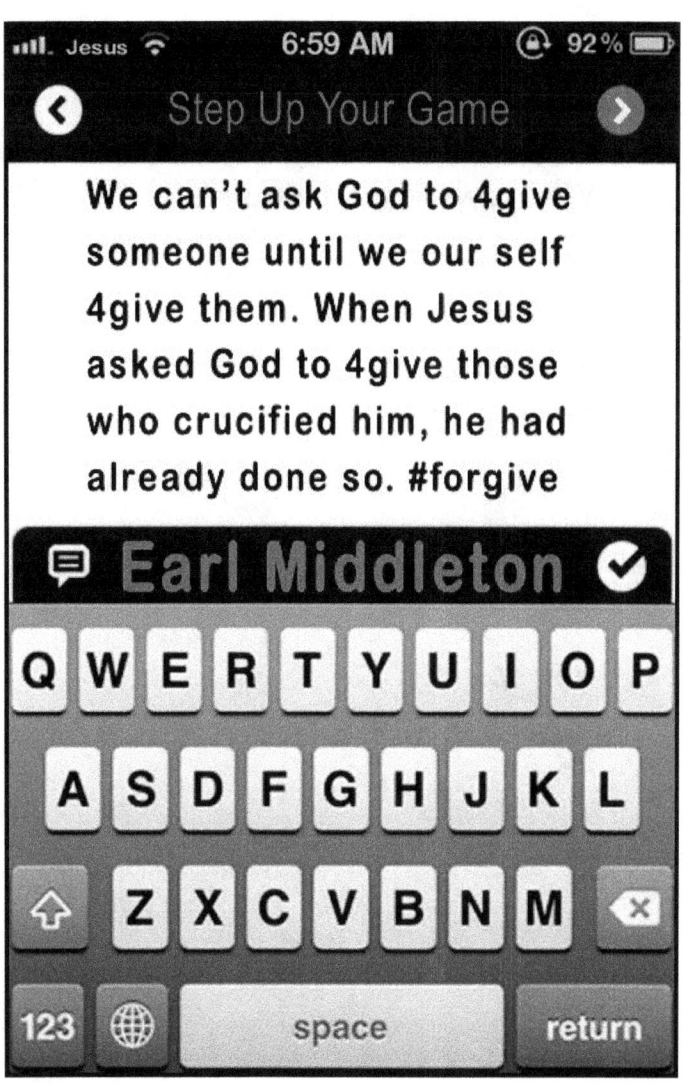

## June 16

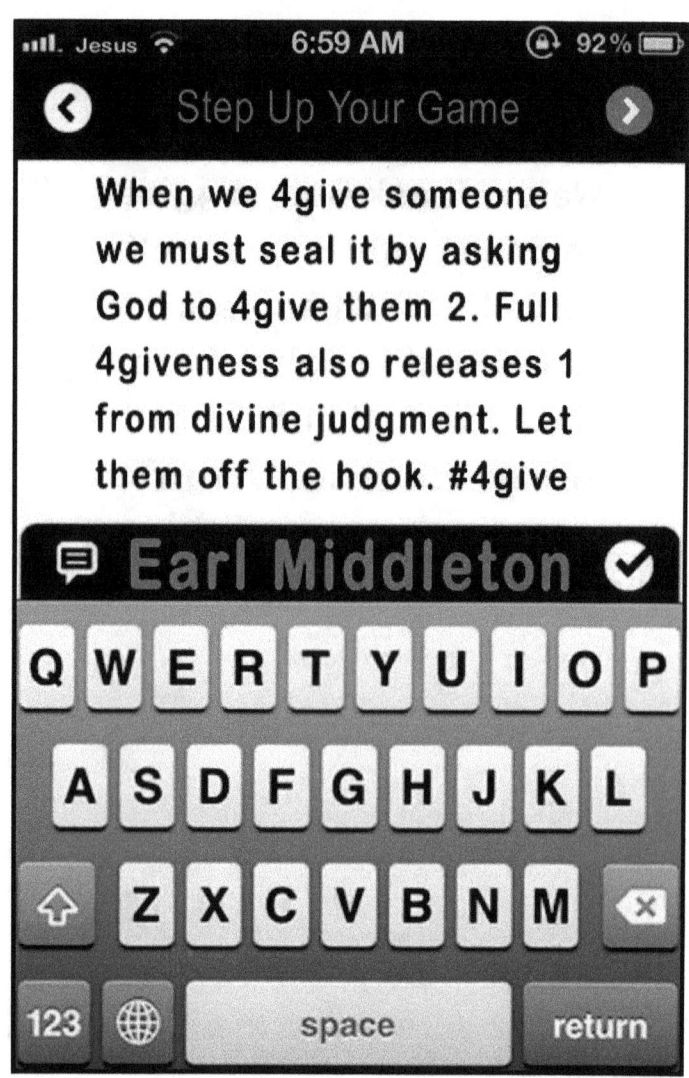

**Step Up Your Game**

When we 4give someone we must seal it by asking God to 4give them 2. Full 4giveness also releases 1 from divine judgment. Let them off the hook. #4give

# June 17

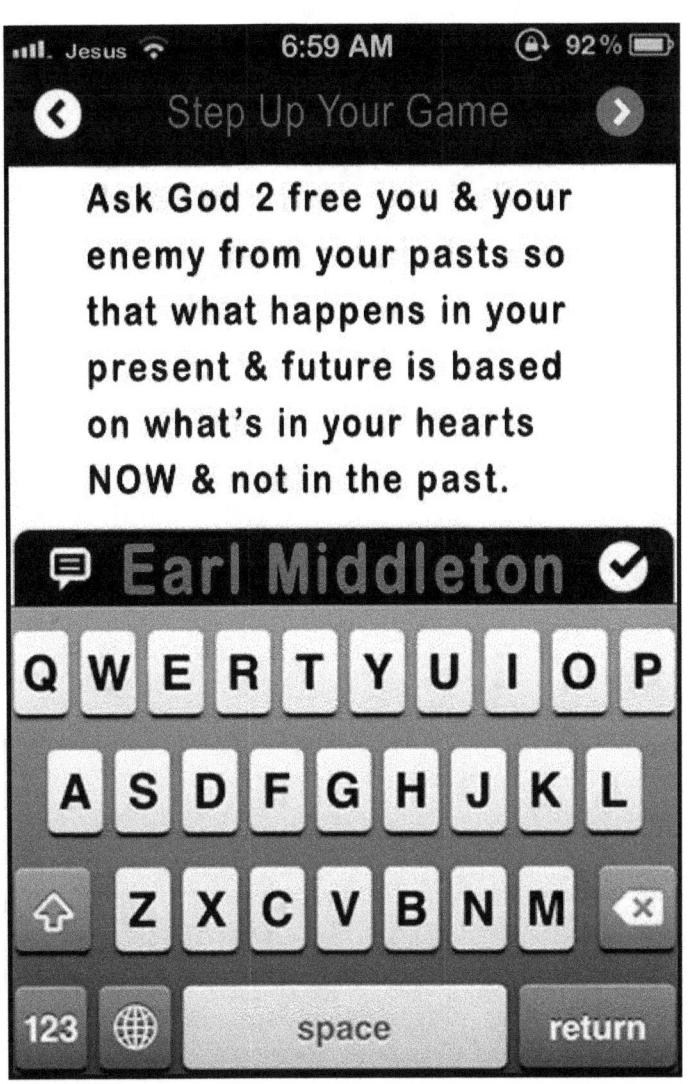

# June 18

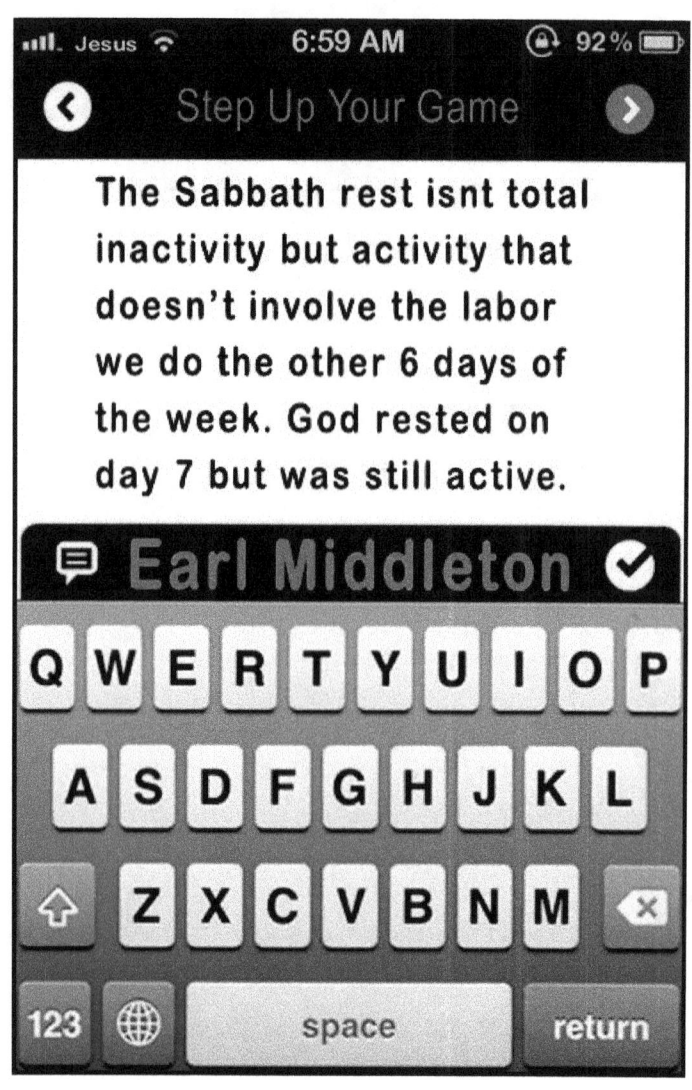

**Step Up Your Game**

The Sabbath rest isnt total inactivity but activity that doesn't involve the labor we do the other 6 days of the week. God rested on day 7 but was still active.

— Earl Middleton

# June 19

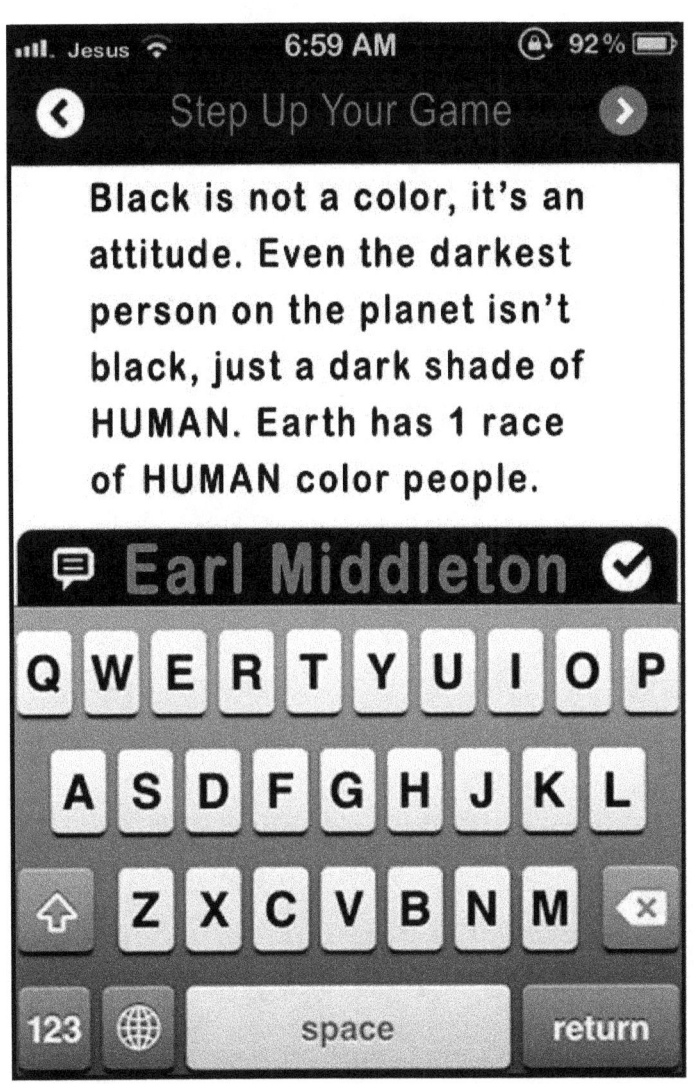

# June 20

# June 21

# June 22

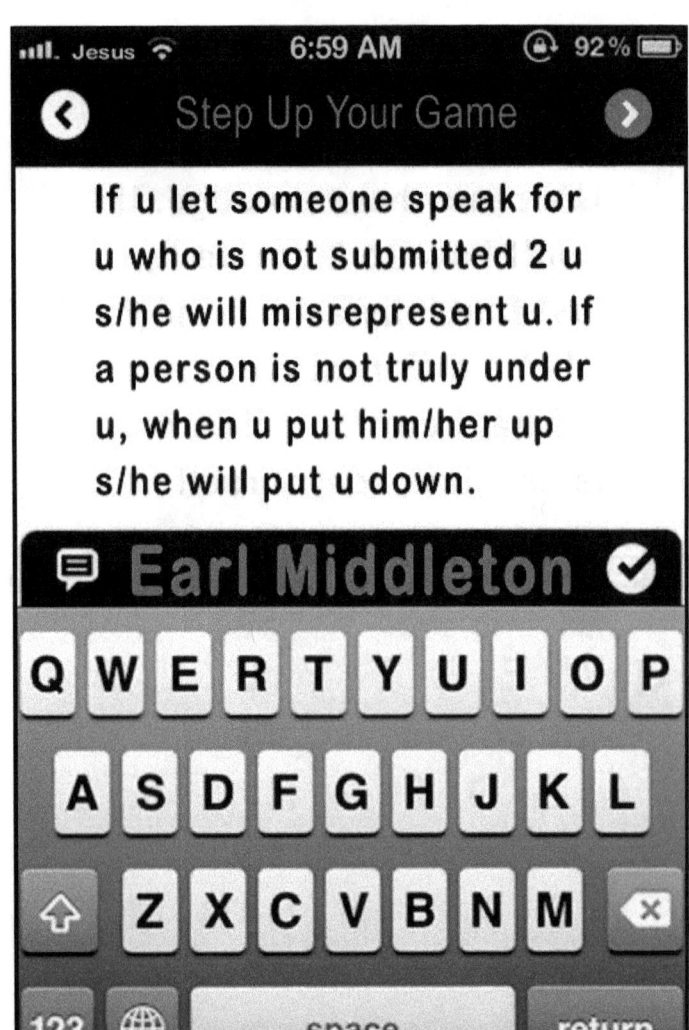

If u let someone speak for u who is not submitted 2 u s/he will misrepresent u. If a person is not truly under u, when u put him/her up s/he will put u down.

— Earl Middleton

# June 23

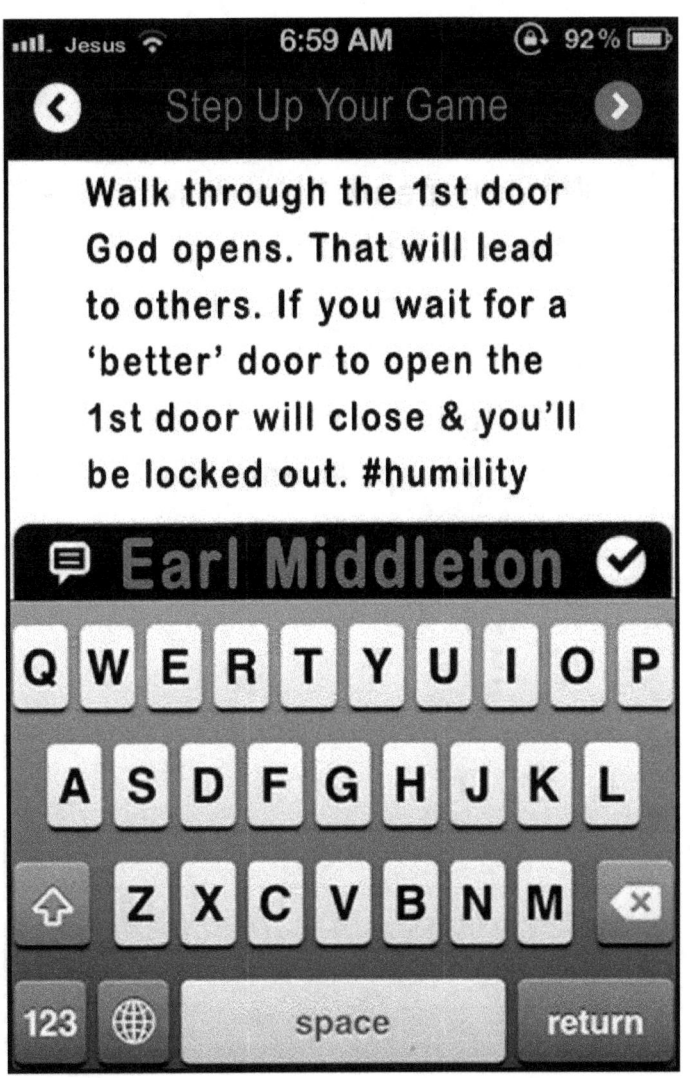

Walk through the 1st door God opens. That will lead to others. If you wait for a 'better' door to open the 1st door will close & you'll be locked out. #humility

# June 24

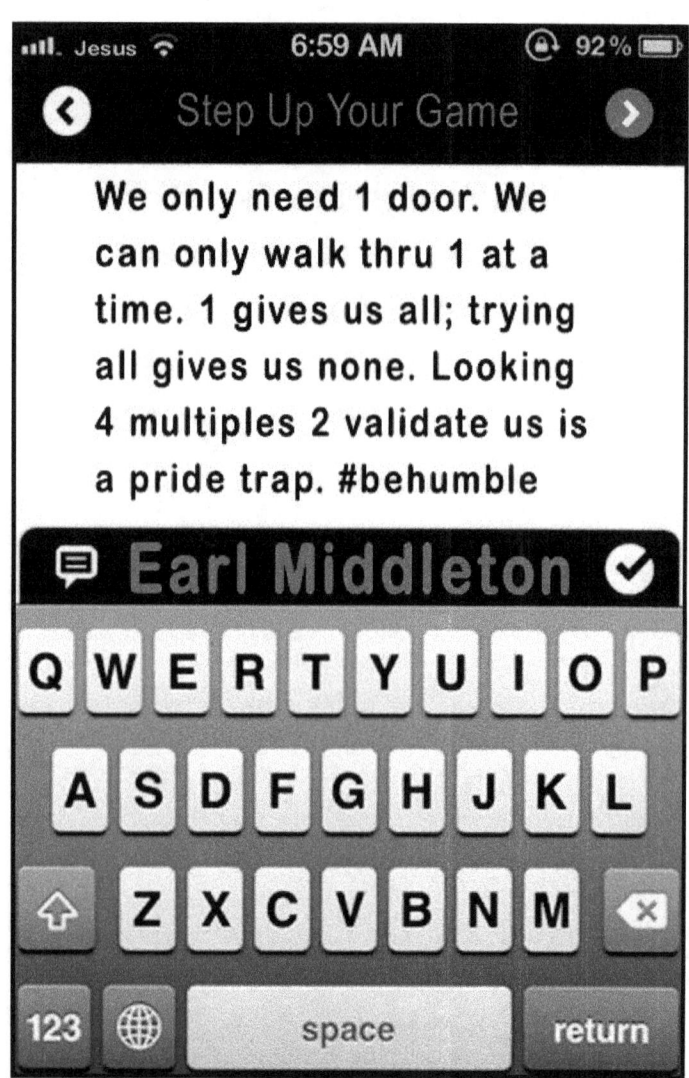

**Step Up Your Game**

We only need 1 door. We can only walk thru 1 at a time. 1 gives us all; trying all gives us none. Looking 4 multiples 2 validate us is a pride trap. #behumble

— Earl Middleton

# June 25

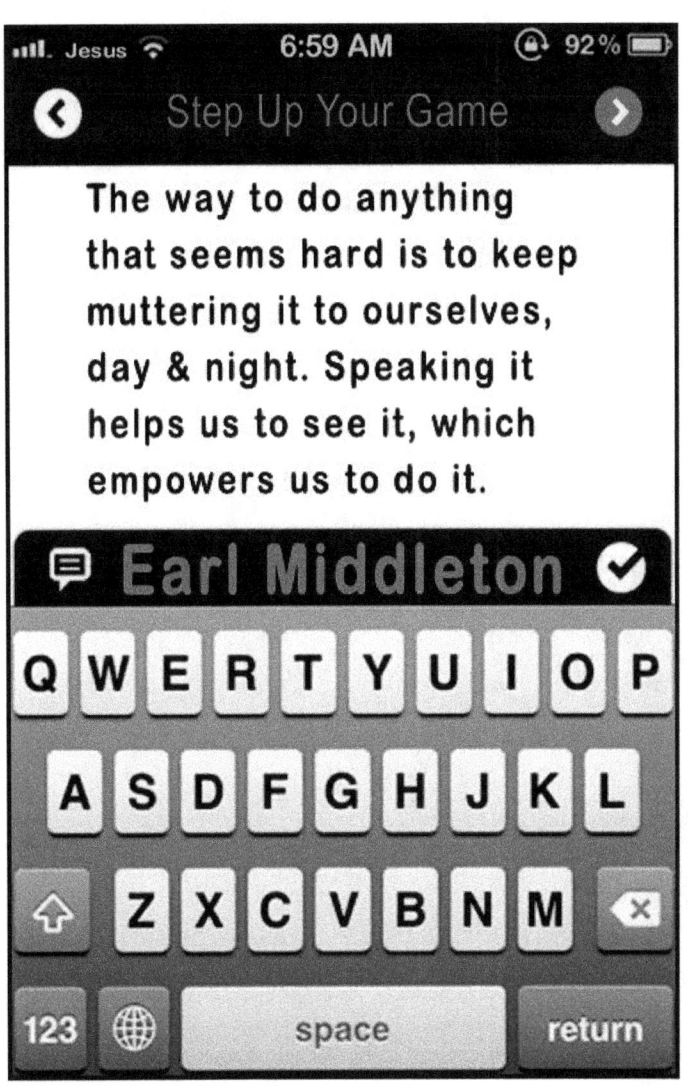

## Step Up Your Game

The way to do anything that seems hard is to keep muttering it to ourselves, day & night. Speaking it helps us to see it, which empowers us to do it.

— Earl Middleton

# June 26

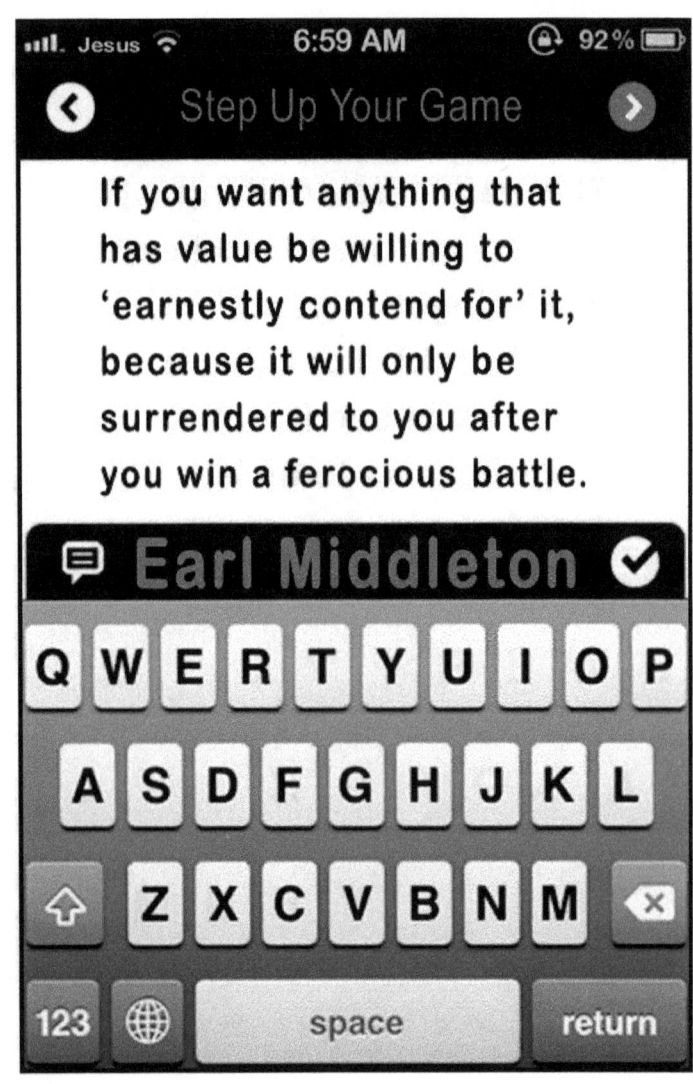

# June 27

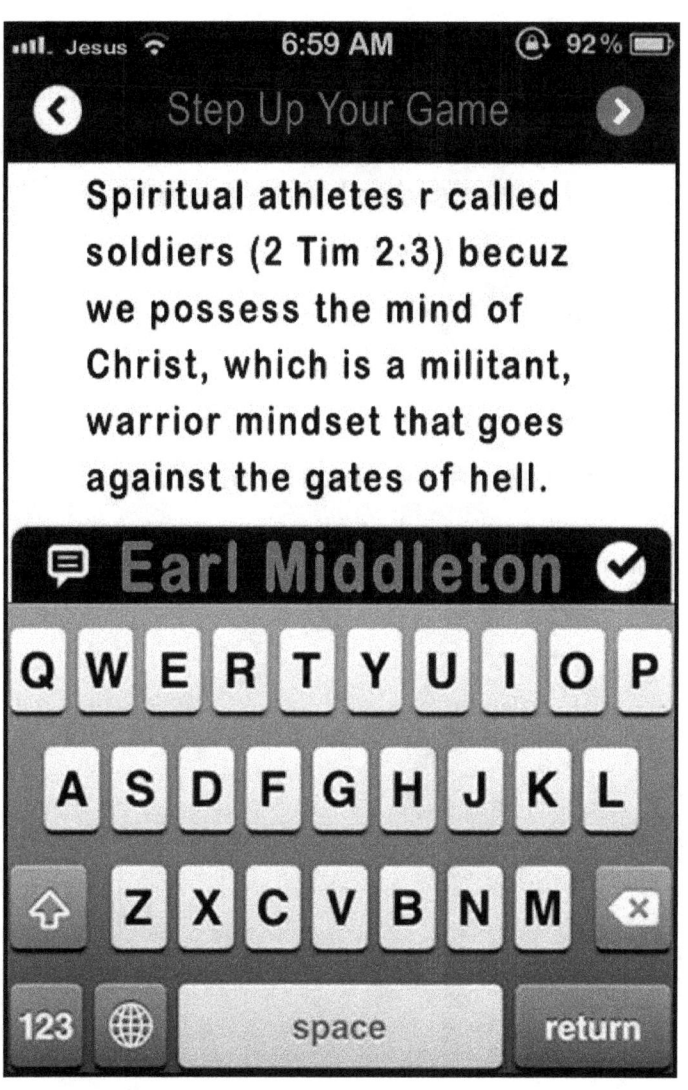

Spiritual athletes r called soldiers (2 Tim 2:3) becuz we possess the mind of Christ, which is a militant, warrior mindset that goes against the gates of hell.

# June 28

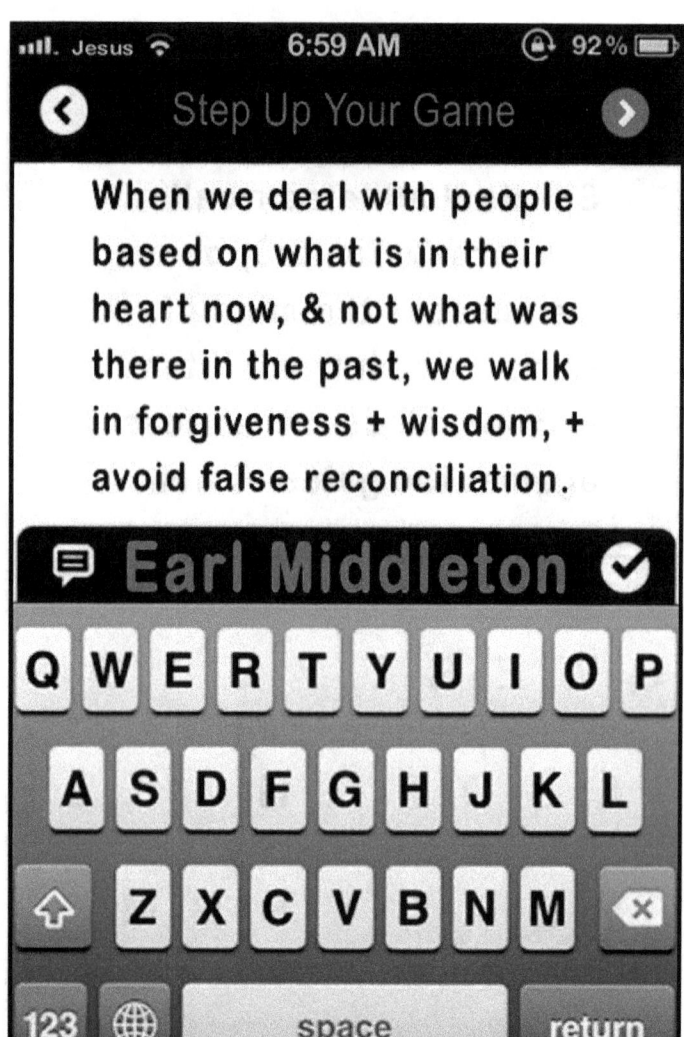

**Step Up Your Game**

When we deal with people based on what is in their heart now, & not what was there in the past, we walk in forgiveness + wisdom, + avoid false reconciliation.

— Earl Middleton

# June 29

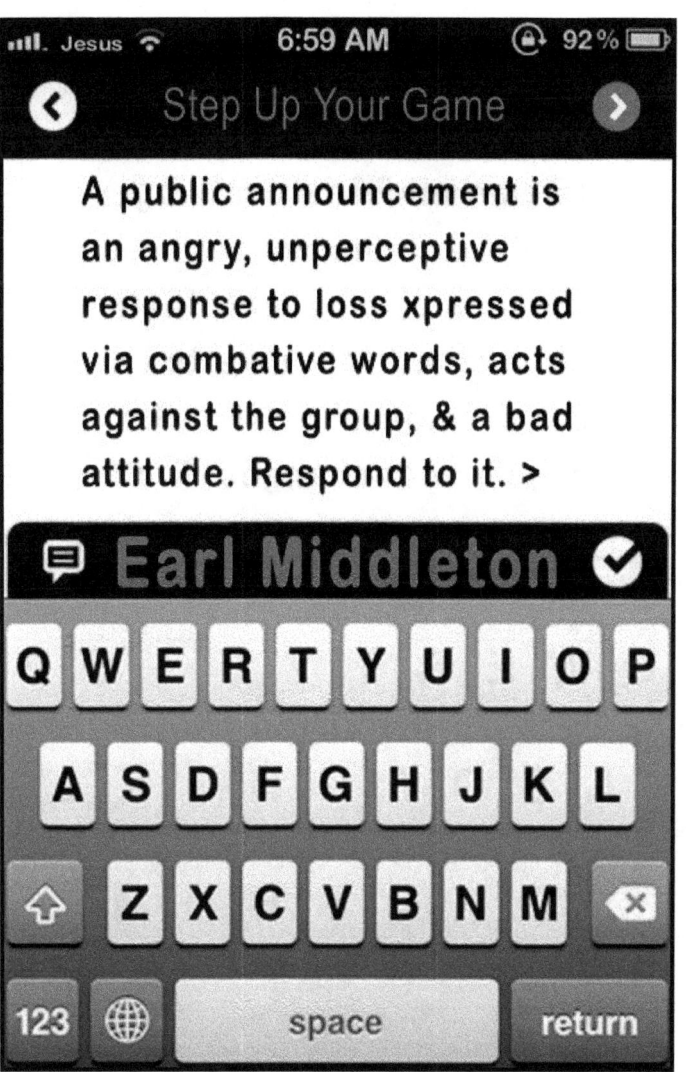

# June 30

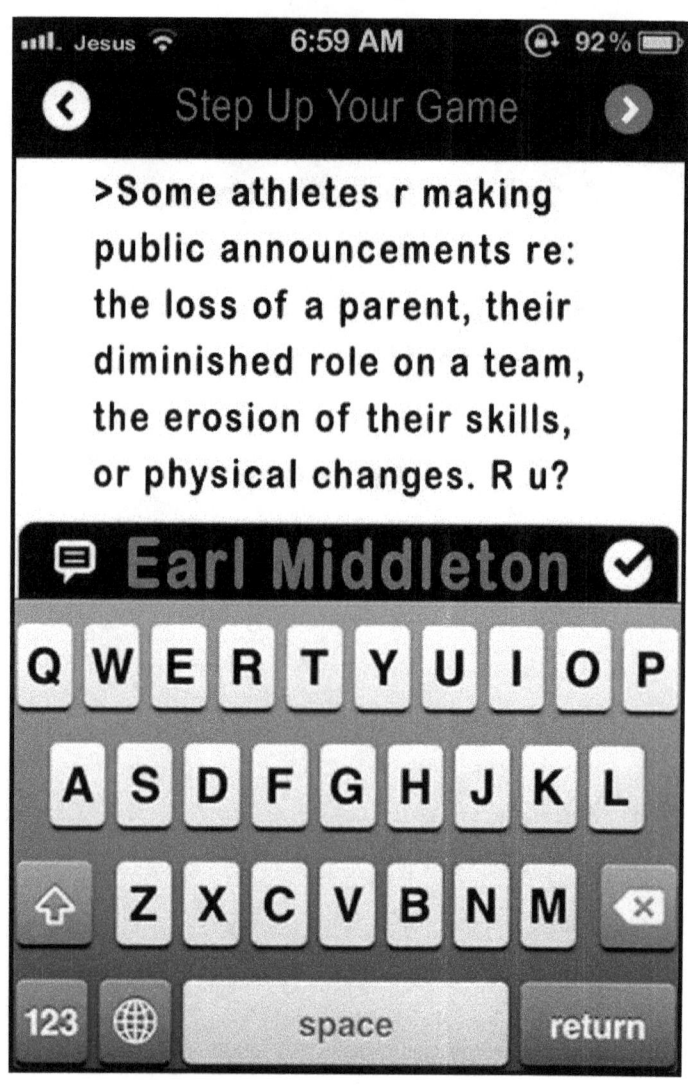

# July 1

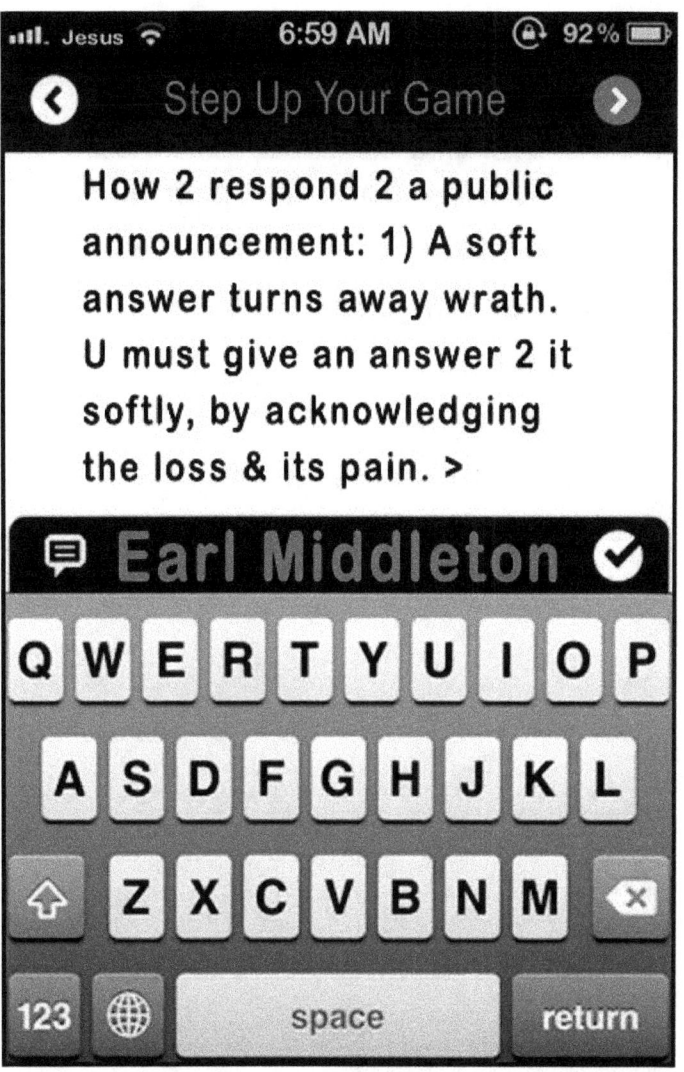

**Step Up Your Game**

How 2 respond 2 a public announcement: 1) A soft answer turns away wrath. U must give an answer 2 it softly, by acknowledging the loss & its pain. >

Earl Middleton

# July 2

**Step Up Your Game**

How 2 respond 2 a public announcement: 2) We r all important members of the same body. Affirm the announcer's importance & place on the team. >

Earl Middleton

# July 3

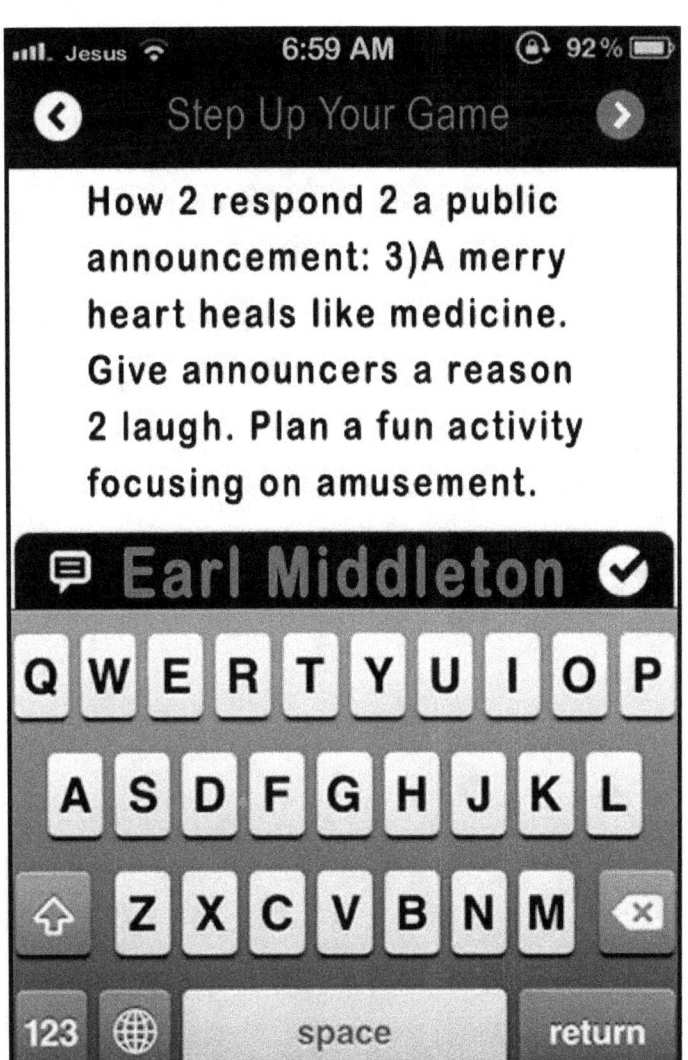

**Step Up Your Game**

How 2 respond 2 a public announcement: 3)A merry heart heals like medicine. Give announcers a reason 2 laugh. Plan a fun activity focusing on amusement.

## July 4

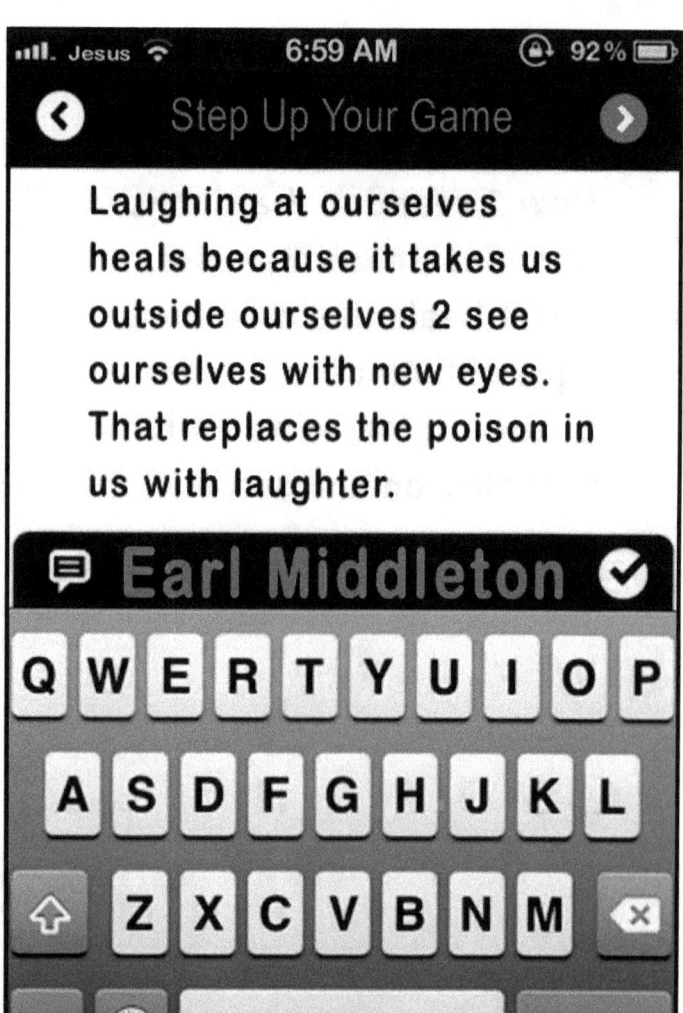

Laughing at ourselves heals because it takes us outside ourselves 2 see ourselves with new eyes. That replaces the poison in us with laughter.

— Earl Middleton

# July 5

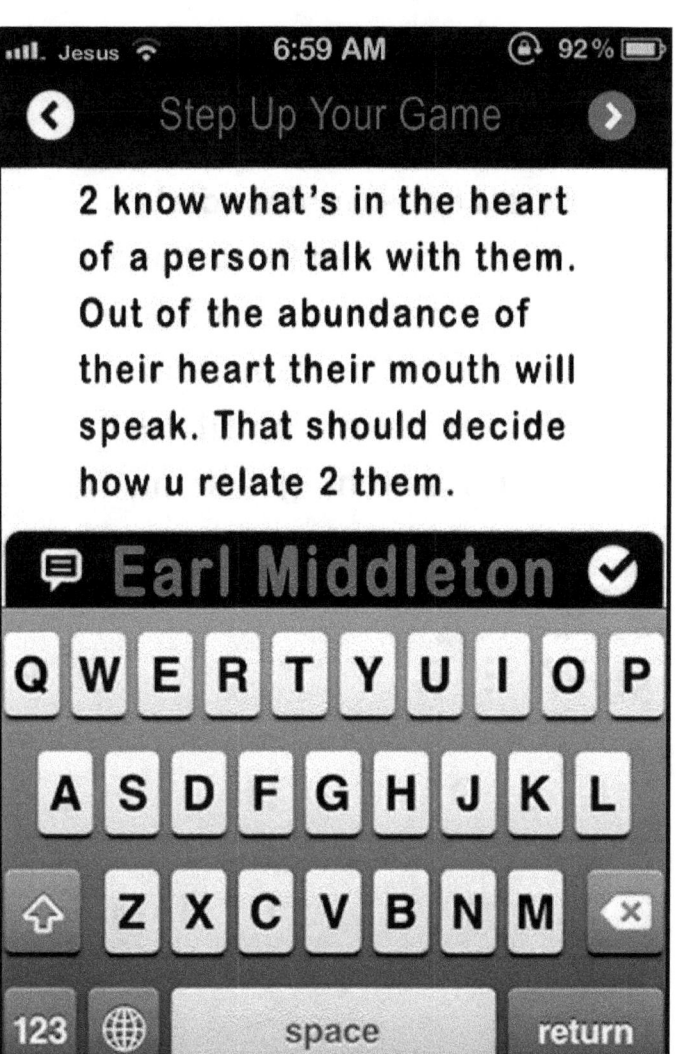

# July 6

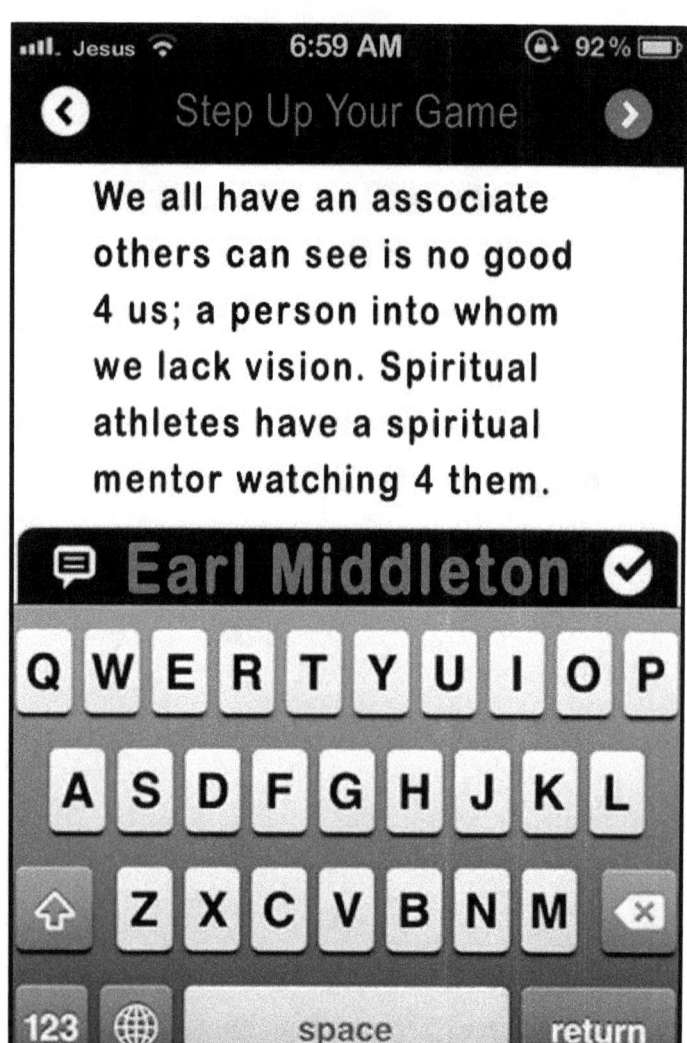

**Step Up Your Game**

We all have an associate others can see is no good 4 us; a person into whom we lack vision. Spiritual athletes have a spiritual mentor watching 4 them.

— Earl Middleton

# July 7

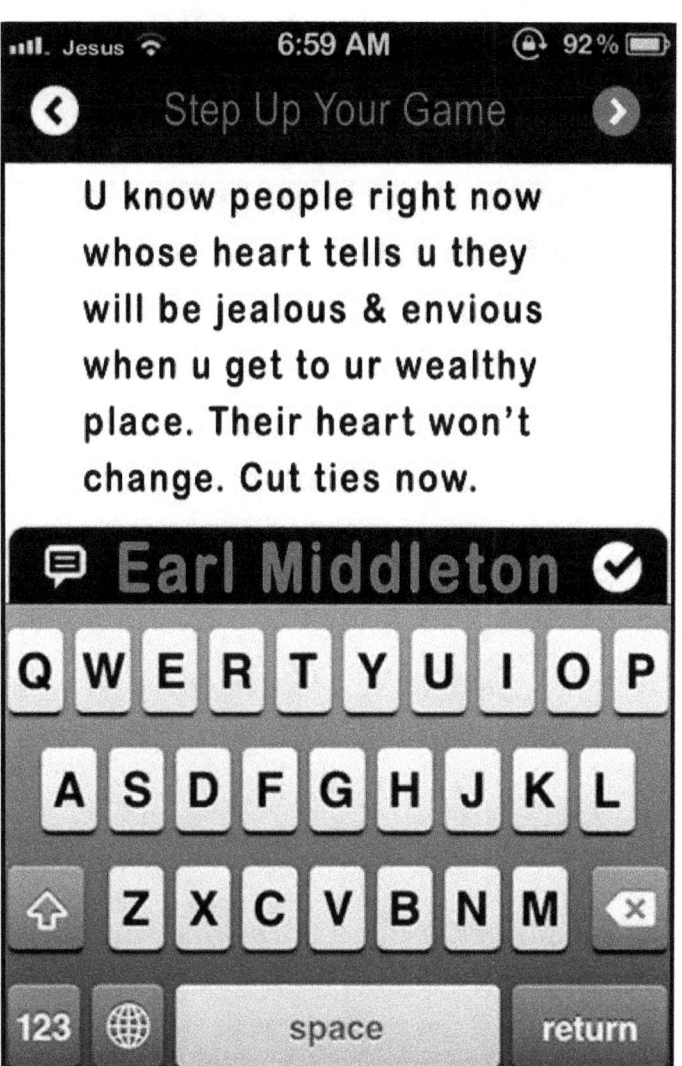

> U know people right now whose heart tells u they will be jealous & envious when u get to ur wealthy place. Their heart won't change. Cut ties now.

## July 8

# July 9

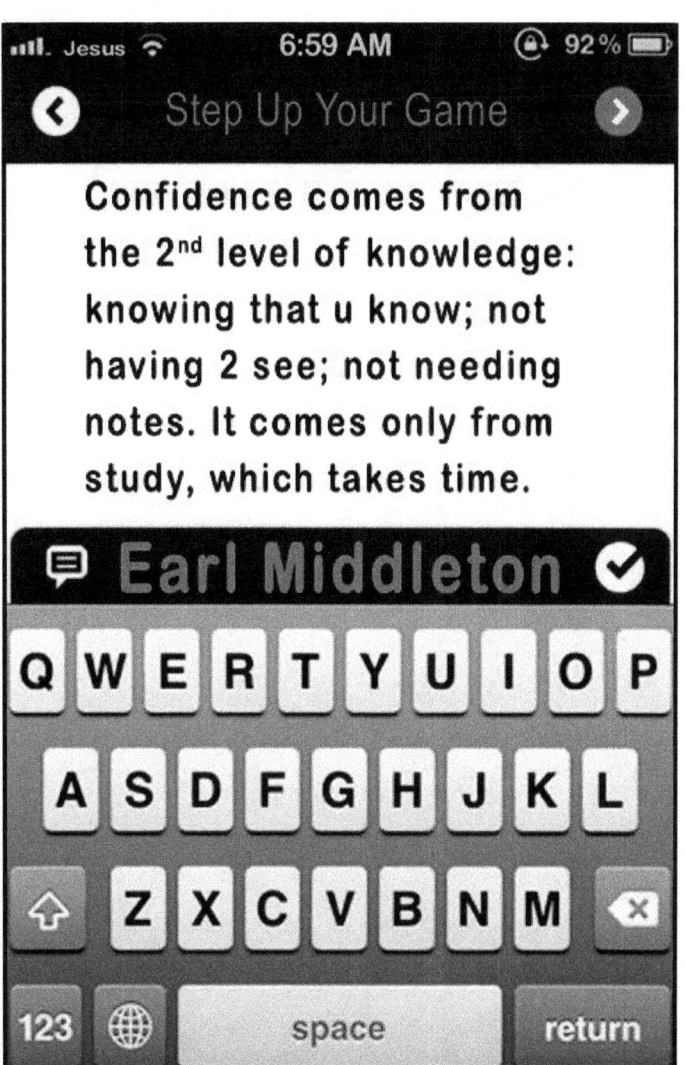

**Confidence comes from the 2nd level of knowledge: knowing that u know; not having 2 see; not needing notes. It comes only from study, which takes time.**

# July 10

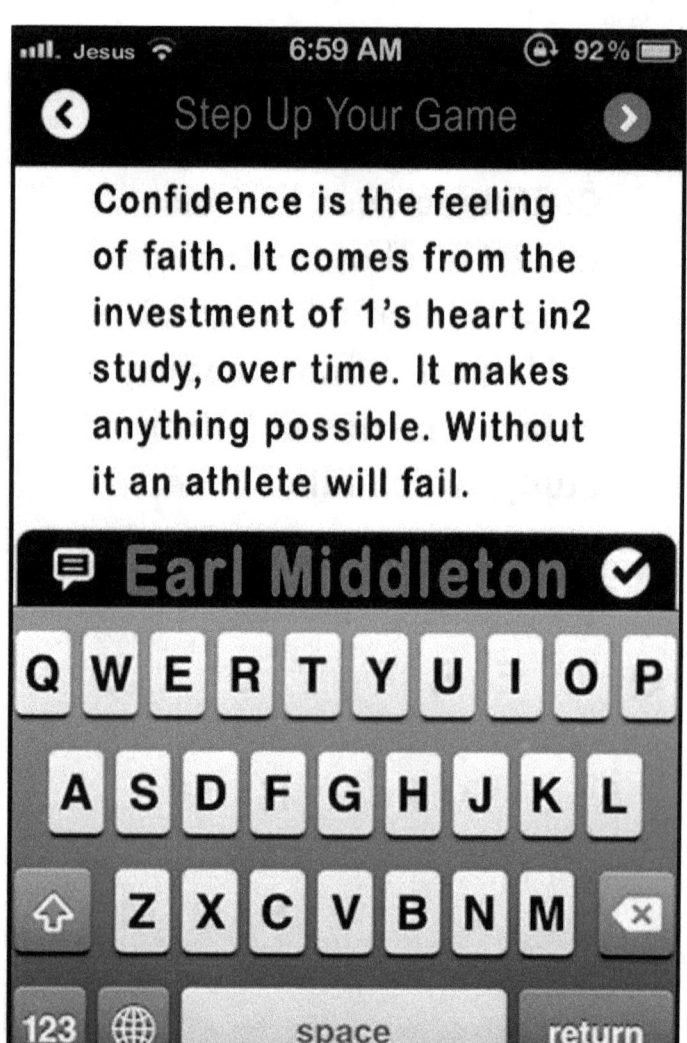

Confidence is the feeling of faith. It comes from the investment of 1's heart in2 study, over time. It makes anything possible. Without it an athlete will fail.

Earl Middleton

# July 11

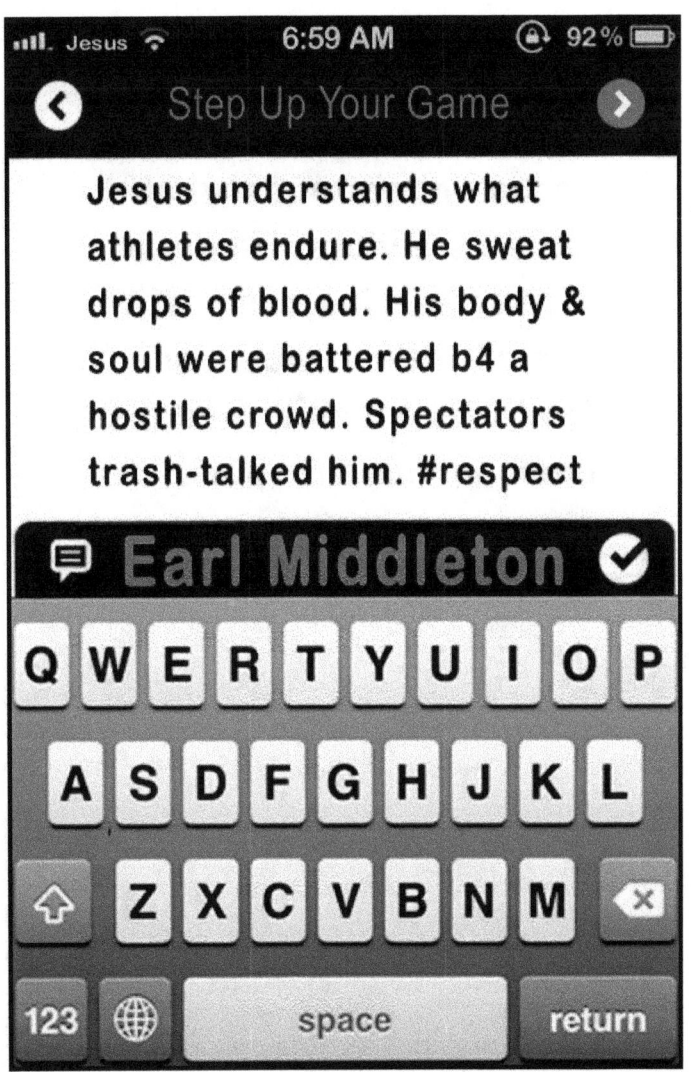

# July 12

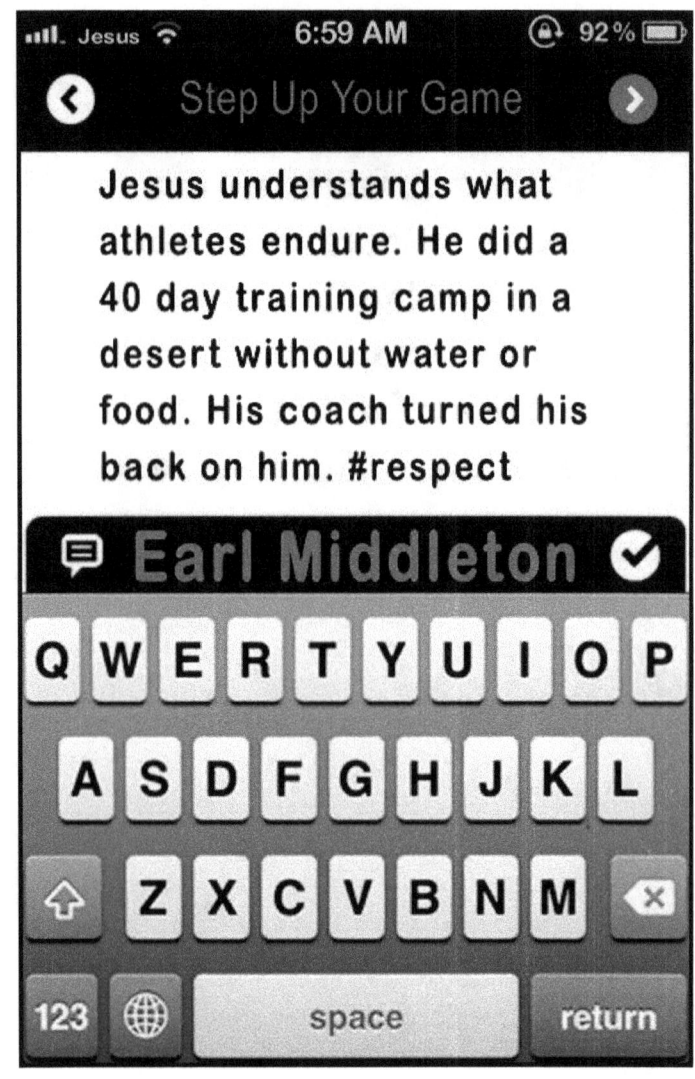

**Step Up Your Game**

Jesus understands what athletes endure. He did a 40 day training camp in a desert without water or food. His coach turned his back on him. #respect

# July 13

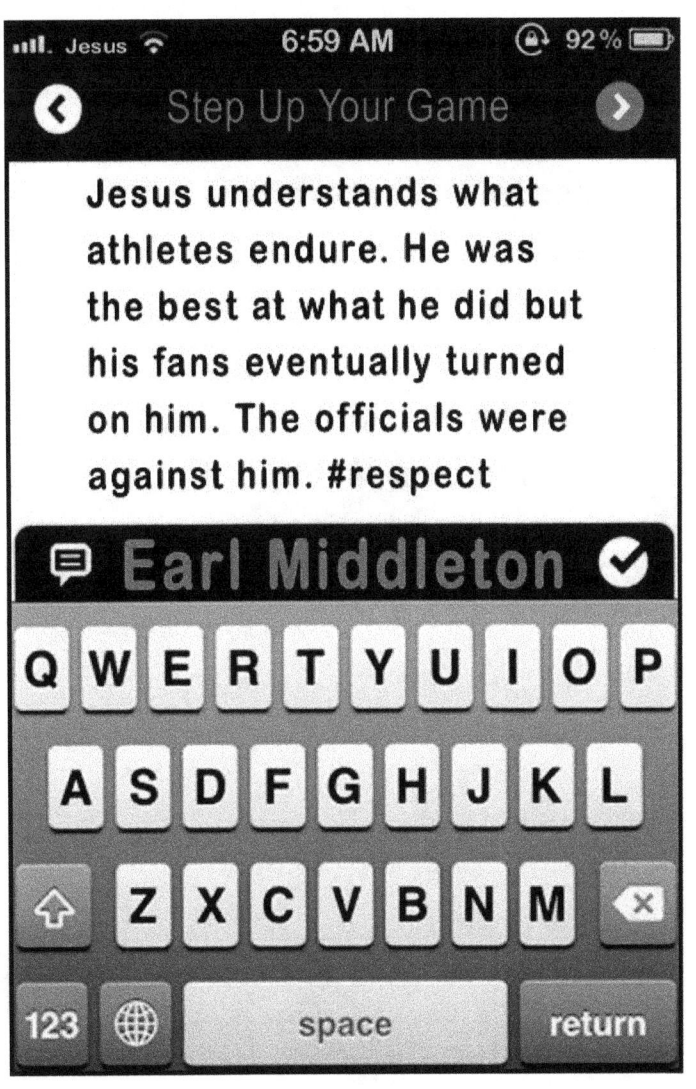

# July 14

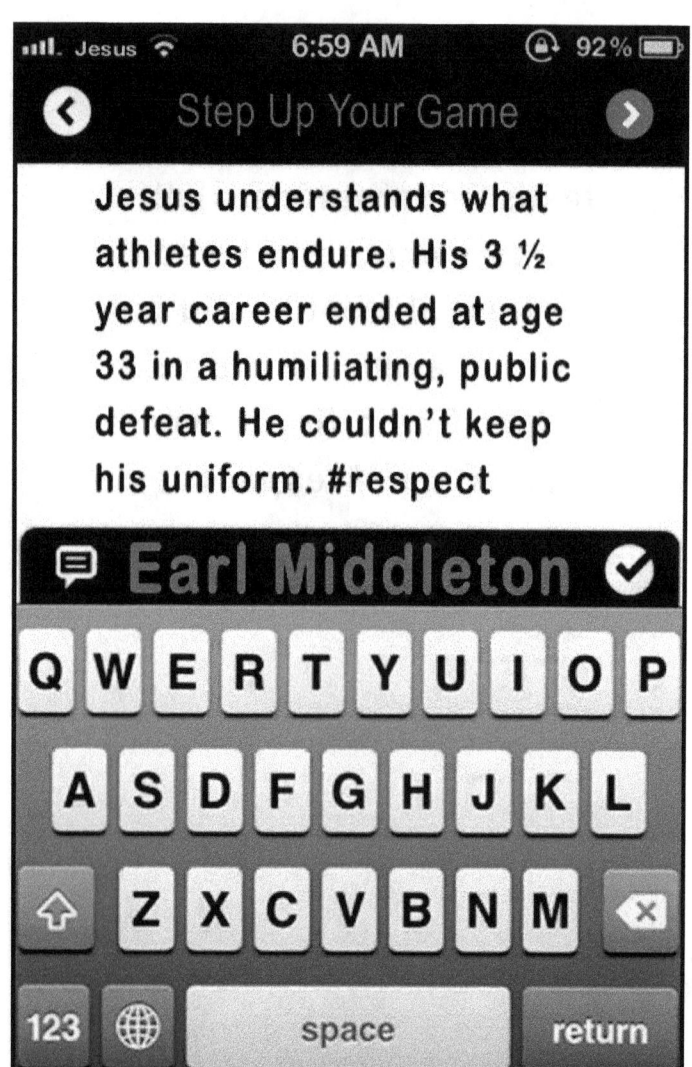

**Step Up Your Game**

Jesus understands what athletes endure. His 3 ½ year career ended at age 33 in a humiliating, public defeat. He couldn't keep his uniform. #respect

— Earl Middleton

# July 15

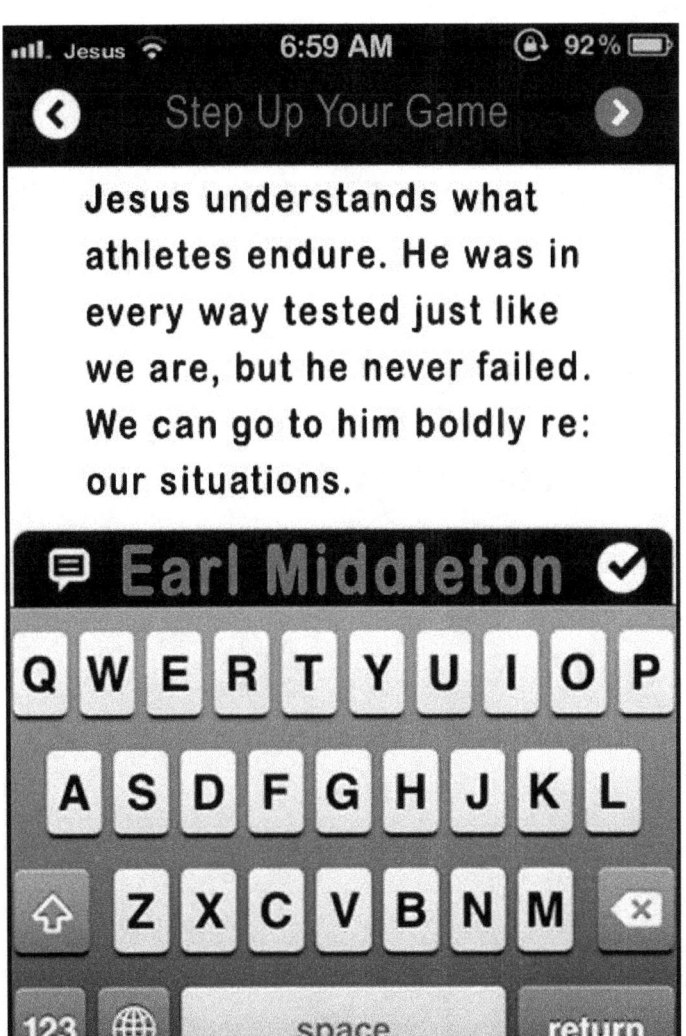

## Step Up Your Game

Jesus understands what athletes endure. He was in every way tested just like we are, but he never failed. We can go to him boldly re: our situations.

— Earl Middleton

# July 16

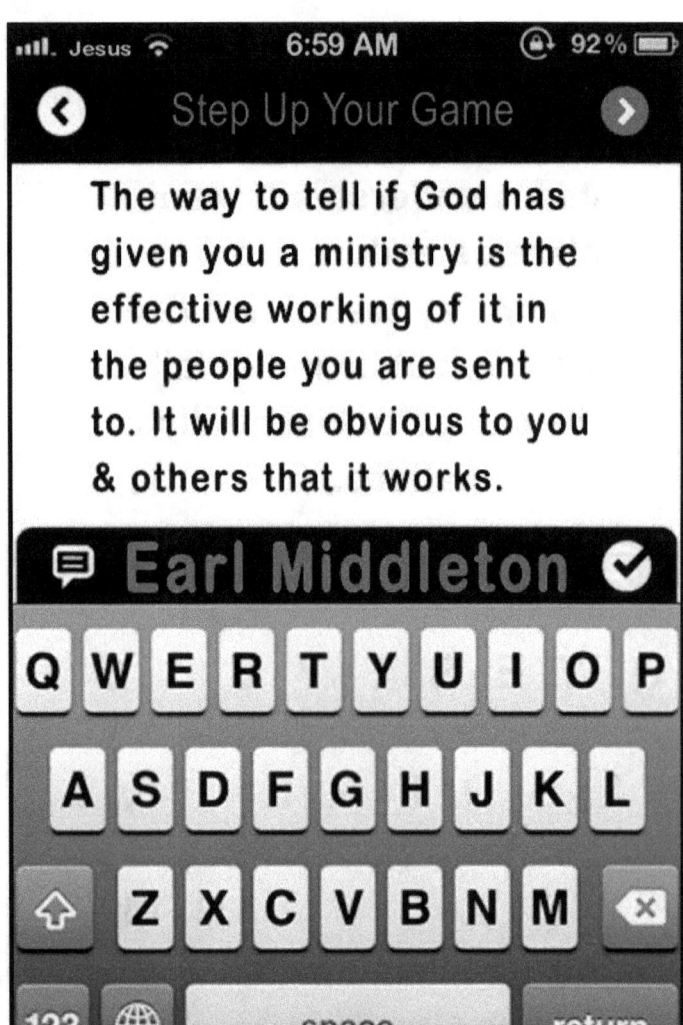

**Step Up Your Game**

The way to tell if God has given you a ministry is the effective working of it in the people you are sent to. It will be obvious to you & others that it works.

— Earl Middleton

# July 17

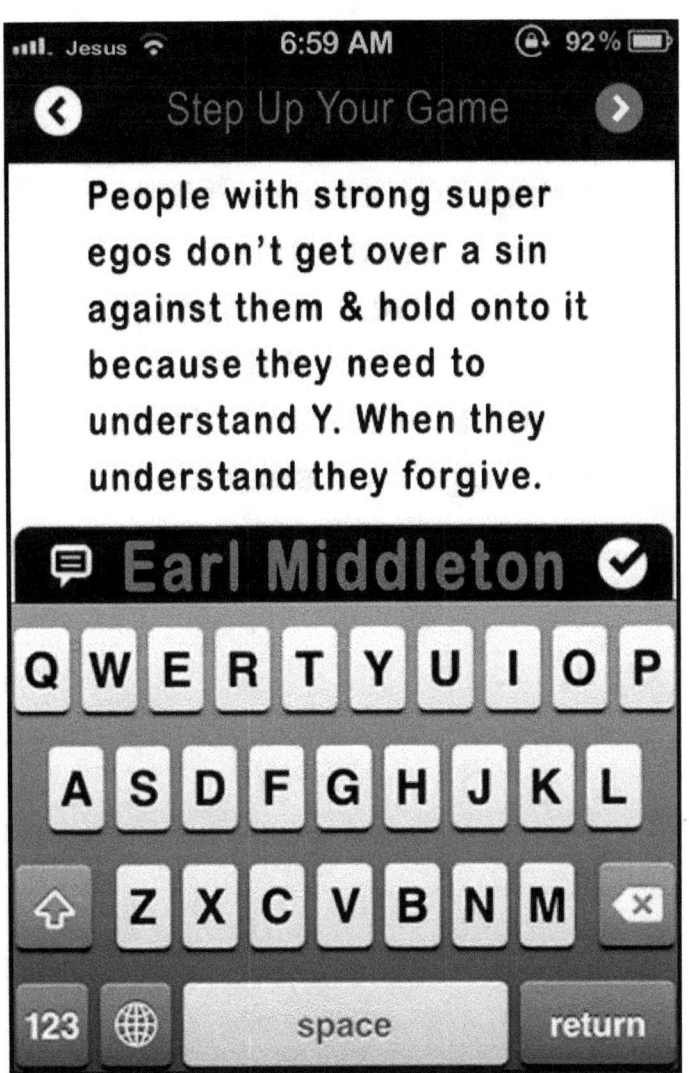

People with strong super egos don't get over a sin against them & hold onto it because they need to understand Y. When they understand they forgive.

— Earl Middleton

# July 18

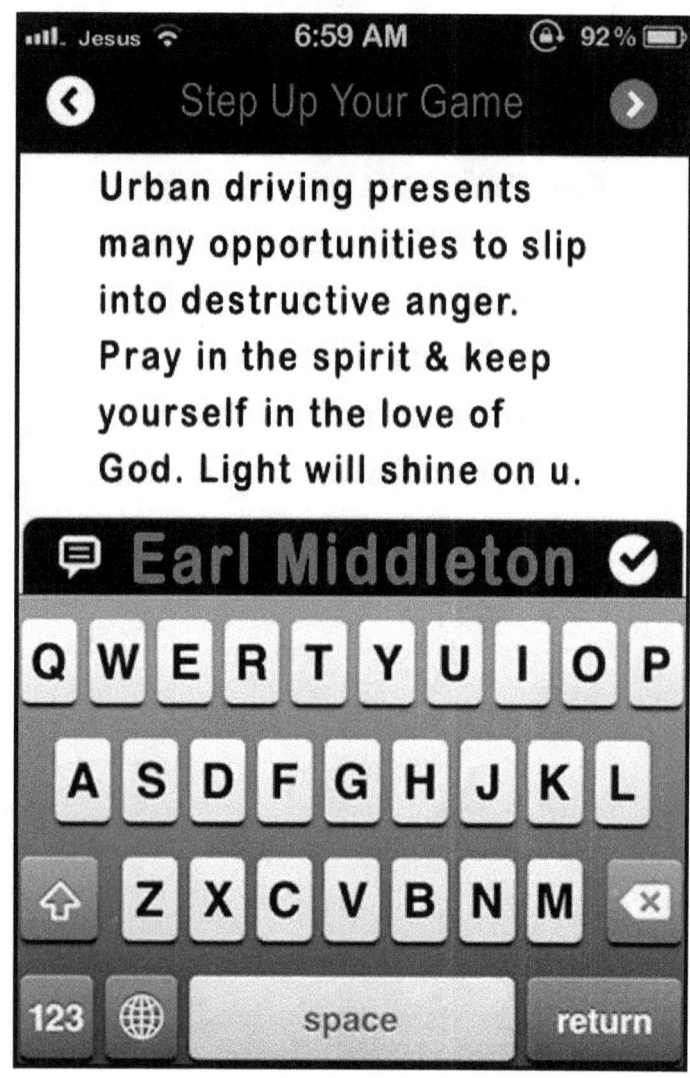

## July 19

# July 20

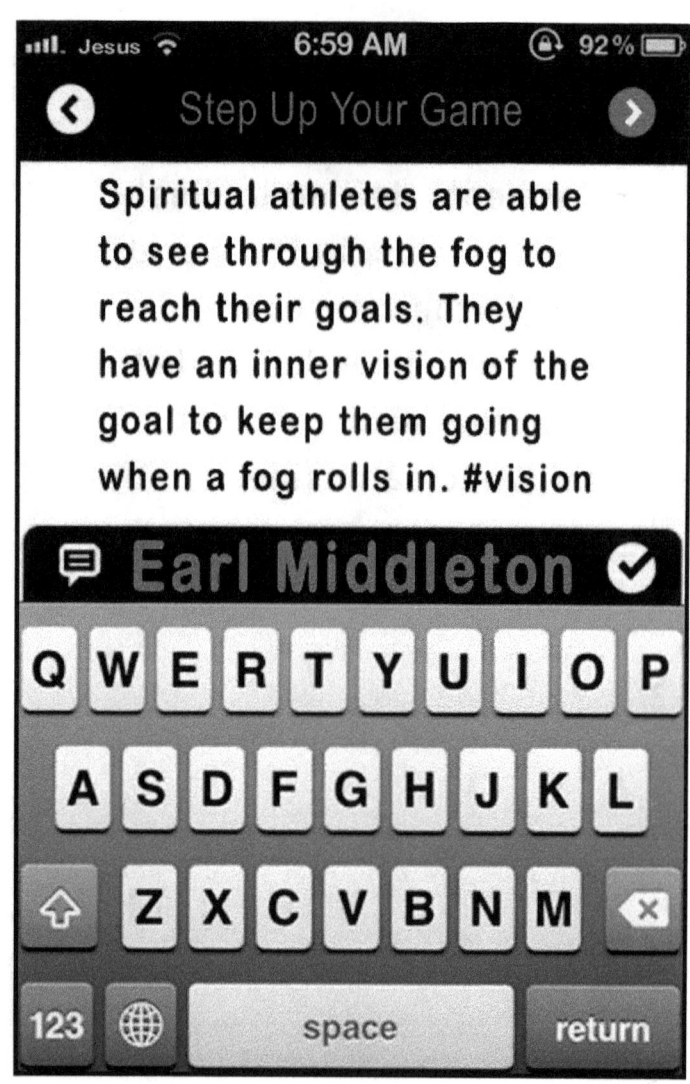

Spiritual athletes are able to see through the fog to reach their goals. They have an inner vision of the goal to keep them going when a fog rolls in. #vision

# July 21

The more on-mission we are the more the enemy attacks. If we lose passion & get weary it's an attack 2 put us off-mission & get us 2 leave our 1st love.

# July 22

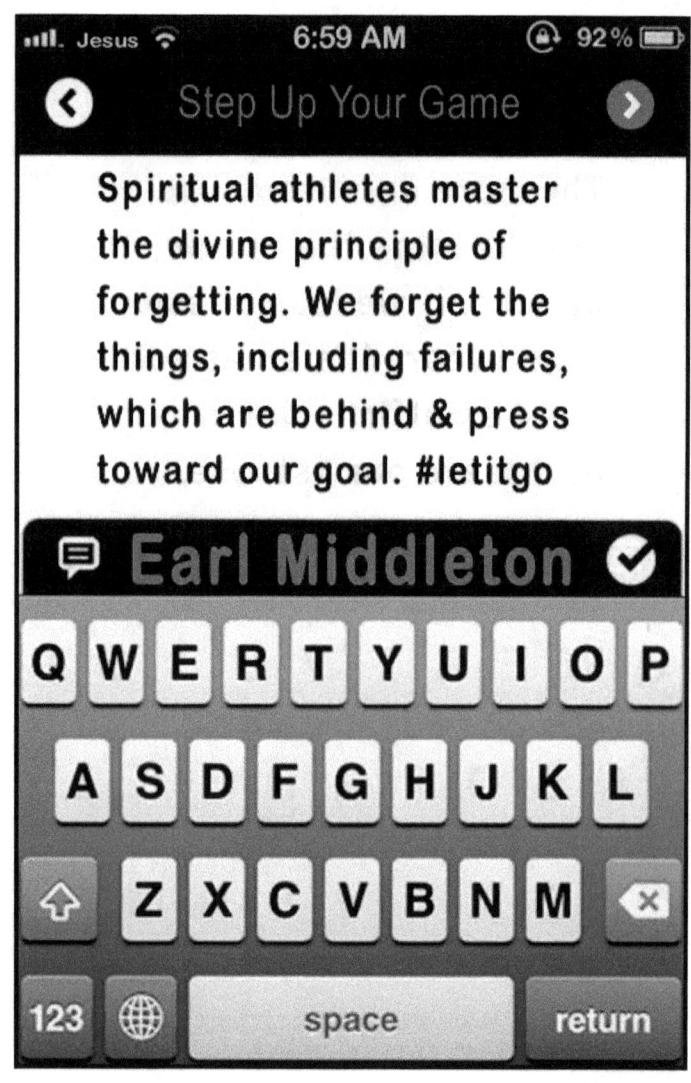

## Step Up Your Game

Spiritual athletes master the divine principle of forgetting. We forget the things, including failures, which are behind & press toward our goal. #letitgo

# July 23

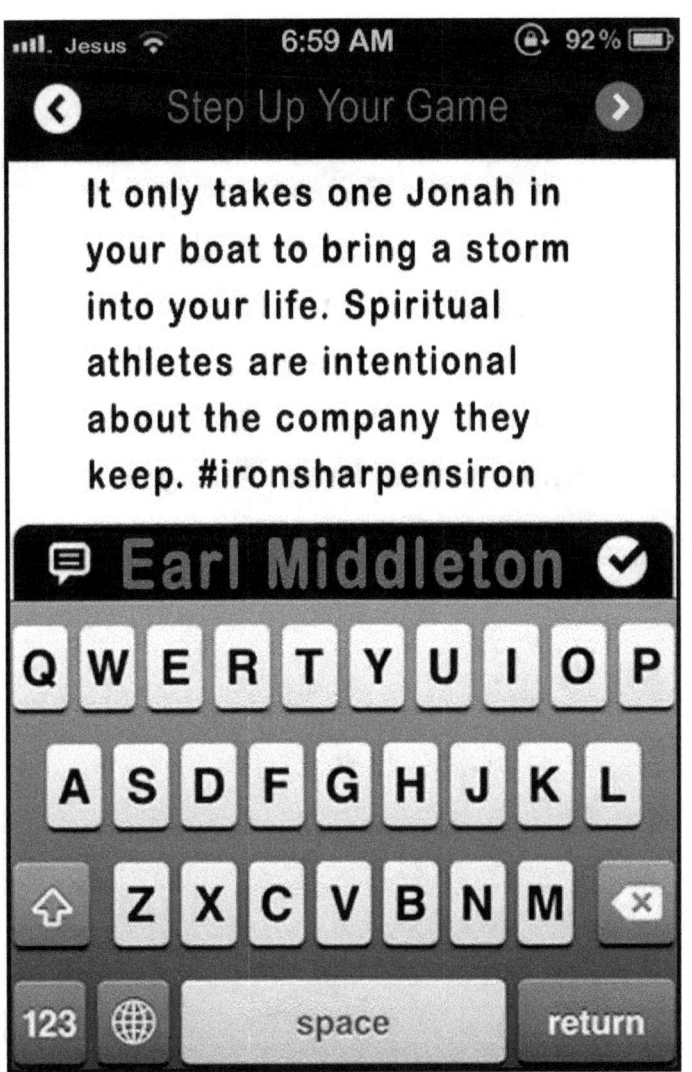

**Step Up Your Game**

It only takes one Jonah in your boat to bring a storm into your life. Spiritual athletes are intentional about the company they keep. #ironsharpensiron

## July 24

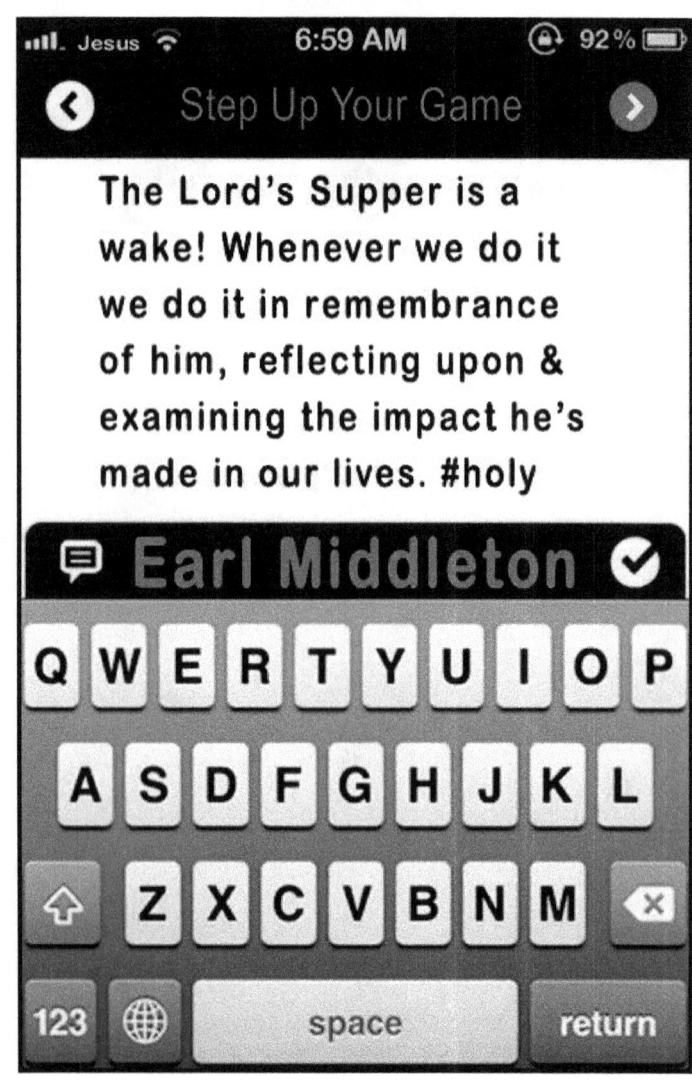

The Lord's Supper is a wake! Whenever we do it we do it in remembrance of him, reflecting upon & examining the impact he's made in our lives. #holy

July 25

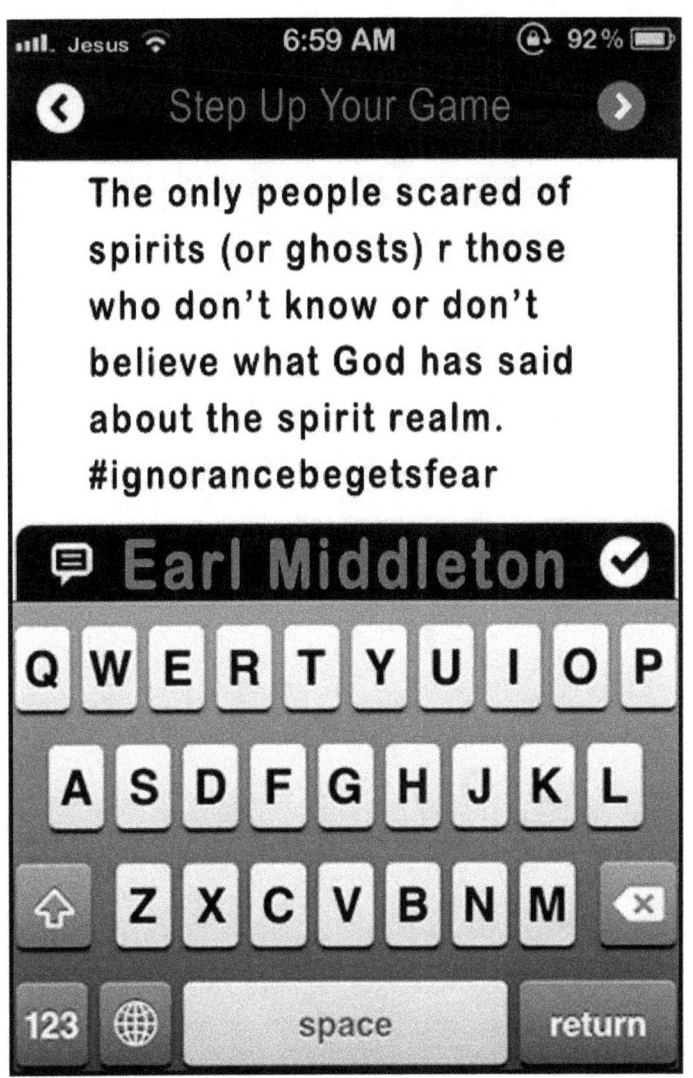

# July 26

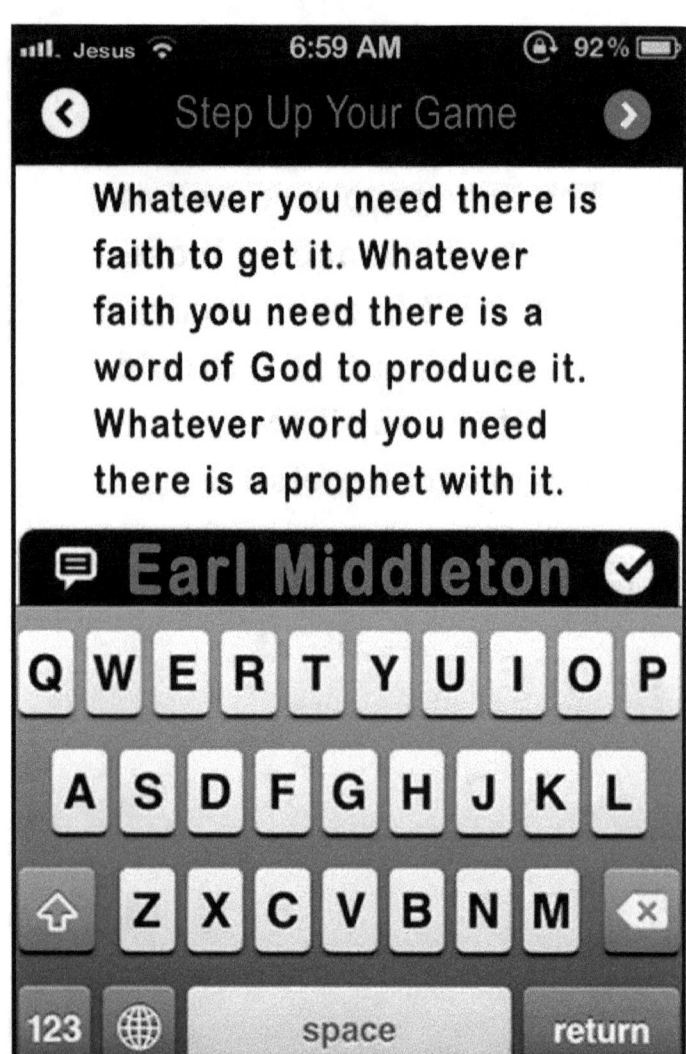

**Step Up Your Game**

Whatever you need there is faith to get it. Whatever faith you need there is a word of God to produce it. Whatever word you need there is a prophet with it.

Earl Middleton

# July 27

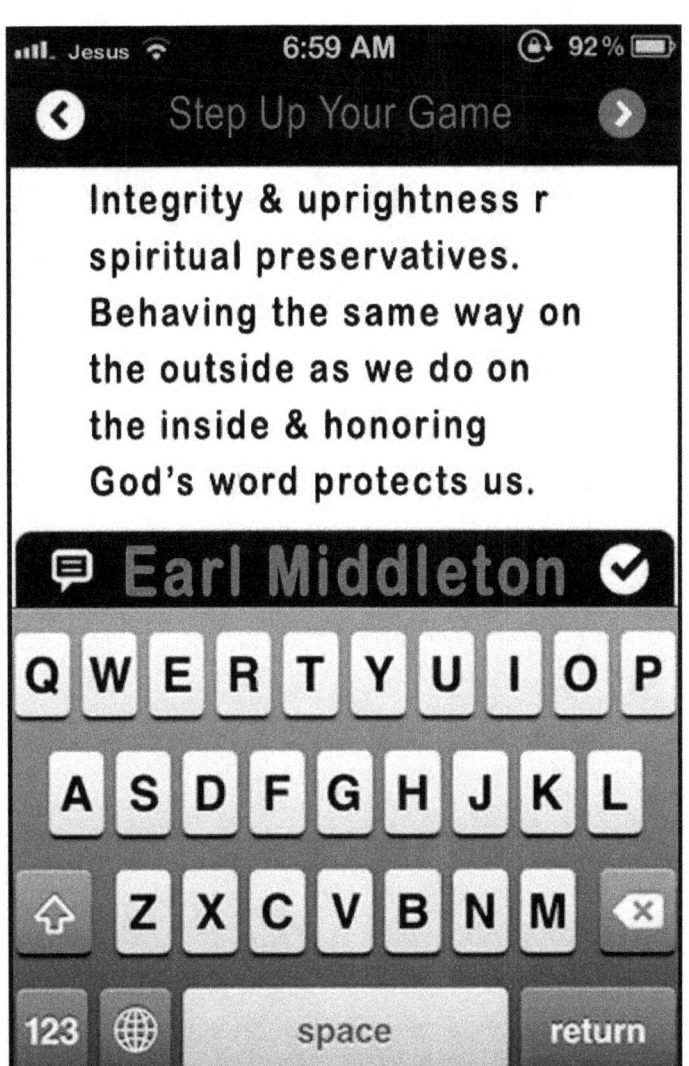

## Step Up Your Game

Integrity & uprightness r spiritual preservatives. Behaving the same way on the outside as we do on the inside & honoring God's word protects us.

— Earl Middleton

# July 28

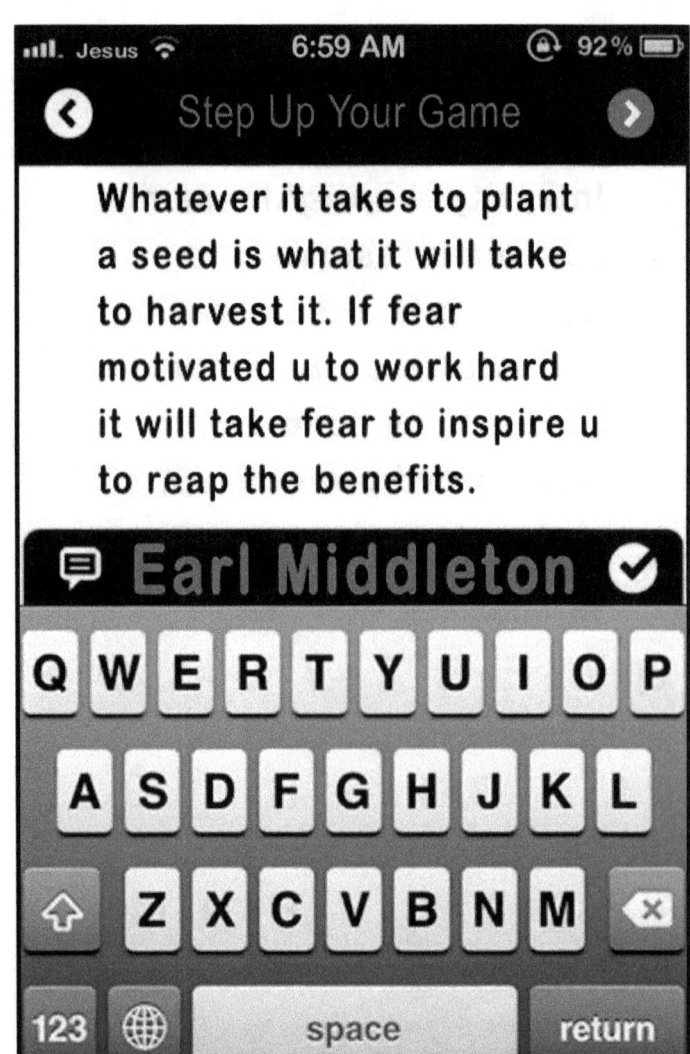

**Step Up Your Game**

Whatever it takes to plant a seed is what it will take to harvest it. If fear motivated u to work hard it will take fear to inspire u to reap the benefits.

— Earl Middleton

# July 29

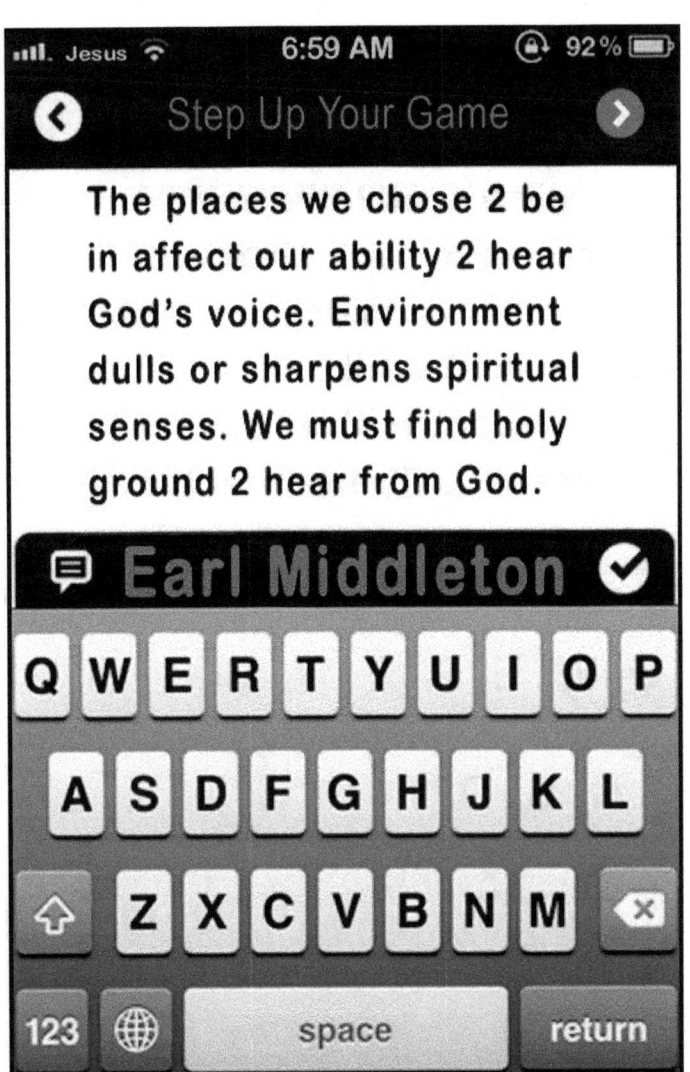

**Step Up Your Game**

The places we chose 2 be in affect our ability 2 hear God's voice. Environment dulls or sharpens spiritual senses. We must find holy ground 2 hear from God.

Earl Middleton

# July 30

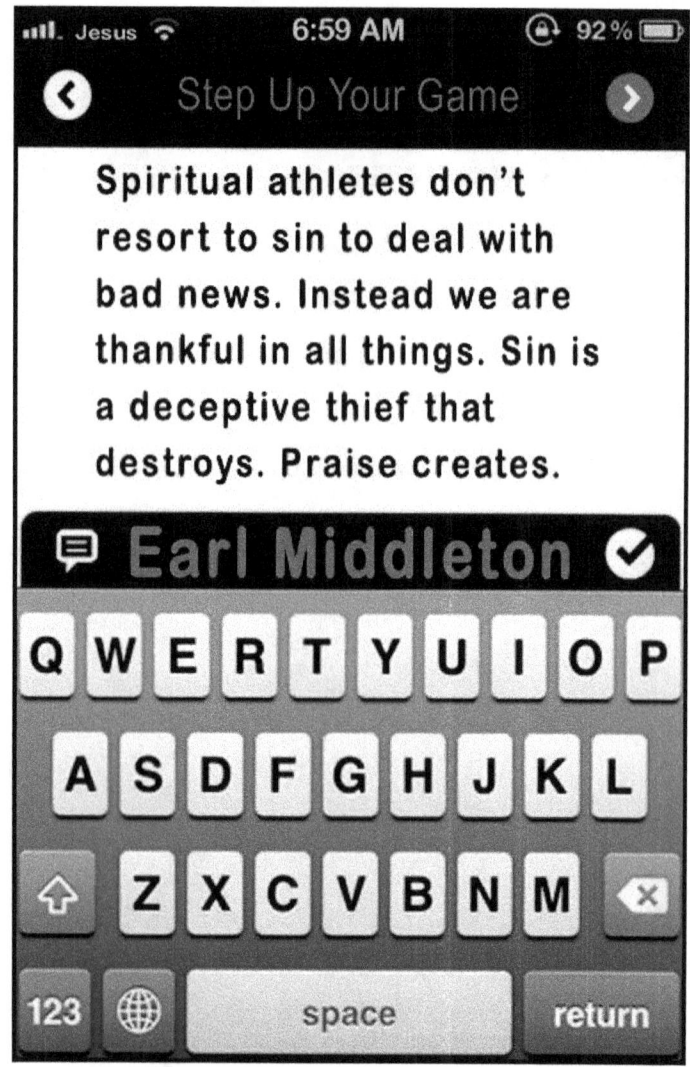

## Step Up Your Game

Spiritual athletes don't resort to sin to deal with bad news. Instead we are thankful in all things. Sin is a deceptive thief that destroys. Praise creates.

— Earl Middleton

# July 31

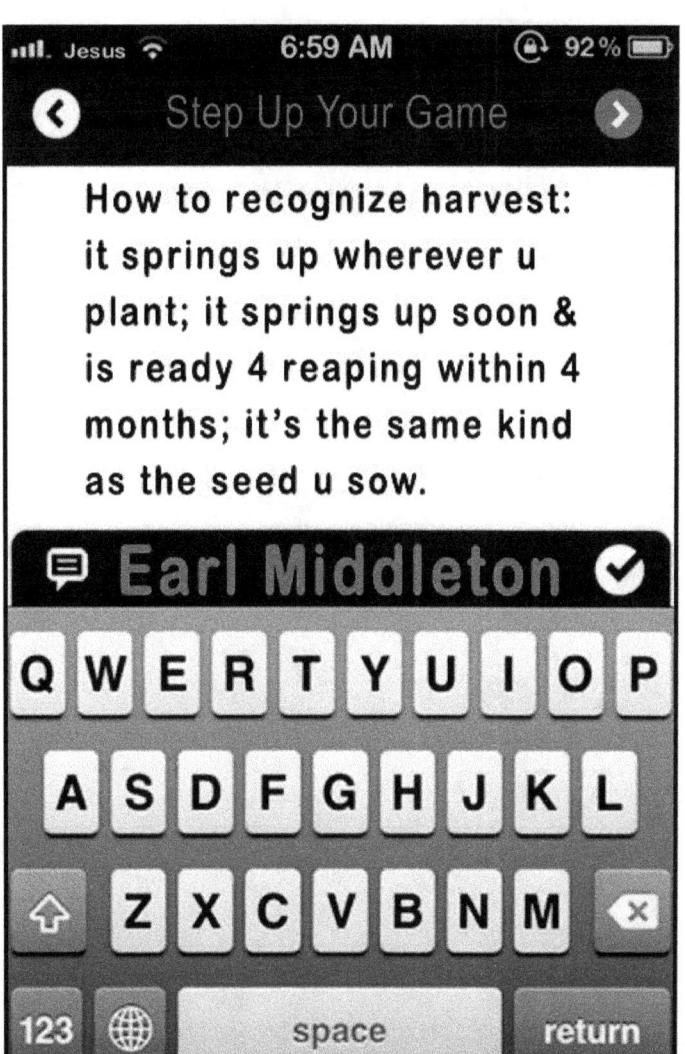

How to recognize harvest: it springs up wherever u plant; it springs up soon & is ready 4 reaping within 4 months; it's the same kind as the seed u sow.

# August 1

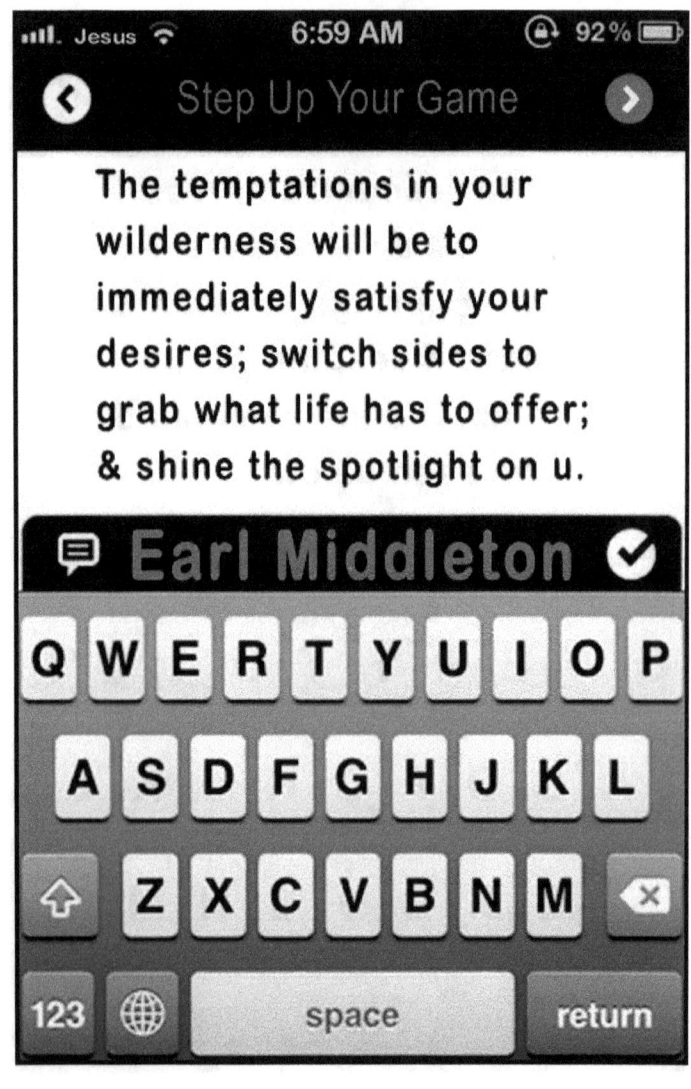

# August 2

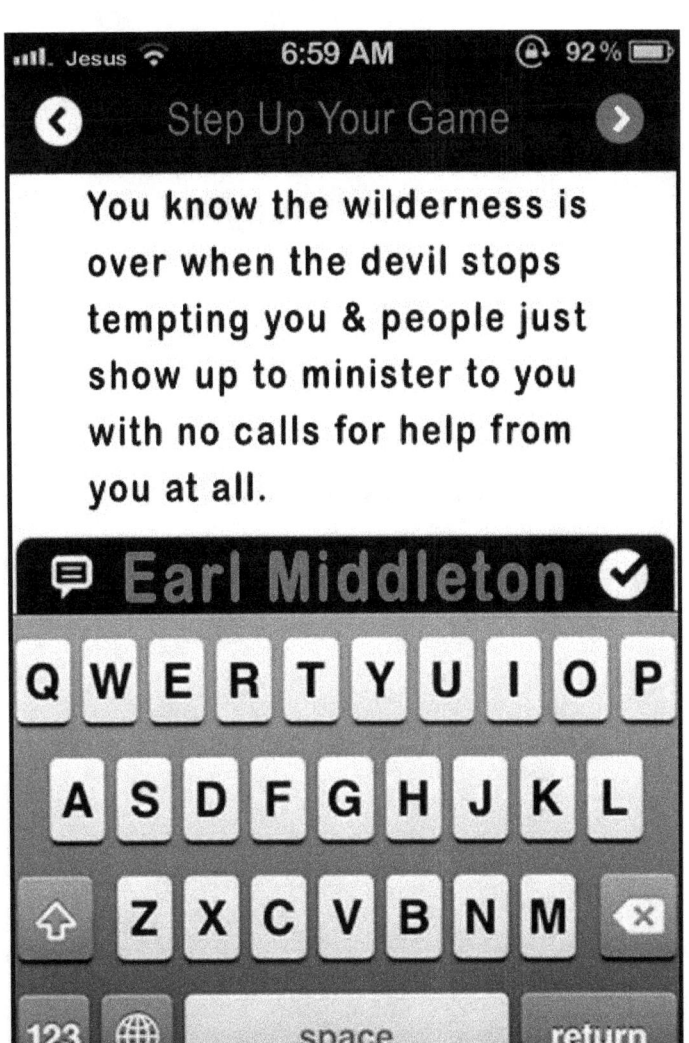

**Step Up Your Game**

You know the wilderness is over when the devil stops tempting you & people just show up to minister to you with no calls for help from you at all.

— Earl Middleton

# August 3

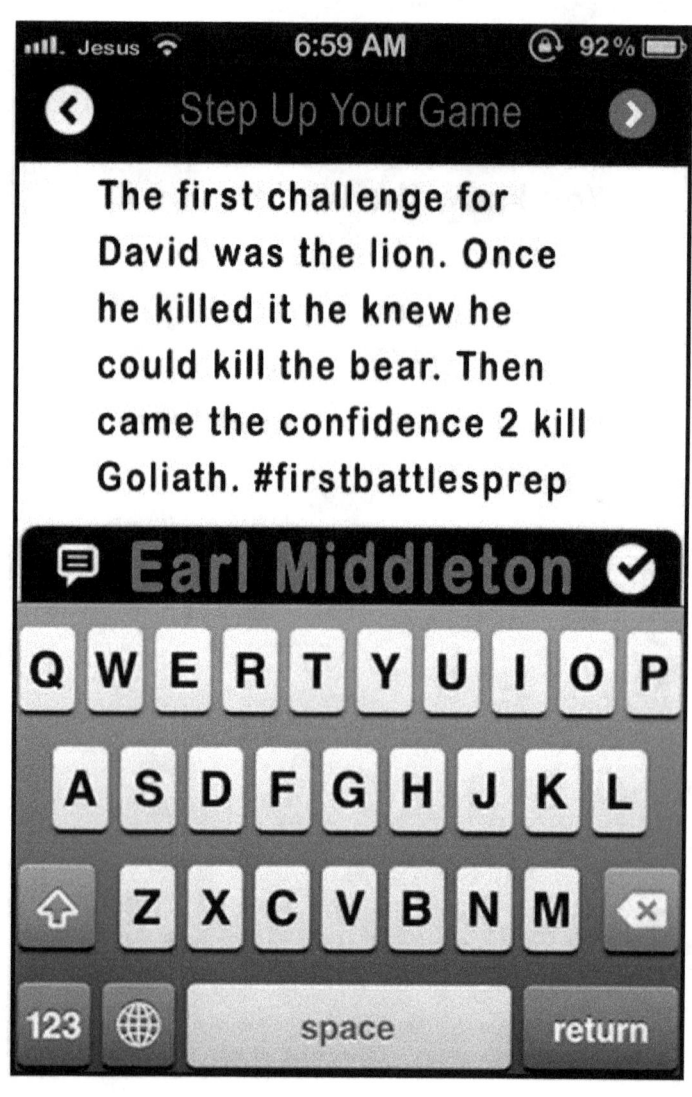

# August 4

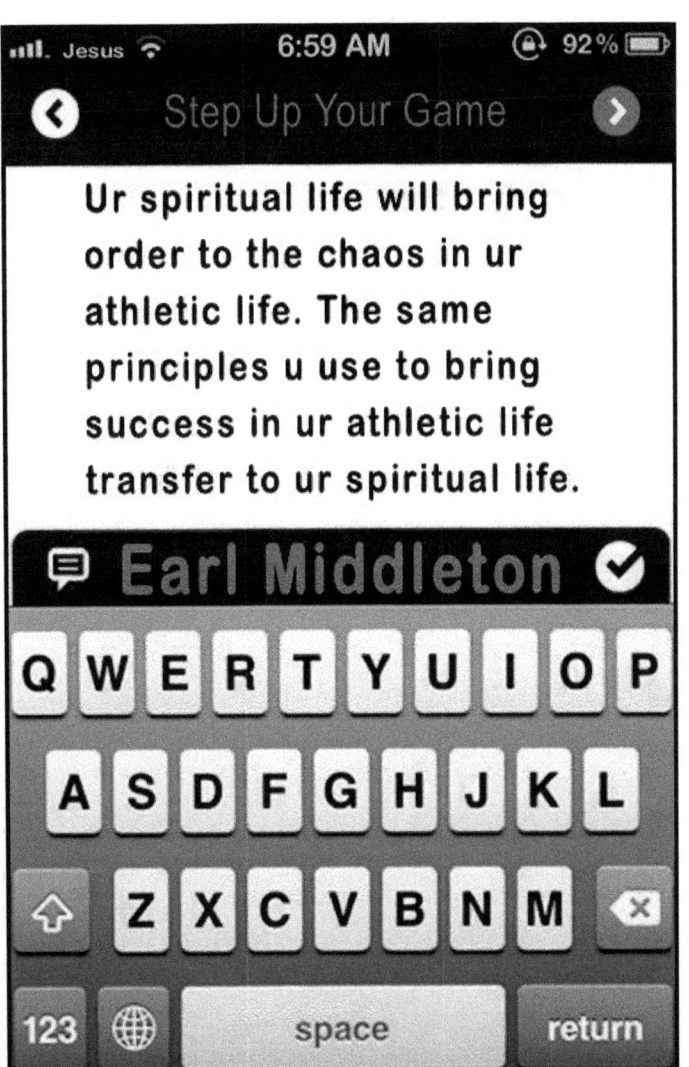

# August 5

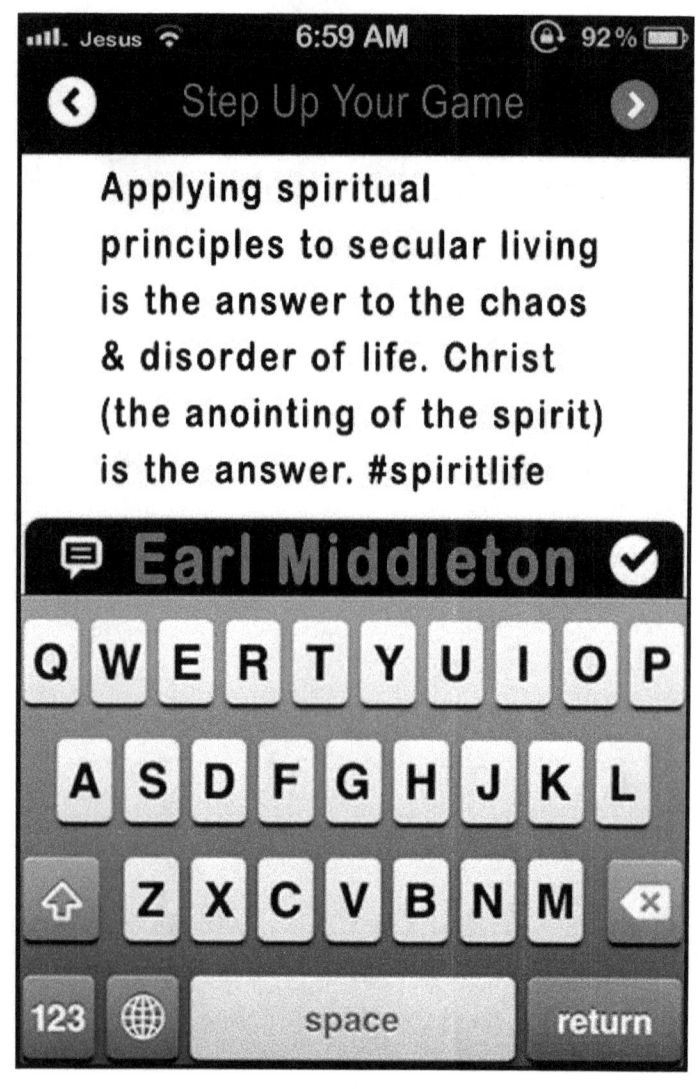

Applying spiritual principles to secular living is the answer to the chaos & disorder of life. Christ (the anointing of the spirit) is the answer. #spiritlife

# August 6

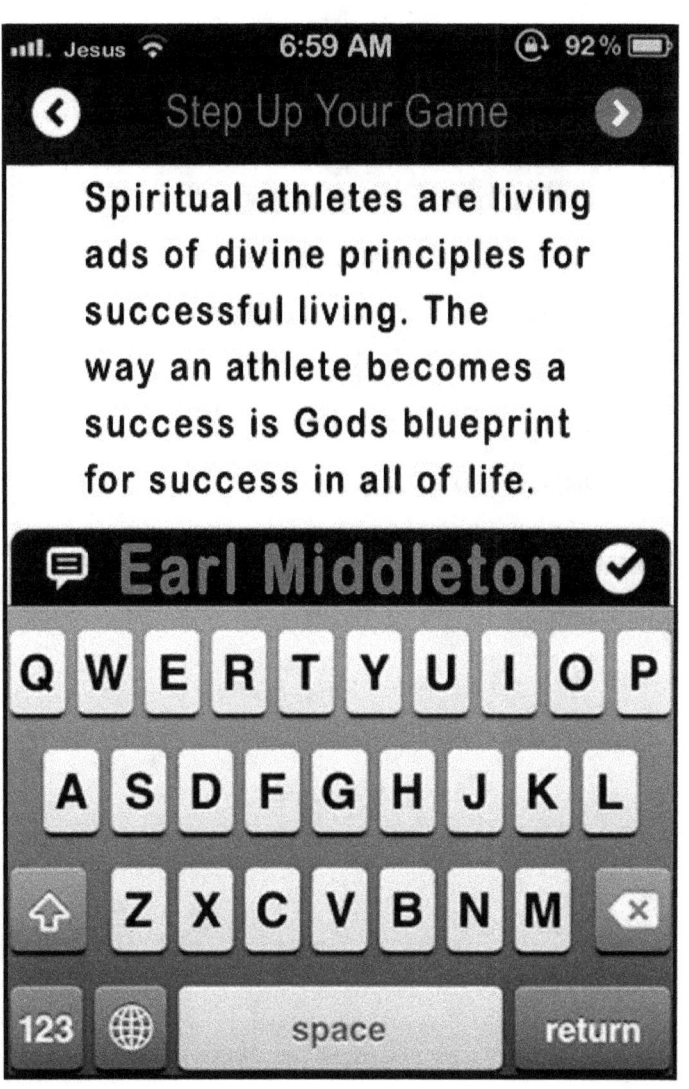

## August 7

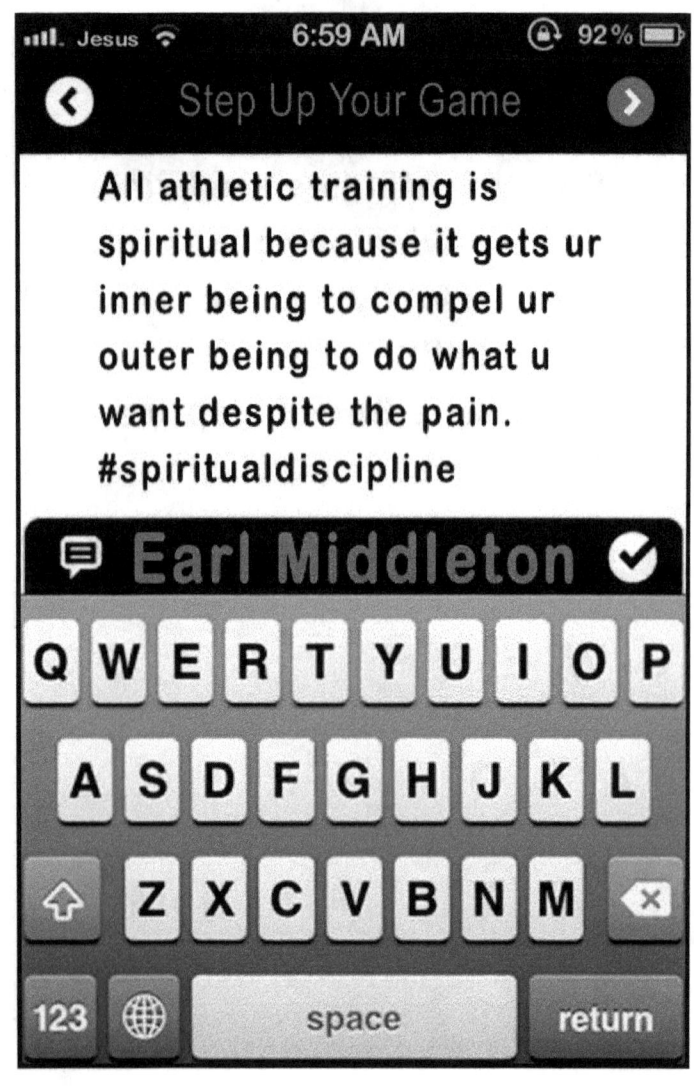

All athletic training is spiritual because it gets ur inner being to compel ur outer being to do what u want despite the pain. #spiritualdiscipline

# August 8

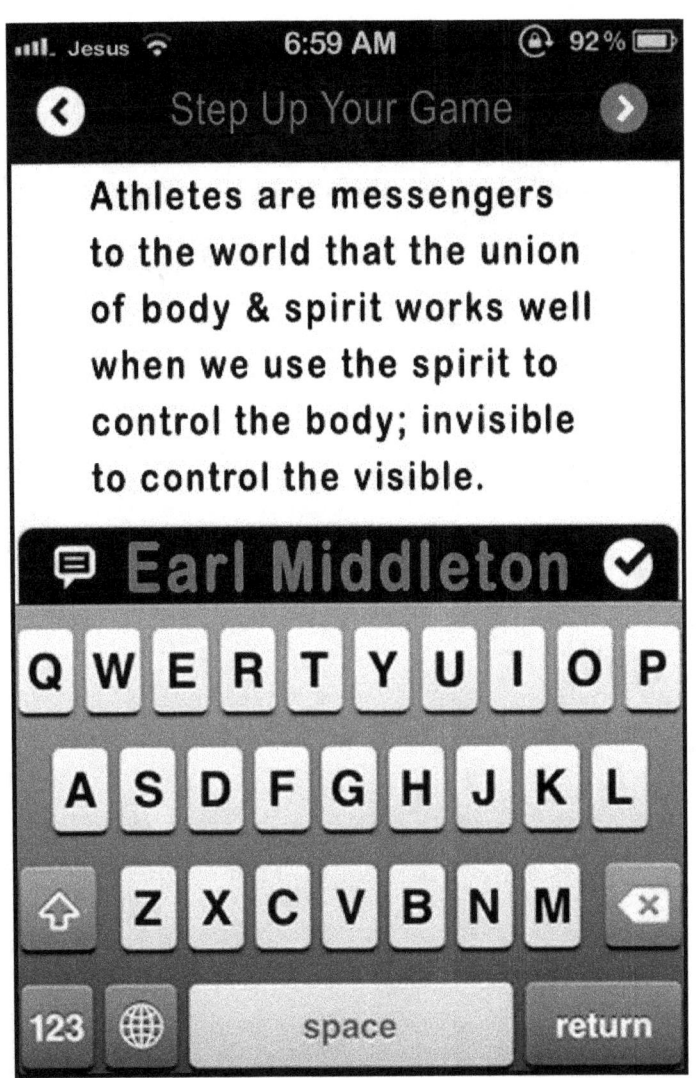

Athletes are messengers to the world that the union of body & spirit works well when we use the spirit to control the body; invisible to control the visible.

Earl Middleton

# August 9

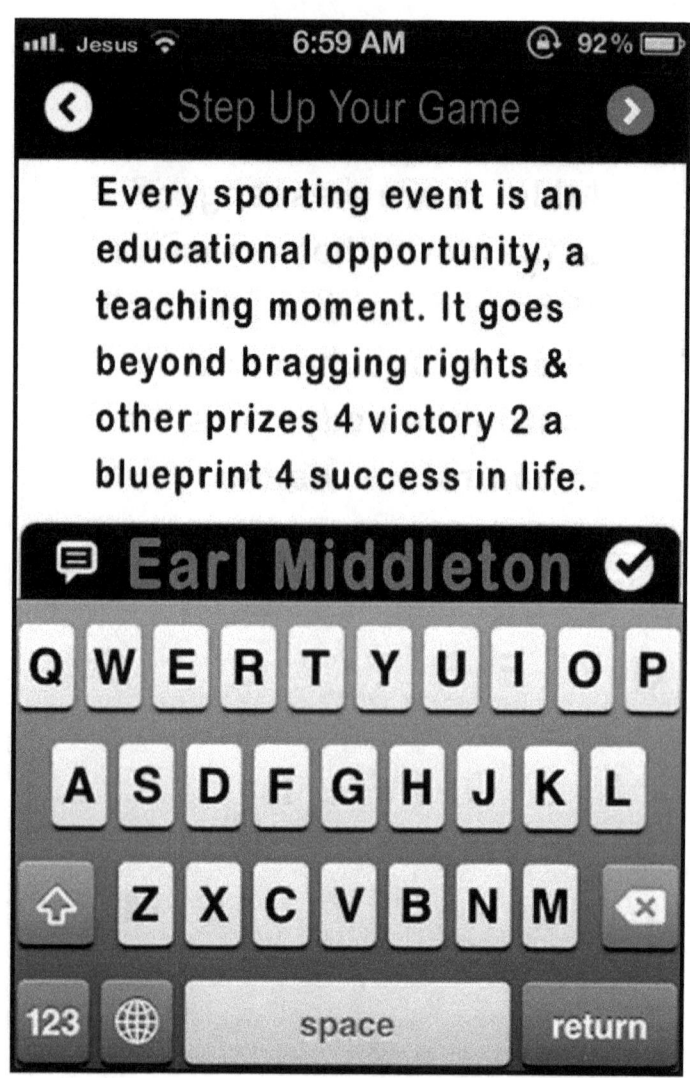

**Step Up Your Game**

Every sporting event is an educational opportunity, a teaching moment. It goes beyond bragging rights & other prizes 4 victory 2 a blueprint 4 success in life.

— Earl Middleton

# August 10

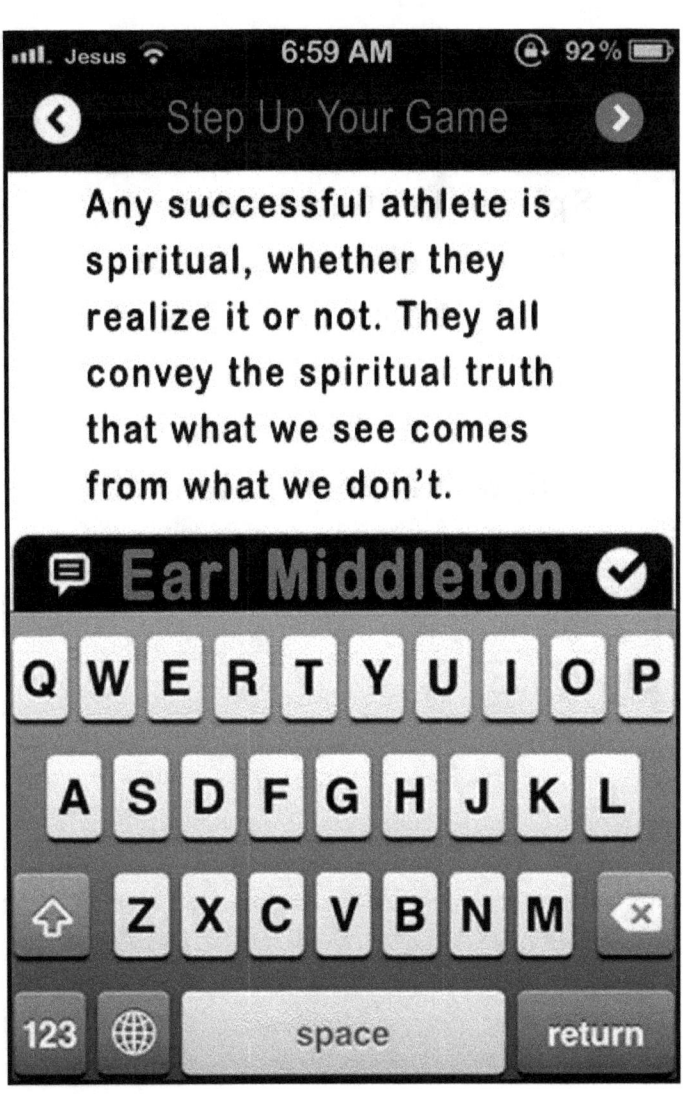

**Step Up Your Game**

Any successful athlete is spiritual, whether they realize it or not. They all convey the spiritual truth that what we see comes from what we don't.

Earl Middleton

# August 11

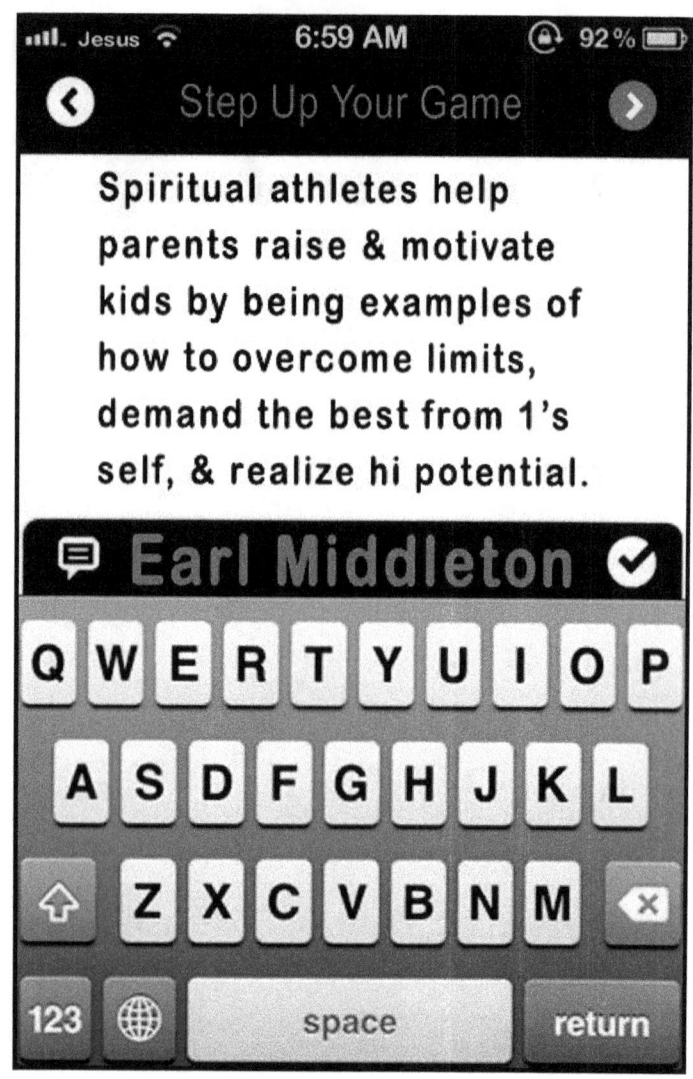

Step Up Your Game

Spiritual athletes help parents raise & motivate kids by being examples of how to overcome limits, demand the best from 1's self, & realize hi potential.

Earl Middleton

# August 12

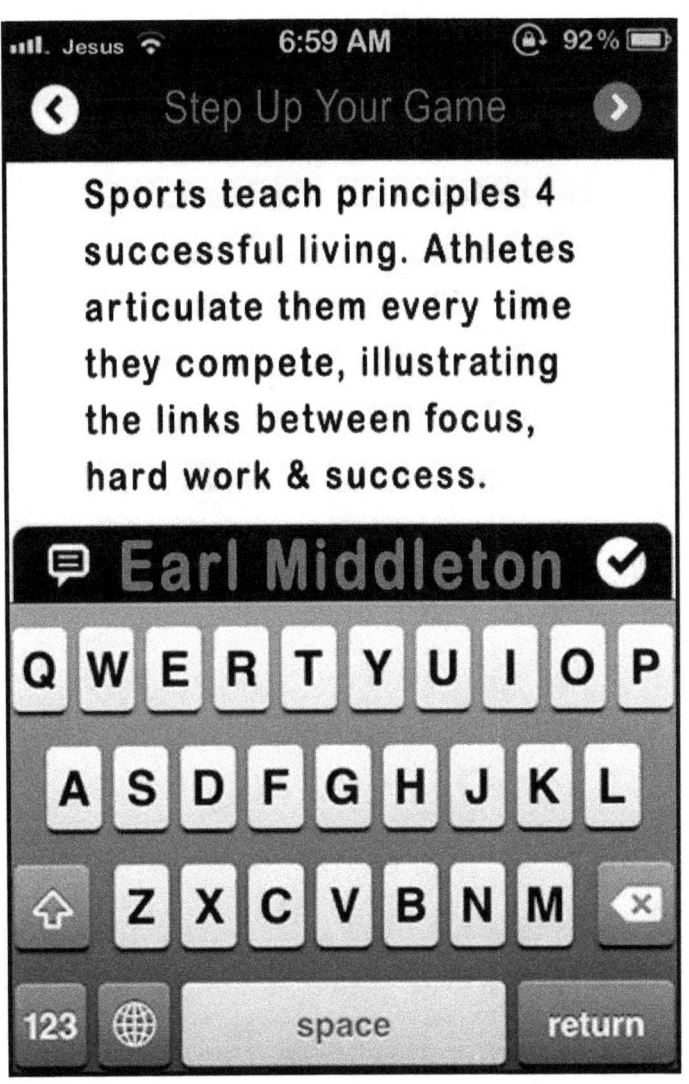

**Step Up Your Game**

Sports teach principles 4 successful living. Athletes articulate them every time they compete, illustrating the links between focus, hard work & success.

— Earl Middleton

# August 13

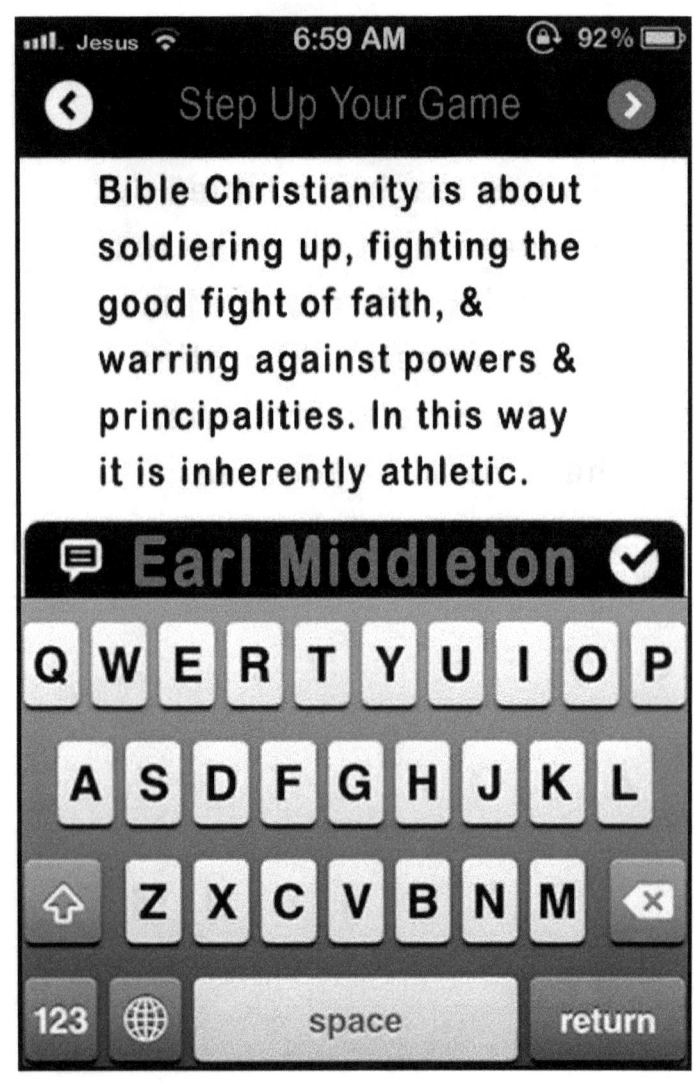

# August 14

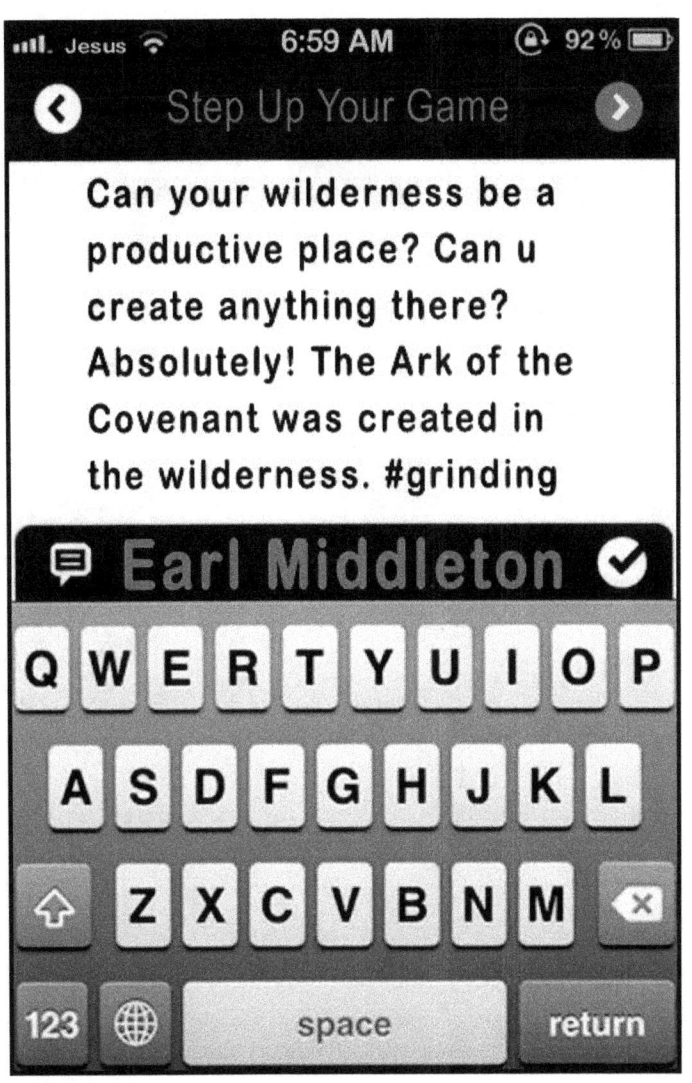

**Step Up Your Game**

Can your wilderness be a productive place? Can u create anything there? Absolutely! The Ark of the Covenant was created in the wilderness. #grinding

# August 15

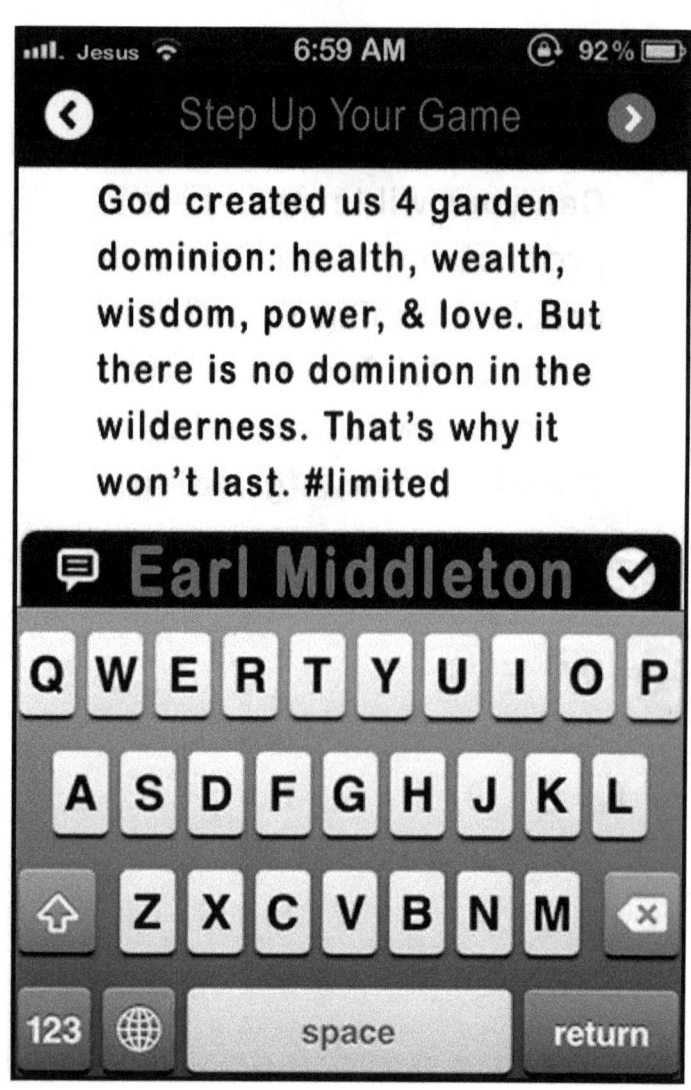

# August 16

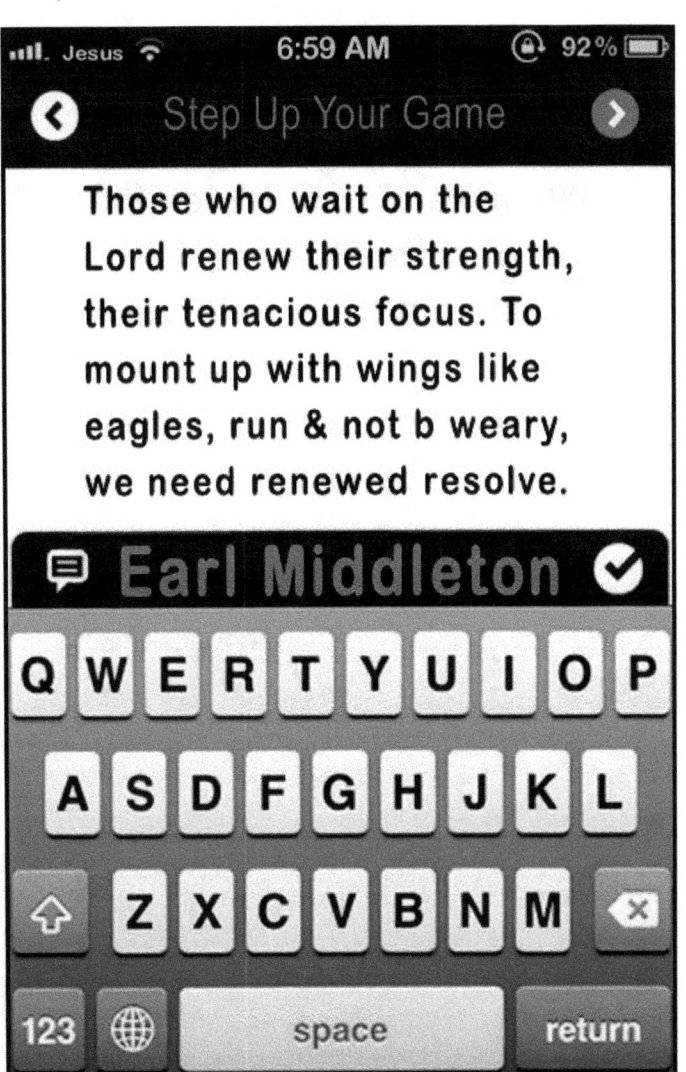

# August 17

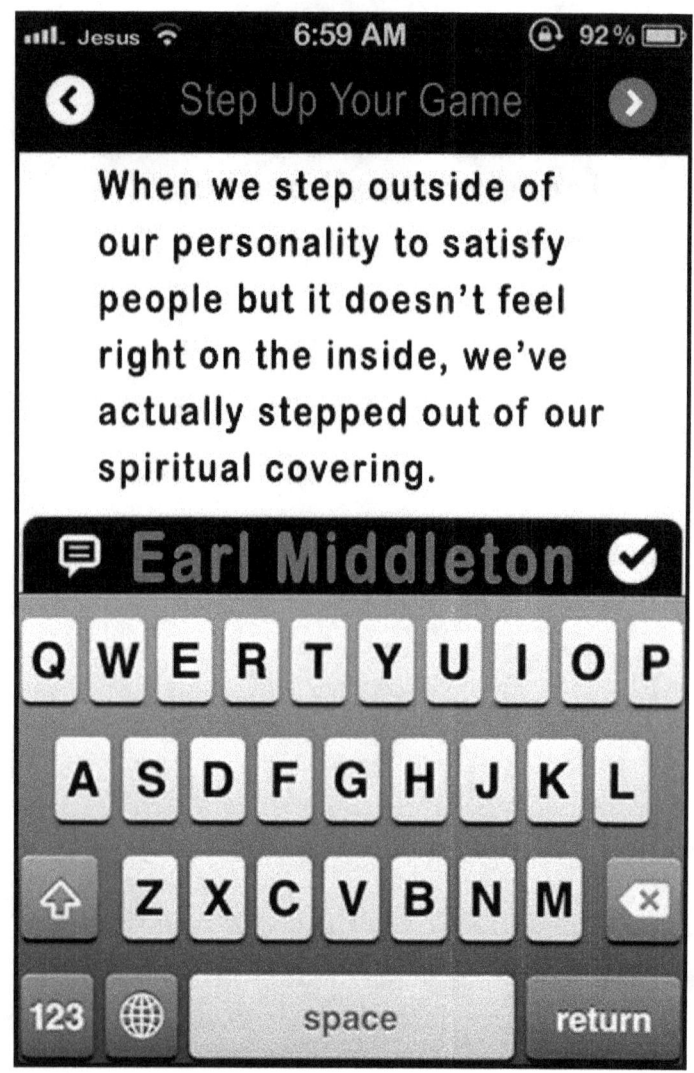

## Step Up Your Game

When we step outside of our personality to satisfy people but it doesn't feel right on the inside, we've actually stepped out of our spiritual covering.

Earl Middleton

# August 18

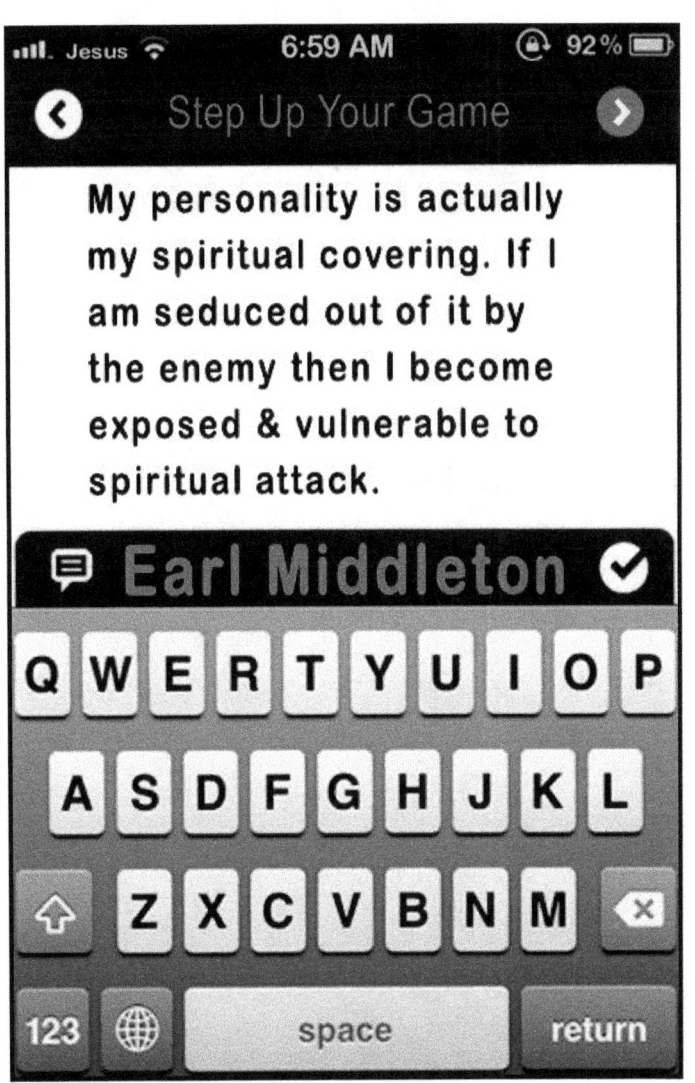

# August 19

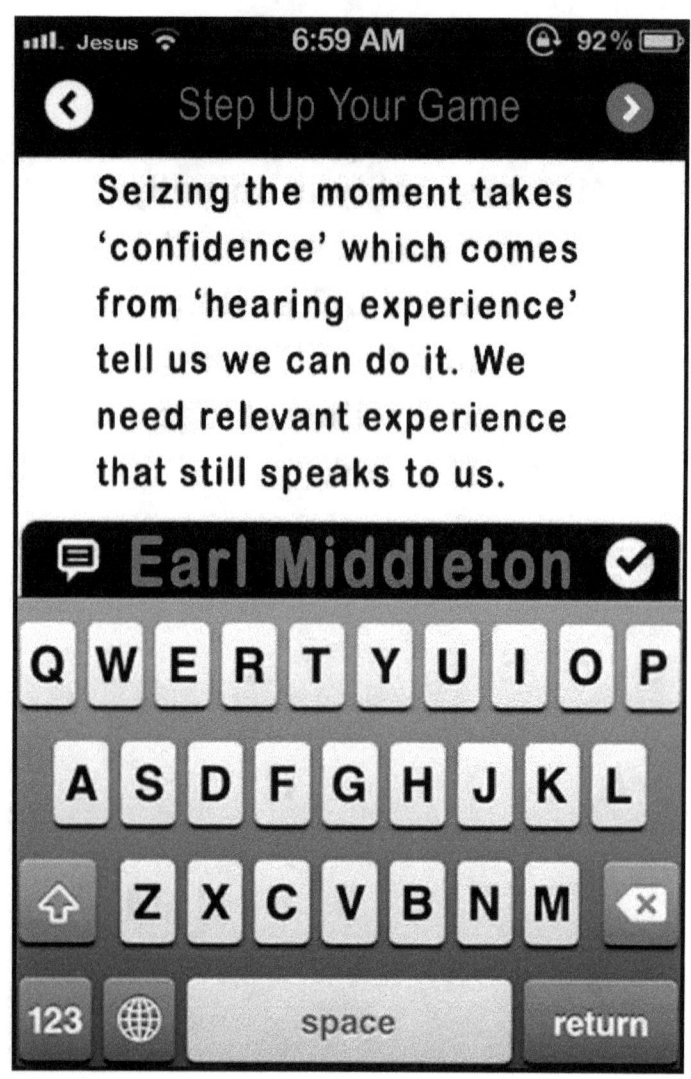

**Step Up Your Game**

Seizing the moment takes 'confidence' which comes from 'hearing experience' tell us we can do it. We need relevant experience that still speaks to us.

— Earl Middleton

# August 20

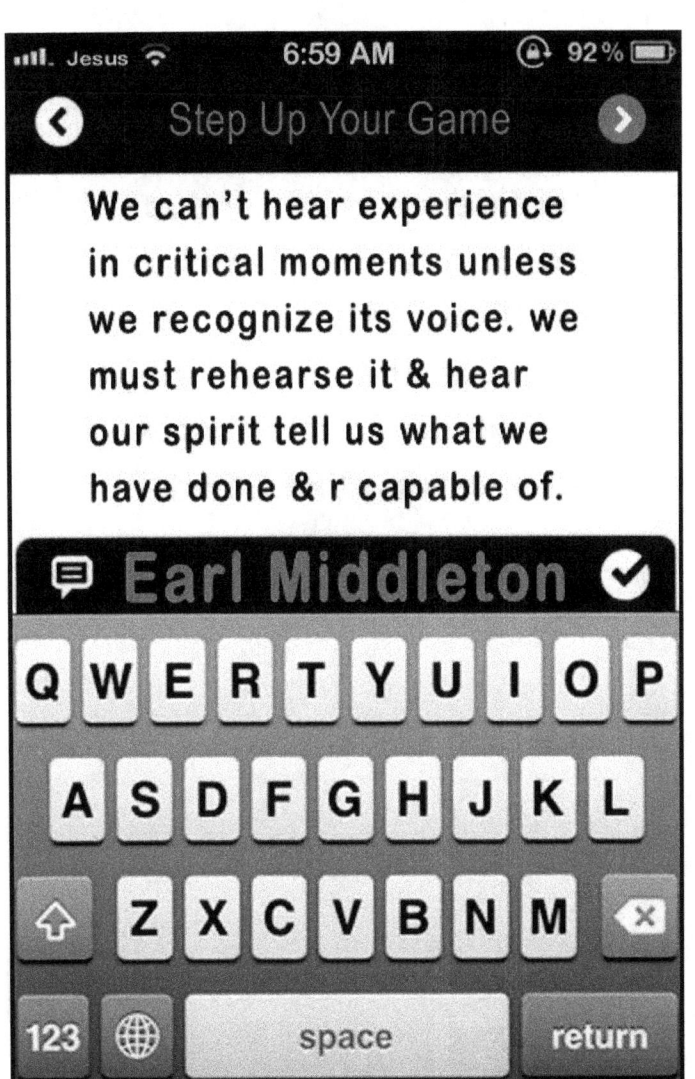

**Step Up Your Game**

We can't hear experience in critical moments unless we recognize its voice. we must rehearse it & hear our spirit tell us what we have done & r capable of.

Earl Middleton

# August 21

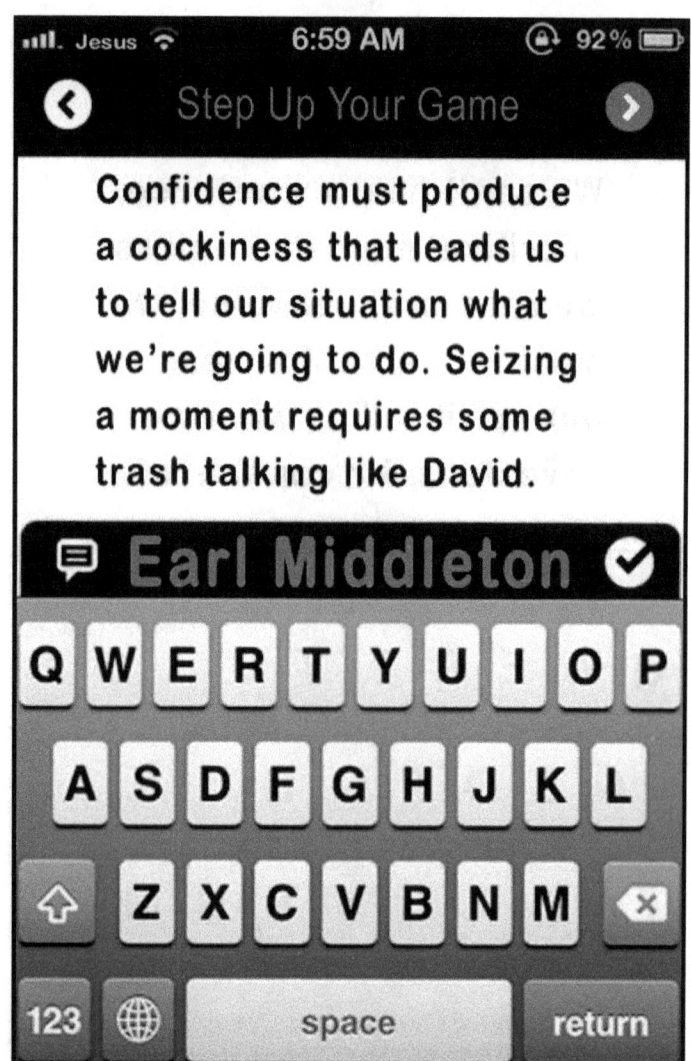

## Step Up Your Game

Confidence must produce a cockiness that leads us to tell our situation what we're going to do. Seizing a moment requires some trash talking like David.

Earl Middleton

# August 22

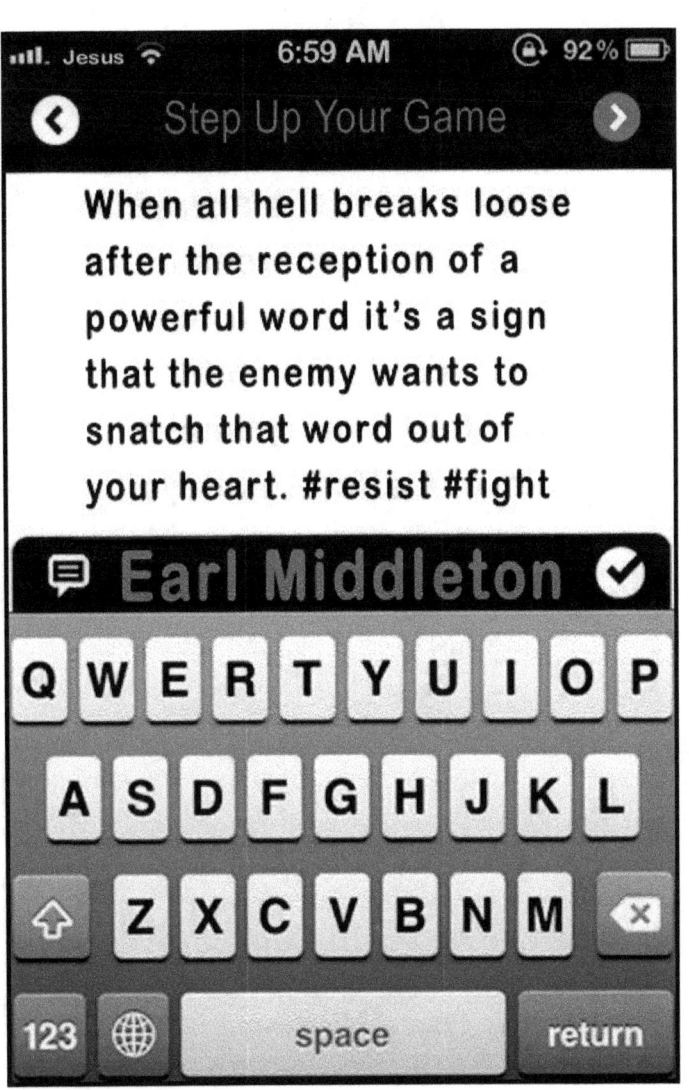

# August 23

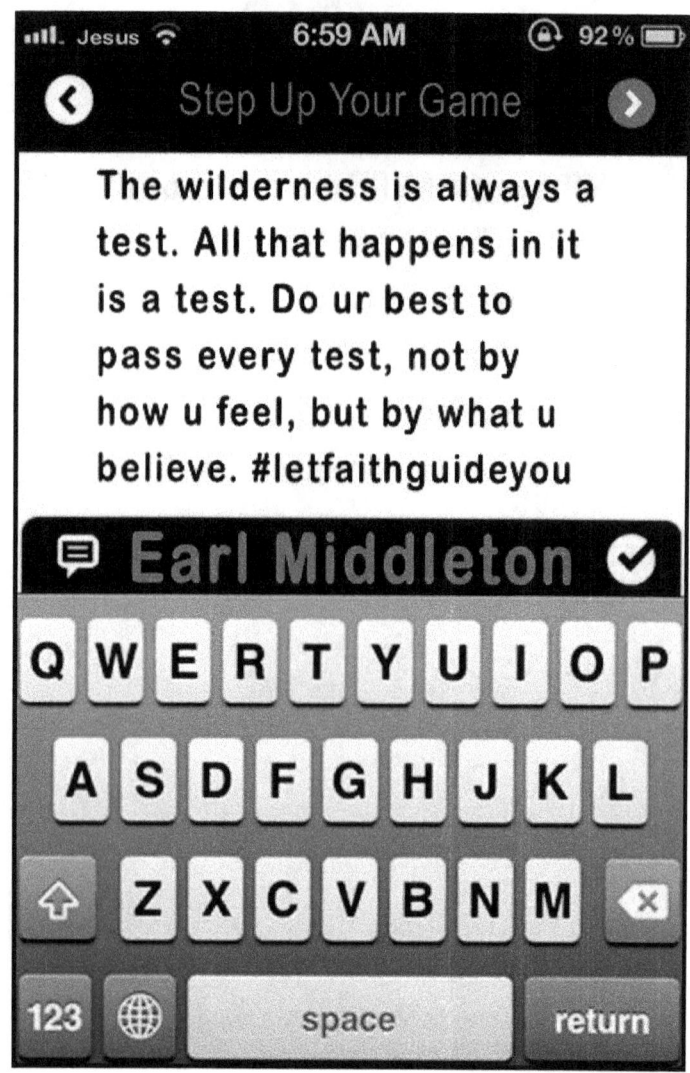

**Step Up Your Game**

The wilderness is always a test. All that happens in it is a test. Do ur best to pass every test, not by how u feel, but by what u believe. #letfaithguideyou

— Earl Middleton

# August 24

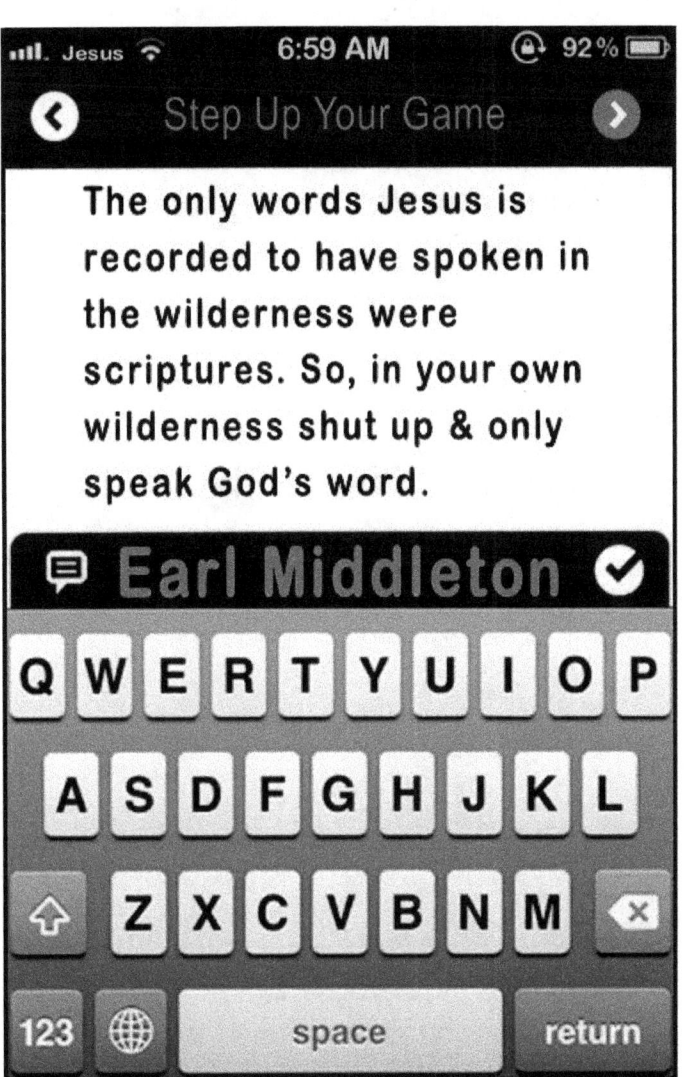

# August 25

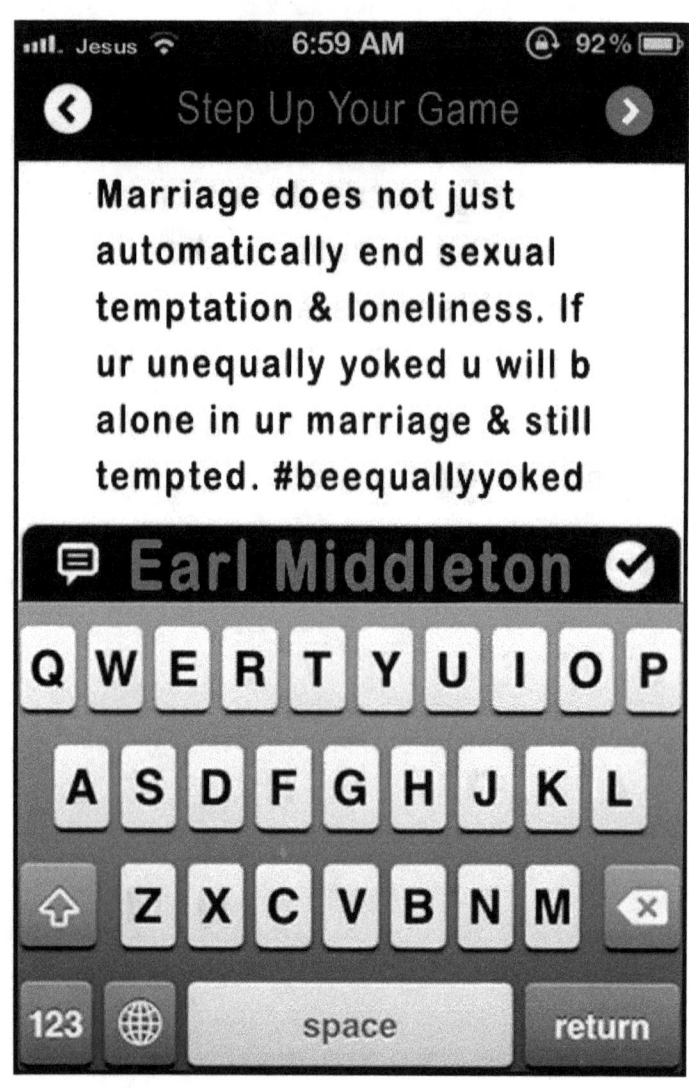

**Step Up Your Game**

Marriage does not just automatically end sexual temptation & loneliness. If ur unequally yoked u will b alone in ur marriage & still tempted. #beequallyyoked

# August 26

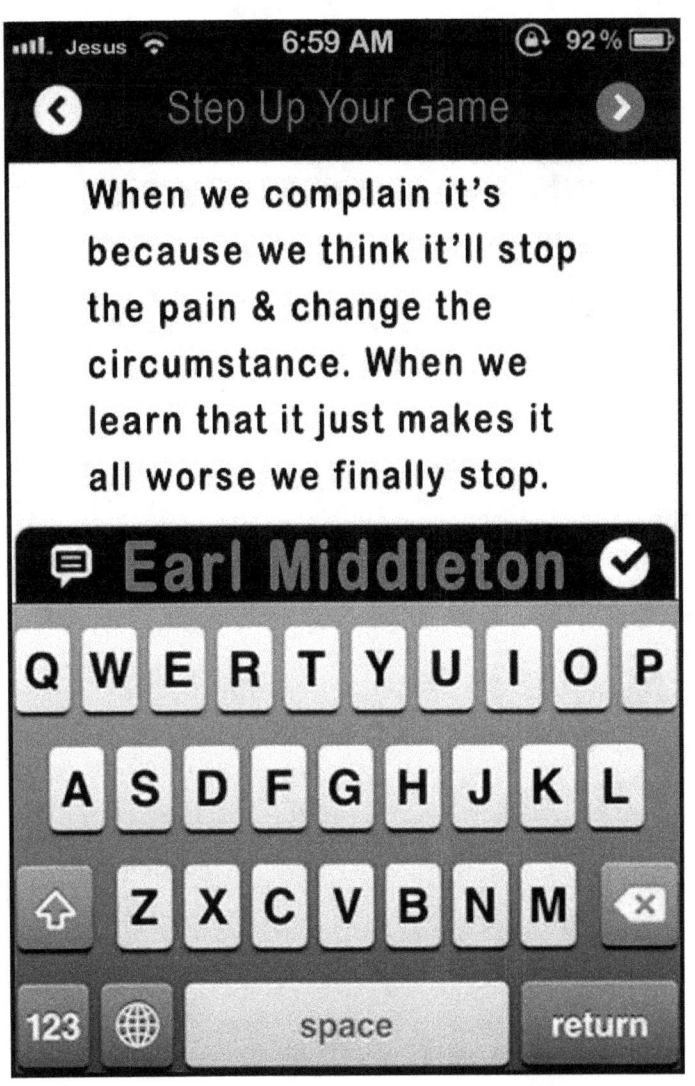

# August 27

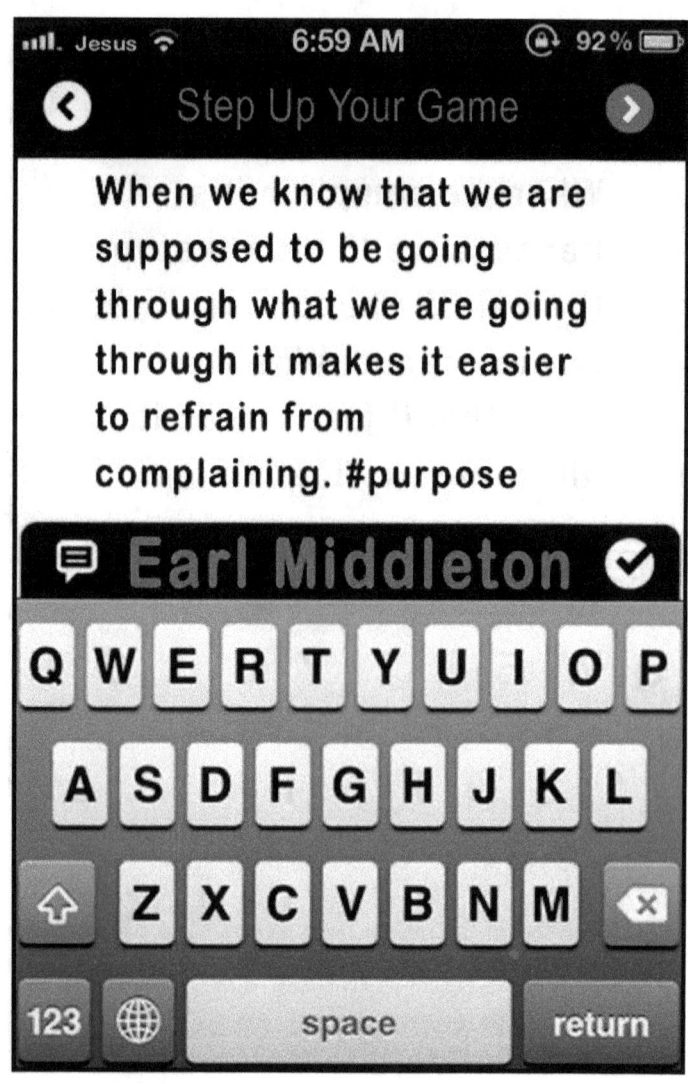

**Step Up Your Game**

When we know that we are supposed to be going through what we are going through it makes it easier to refrain from complaining. #purpose

Earl Middleton

# August 28

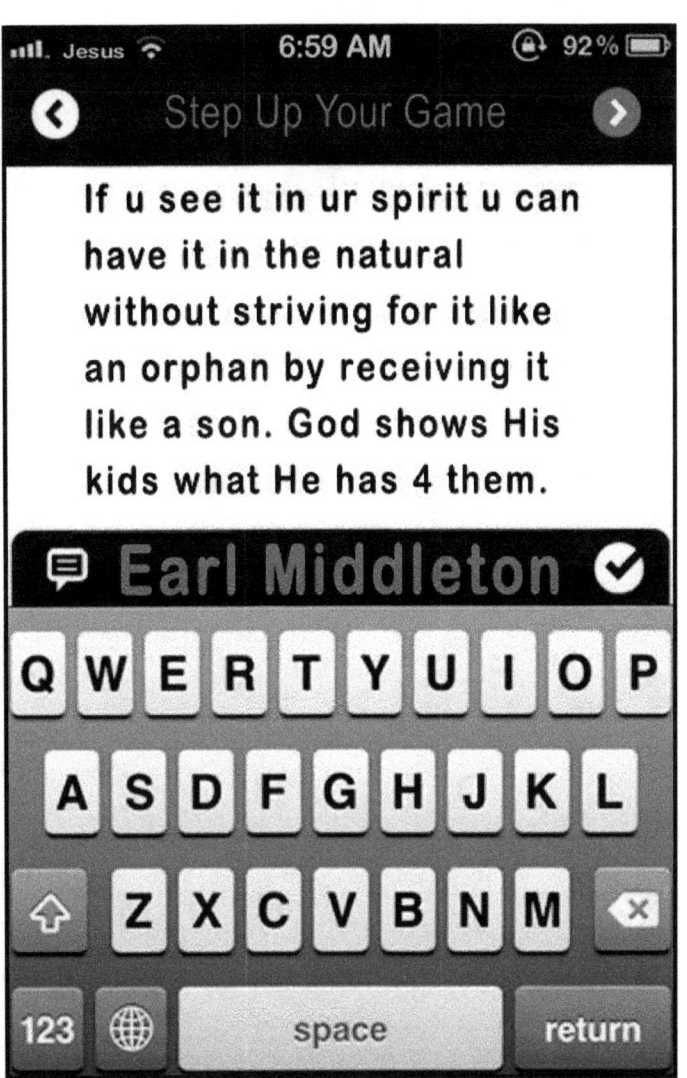

# August 29

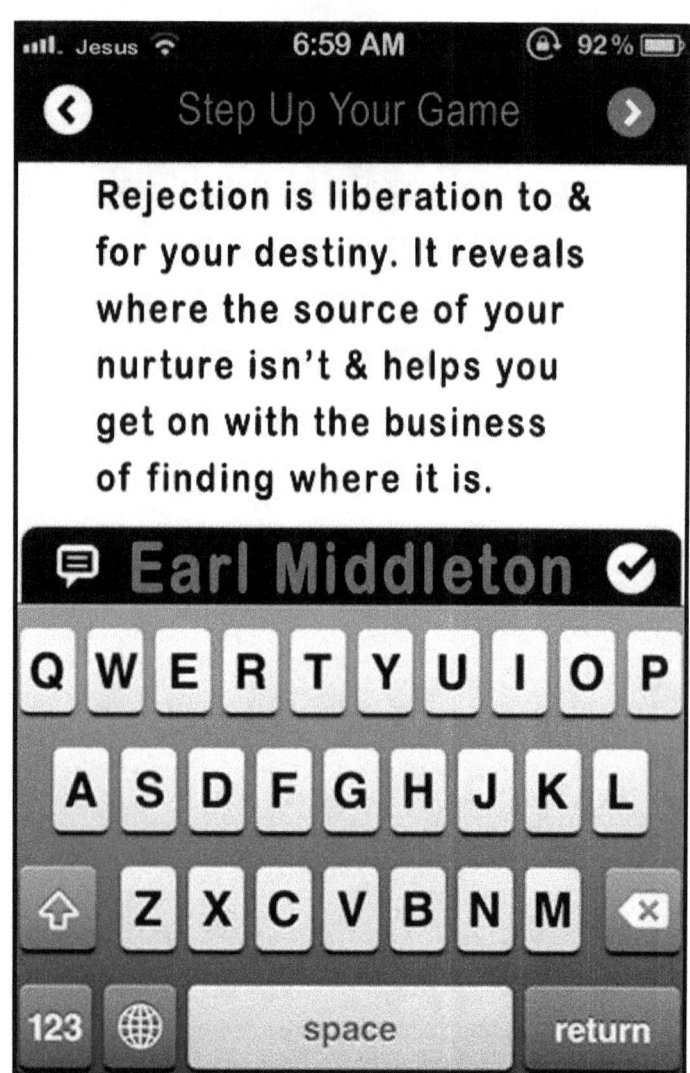

Rejection is liberation to & for your destiny. It reveals where the source of your nurture isn't & helps you get on with the business of finding where it is.

Earl Middleton

## August 30

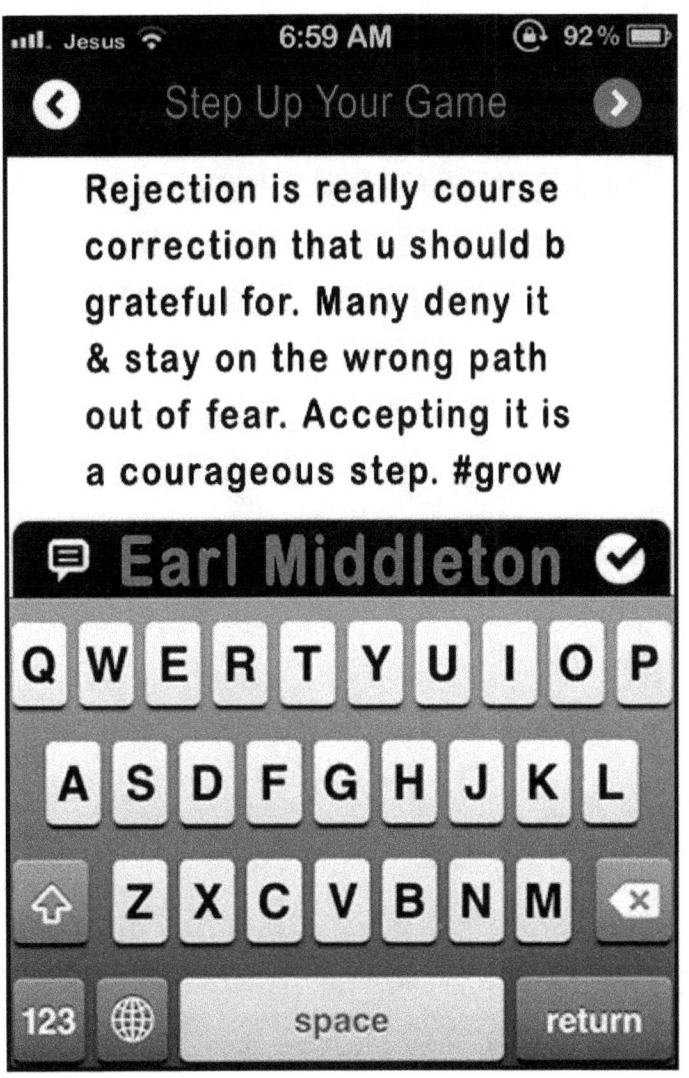

**Step Up Your Game**

Rejection is really course correction that u should b grateful for. Many deny it & stay on the wrong path out of fear. Accepting it is a courageous step. #grow

# August 31

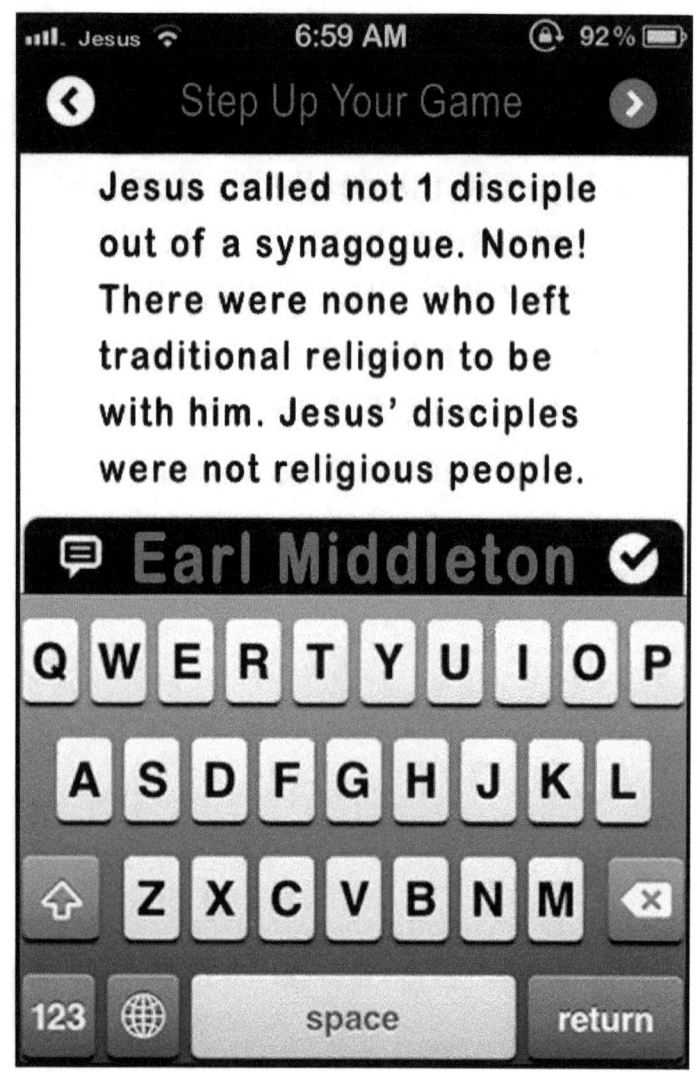

# September 1

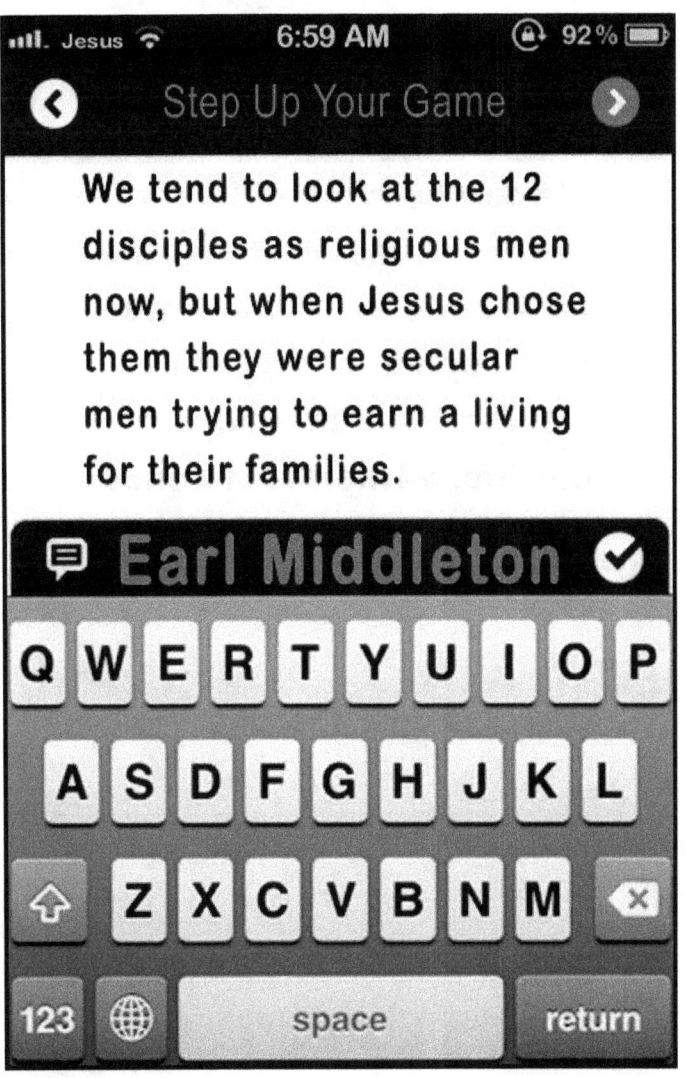

# September 2

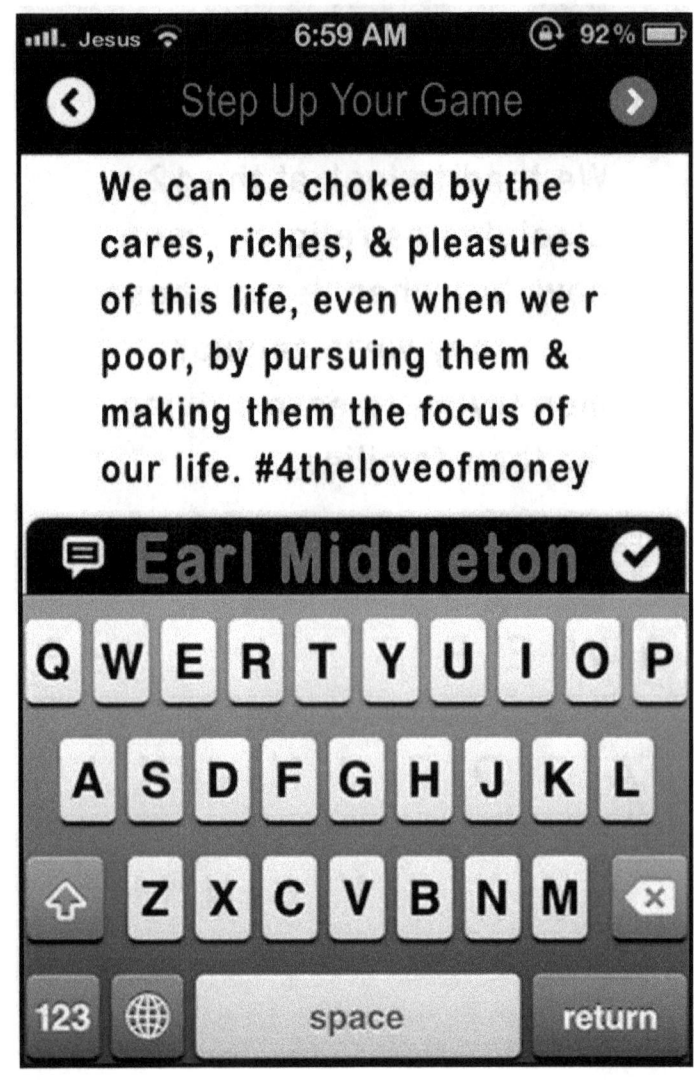

> We can be choked by the cares, riches, & pleasures of this life, even when we r poor, by pursuing them & making them the focus of our life. #4theloveofmoney

# September 3

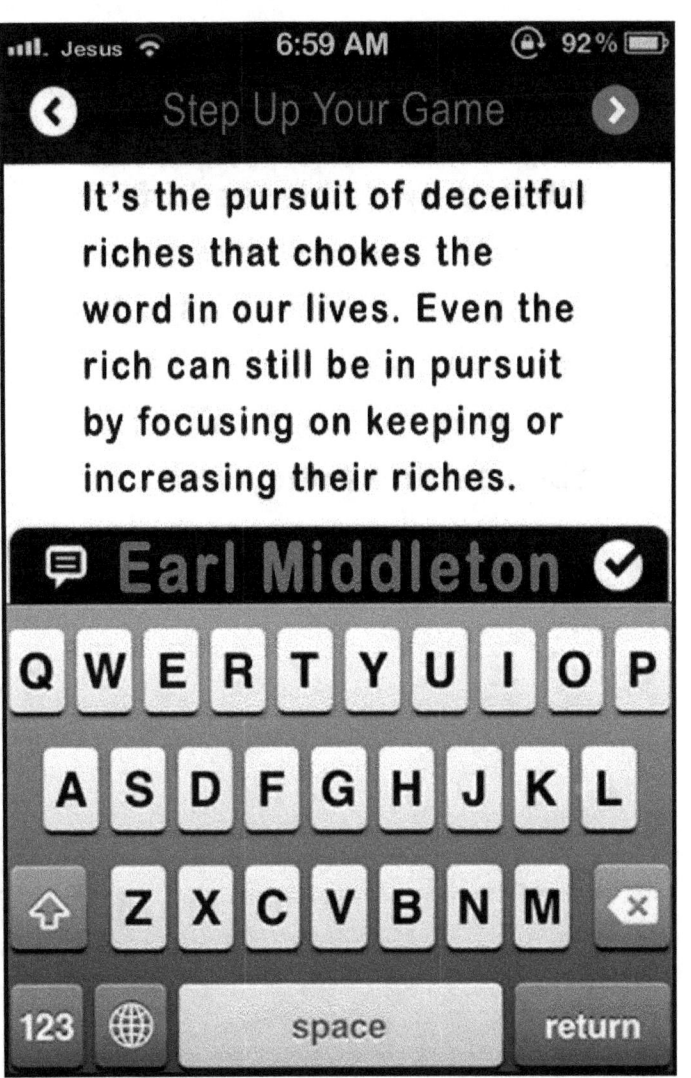

It's the pursuit of deceitful riches that chokes the word in our lives. Even the rich can still be in pursuit by focusing on keeping or increasing their riches.

# September 4

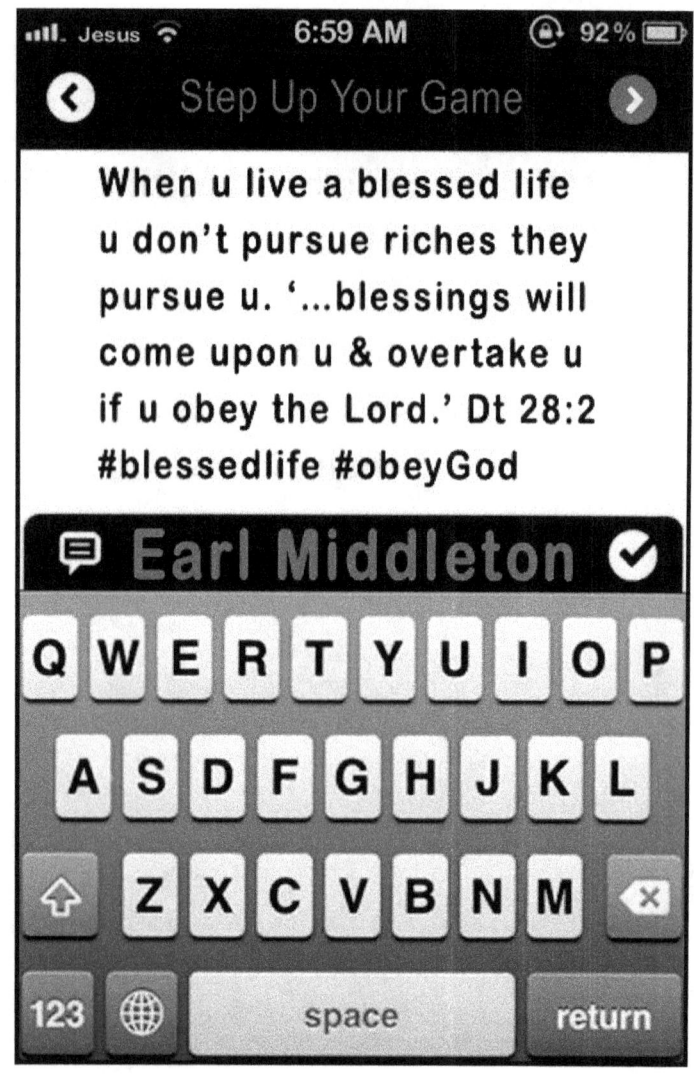

## September 5

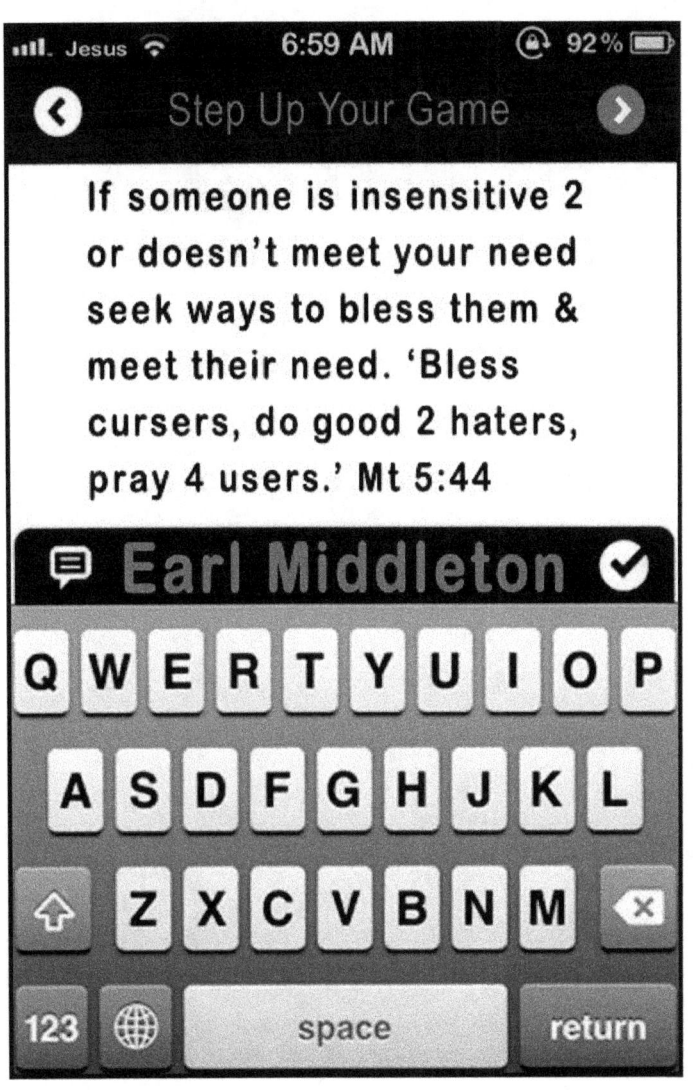

If someone is insensitive 2 or doesn't meet your need seek ways to bless them & meet their need. 'Bless cursers, do good 2 haters, pray 4 users.' Mt 5:44

# September 6

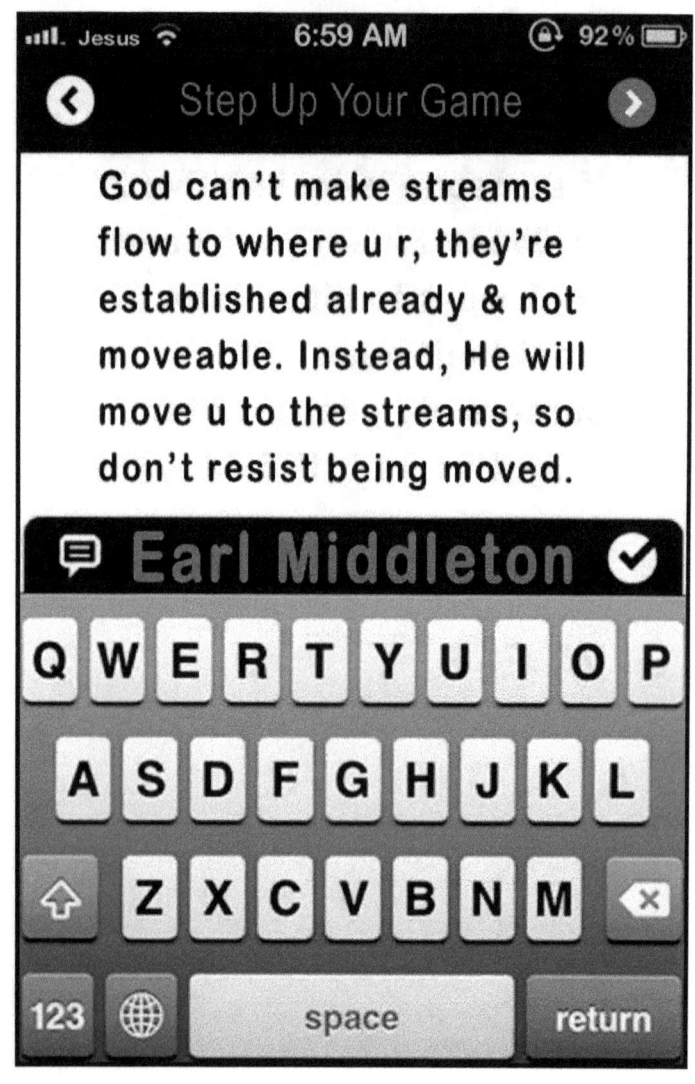

God can't make streams flow to where u r, they're established already & not moveable. Instead, He will move u to the streams, so don't resist being moved.

— Earl Middleton

# September 7

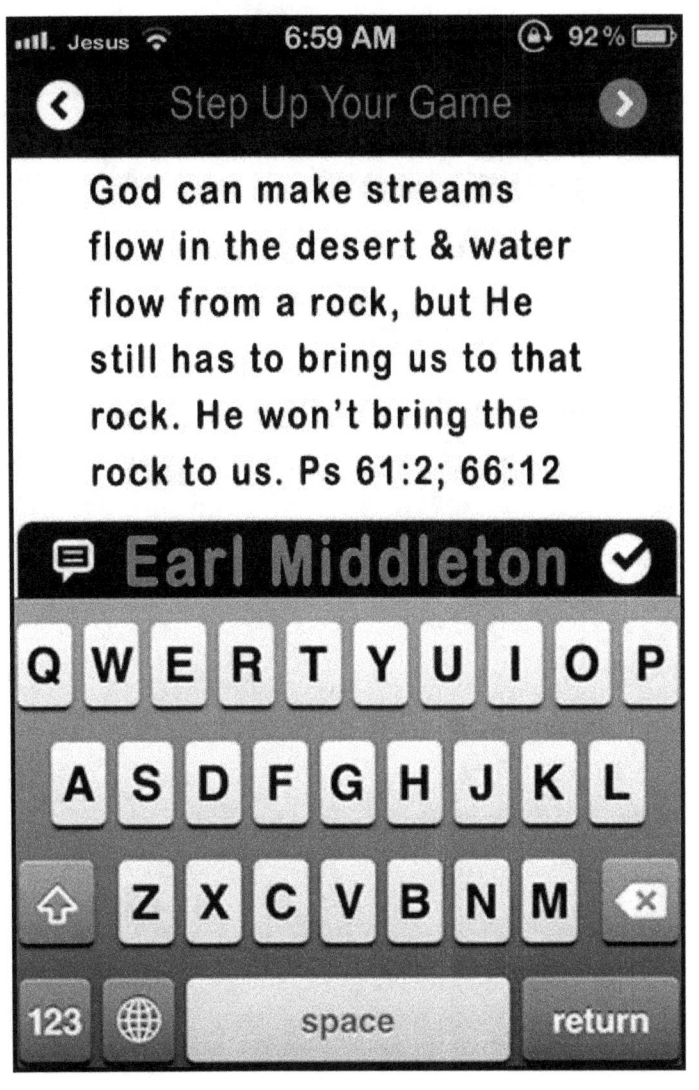

# September 8

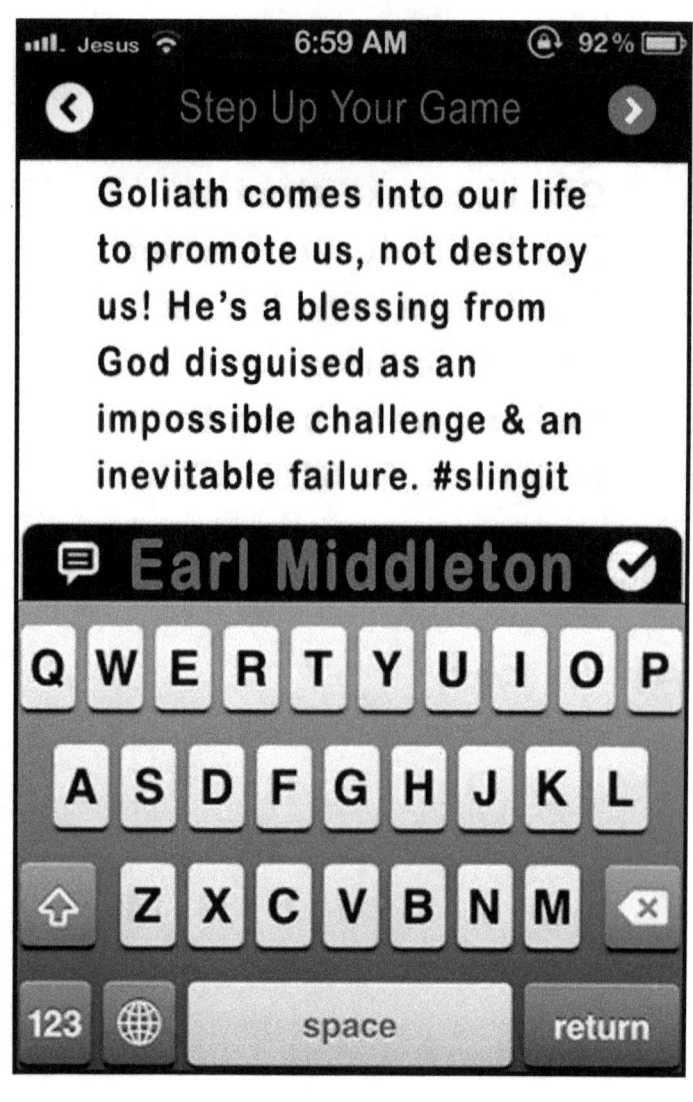

# September 9

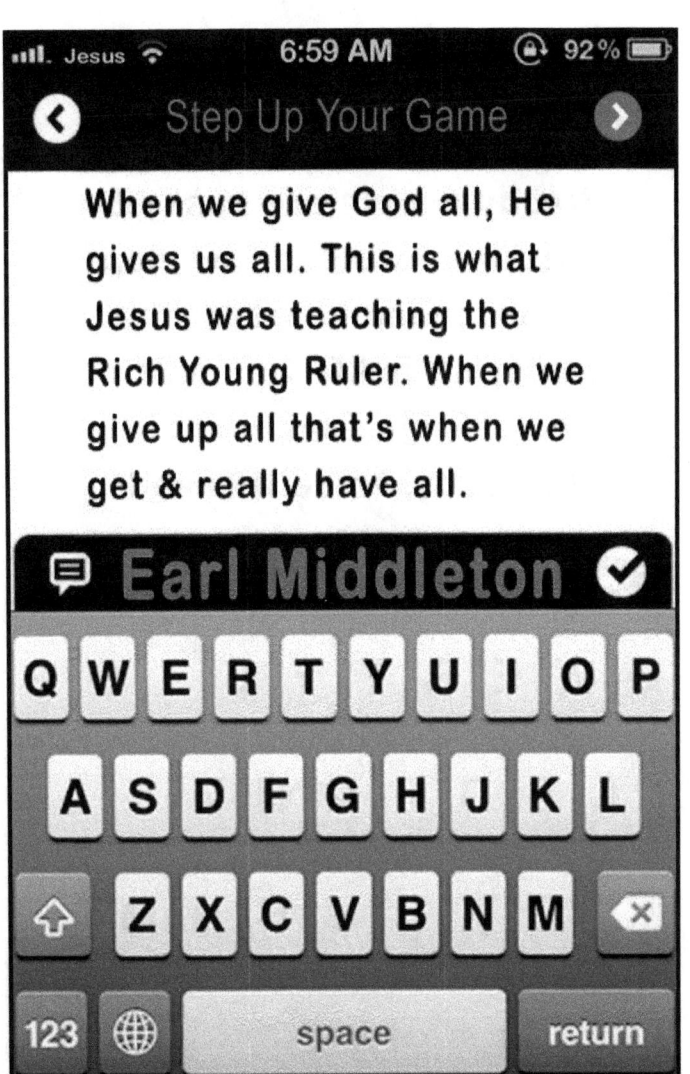

When we give God all, He gives us all. This is what Jesus was teaching the Rich Young Ruler. When we give up all that's when we get & really have all.

— Earl Middleton

# September 10

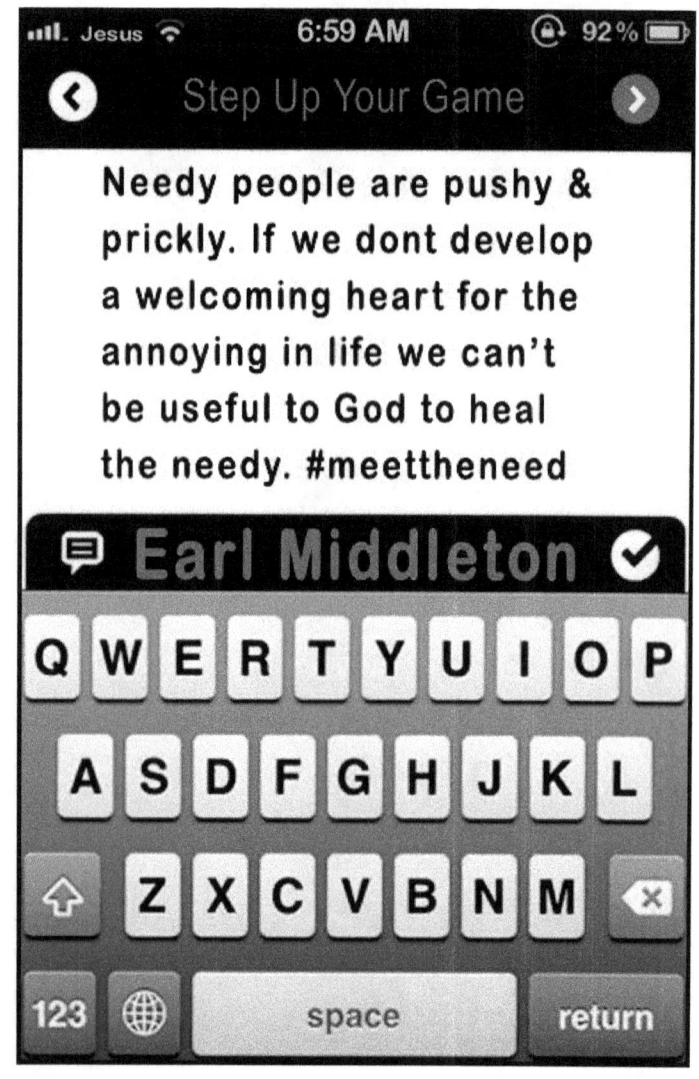

**Step Up Your Game**

Needy people are pushy & prickly. If we dont develop a welcoming heart for the annoying in life we can't be useful to God to heal the needy. #meettheneed

Earl Middleton

# September 11

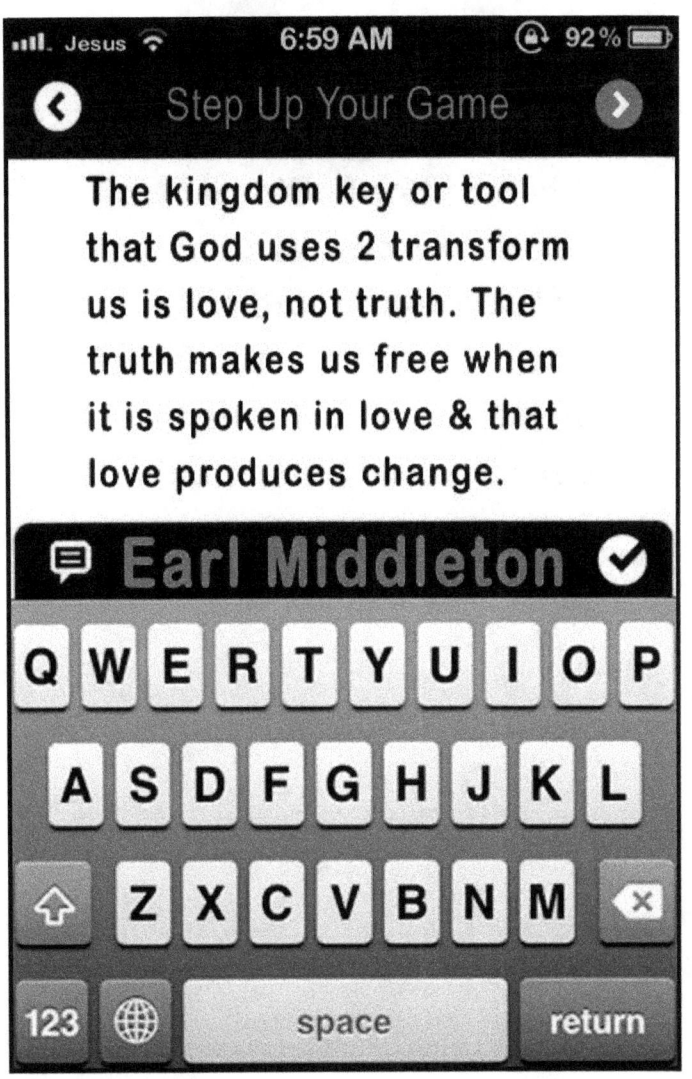

The kingdom key or tool that God uses 2 transform us is love, not truth. The truth makes us free when it is spoken in love & that love produces change.

# September 12

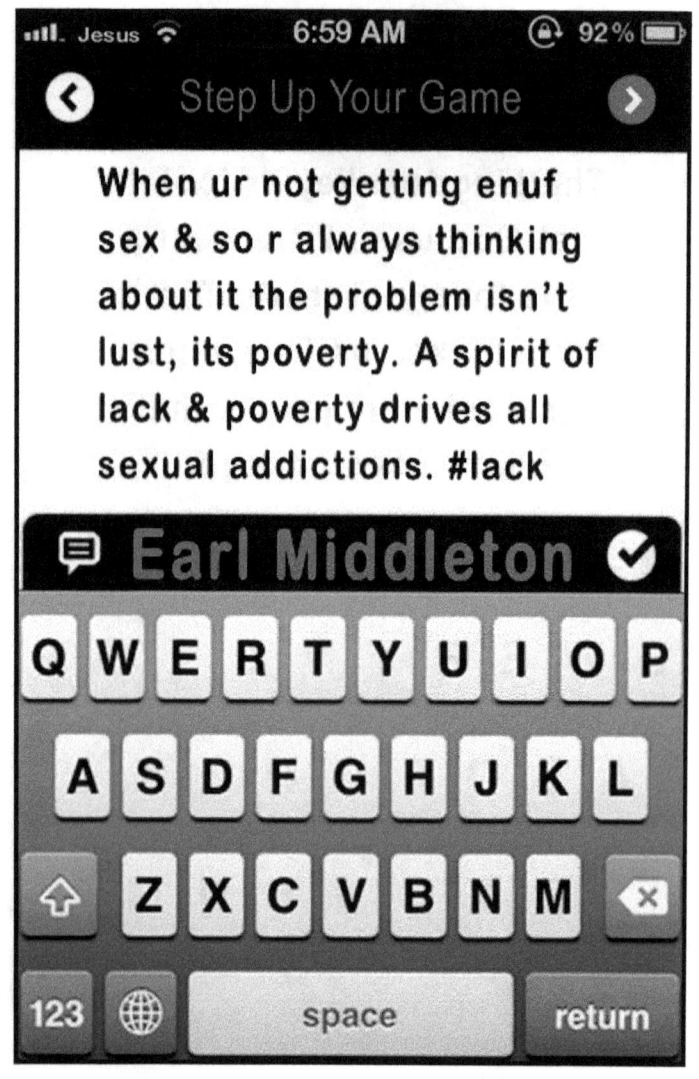

# September 13

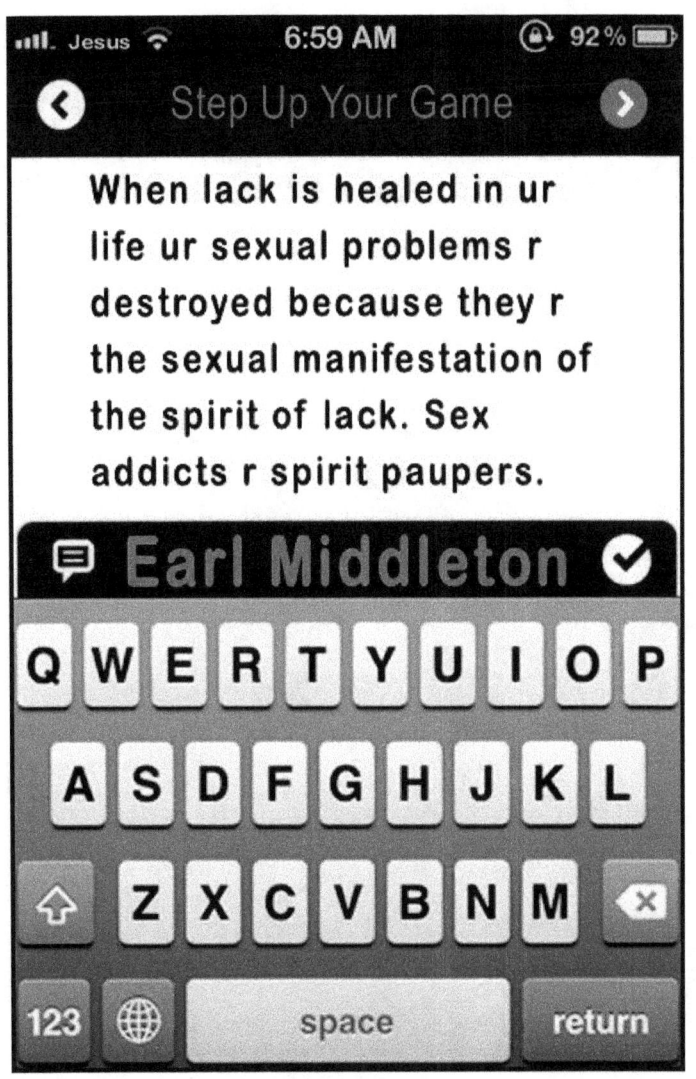

## September 14

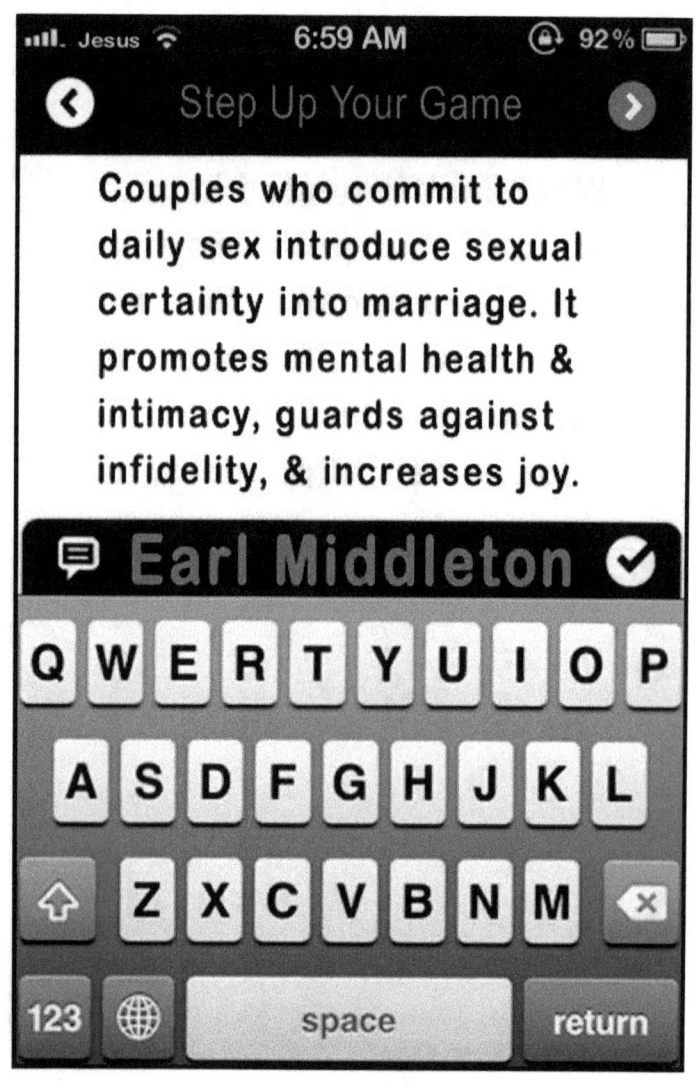

# September 15

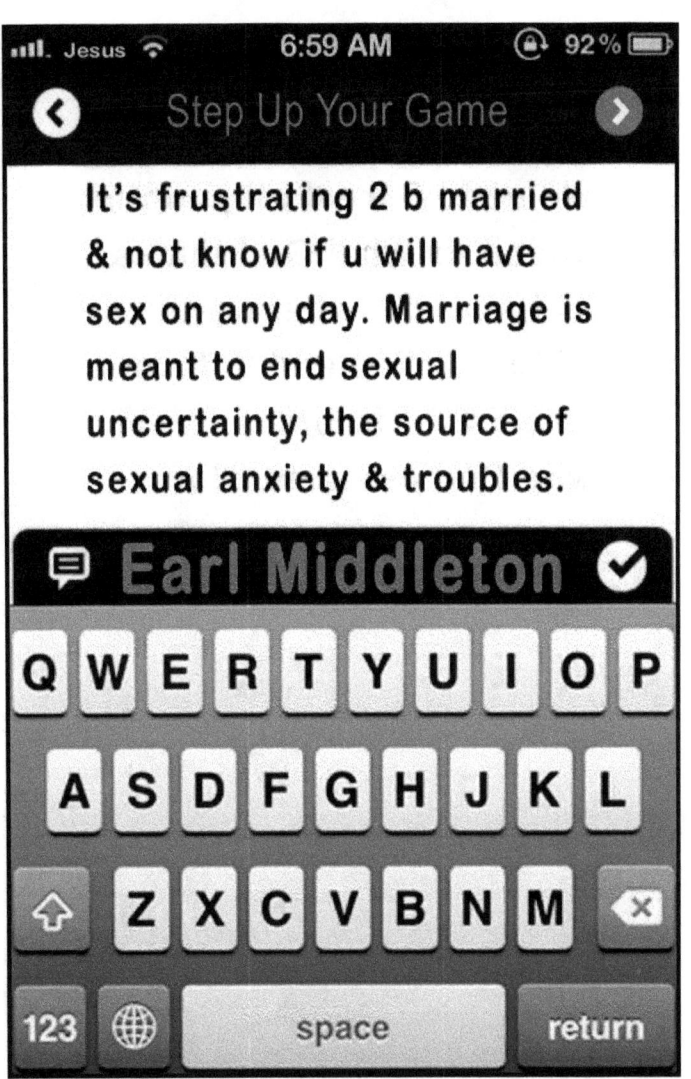

It's frustrating 2 b married & not know if u will have sex on any day. Marriage is meant to end sexual uncertainty, the source of sexual anxiety & troubles.

— Earl Middleton

# September 16

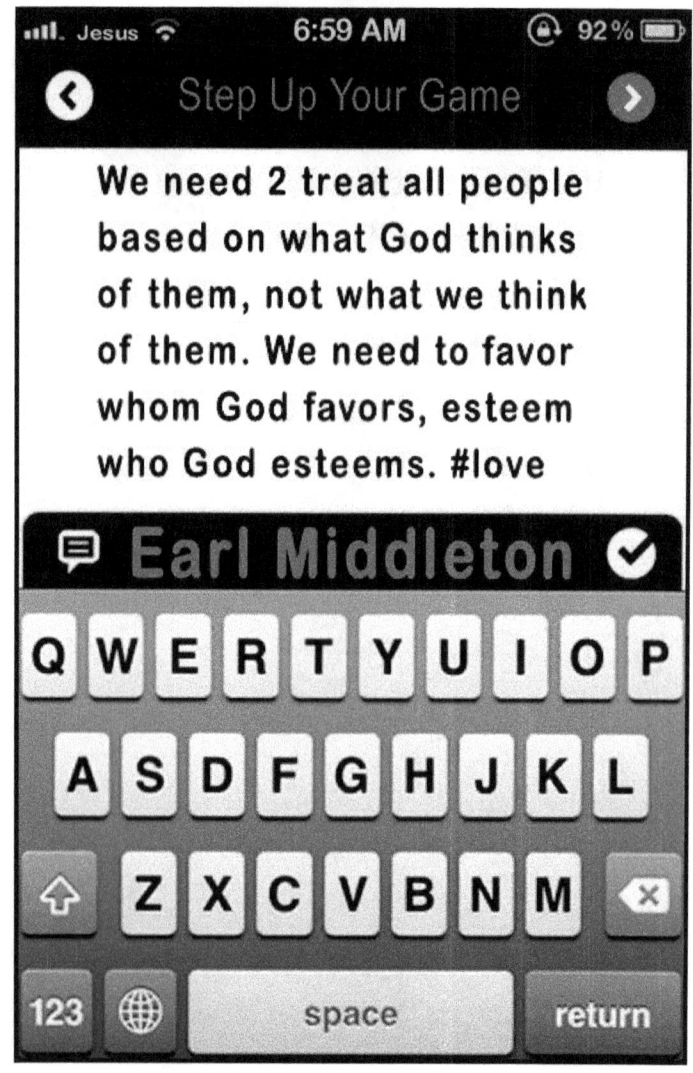

# September 17

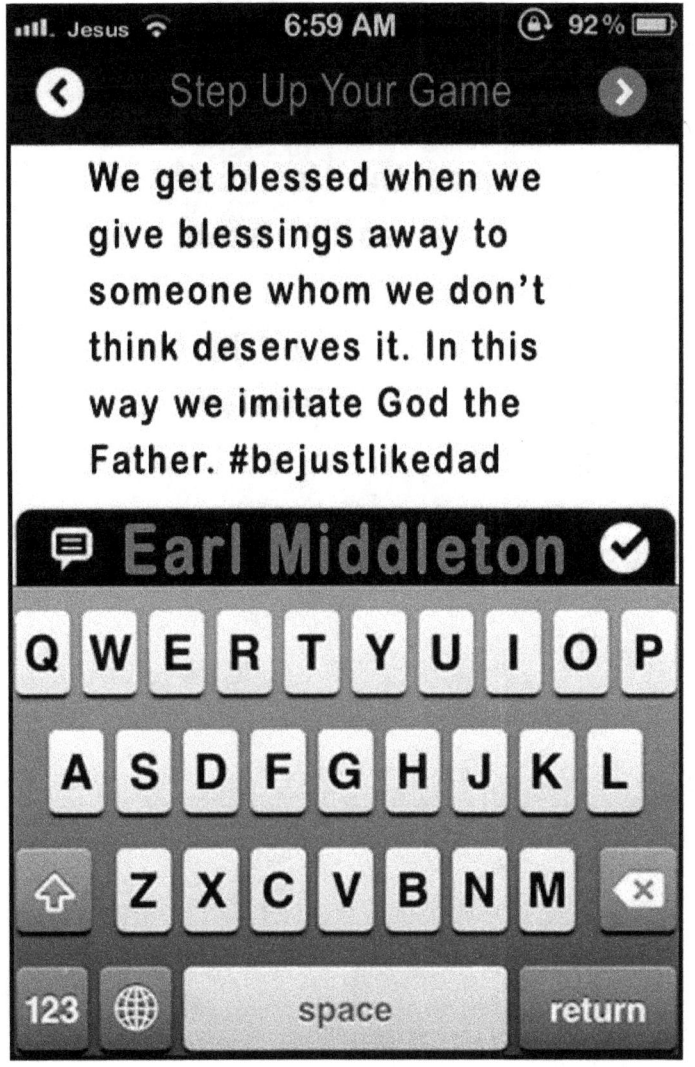

**Step Up Your Game**

We get blessed when we give blessings away to someone whom we don't think deserves it. In this way we imitate God the Father. #bejustlikedad

# September 18

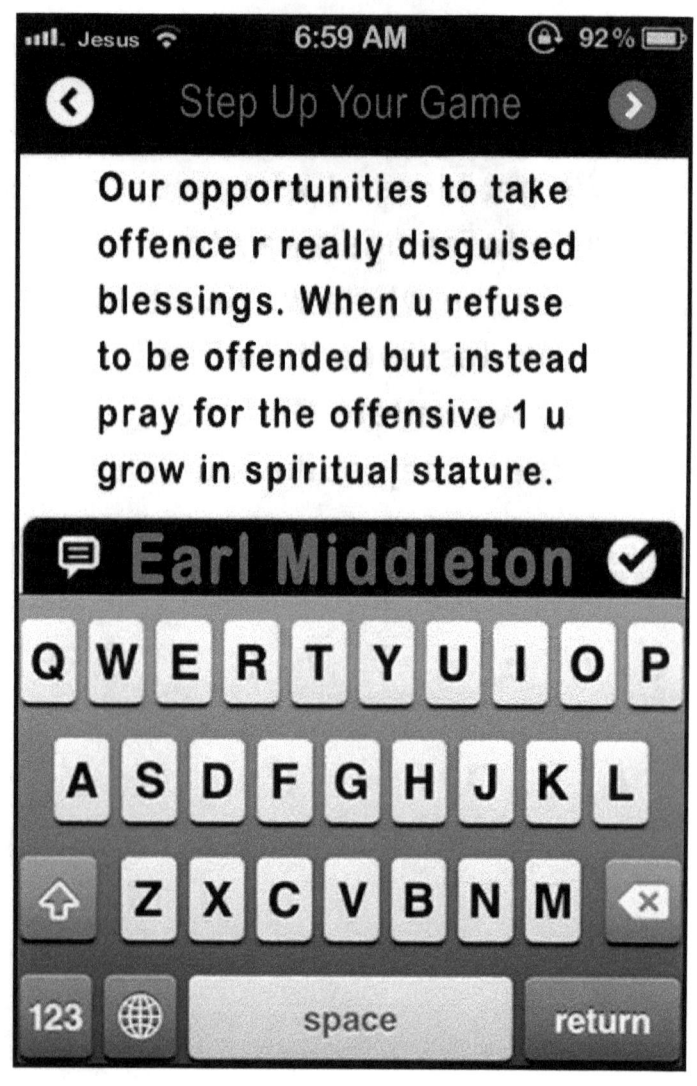

> Our opportunities to take offence r really disguised blessings. When u refuse to be offended but instead pray for the offensive 1 u grow in spiritual stature.
>
> — Earl Middleton

# September 19

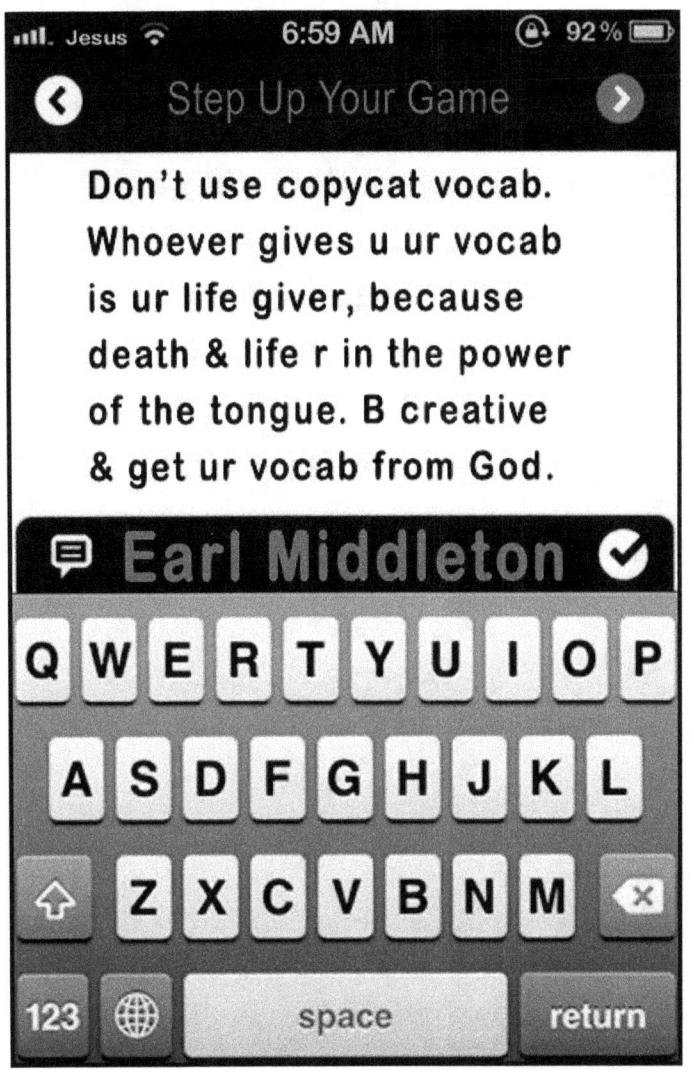

# September 20

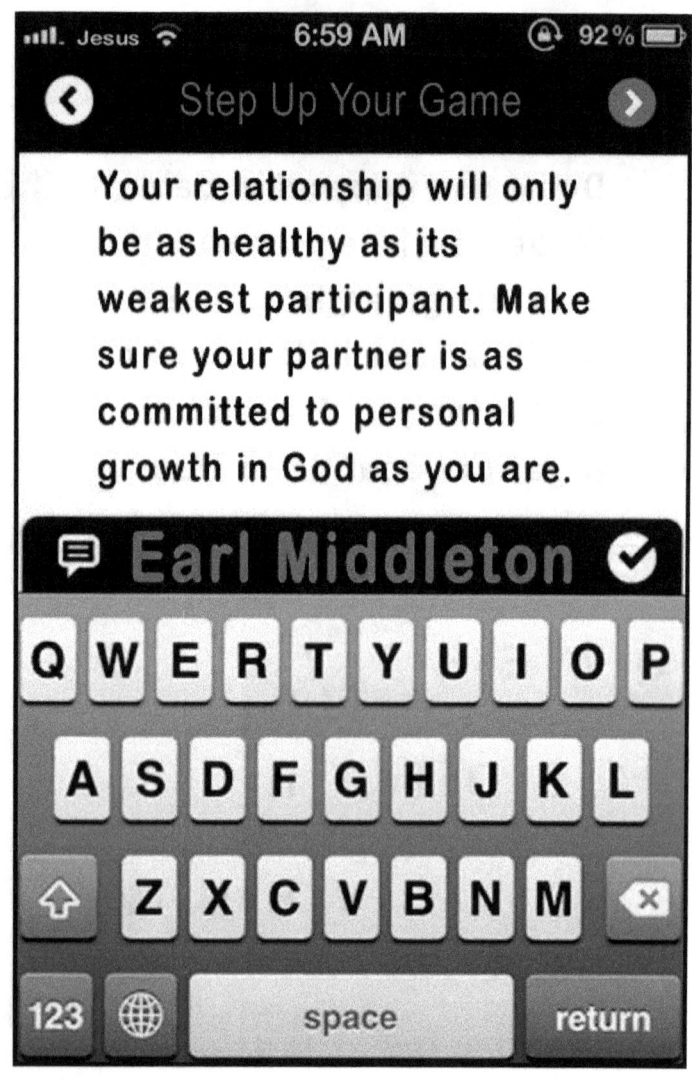

Your relationship will only be as healthy as its weakest participant. Make sure your partner is as committed to personal growth in God as you are.

# September 21

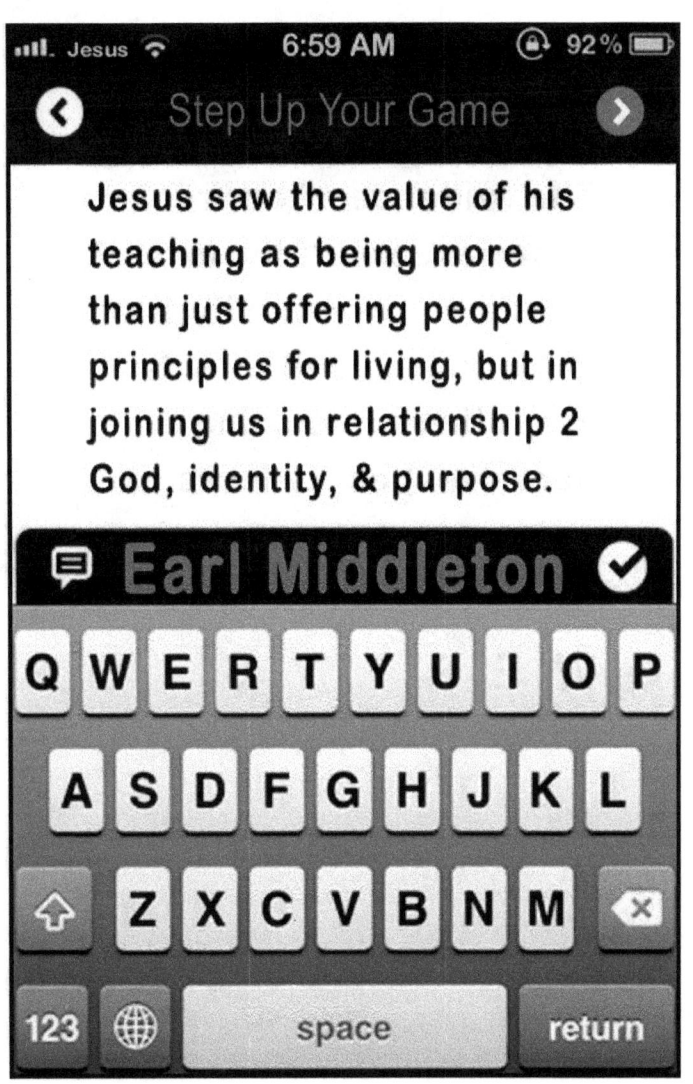

**Step Up Your Game**

Jesus saw the value of his teaching as being more than just offering people principles for living, but in joining us in relationship 2 God, identity, & purpose.

Earl Middleton

# September 22

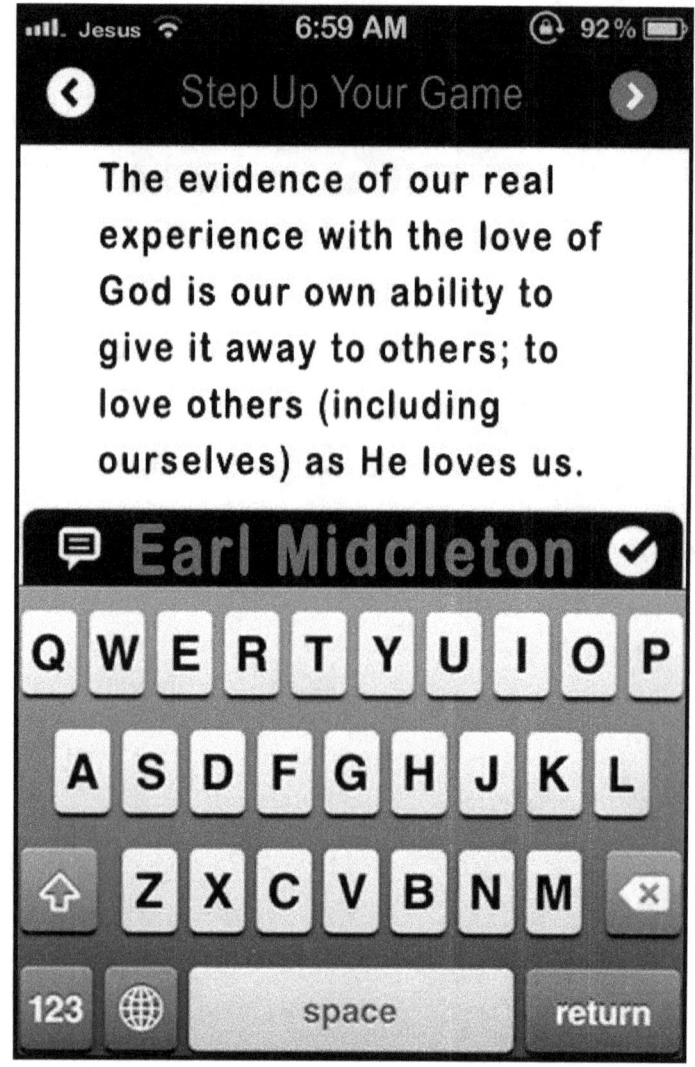

**Step Up Your Game**

The evidence of our real experience with the love of God is our own ability to give it away to others; to love others (including ourselves) as He loves us.

Earl Middleton

# September 23

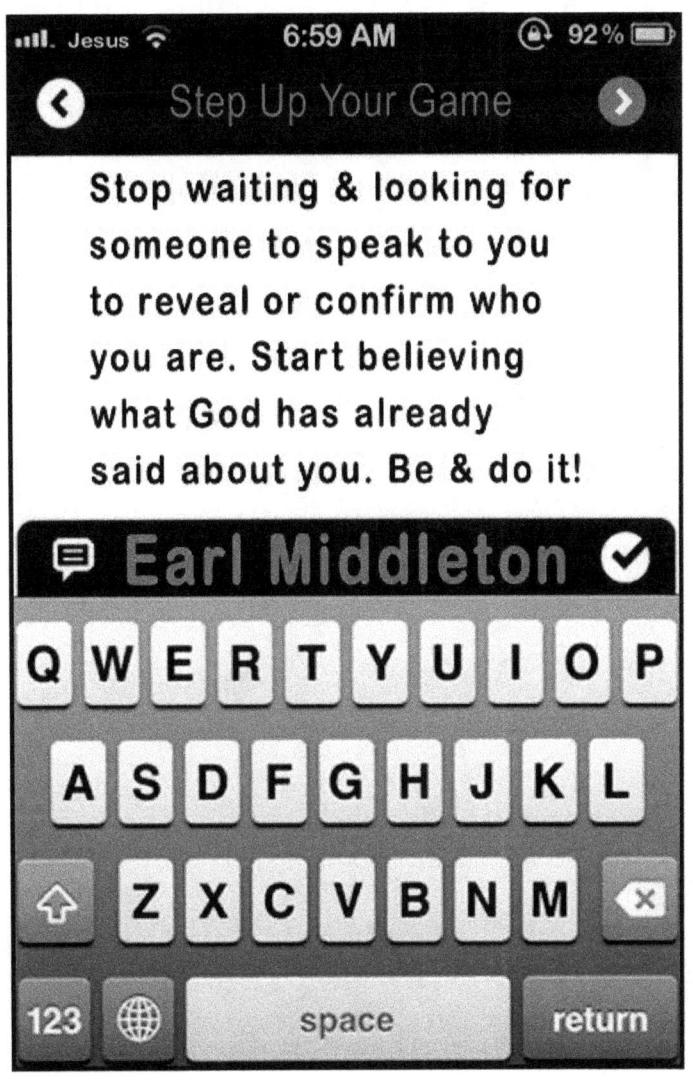

# September 24

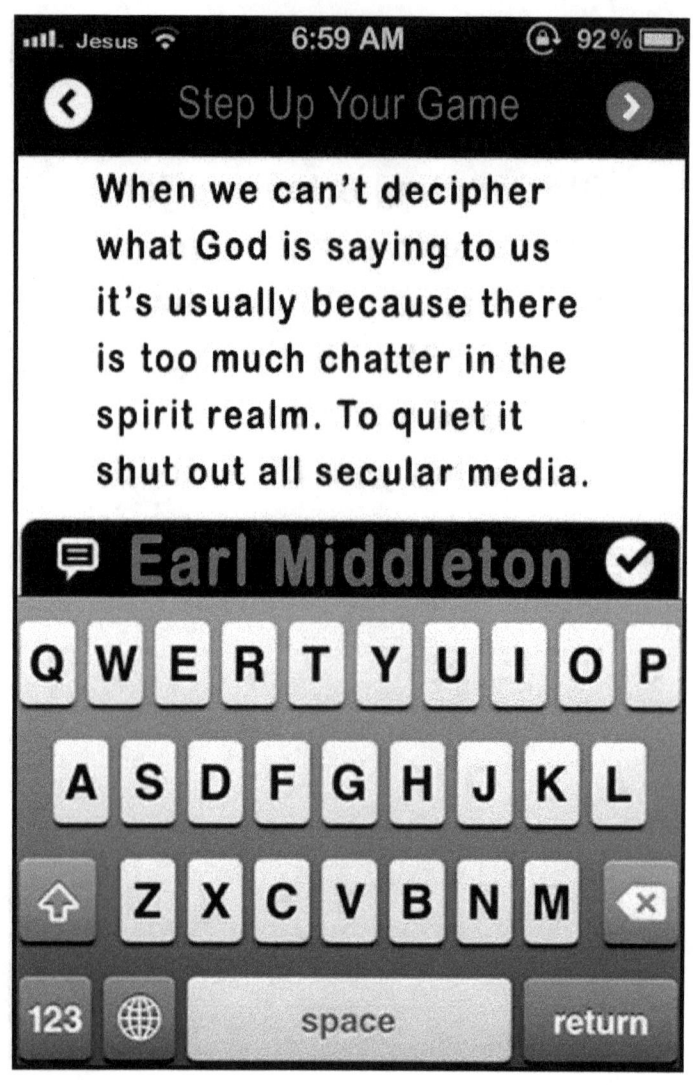

# September 25

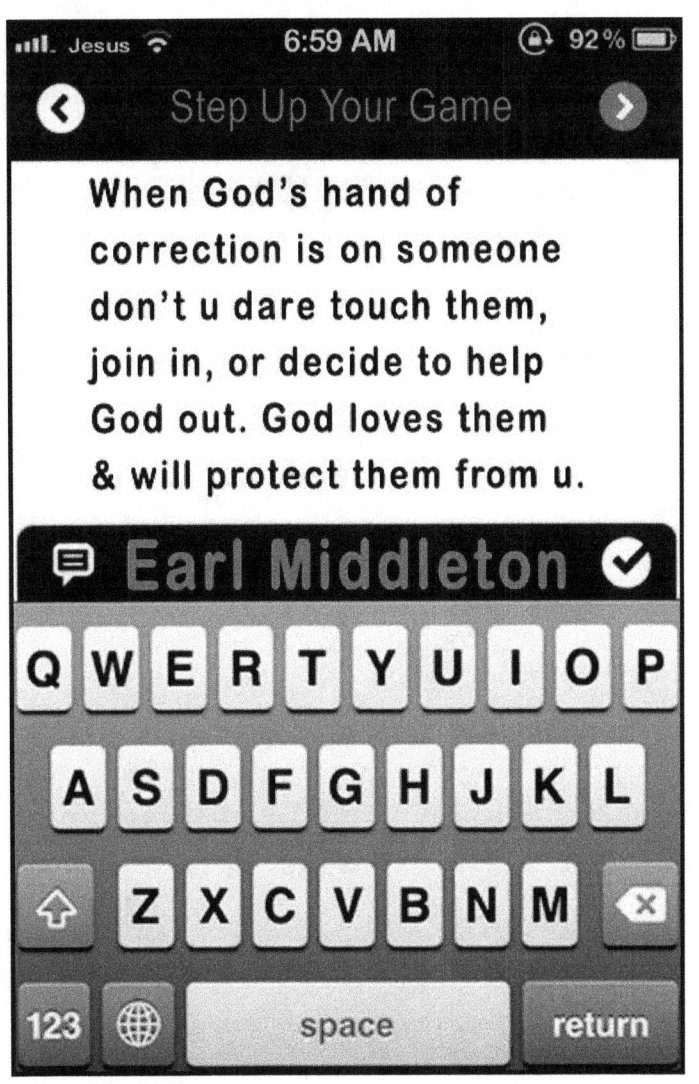

# September 26

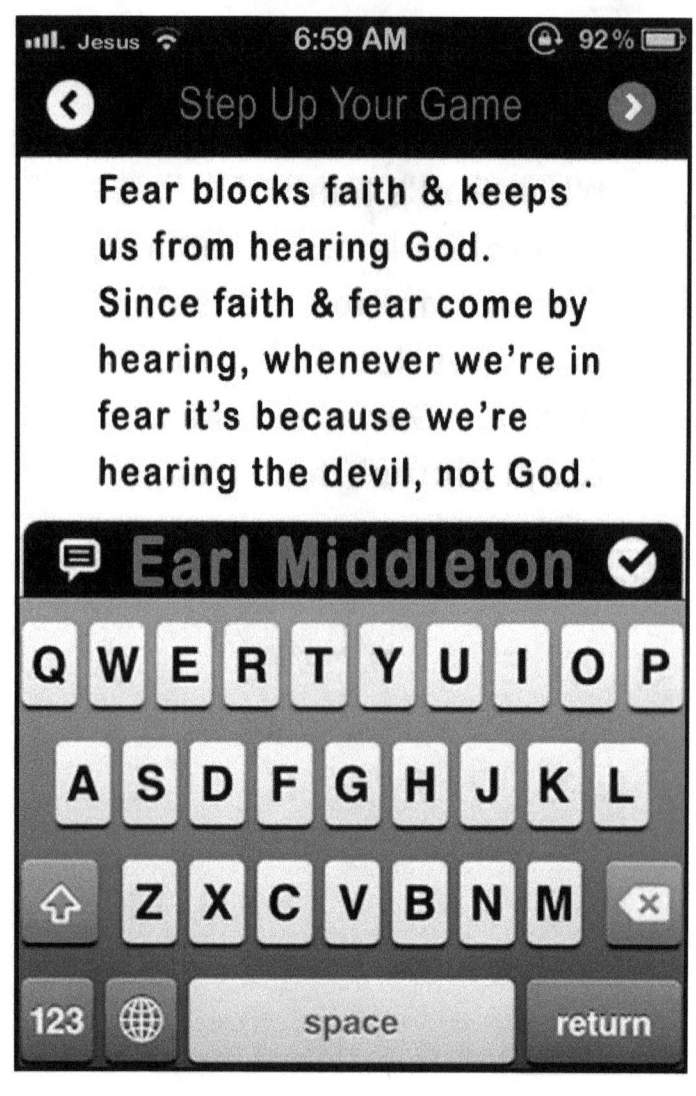

Fear blocks faith & keeps us from hearing God. Since faith & fear come by hearing, whenever we're in fear it's because we're hearing the devil, not God.

Earl Middleton

# September 27

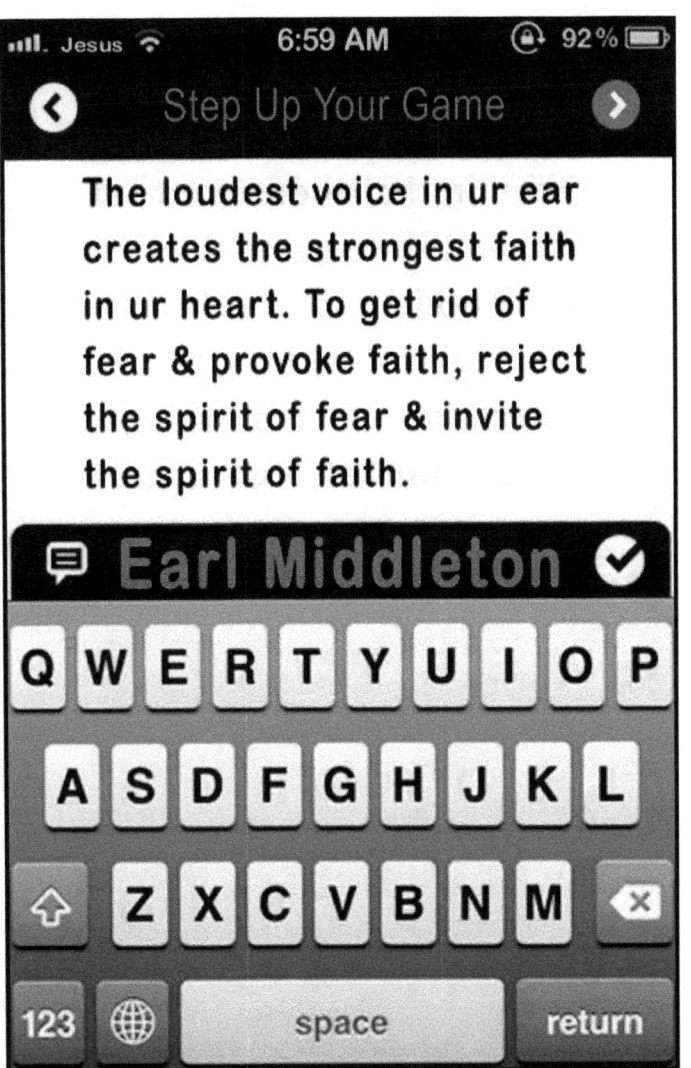

The loudest voice in ur ear creates the strongest faith in ur heart. To get rid of fear & provoke faith, reject the spirit of fear & invite the spirit of faith.

— Earl Middleton

# September 28

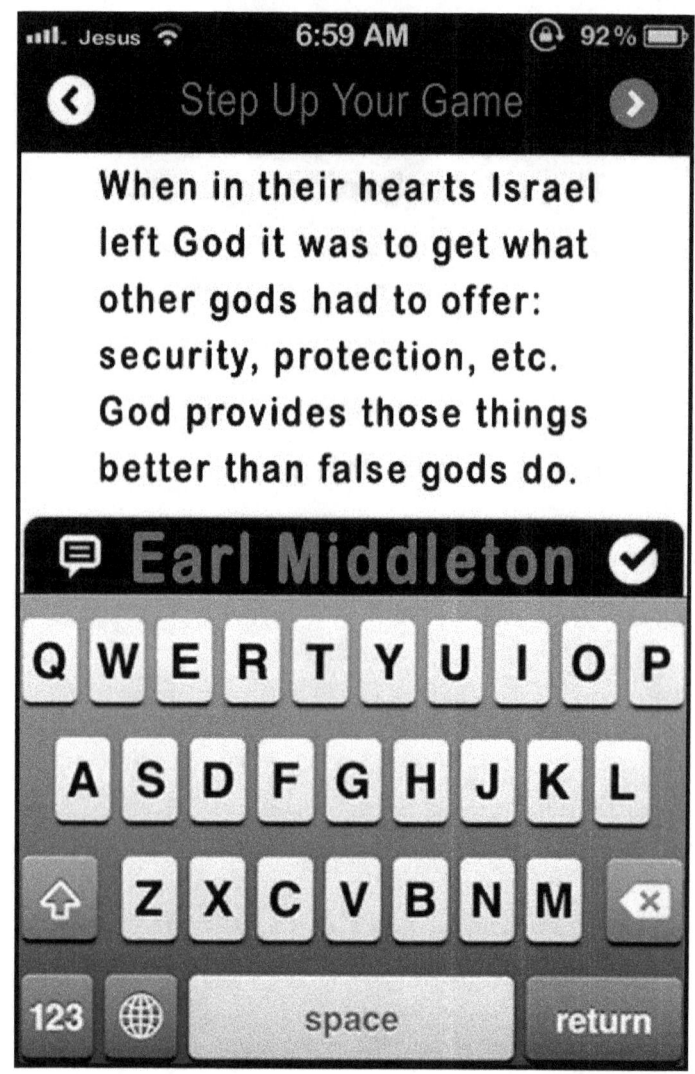

When in their hearts Israel left God it was to get what other gods had to offer: security, protection, etc. God provides those things better than false gods do.

— Earl Middleton

# September 29

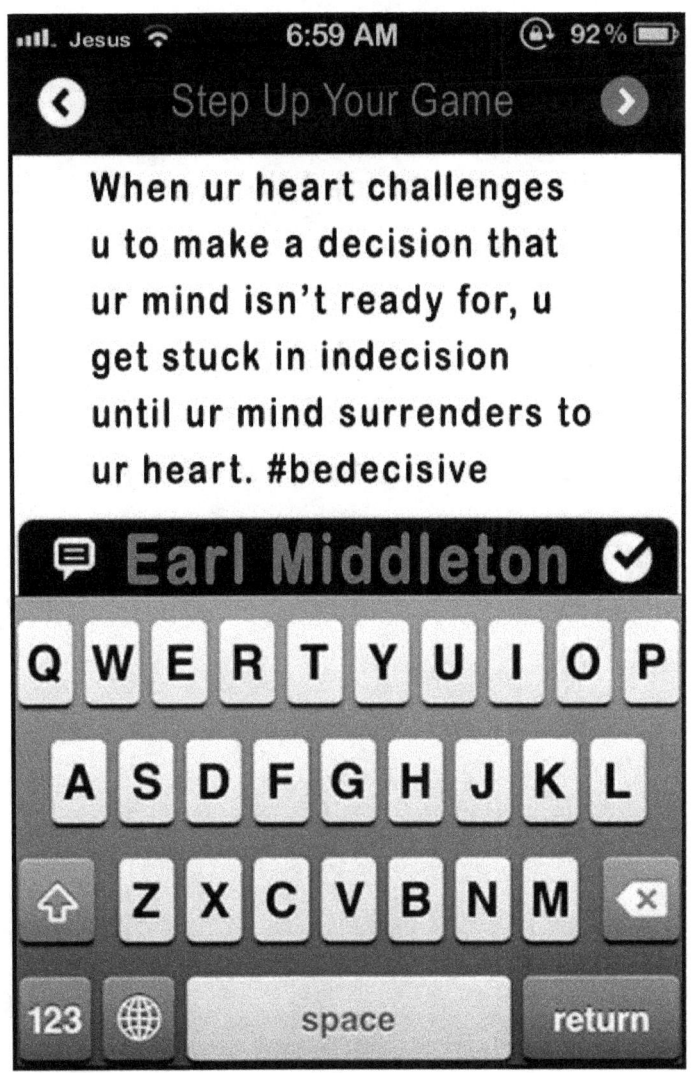

# September 30

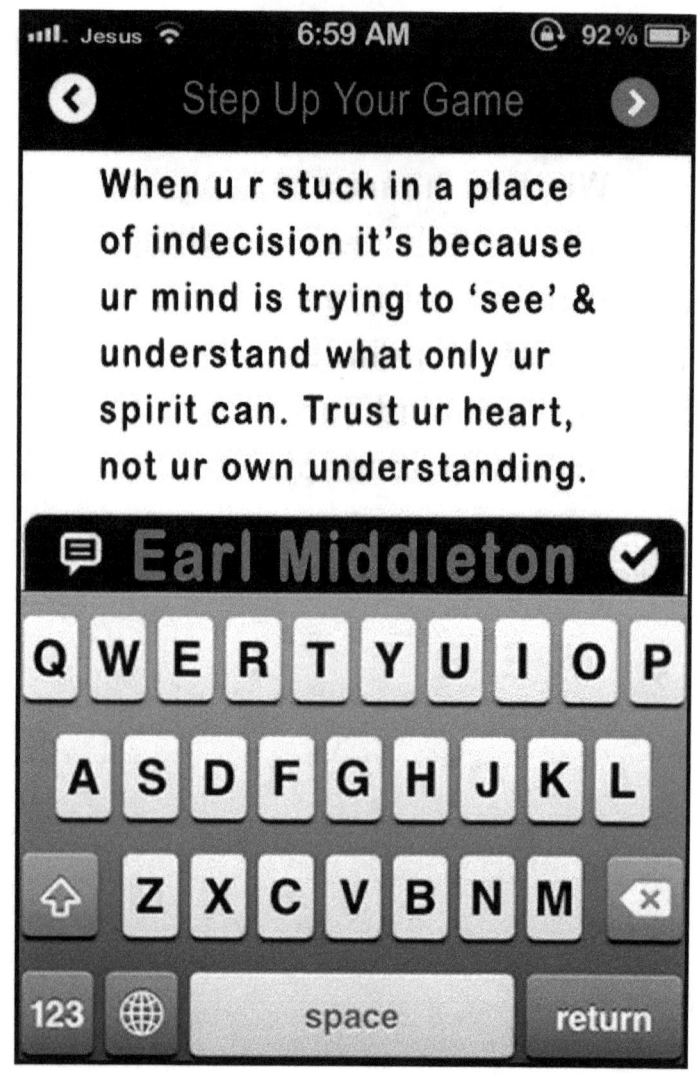

When u r stuck in a place of indecision it's because ur mind is trying to 'see' & understand what only ur spirit can. Trust ur heart, not ur own understanding.

— Earl Middleton

# October 1

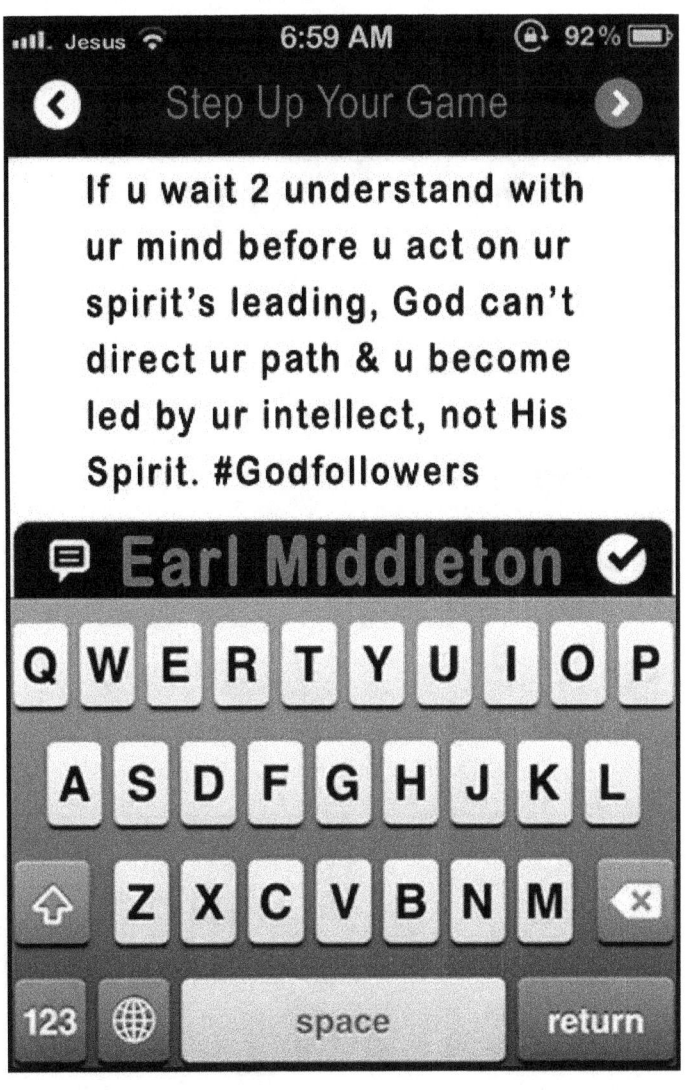

**Step Up Your Game**

If u wait 2 understand with ur mind before u act on ur spirit's leading, God can't direct ur path & u become led by ur intellect, not His Spirit. #Godfollowers

— Earl Middleton

# October 2

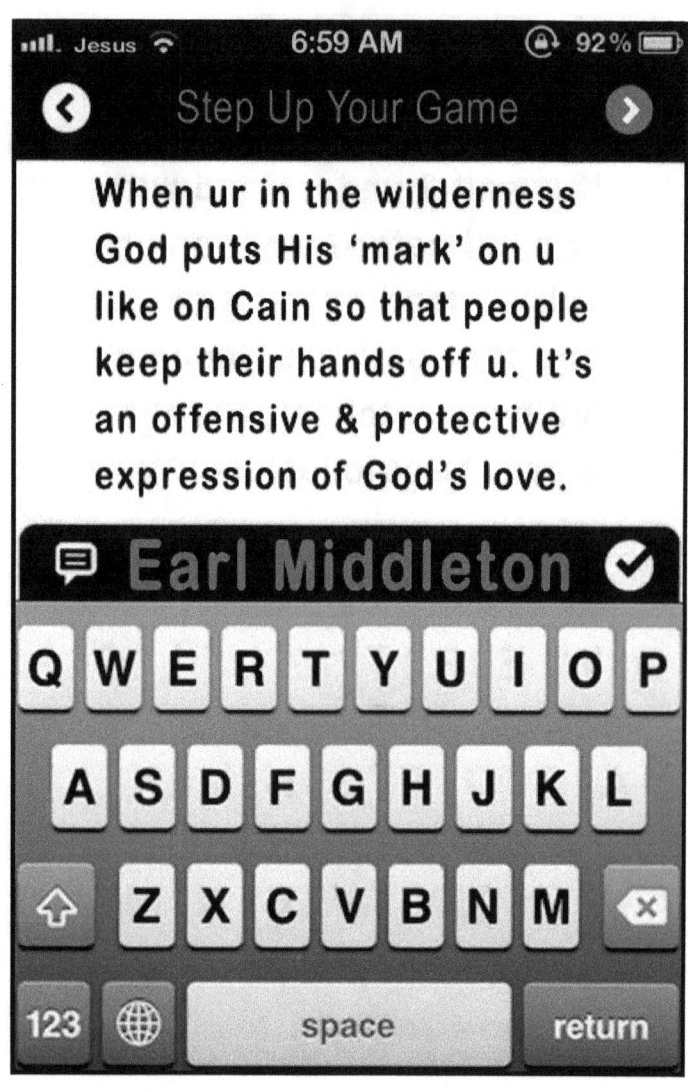

**Step Up Your Game**

When ur in the wilderness God puts His 'mark' on u like on Cain so that people keep their hands off u. It's an offensive & protective expression of God's love.

Earl Middleton

# October 3

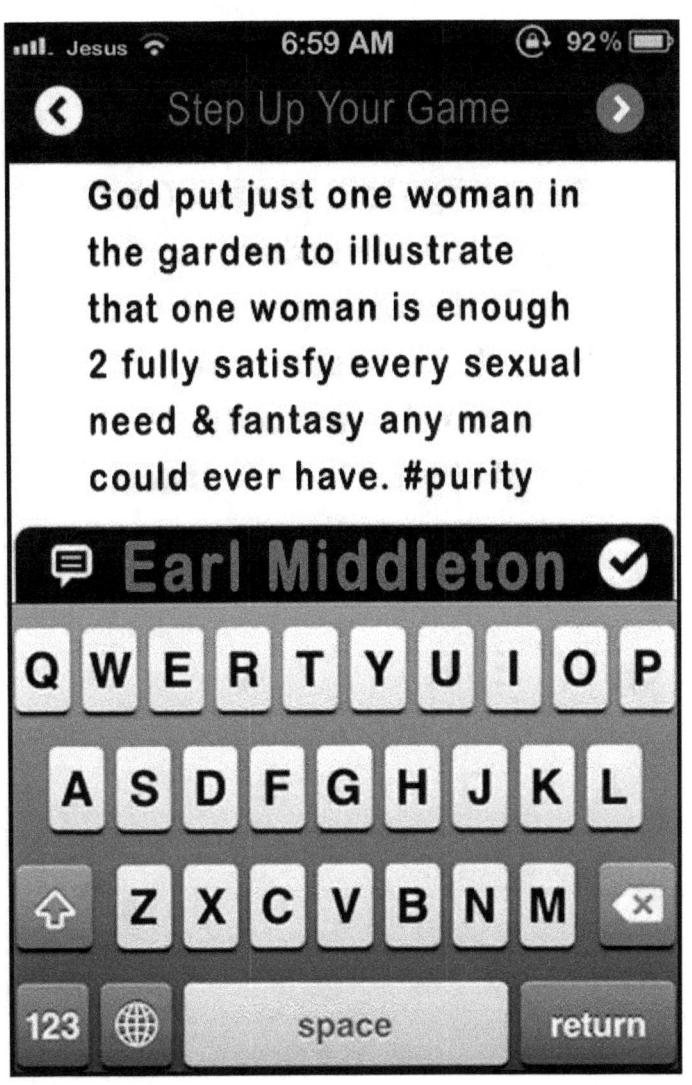

# October 4

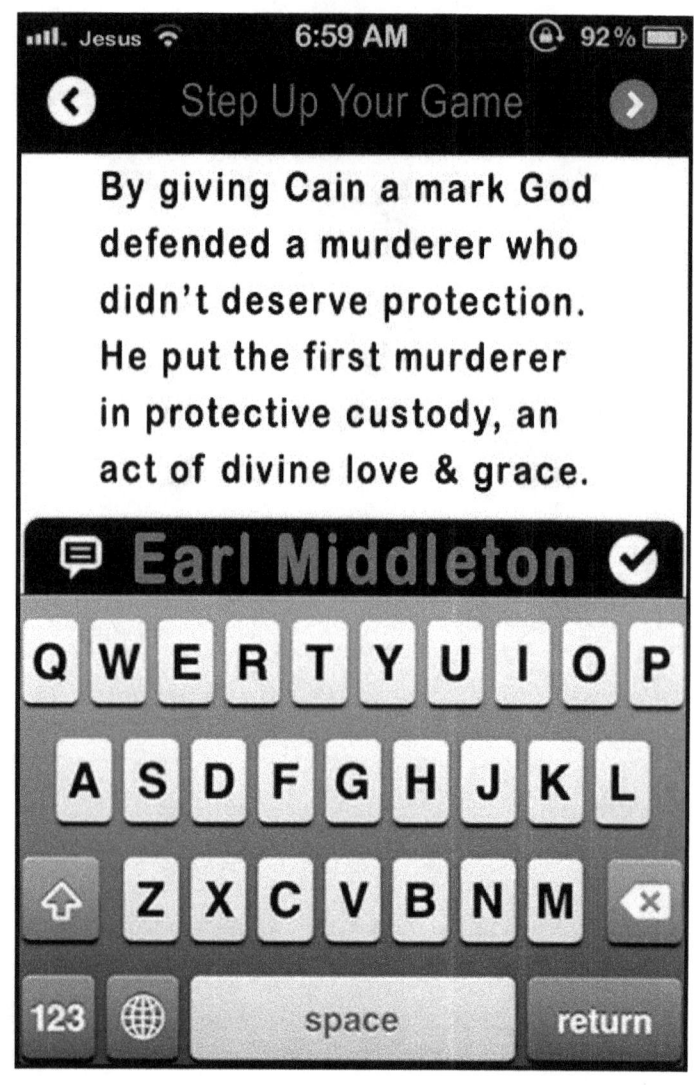

**Step Up Your Game**

By giving Cain a mark God defended a murderer who didn't deserve protection. He put the first murderer in protective custody, an act of divine love & grace.

— Earl Middleton

# October 5

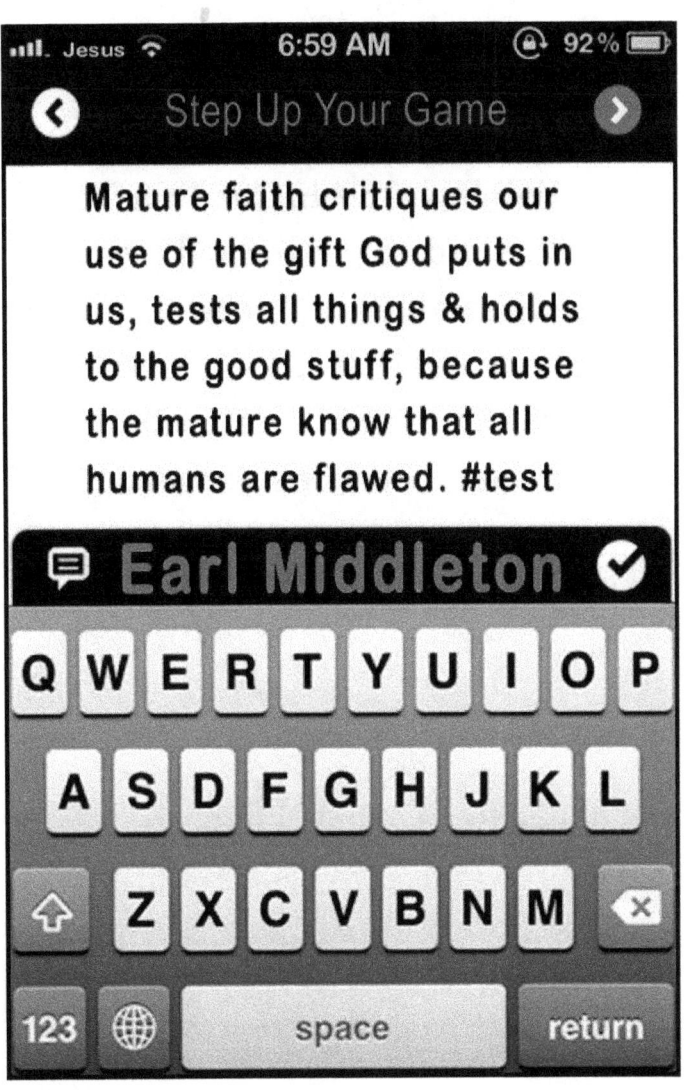

**Step Up Your Game**

Mature faith critiques our use of the gift God puts in us, tests all things & holds to the good stuff, because the mature know that all humans are flawed. #test

Earl Middleton

# October 6

## Step Up Your Game

Whatever God births in a fallen world comes with an expiration date. When it's over, trust God to give you something else to do. Release what has expired.

— Earl Middleton

## October 7

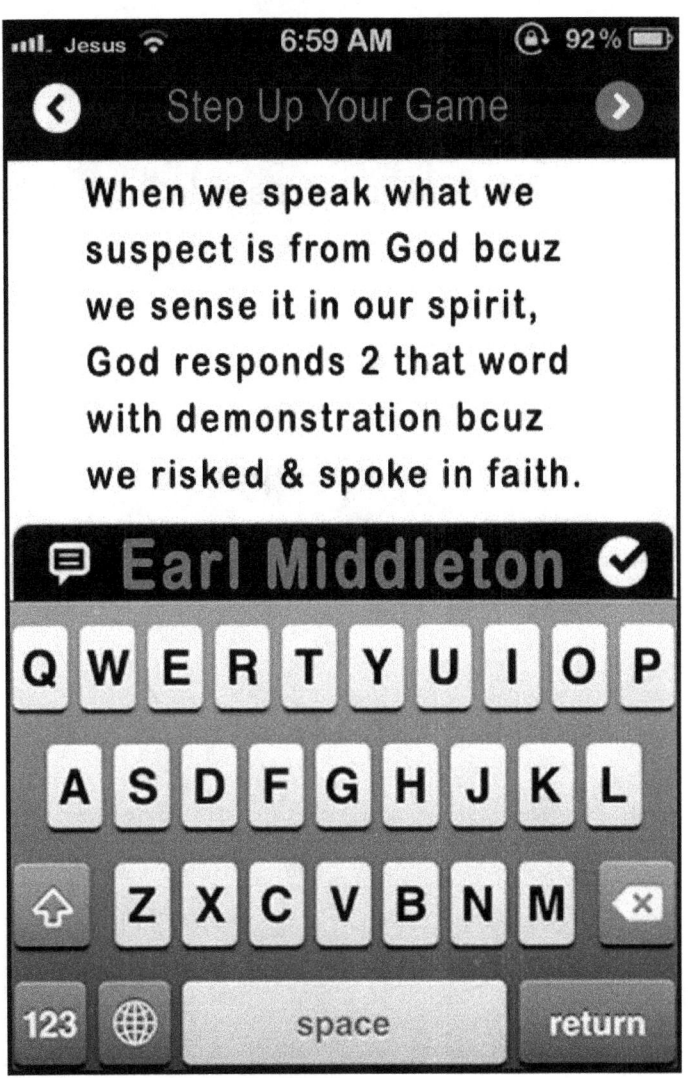

When we speak what we suspect is from God bcuz we sense it in our spirit, God responds 2 that word with demonstration bcuz we risked & spoke in faith.

# October 8

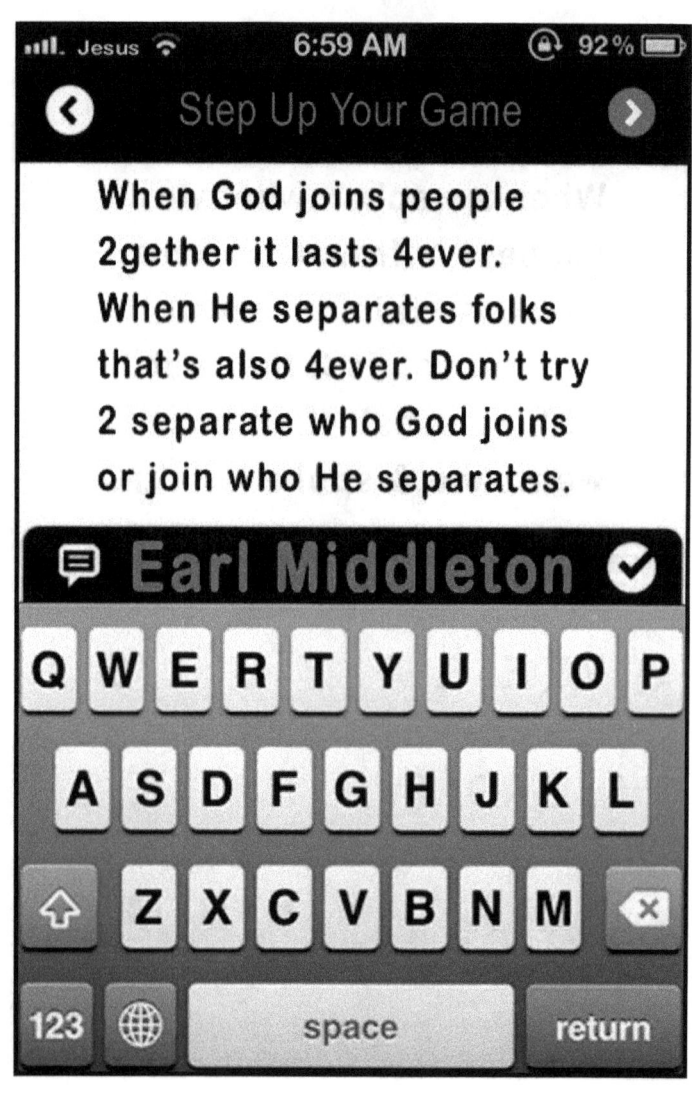

# October 9

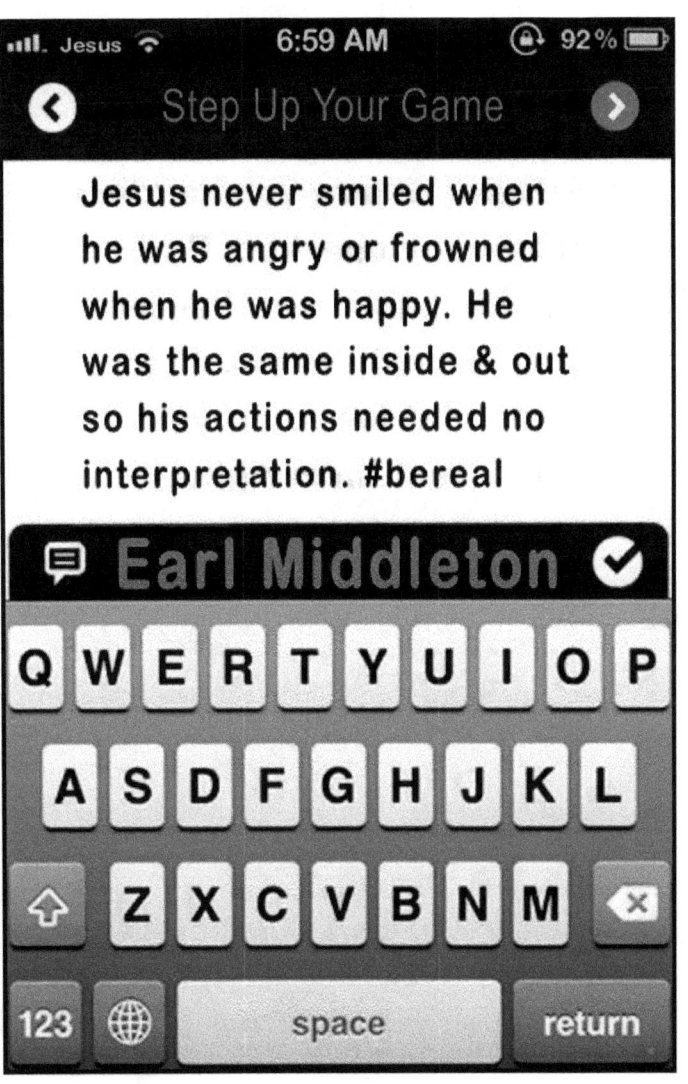

# October 10

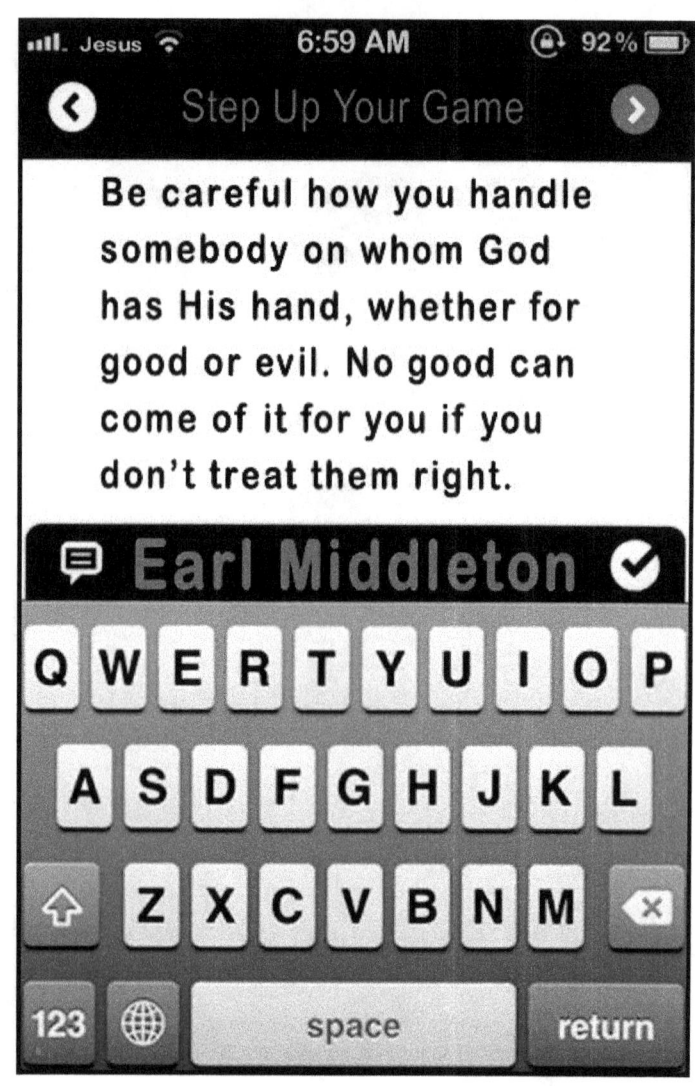

# October 11

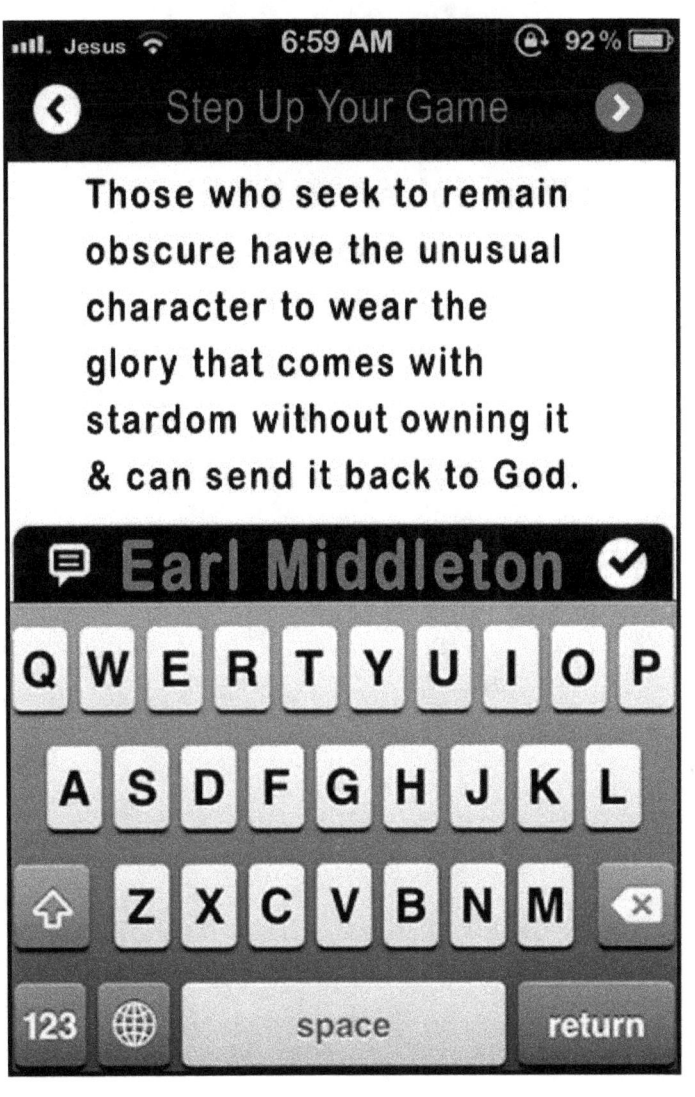

# October 12

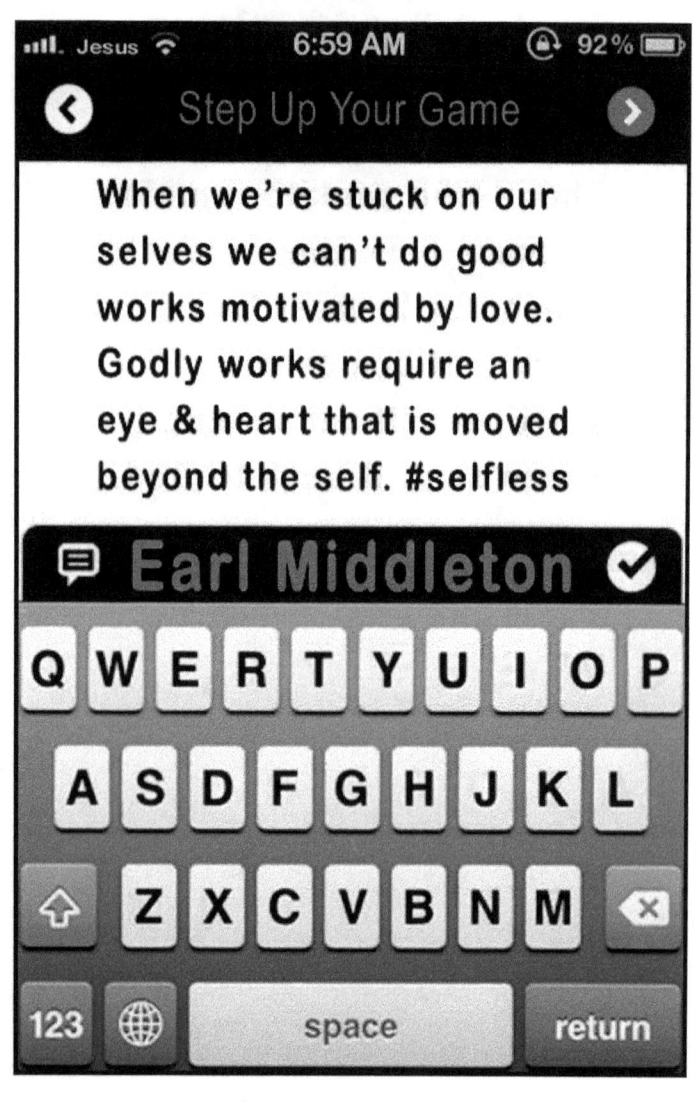

When we're stuck on our selves we can't do good works motivated by love. Godly works require an eye & heart that is moved beyond the self. #selfless

# October 13

# October 14

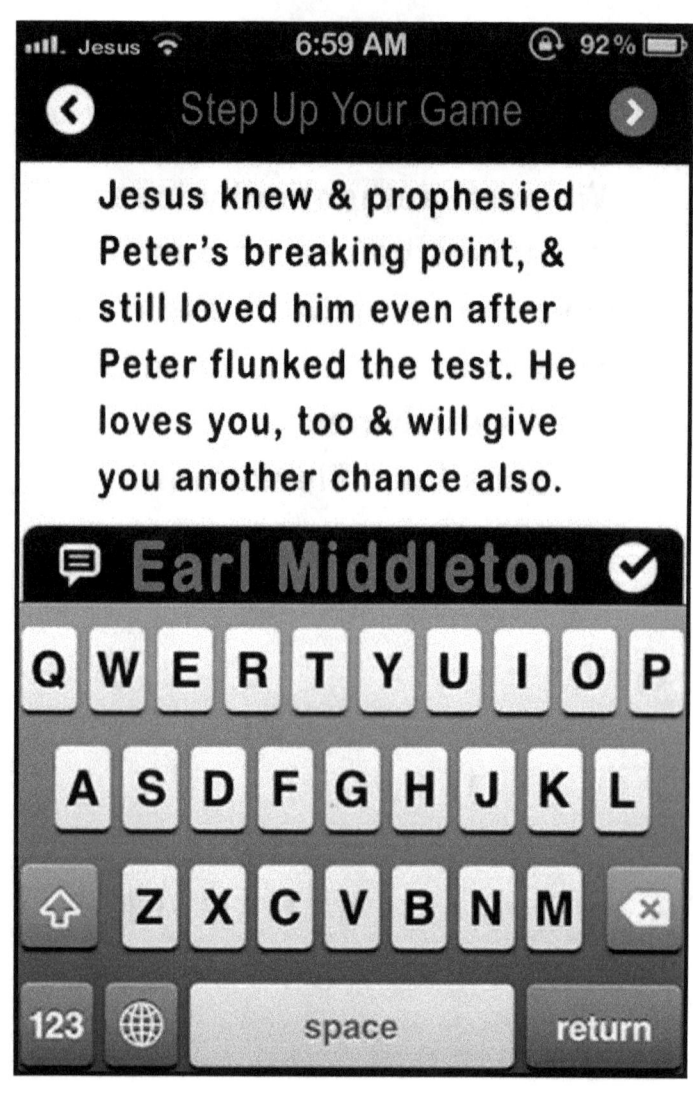

Jesus knew & prophesied Peter's breaking point, & still loved him even after Peter flunked the test. He loves you, too & will give you another chance also.

— Earl Middleton

# October 15

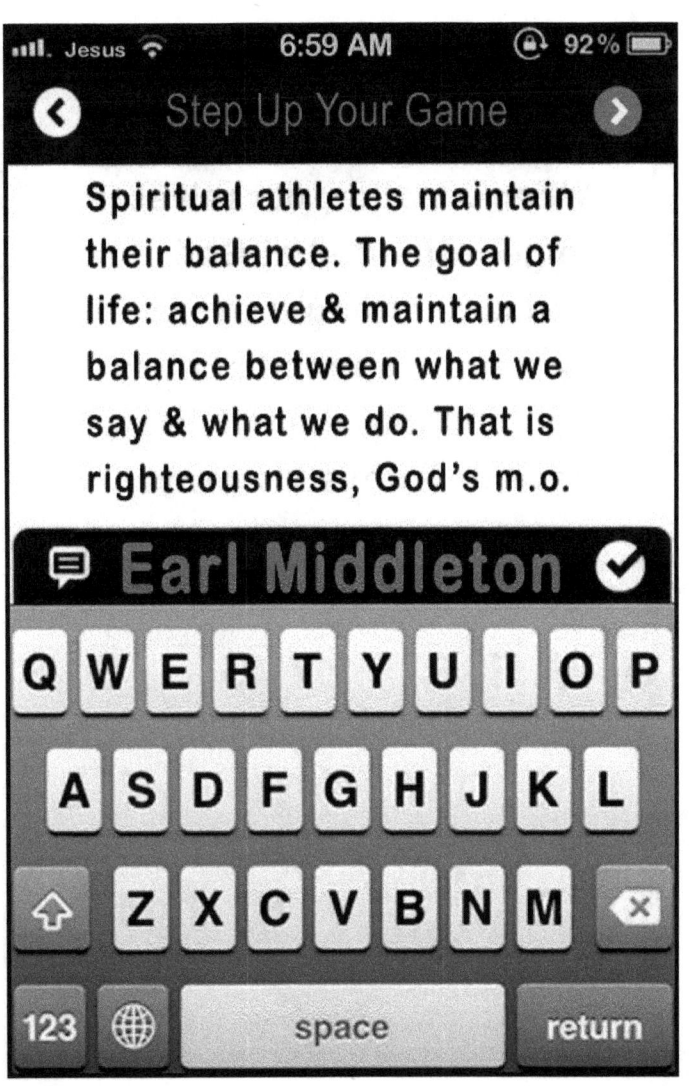

**Step Up Your Game**

Spiritual athletes maintain their balance. The goal of life: achieve & maintain a balance between what we say & what we do. That is righteousness, God's m.o.

Earl Middleton

# October 16

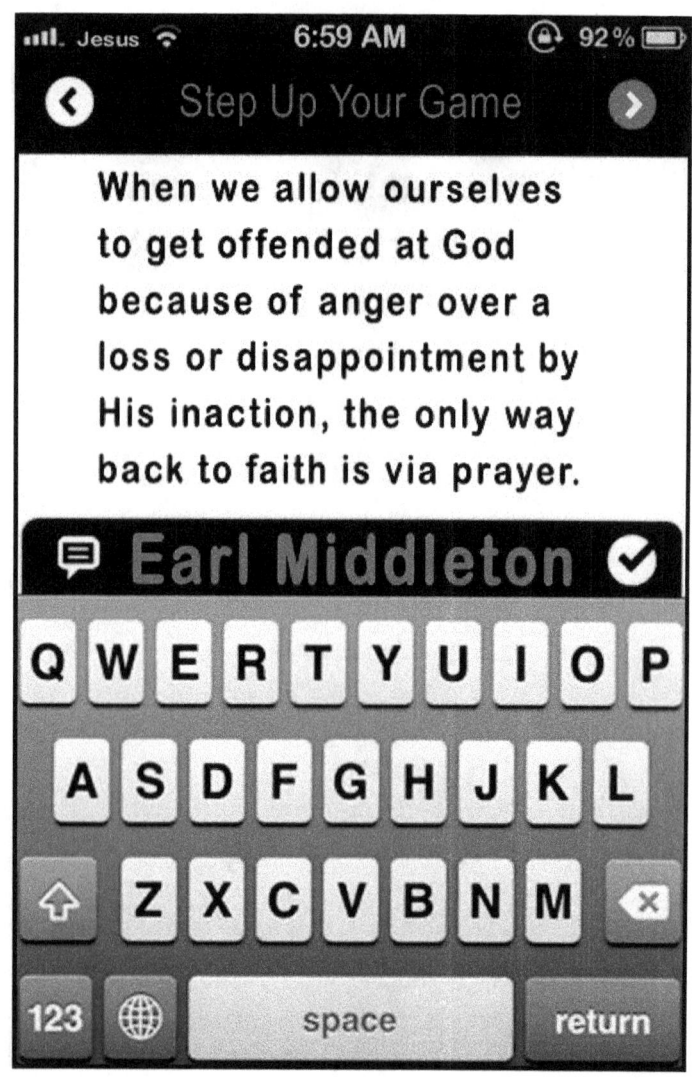

# October 17

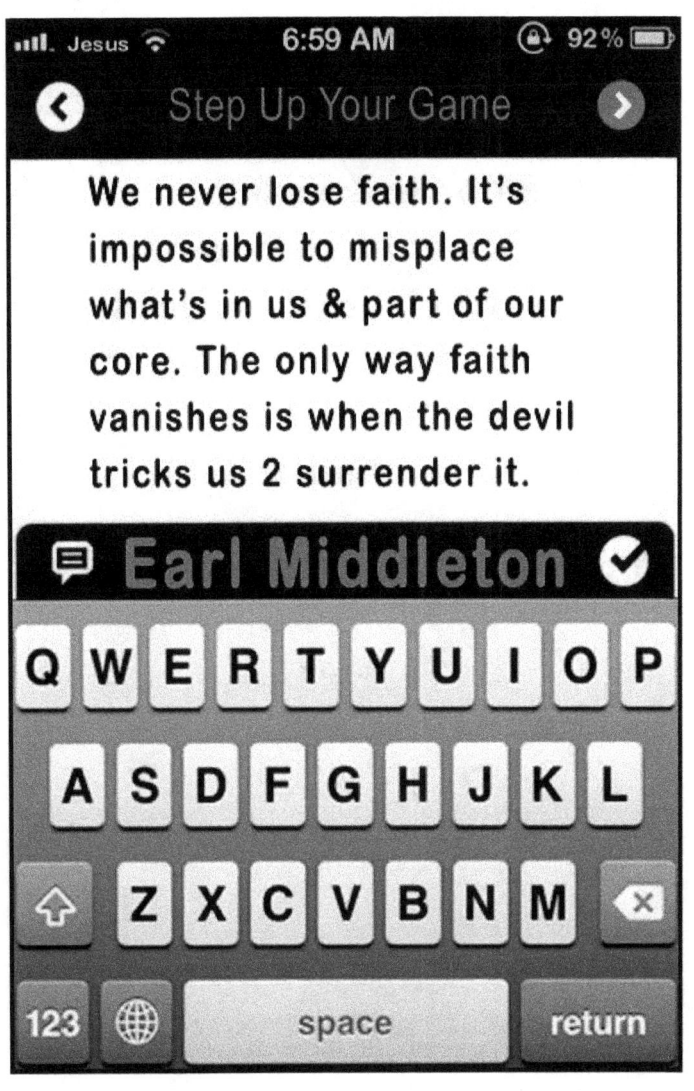

We never lose faith. It's impossible to misplace what's in us & part of our core. The only way faith vanishes is when the devil tricks us 2 surrender it.

— Earl Middleton

# October 18

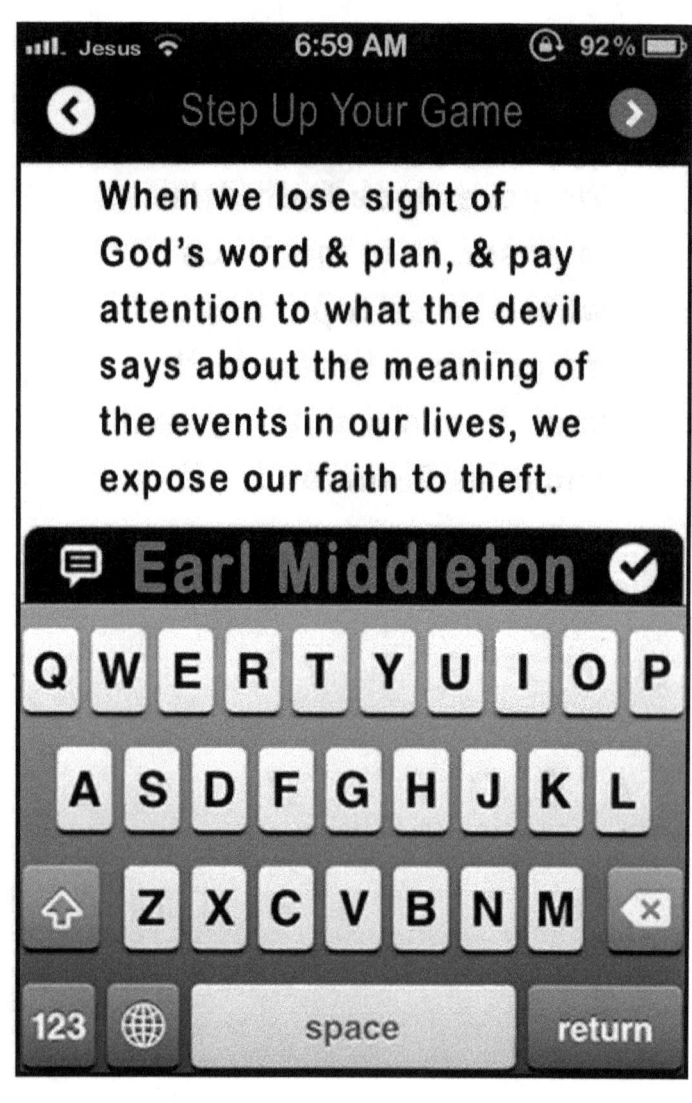

**Step Up Your Game**

When we lose sight of God's word & plan, & pay attention to what the devil says about the meaning of the events in our lives, we expose our faith to theft.

Earl Middleton

# October 19

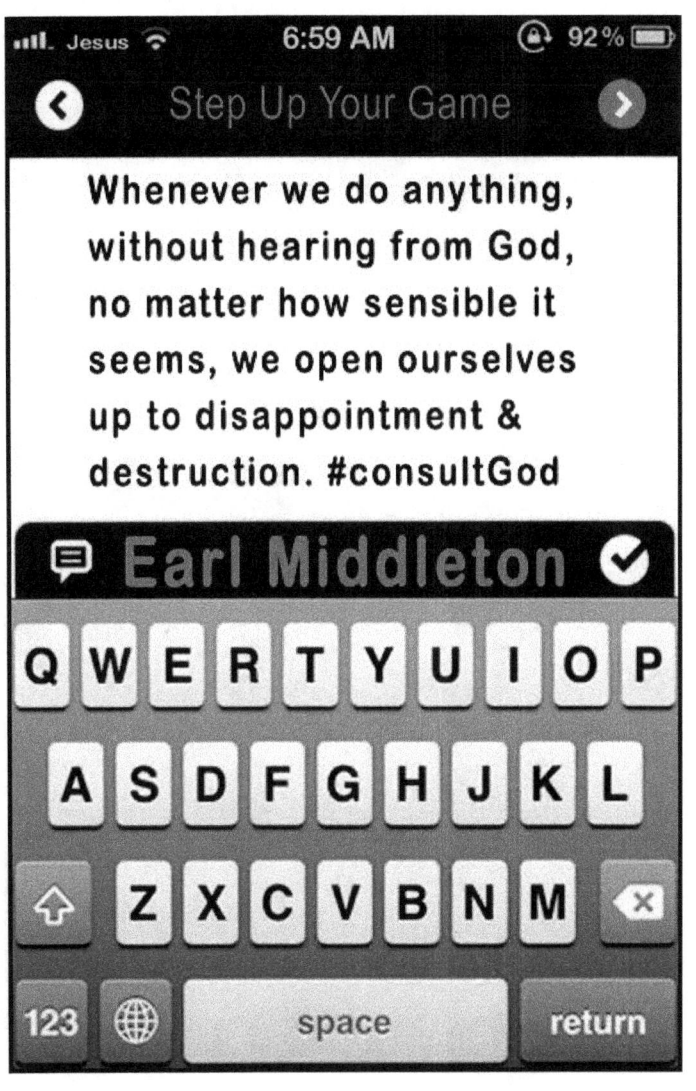

Whenever we do anything, without hearing from God, no matter how sensible it seems, we open ourselves up to disappointment & destruction. #consultGod

# October 20

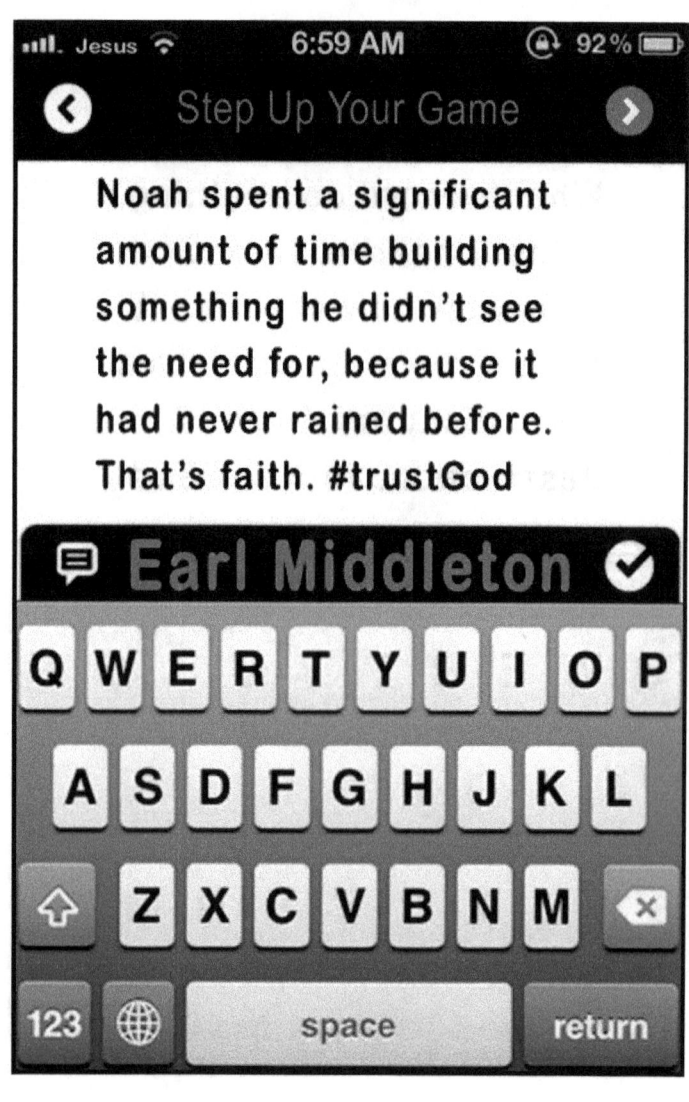

# October 21

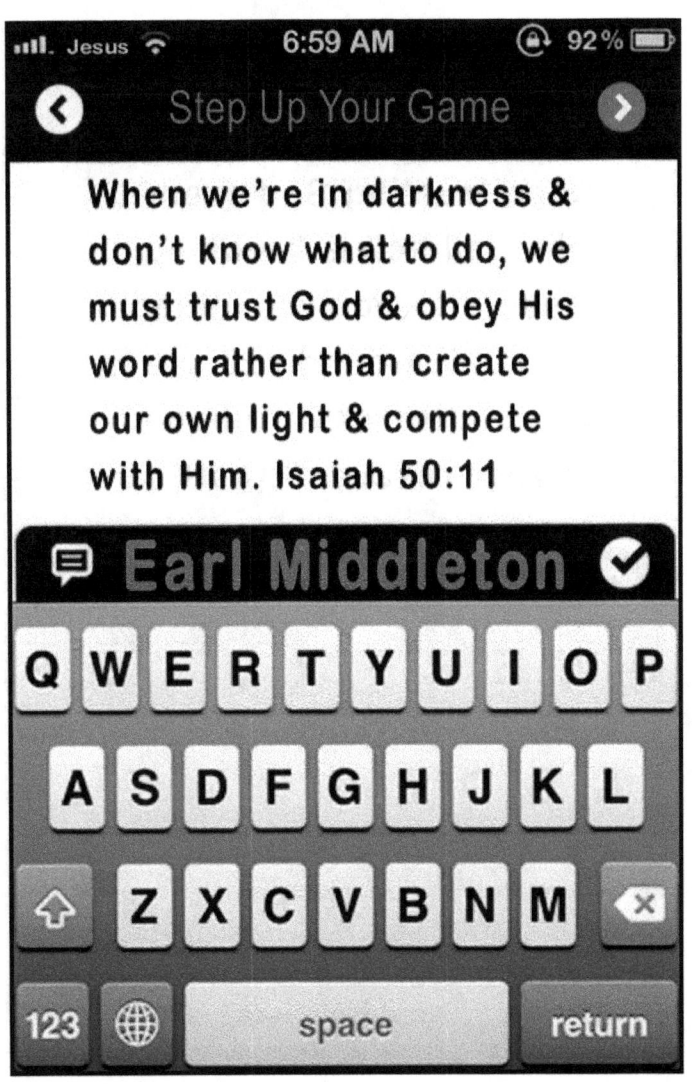

When we're in darkness & don't know what to do, we must trust God & obey His word rather than create our own light & compete with Him. Isaiah 50:11

— Earl Middleton

# October 22

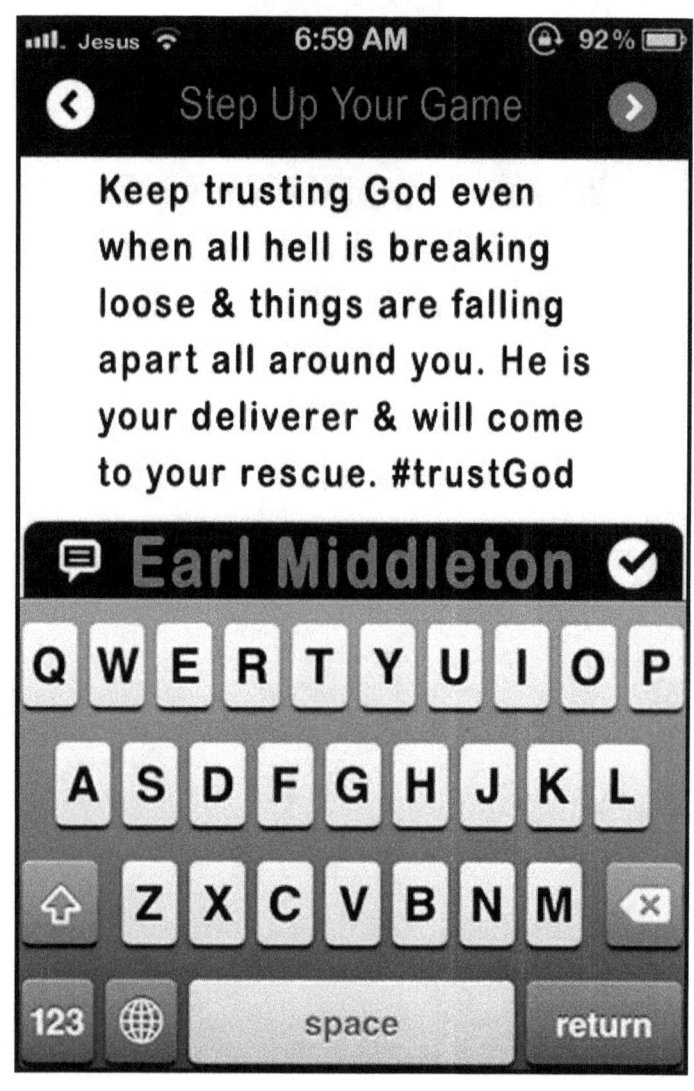

# October 23

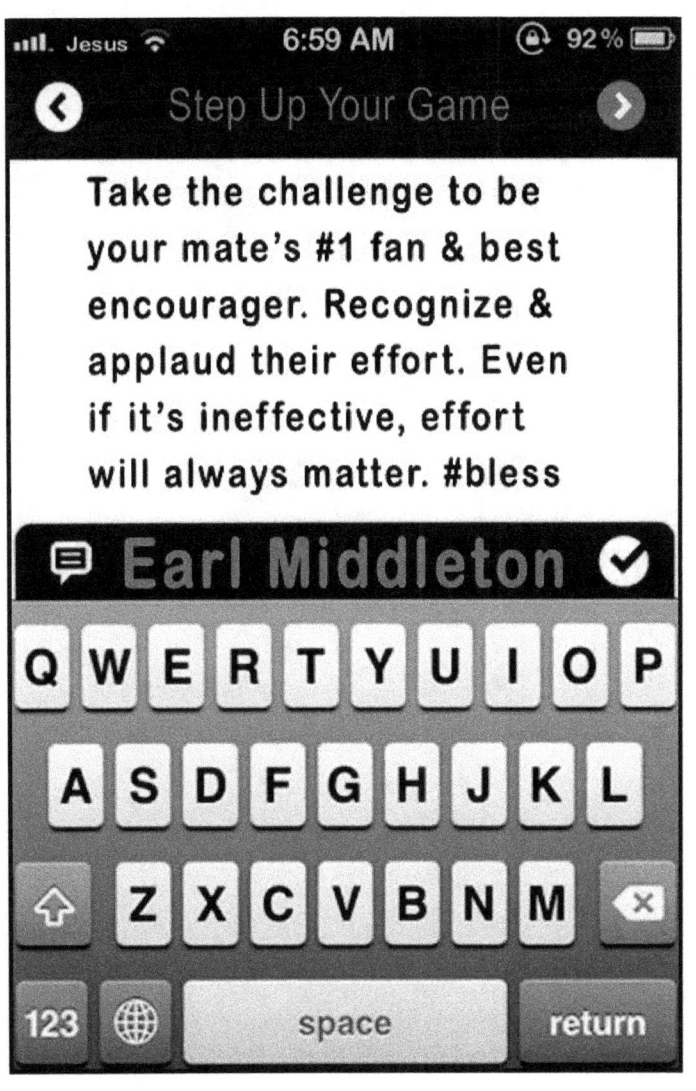

# October 24

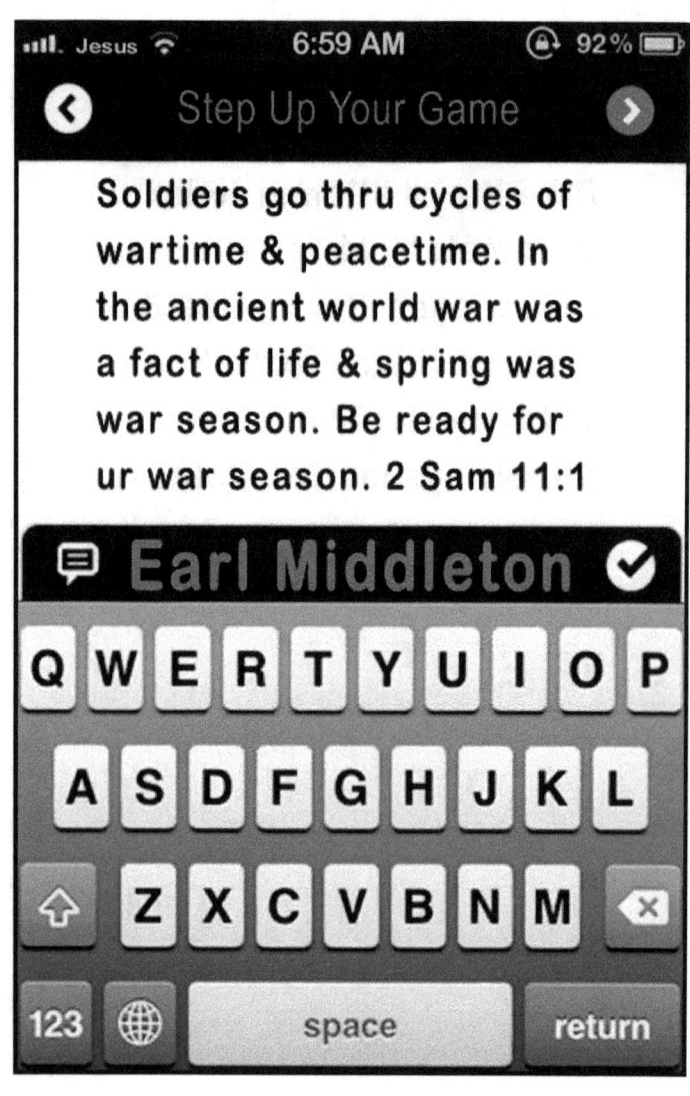

**Step Up Your Game**

Soldiers go thru cycles of wartime & peacetime. In the ancient world war was a fact of life & spring was war season. Be ready for ur war season. 2 Sam 11:1

Earl Middleton

# October 25

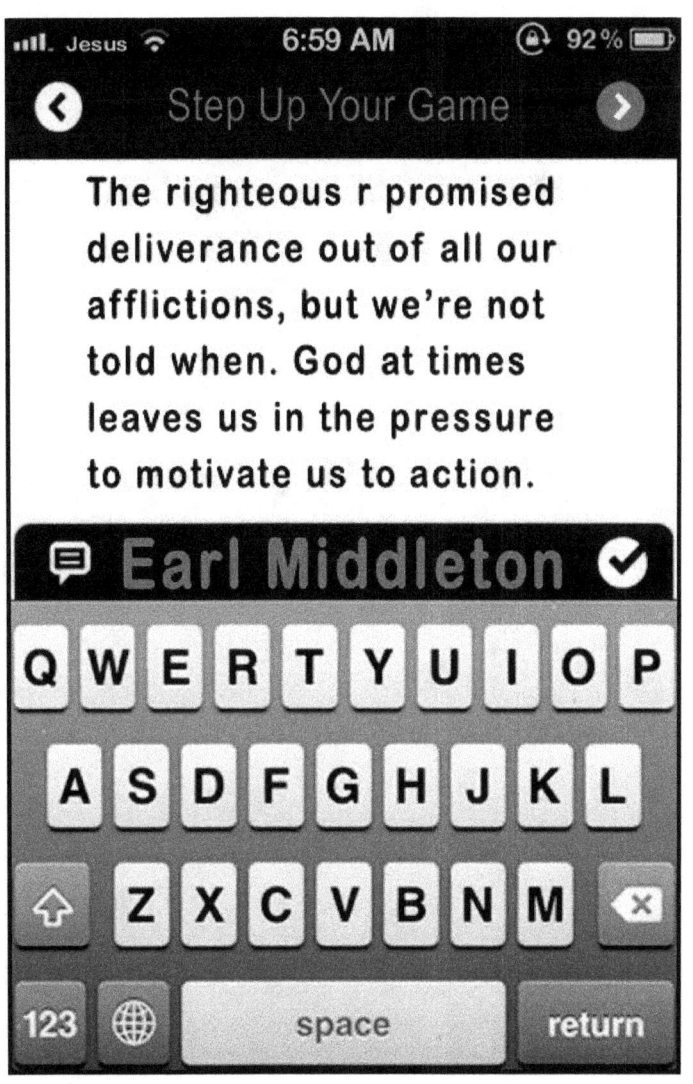

# October 26

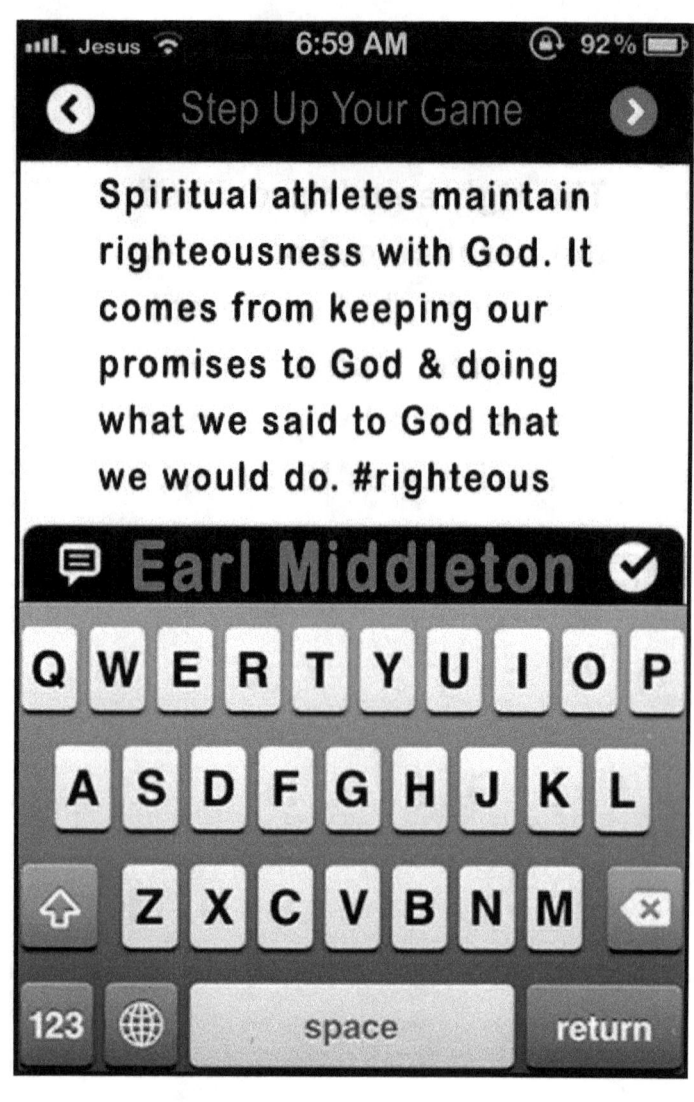

**Step Up Your Game**

Spiritual athletes maintain righteousness with God. It comes from keeping our promises to God & doing what we said to God that we would do. #righteous

Earl Middleton

# October 27

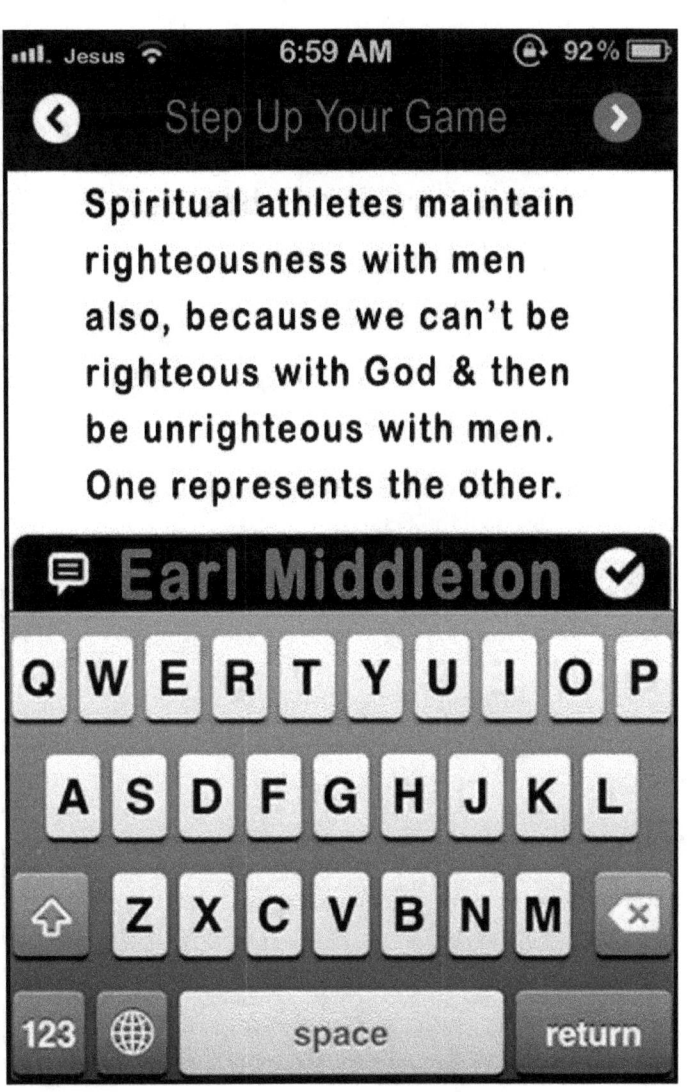

## Step Up Your Game

Spiritual athletes maintain righteousness with men also, because we can't be righteous with God & then be unrighteous with men. One represents the other.

— Earl Middleton

# October 28

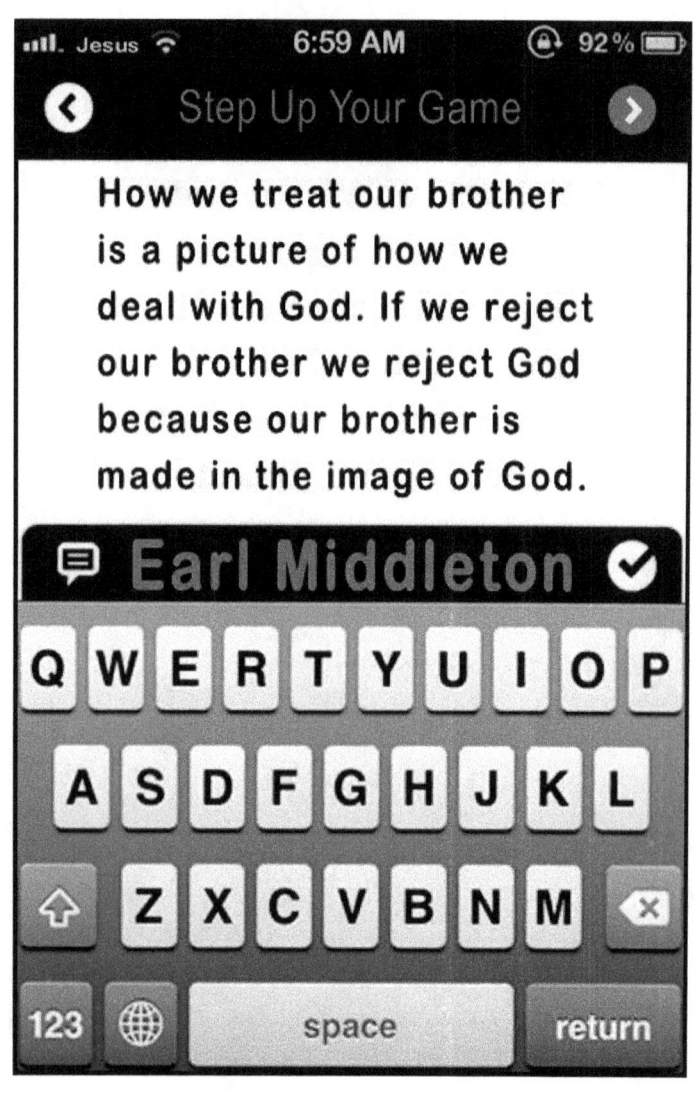

How we treat our brother is a picture of how we deal with God. If we reject our brother we reject God because our brother is made in the image of God.

Earl Middleton

# October 29

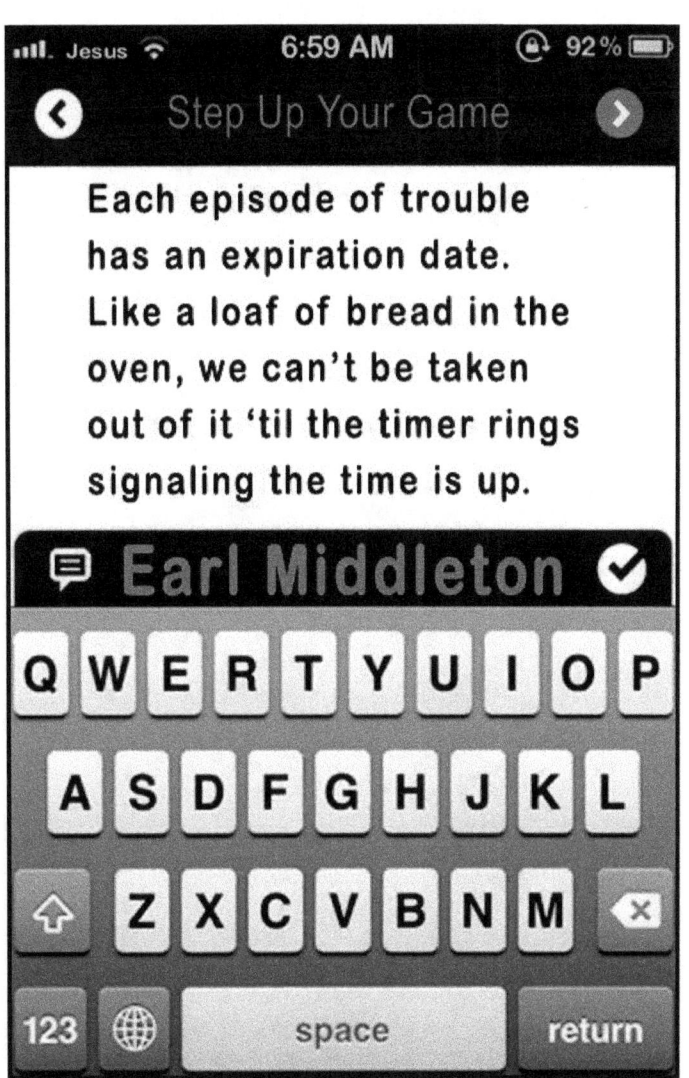

Each episode of trouble has an expiration date. Like a loaf of bread in the oven, we can't be taken out of it 'til the timer rings signaling the time is up.

Earl Middleton

# October 30

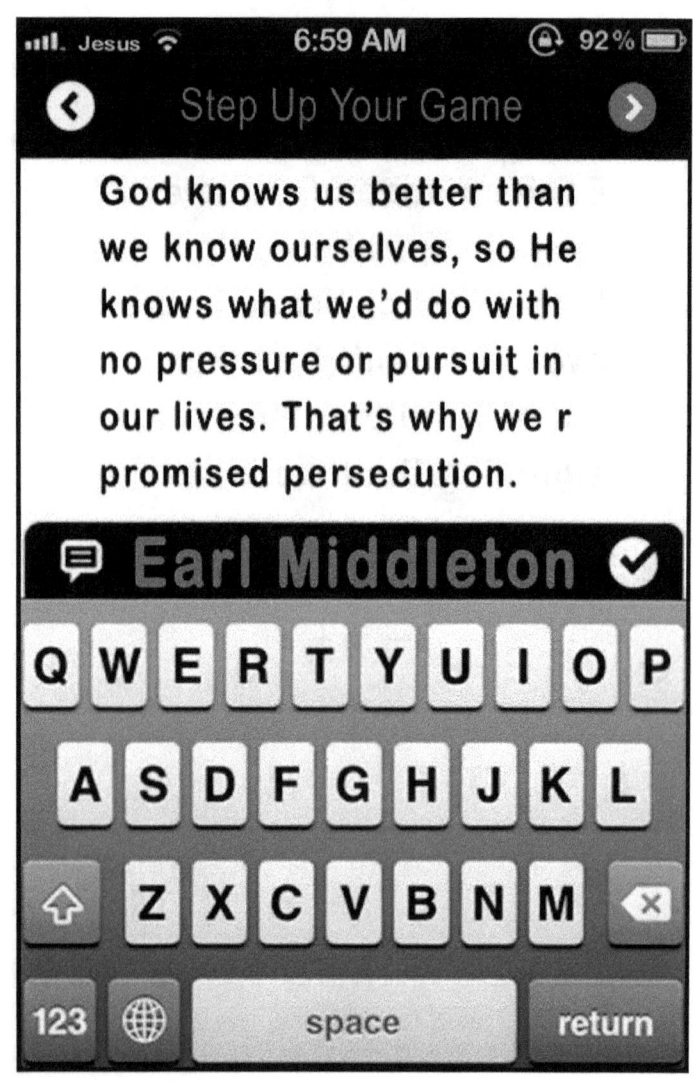

# October 31

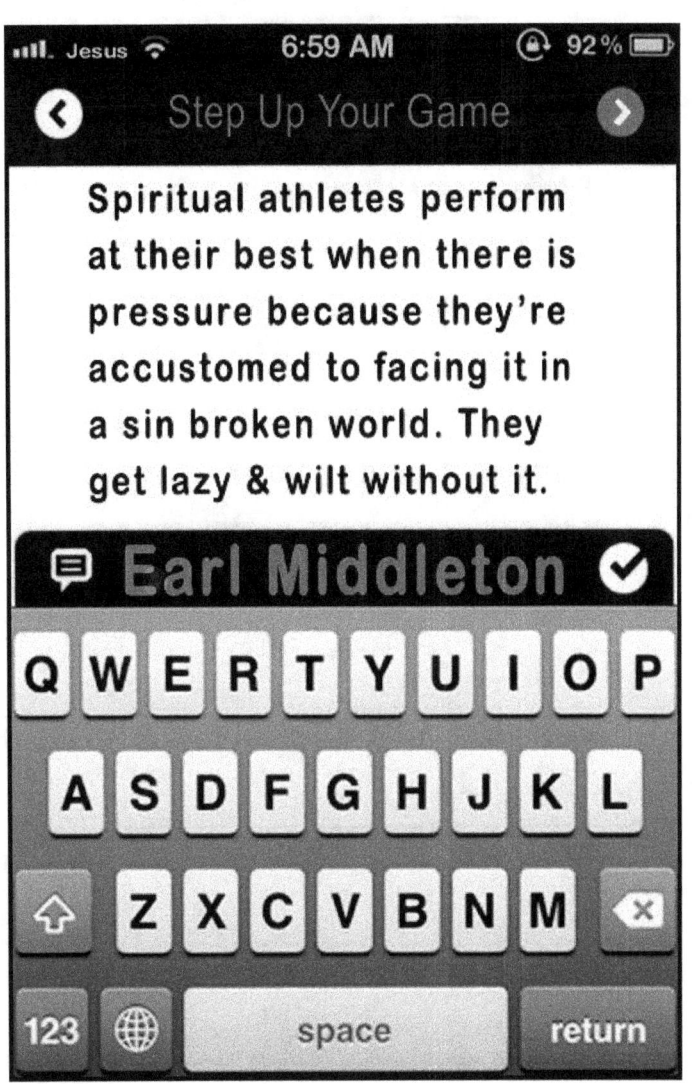

# November 1

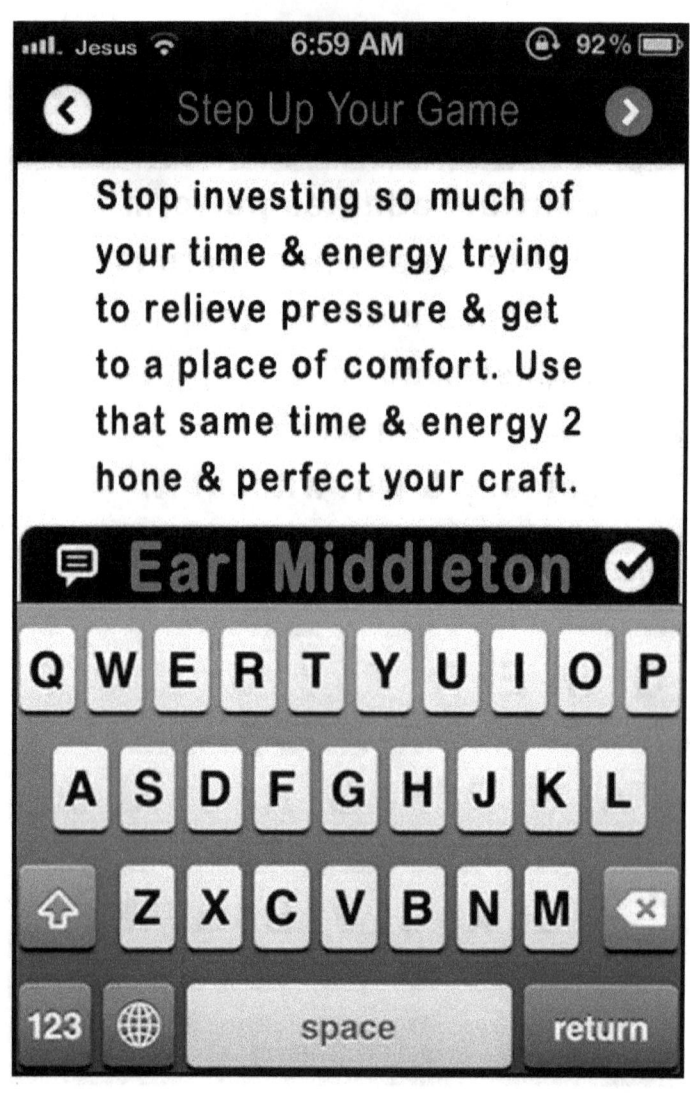

**Step Up Your Game**

Stop investing so much of your time & energy trying to relieve pressure & get to a place of comfort. Use that same time & energy 2 hone & perfect your craft.

Earl Middleton

# November 2

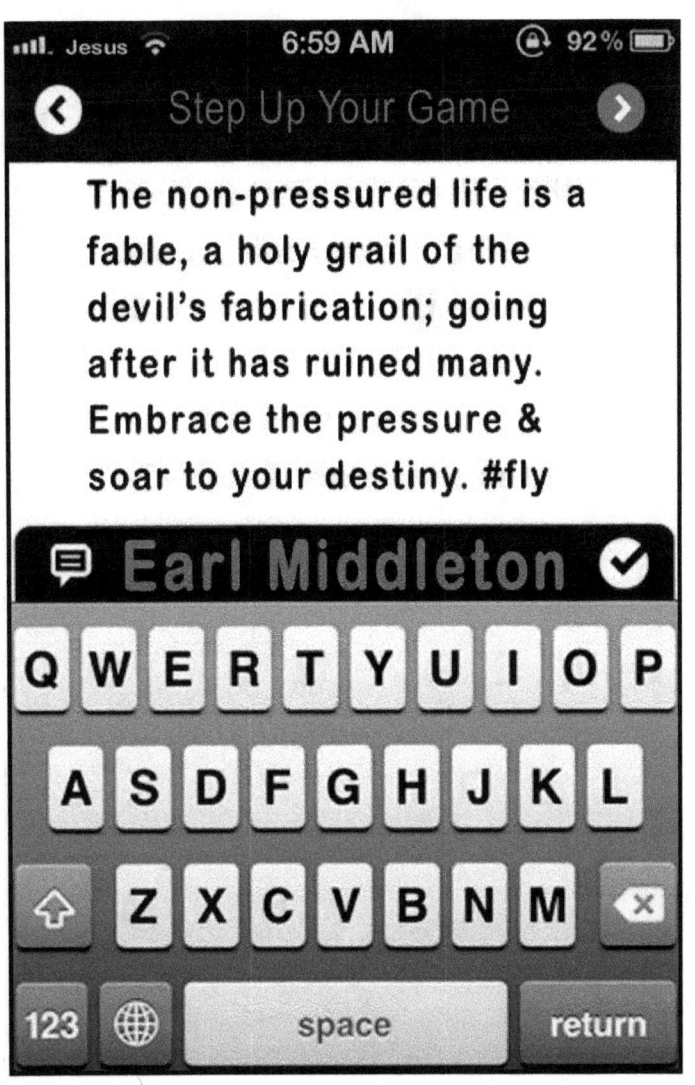

# November 3

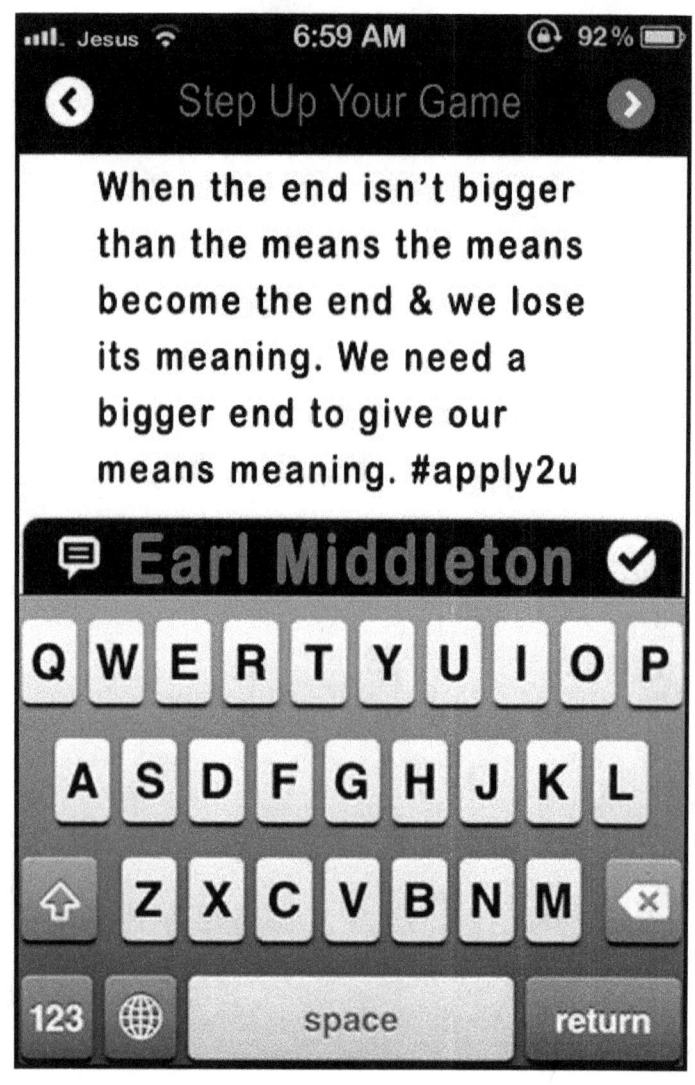

When the end isn't bigger than the means the means become the end & we lose its meaning. We need a bigger end to give our means meaning. #apply2u

— Earl Middleton

# November 4

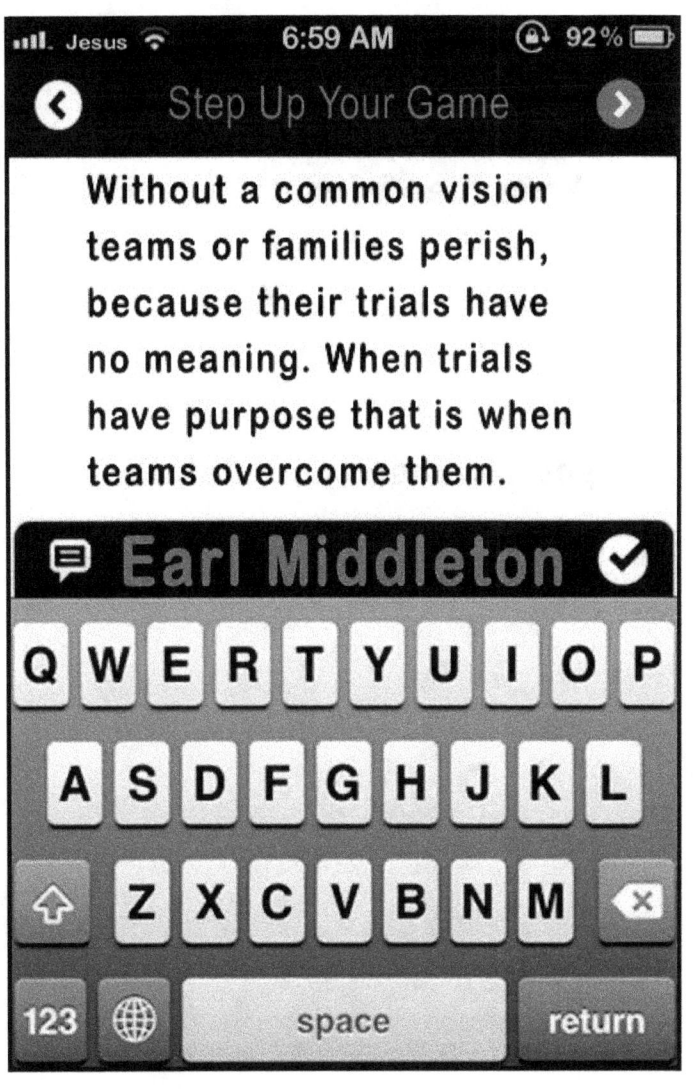

Without a common vision teams or families perish, because their trials have no meaning. When trials have purpose that is when teams overcome them.

Earl Middleton

# November 5

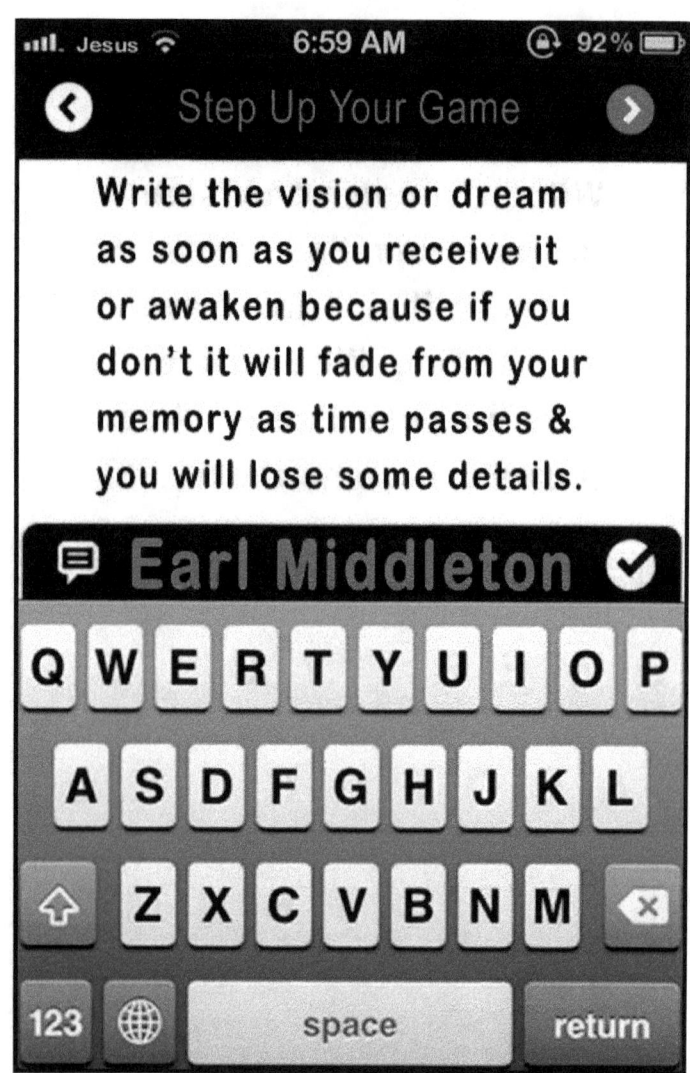

> Write the vision or dream as soon as you receive it or awaken because if you don't it will fade from your memory as time passes & you will lose some details.

# November 6

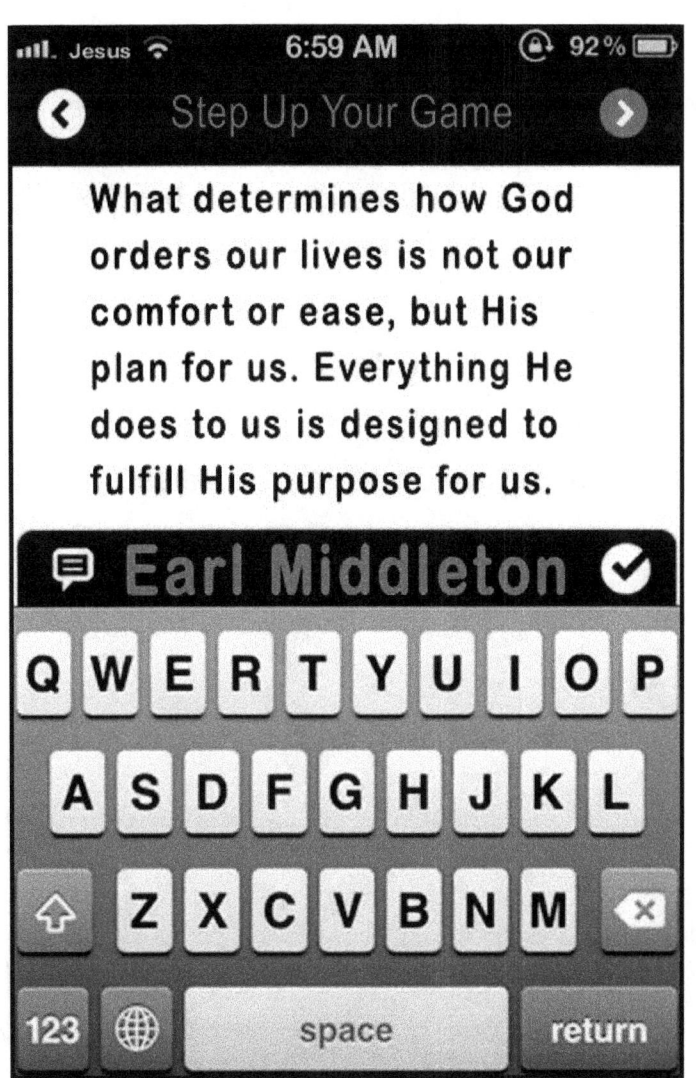

What determines how God orders our lives is not our comfort or ease, but His plan for us. Everything He does to us is designed to fulfill His purpose for us.

Earl Middleton

# November 7

## Step Up Your Game

If your vision is only about your comfort it's YOUR's, not God's. God's vision is about Kingdom purpose fulfillment, heroic mission completion, & met needs.

— Earl Middleton

# November 8

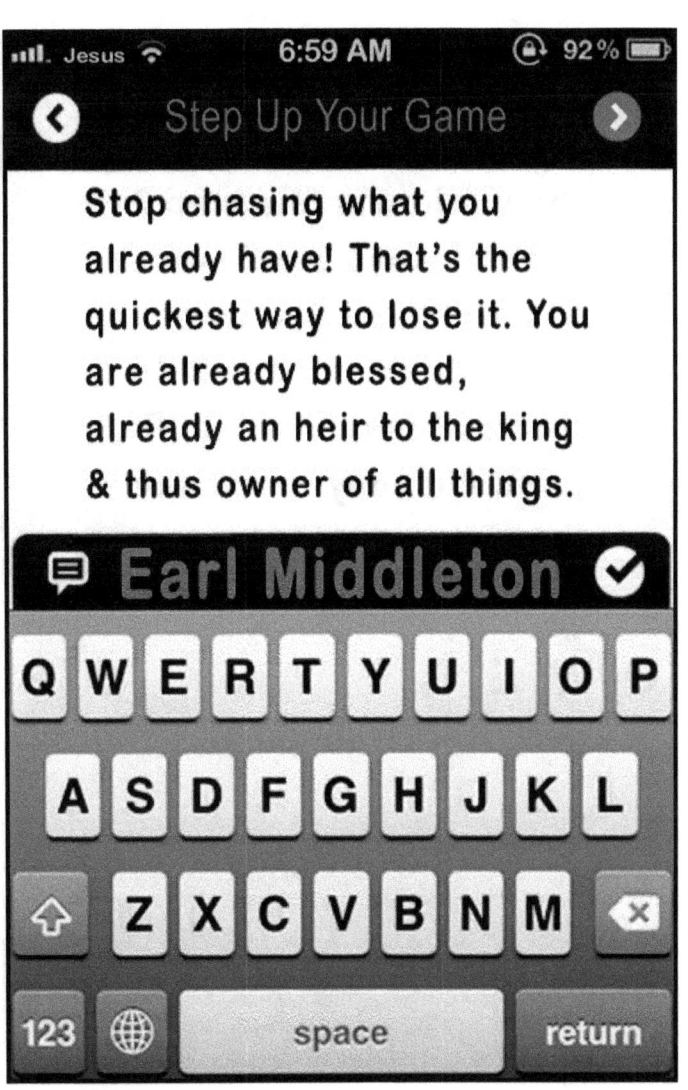

# November 9

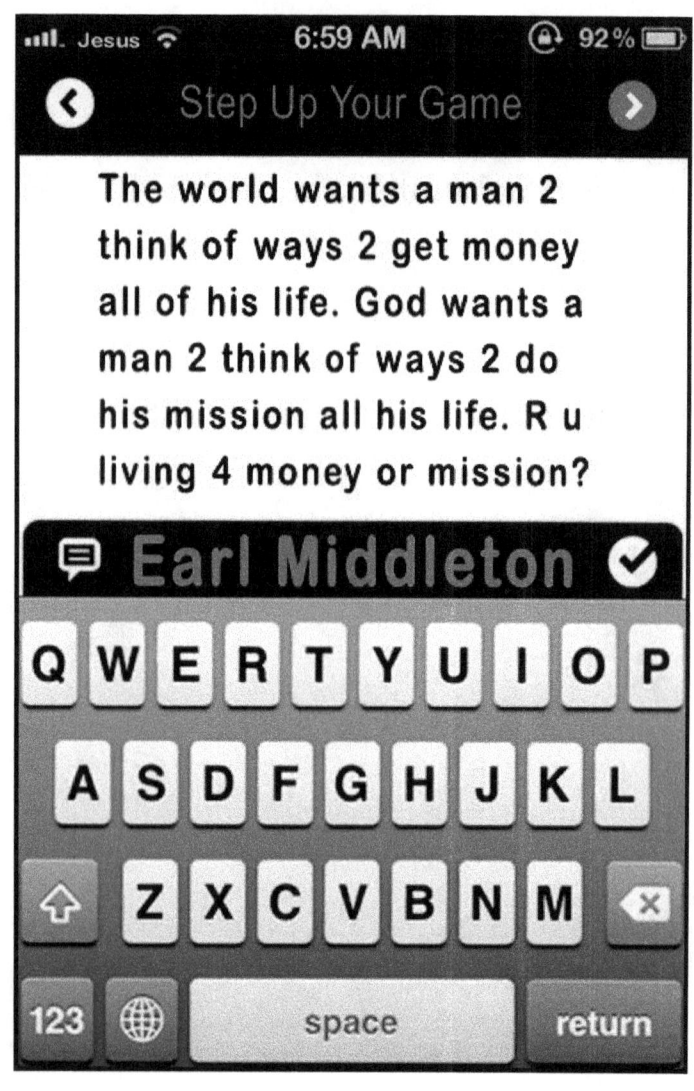

# November 10

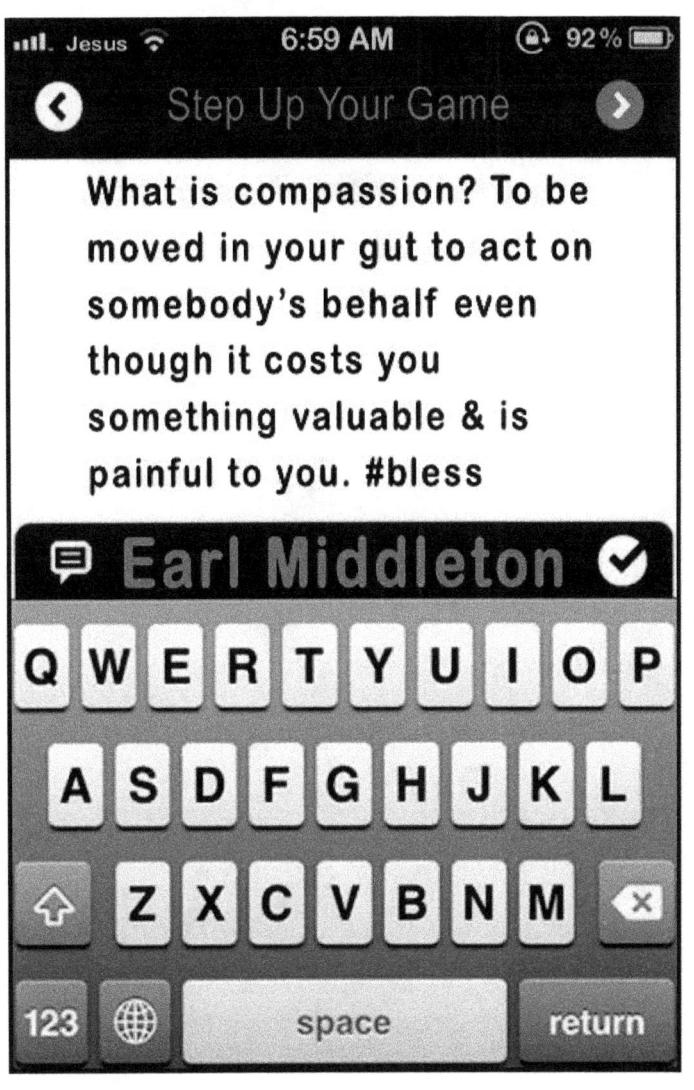

What is compassion? To be moved in your gut to act on somebody's behalf even though it costs you something valuable & is painful to you. #bless

# November 11

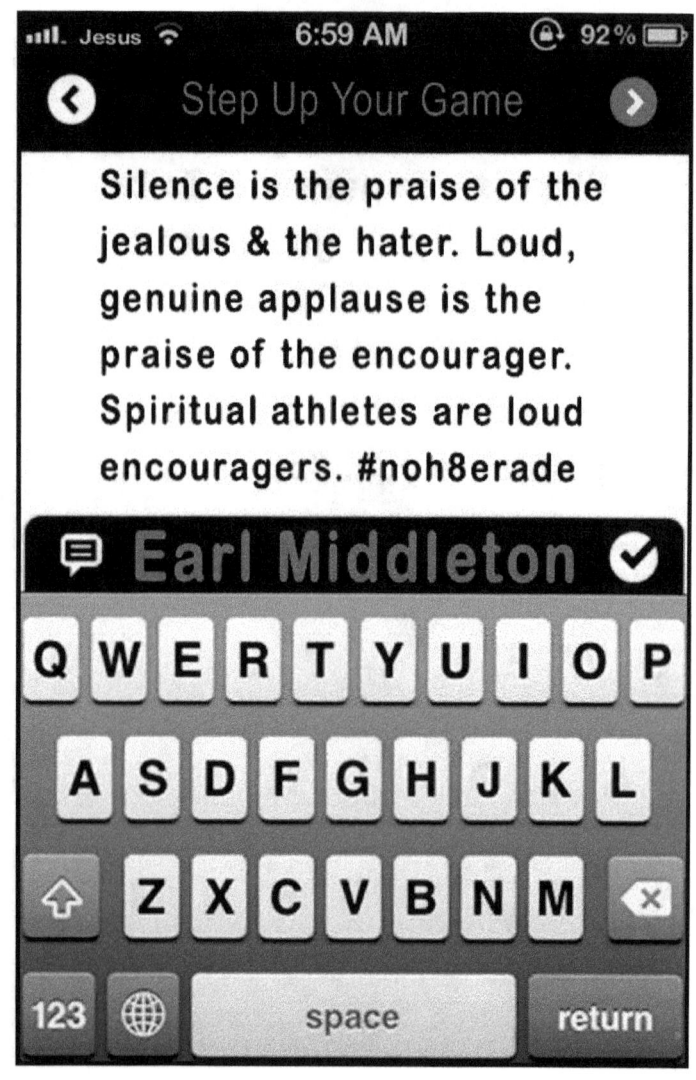

**Step Up Your Game**

Silence is the praise of the jealous & the hater. Loud, genuine applause is the praise of the encourager. Spiritual athletes are loud encouragers. #noh8erade

Earl Middleton

# November 12

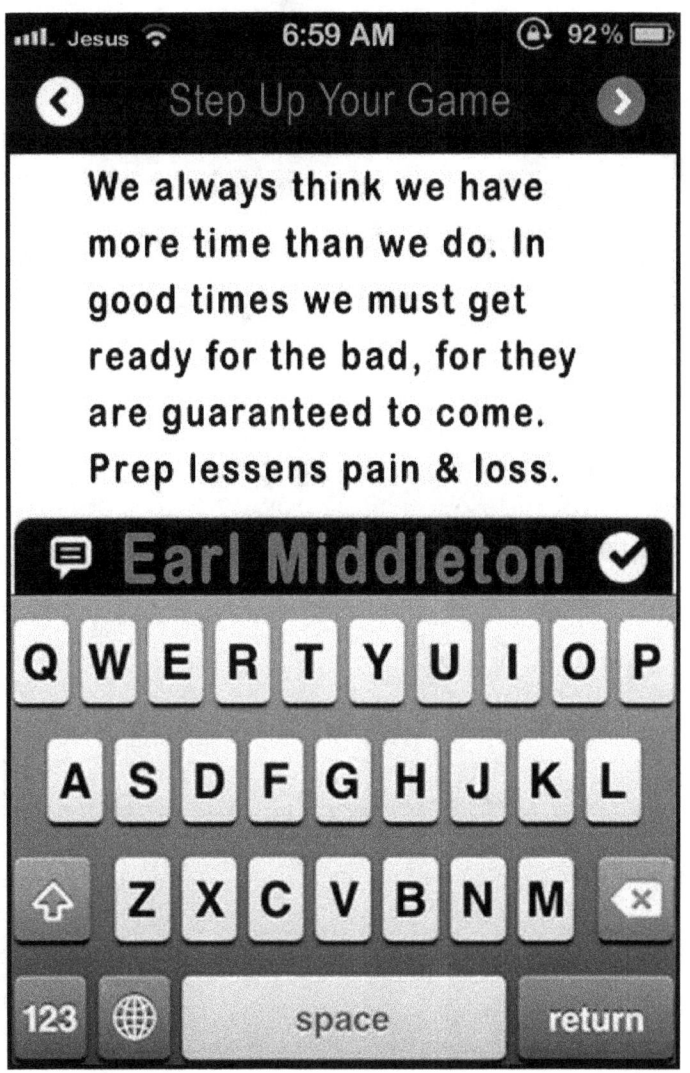

# November 13

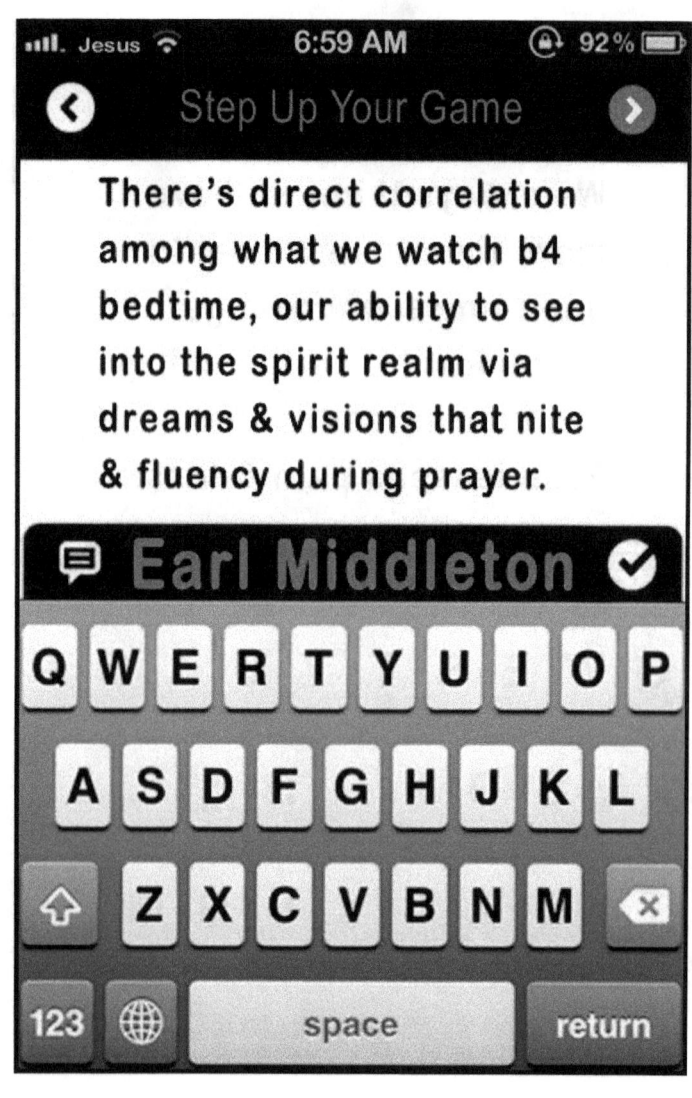

> There's direct correlation among what we watch b4 bedtime, our ability to see into the spirit realm via dreams & visions that nite & fluency during prayer.
>
> — Earl Middleton

# November 14

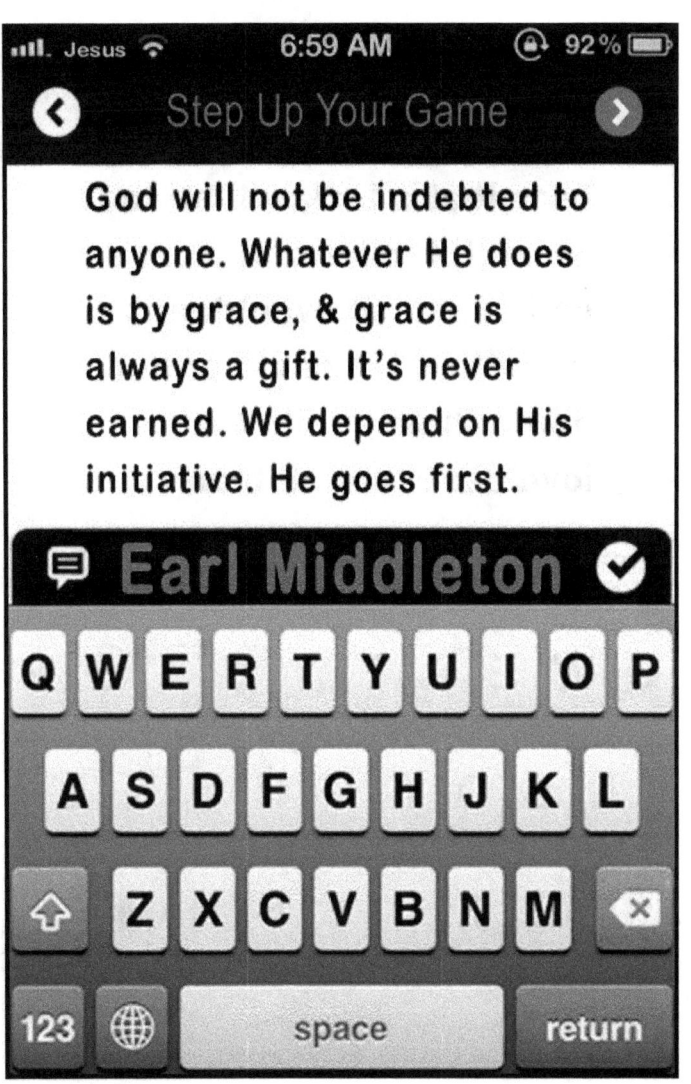

**Step Up Your Game**

God will not be indebted to anyone. Whatever He does is by grace, & grace is always a gift. It's never earned. We depend on His initiative. He goes first.

— Earl Middleton

# November 15

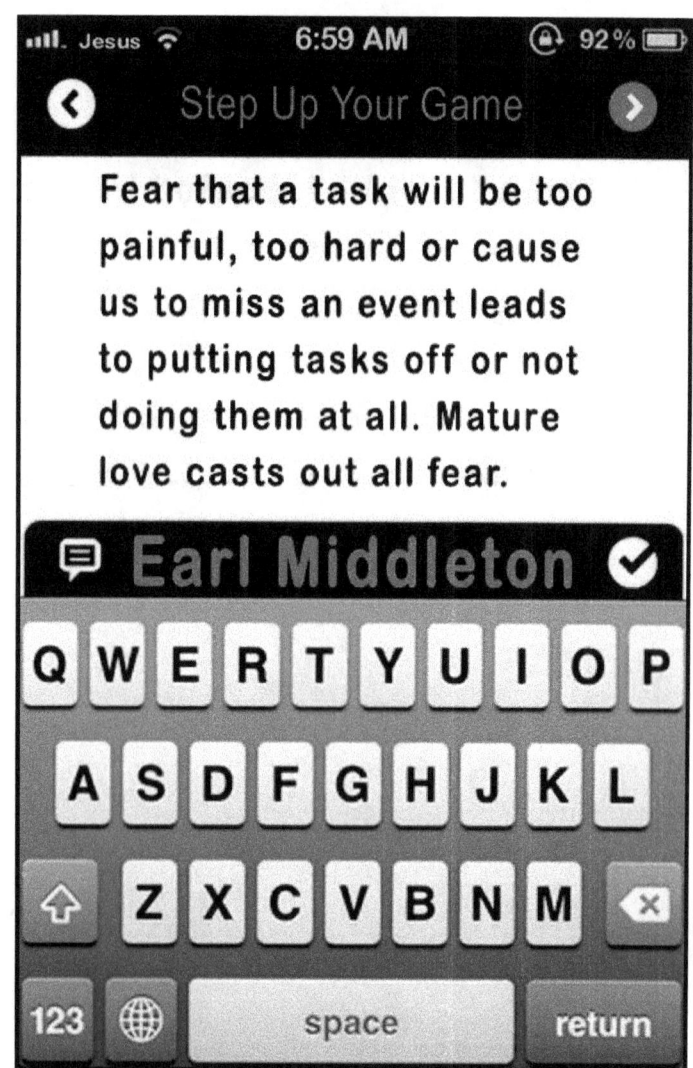

# November 16

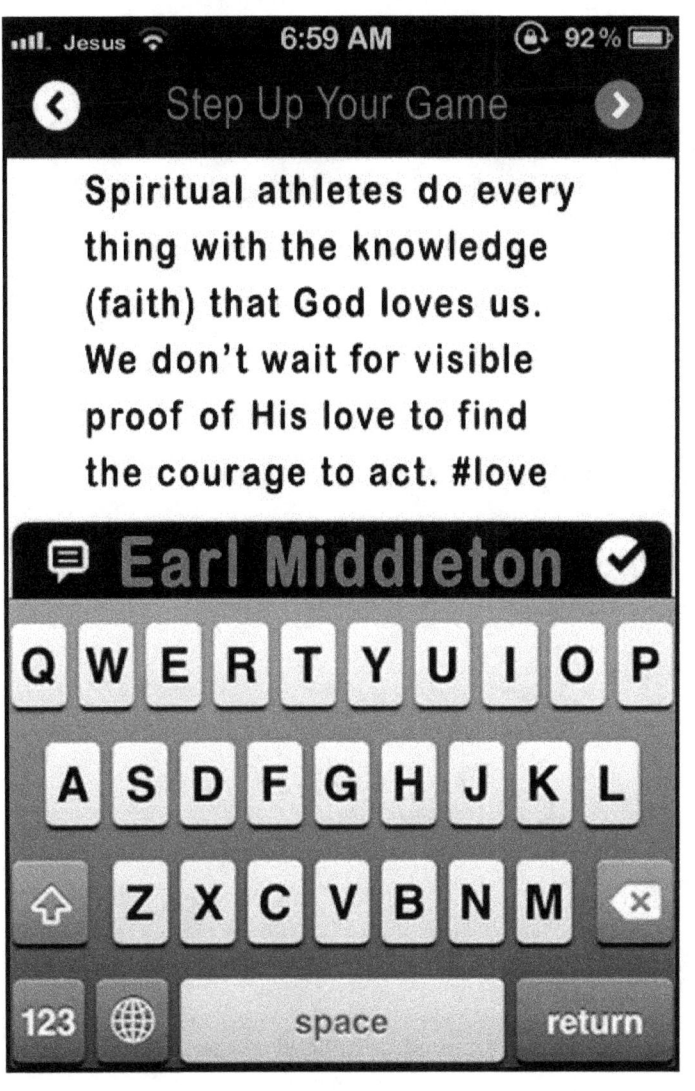

## Step Up Your Game

Spiritual athletes do every thing with the knowledge (faith) that God loves us. We don't wait for visible proof of His love to find the courage to act. #love

Earl Middleton

# November 17

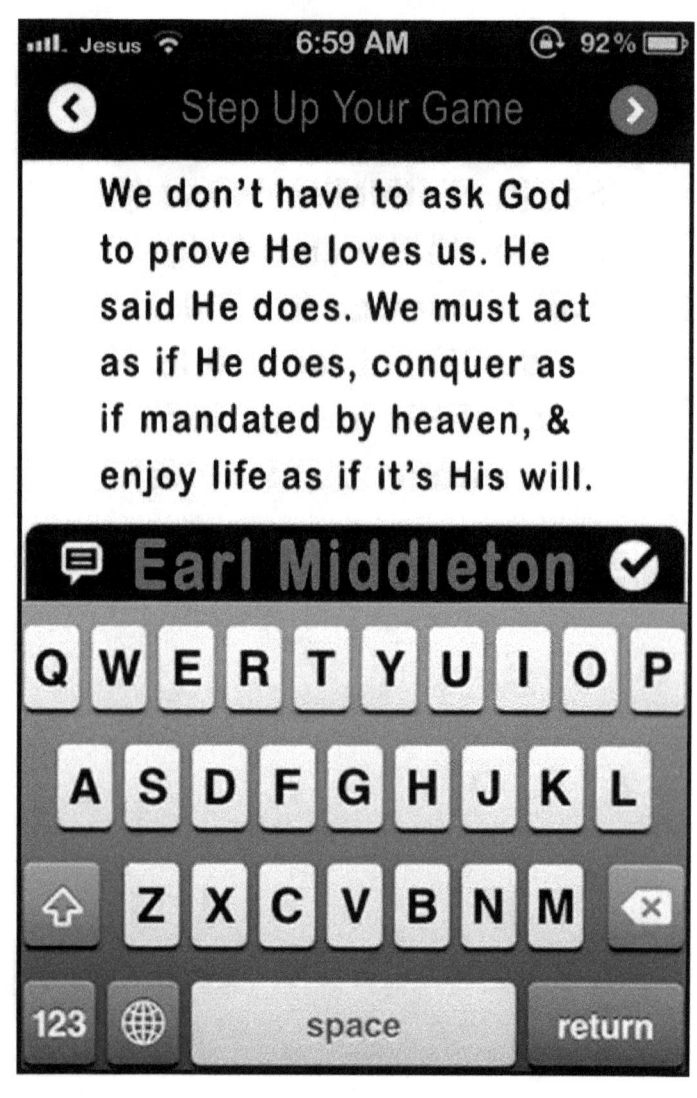

We don't have to ask God to prove He loves us. He said He does. We must act as if He does, conquer as if mandated by heaven, & enjoy life as if it's His will.

# November 18

God waits to open doors until we are ready to walk thru them, or else a thief could slip in thru our door. Ur door is just 4 u & opens only when ur time comes.

Earl Middleton

# November 19

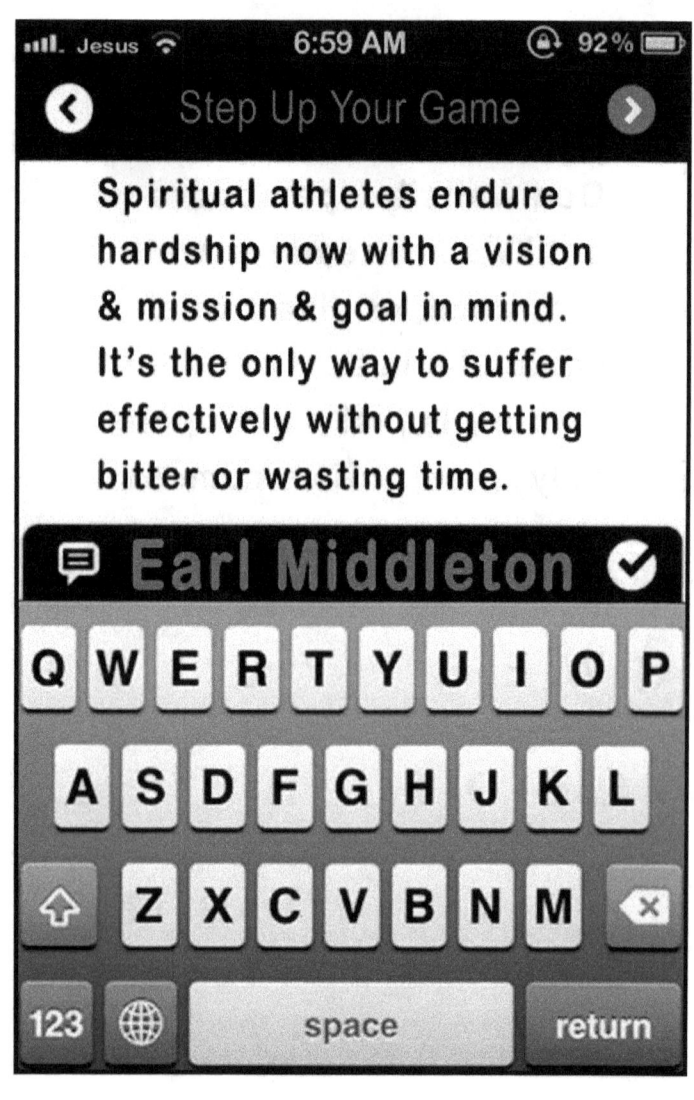

**Step Up Your Game**

Spiritual athletes endure hardship now with a vision & mission & goal in mind. It's the only way to suffer effectively without getting bitter or wasting time.

Earl Middleton

# November 20

# November 21

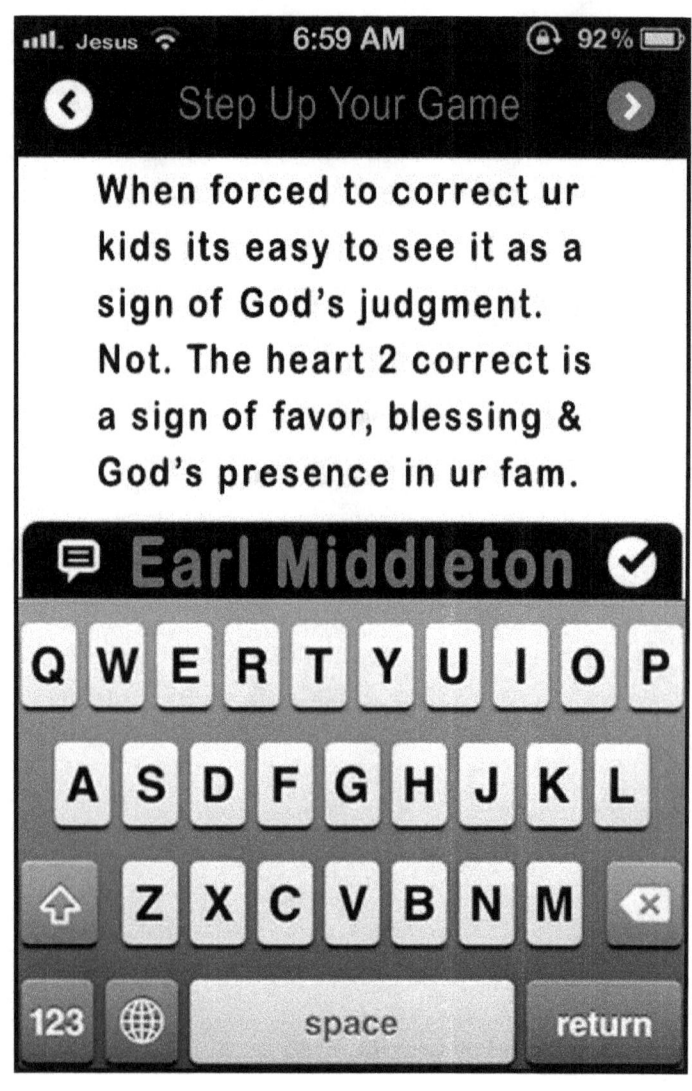

When forced to correct ur kids its easy to see it as a sign of God's judgment. Not. The heart 2 correct is a sign of favor, blessing & God's presence in ur fam.

# November 22

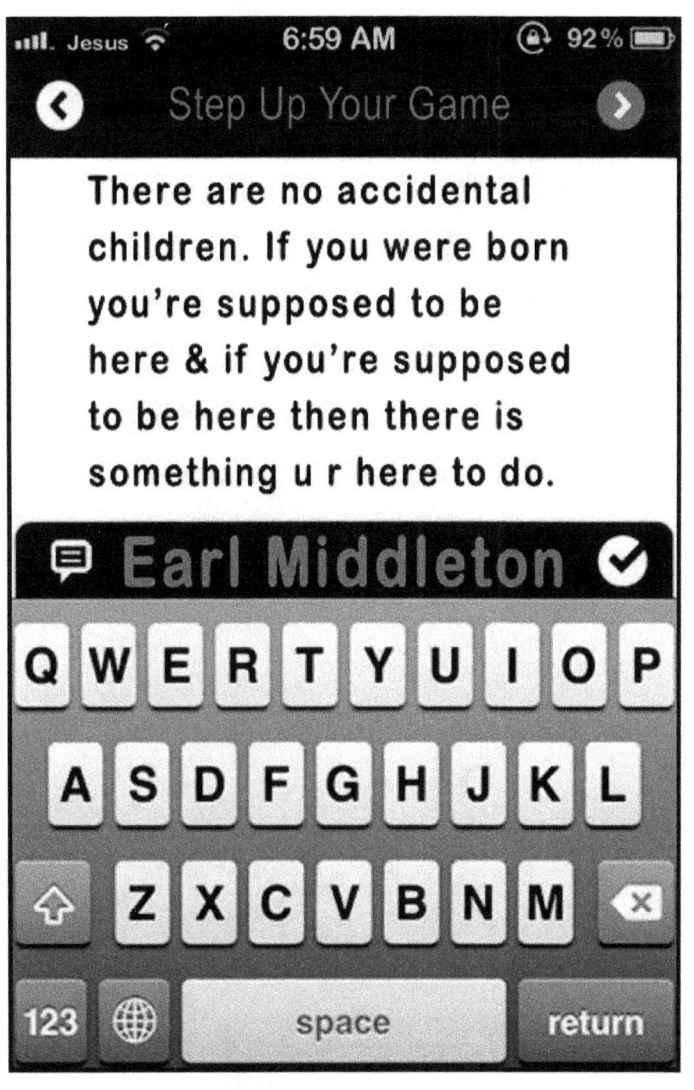

# November 23

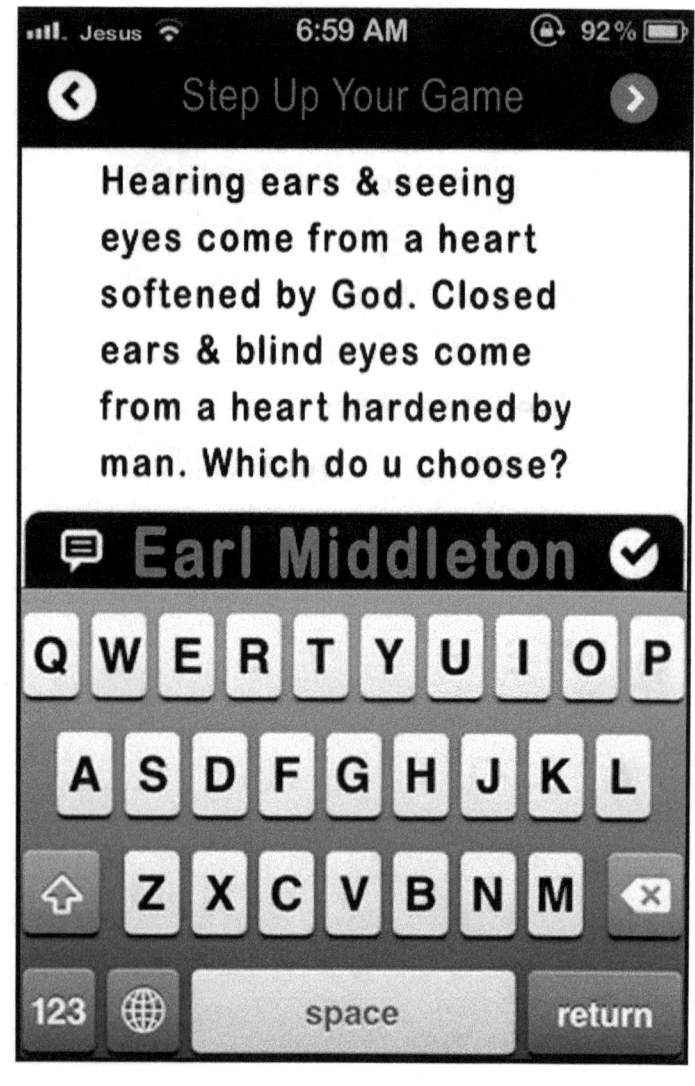

# November 24

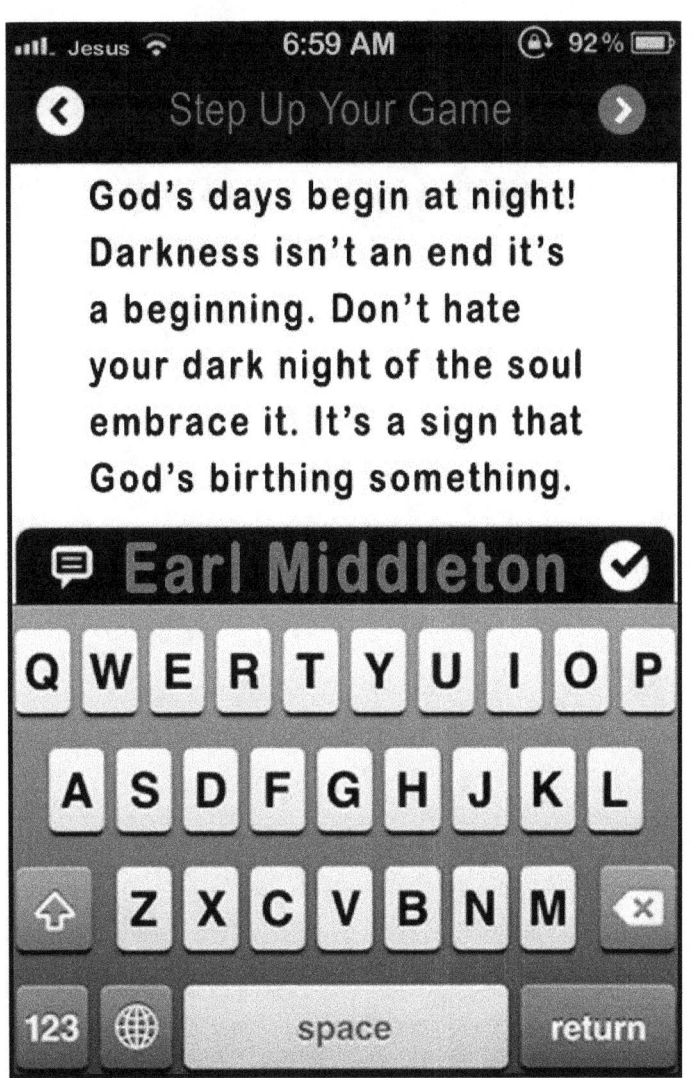

# November 25

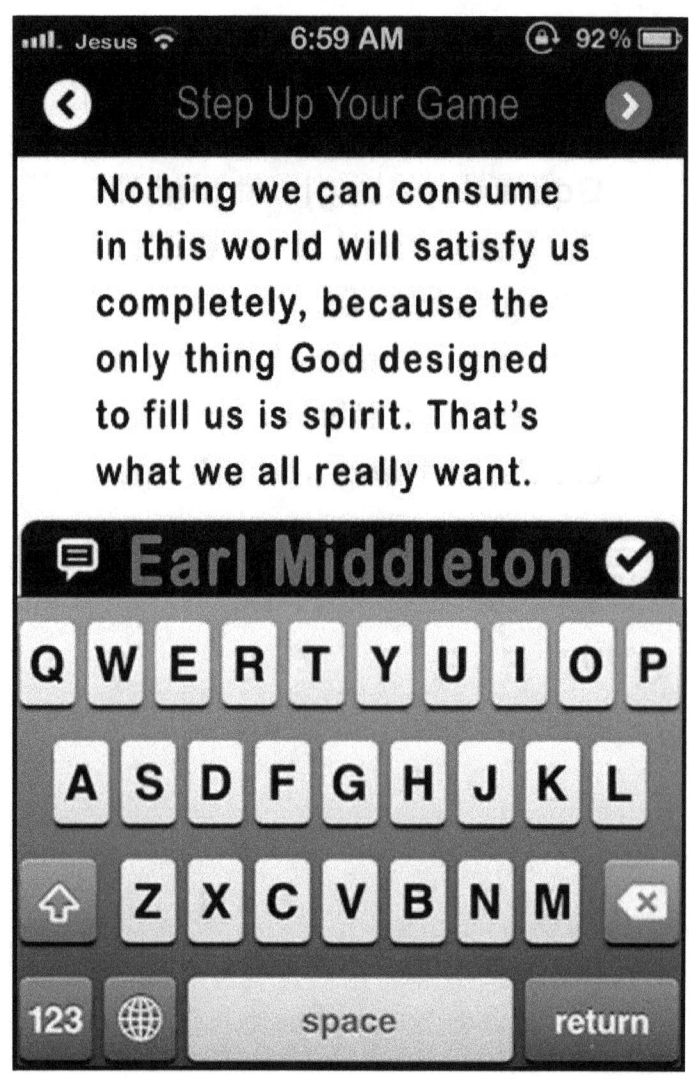

Nothing we can consume in this world will satisfy us completely, because the only thing God designed to fill us is spirit. That's what we all really want.

# November 26

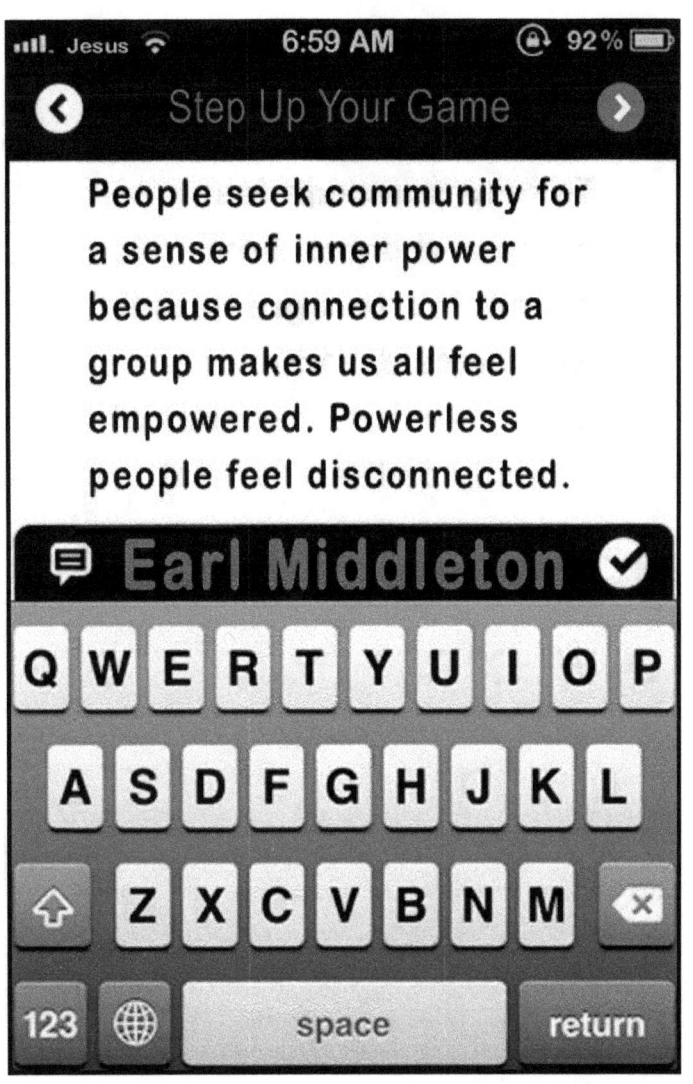

# November 27

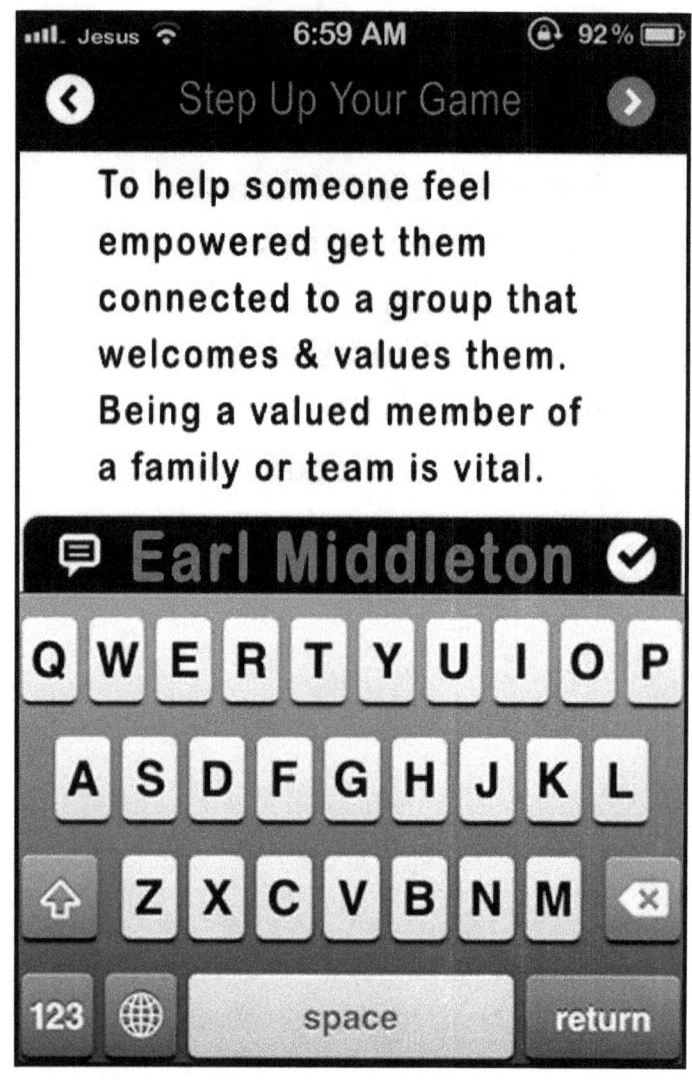

## Step Up Your Game

To help someone feel empowered get them connected to a group that welcomes & values them. Being a valued member of a family or team is vital.

Earl Middleton

# November 28

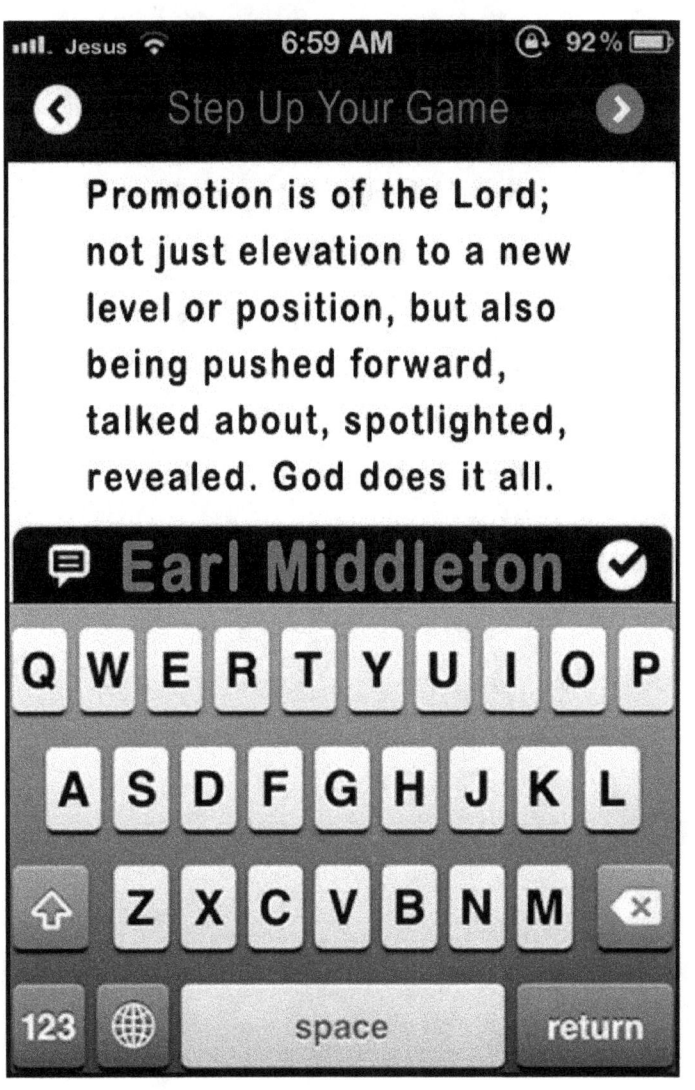

## Step Up Your Game

Promotion is of the Lord; not just elevation to a new level or position, but also being pushed forward, talked about, spotlighted, revealed. God does it all.

Earl Middleton

# November 29

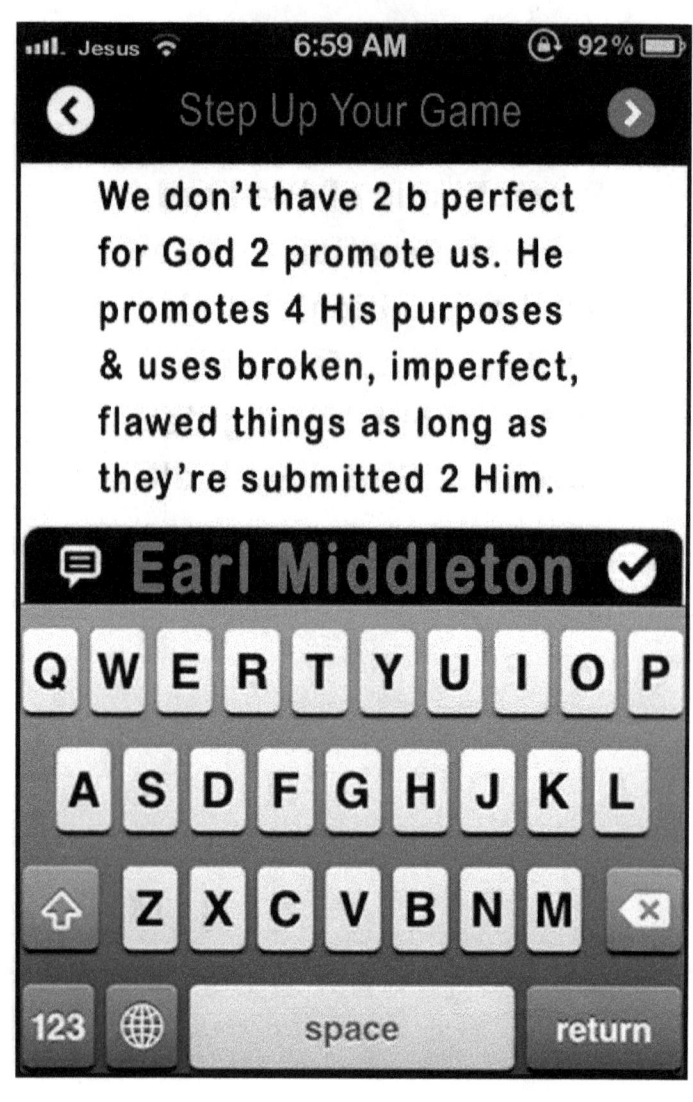

**Step Up Your Game**

We don't have 2 b perfect for God 2 promote us. He promotes 4 His purposes & uses broken, imperfect, flawed things as long as they're submitted 2 Him.

— Earl Middleton

# November 30

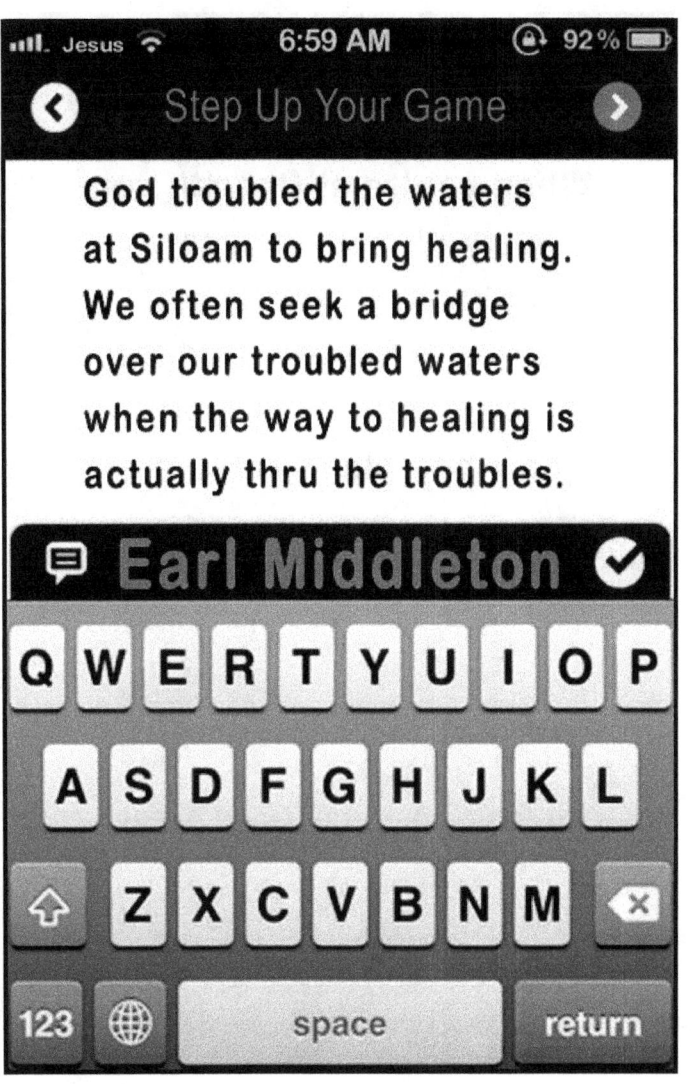

# December 1

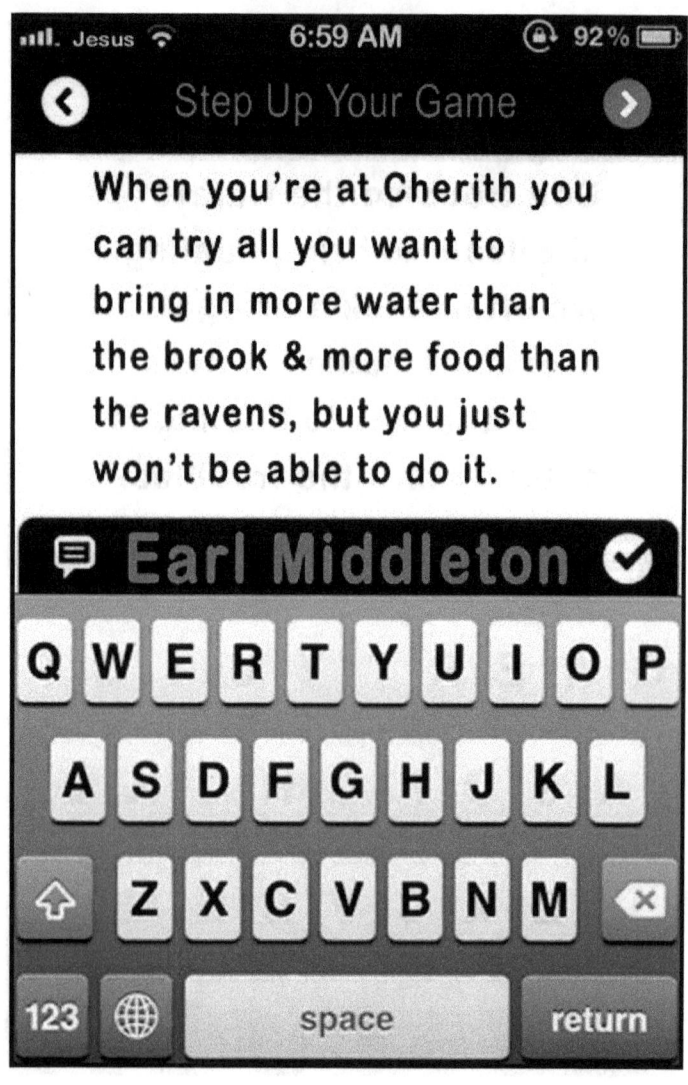

When you're at Cherith you can try all you want to bring in more water than the brook & more food than the ravens, but you just won't be able to do it.

— Earl Middleton

# December 2

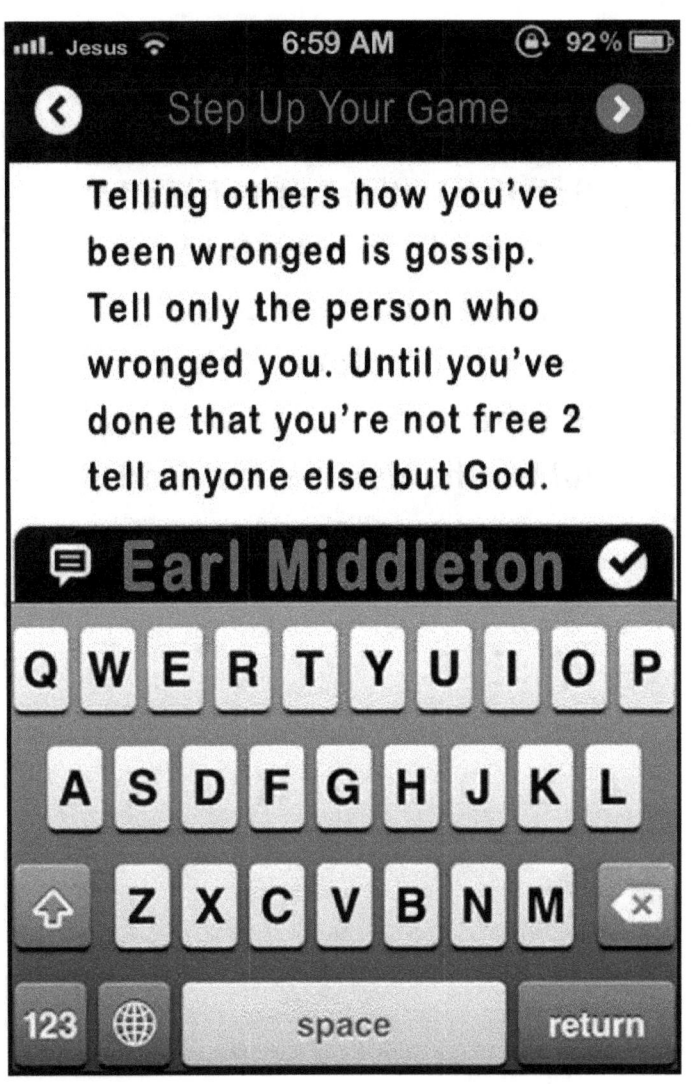

# December 3

## Step Up Your Game

Spiritual athletes refuse to contribute to a culture of blame by blaming their failures on others. Blame is a behavior of powerless folks who don't know God.

— Earl Middleton

# December 4

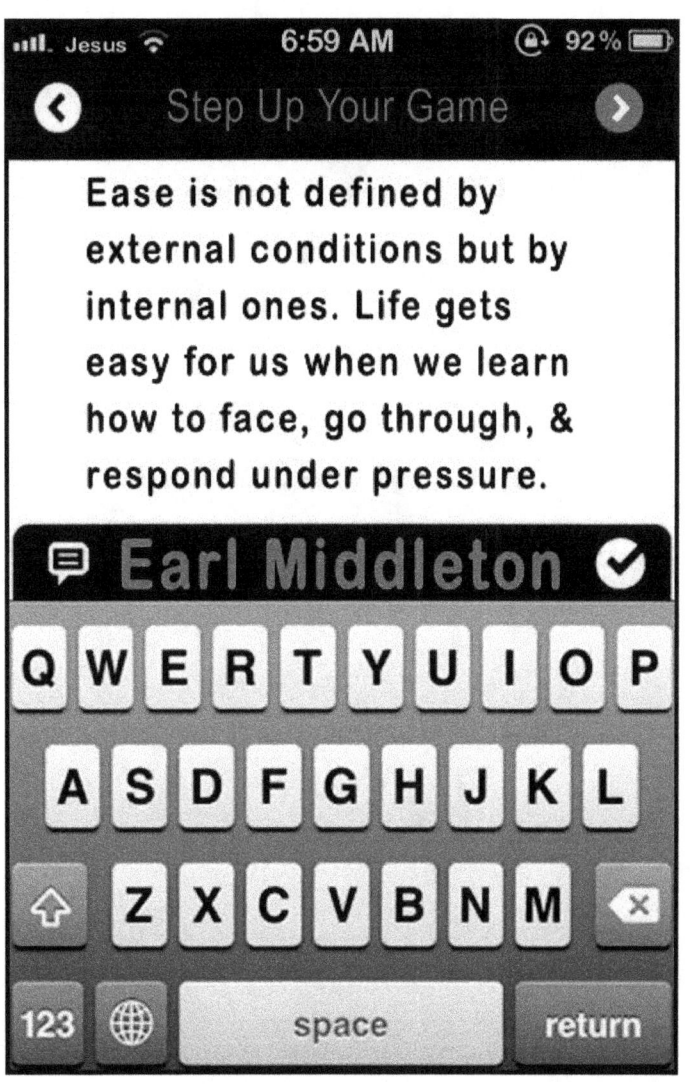

> Ease is not defined by external conditions but by internal ones. Life gets easy for us when we learn how to face, go through, & respond under pressure.

# December 5

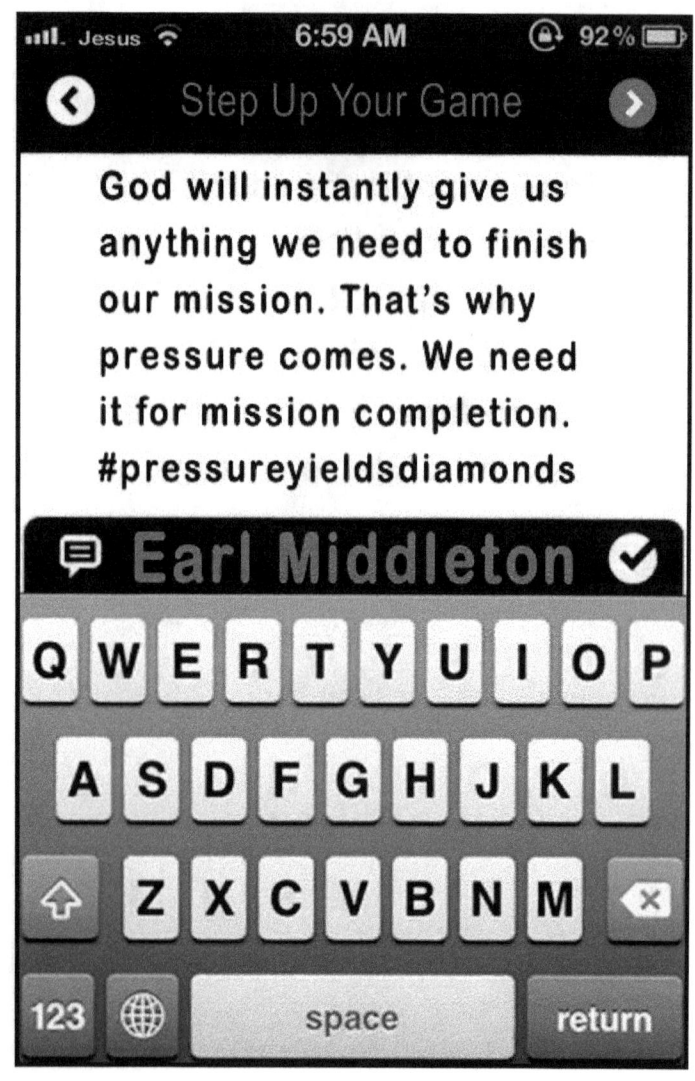

# December 6

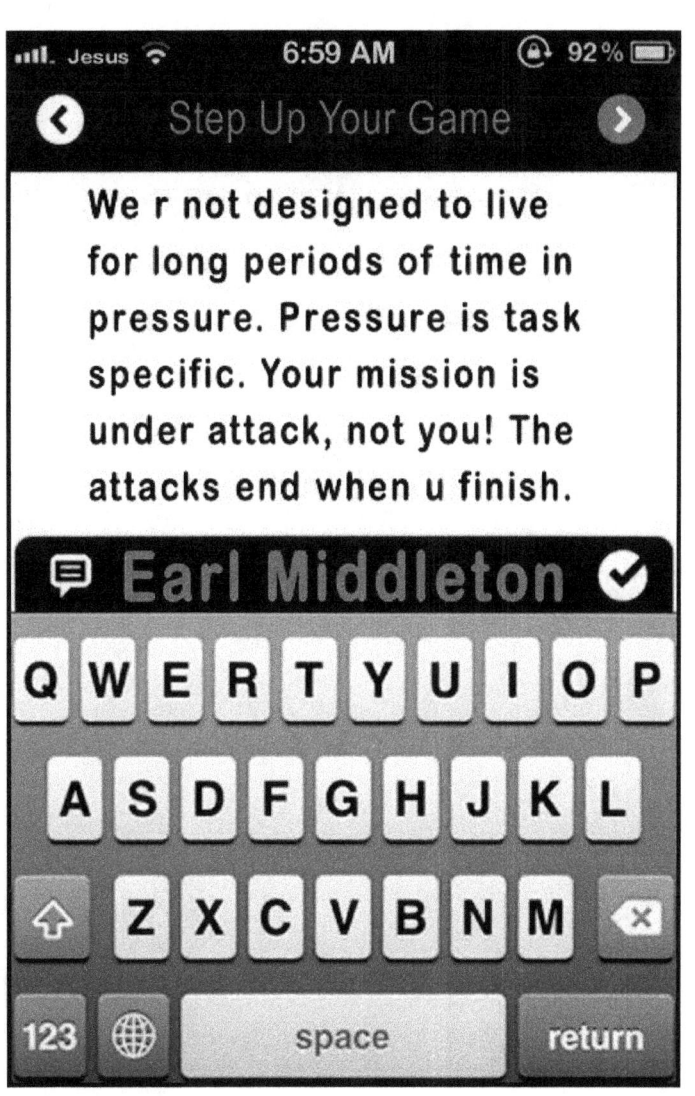

# December 7

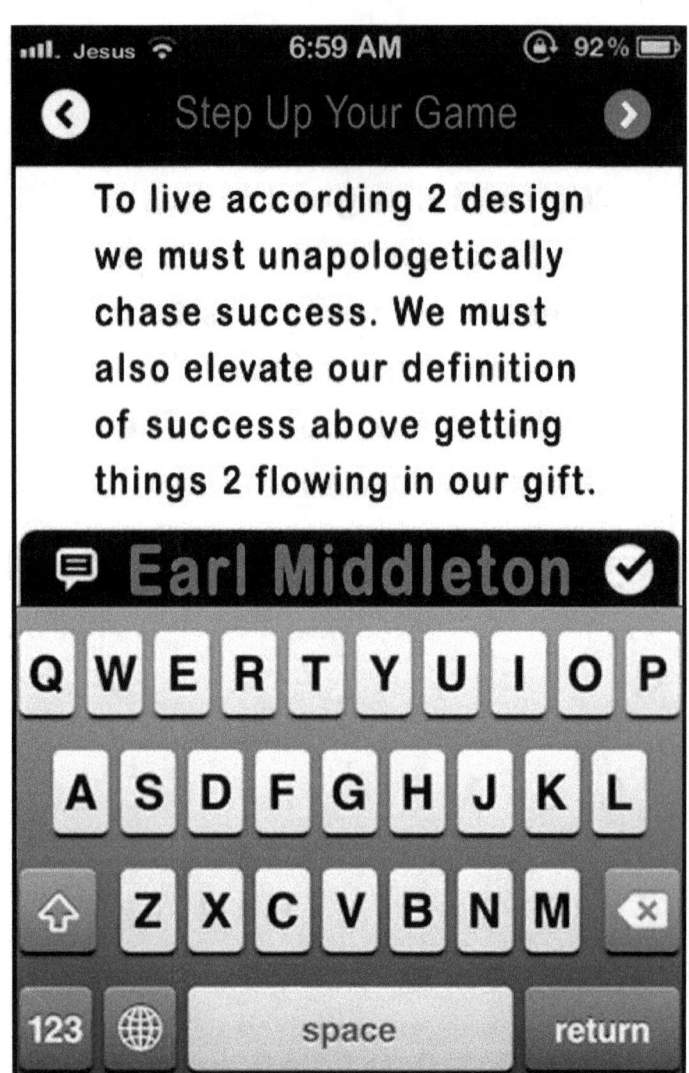

To live according 2 design we must unapologetically chase success. We must also elevate our definition of success above getting things 2 flowing in our gift.

# December 8

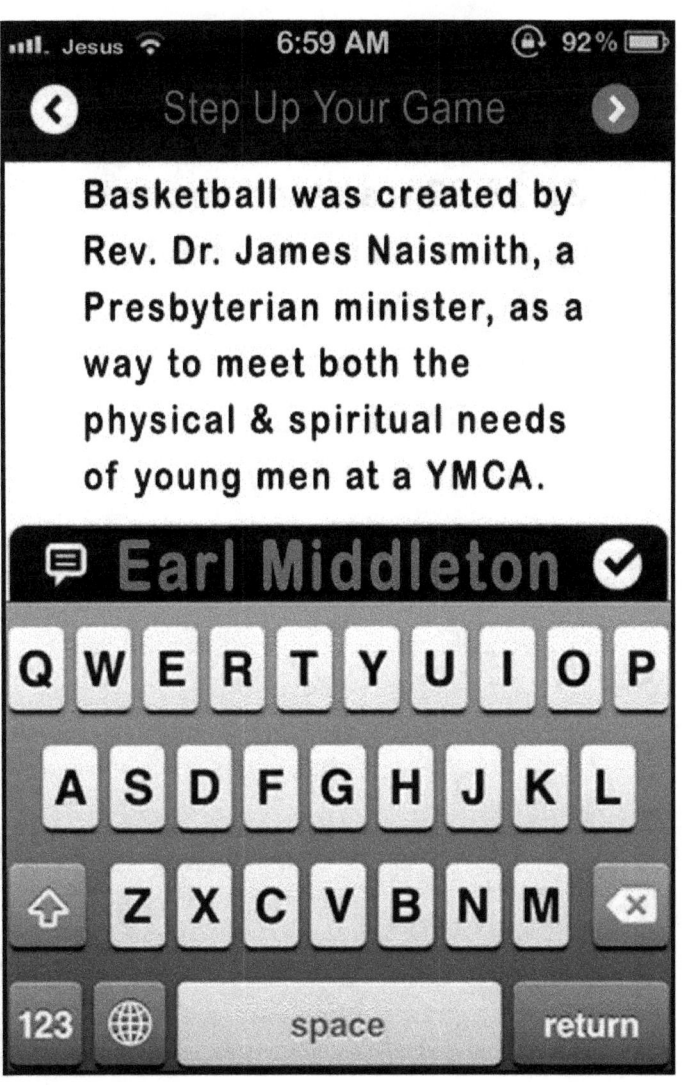

# December 9

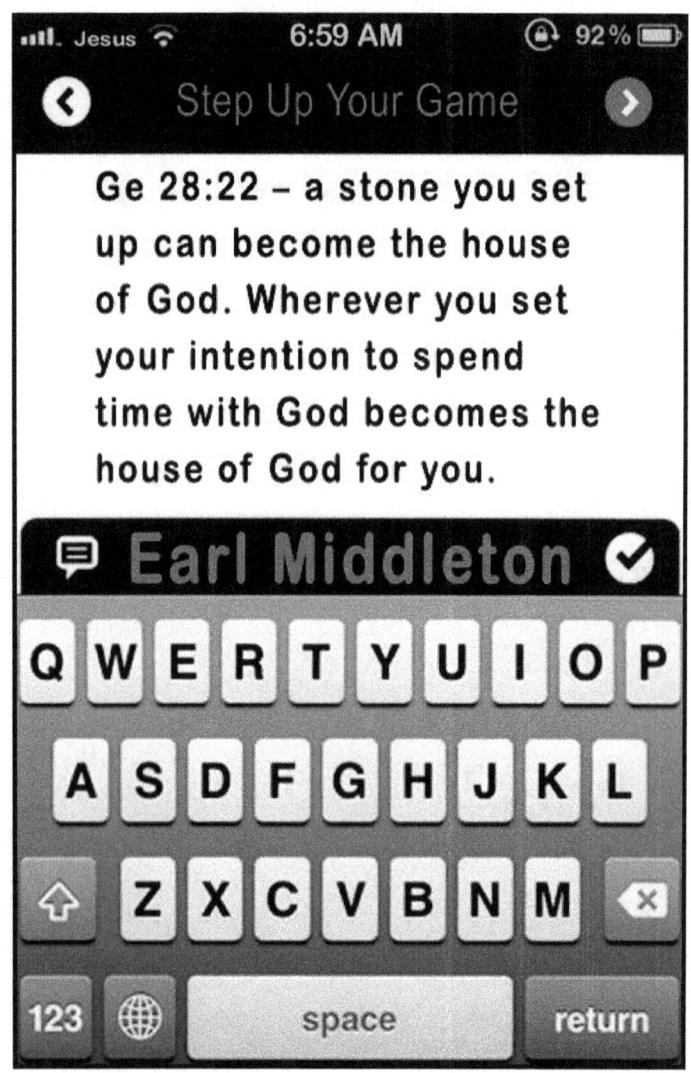

Ge 28:22 – a stone you set up can become the house of God. Wherever you set your intention to spend time with God becomes the house of God for you.

Earl Middleton

# December 10

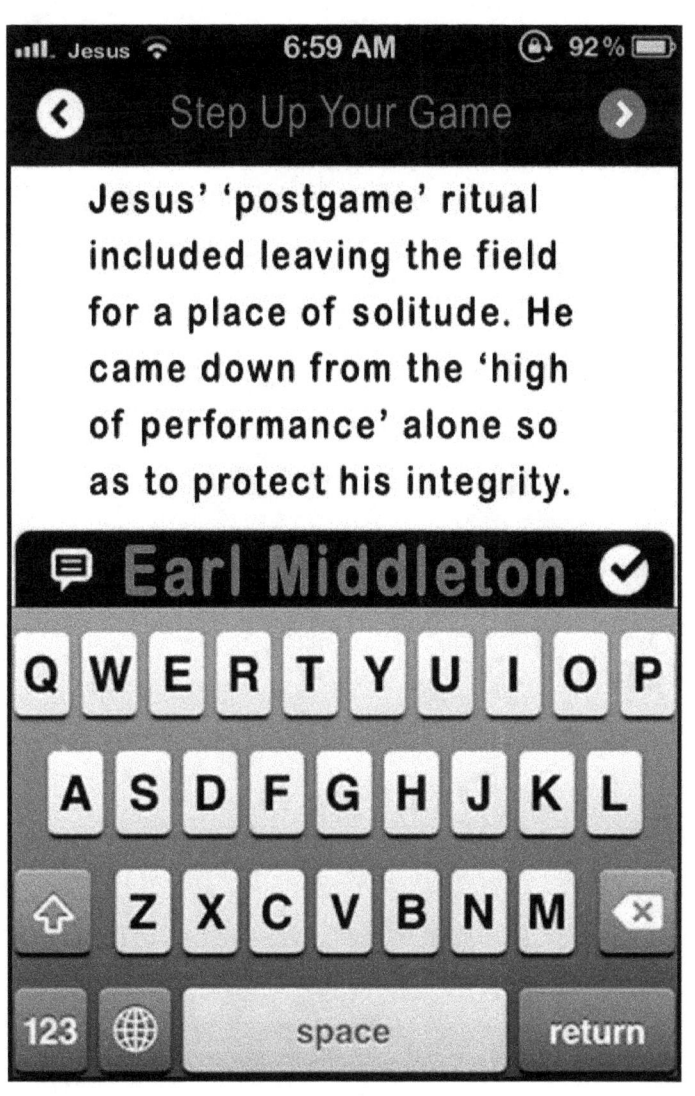

# December 11

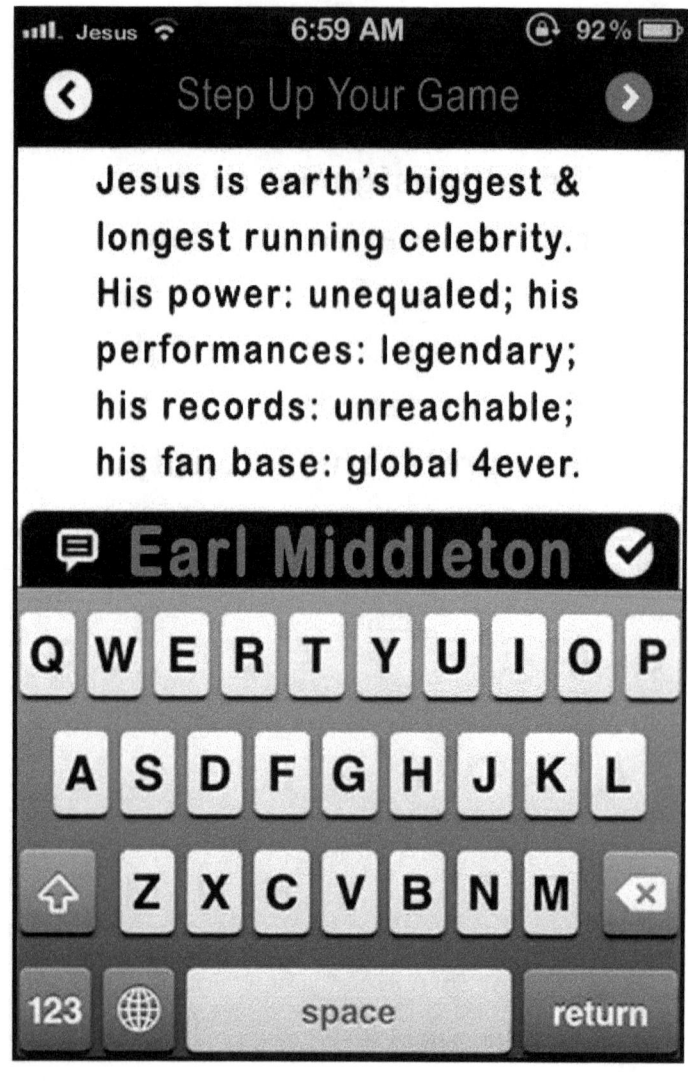

# December 12

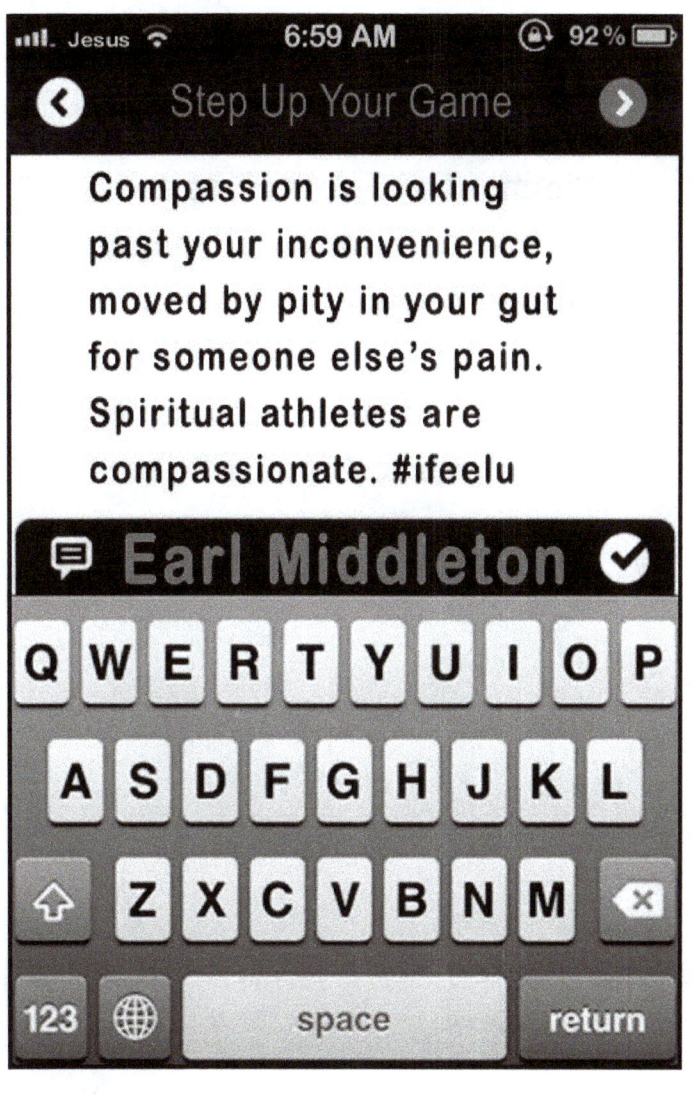

# December 13

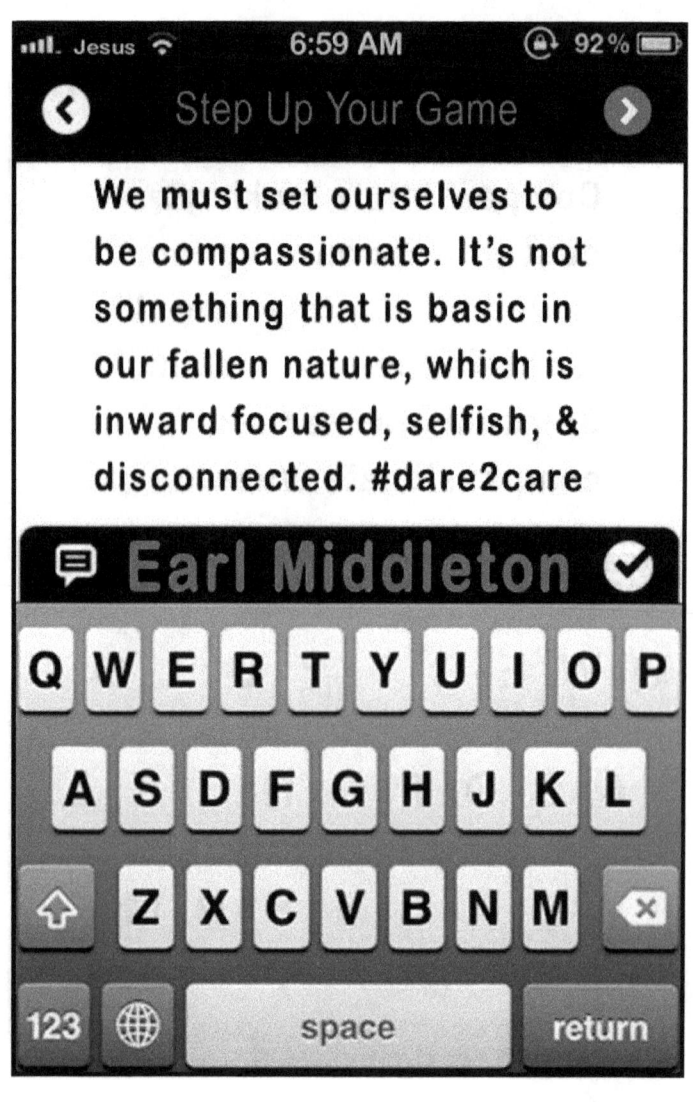

> We must set ourselves to be compassionate. It's not something that is basic in our fallen nature, which is inward focused, selfish, & disconnected. #dare2care

# December 14

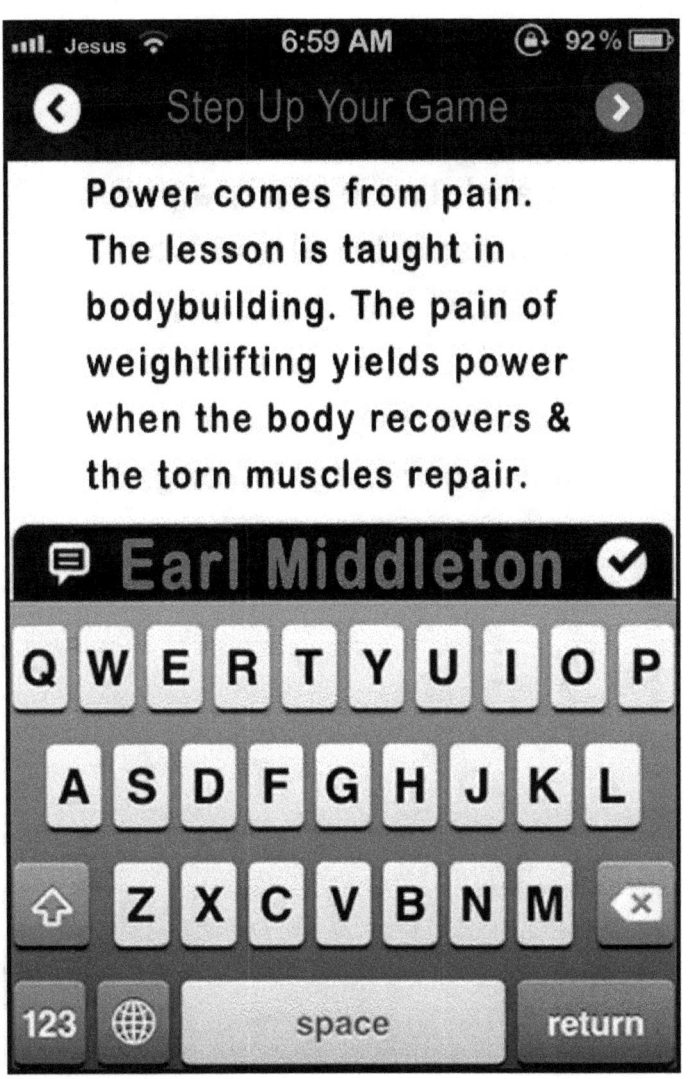

Power comes from pain. The lesson is taught in bodybuilding. The pain of weightlifting yields power when the body recovers & the torn muscles repair.

— Earl Middleton

# December 15

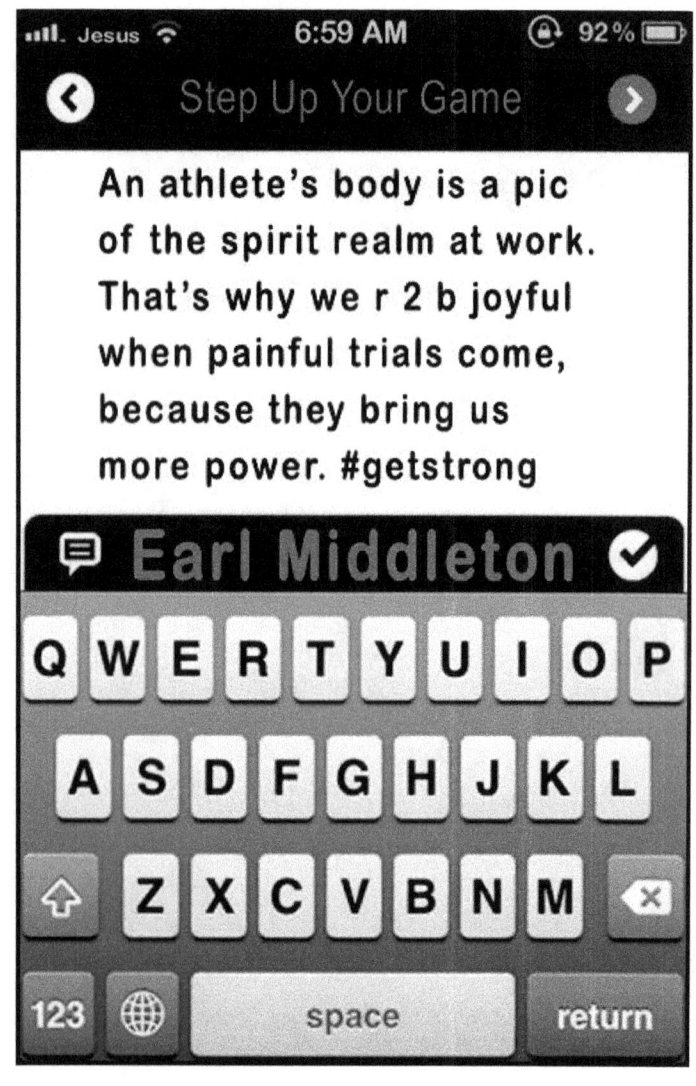

# December 16

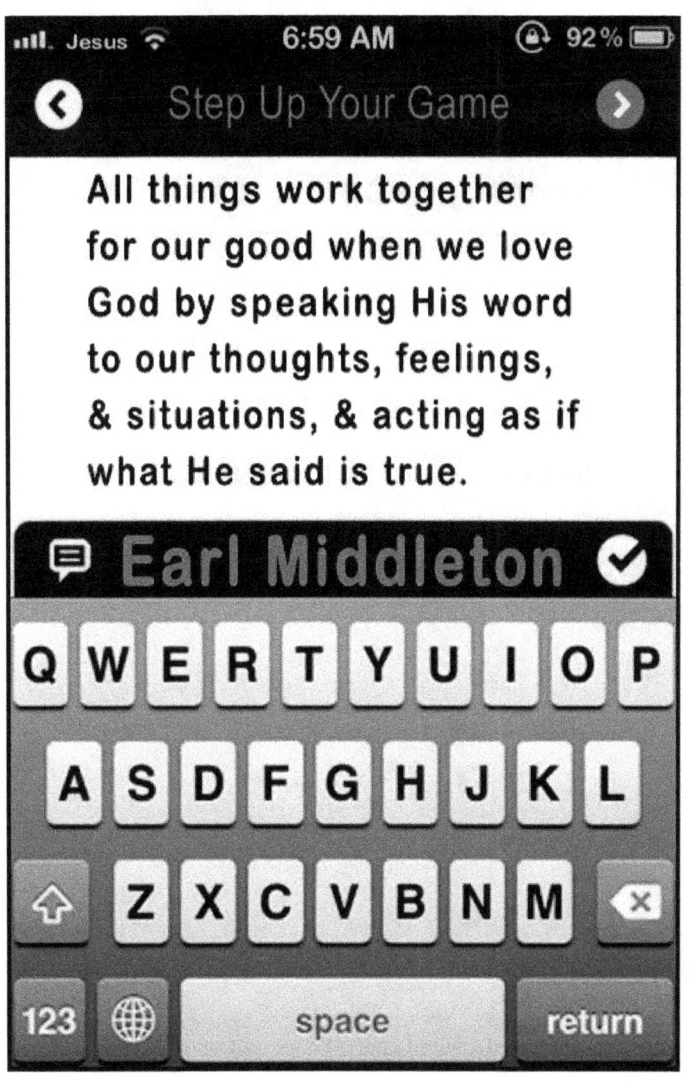

# December 17

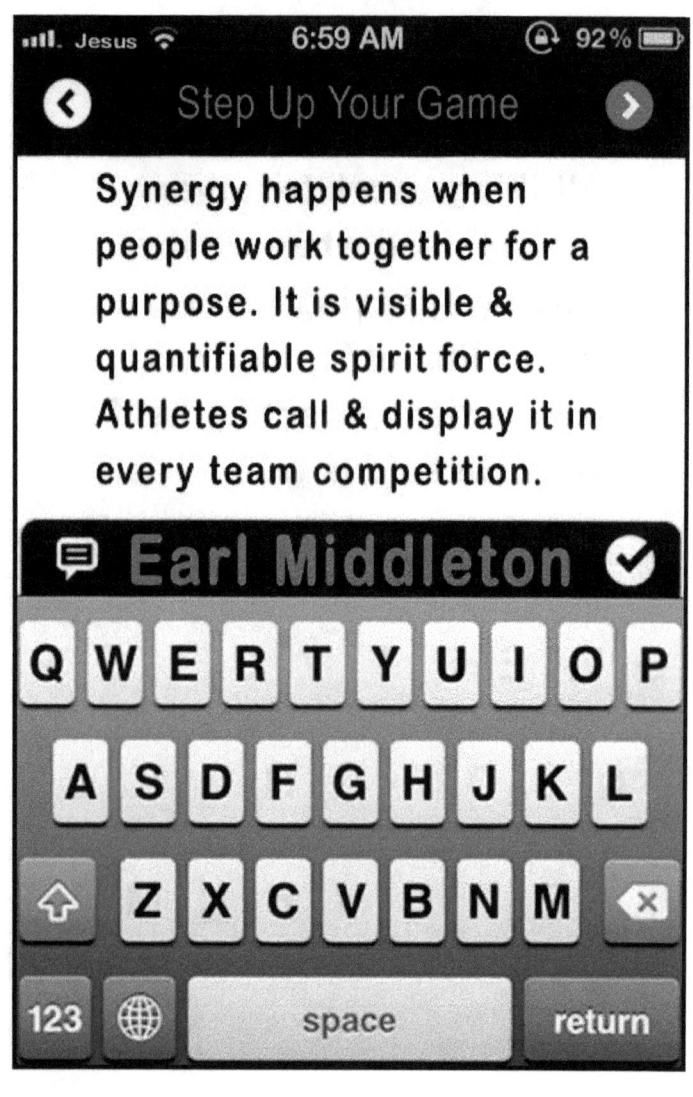

# December 18

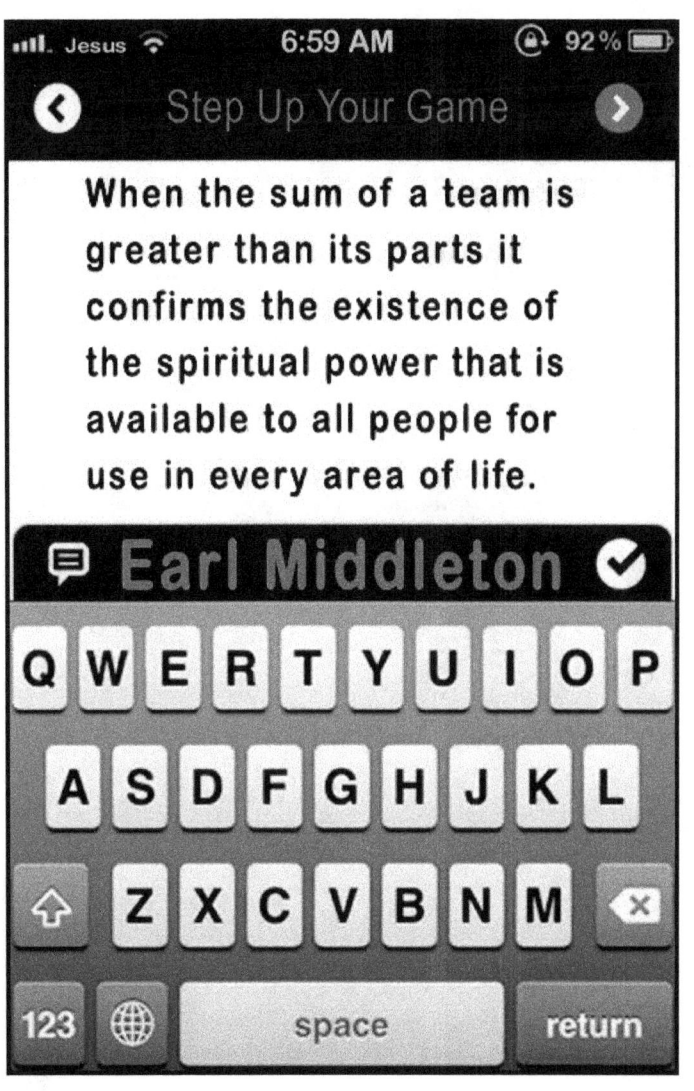

When the sum of a team is greater than its parts it confirms the existence of the spiritual power that is available to all people for use in every area of life.

**Earl Middleton**

# December 19

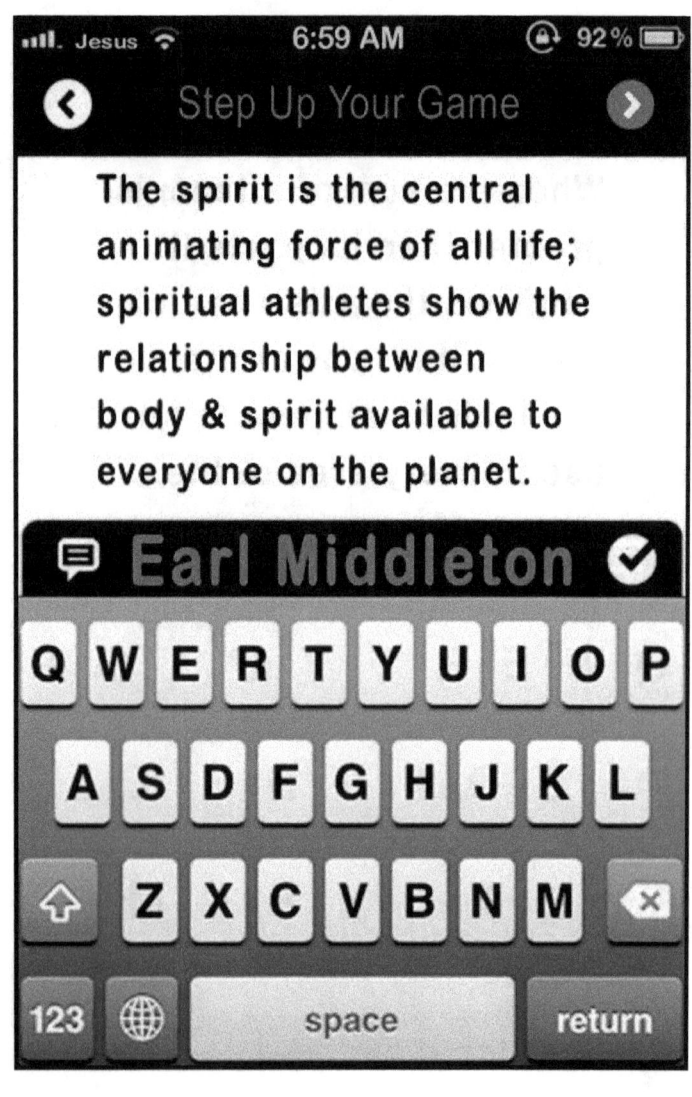

The spirit is the central animating force of all life; spiritual athletes show the relationship between body & spirit available to everyone on the planet.

Earl Middleton

# December 20

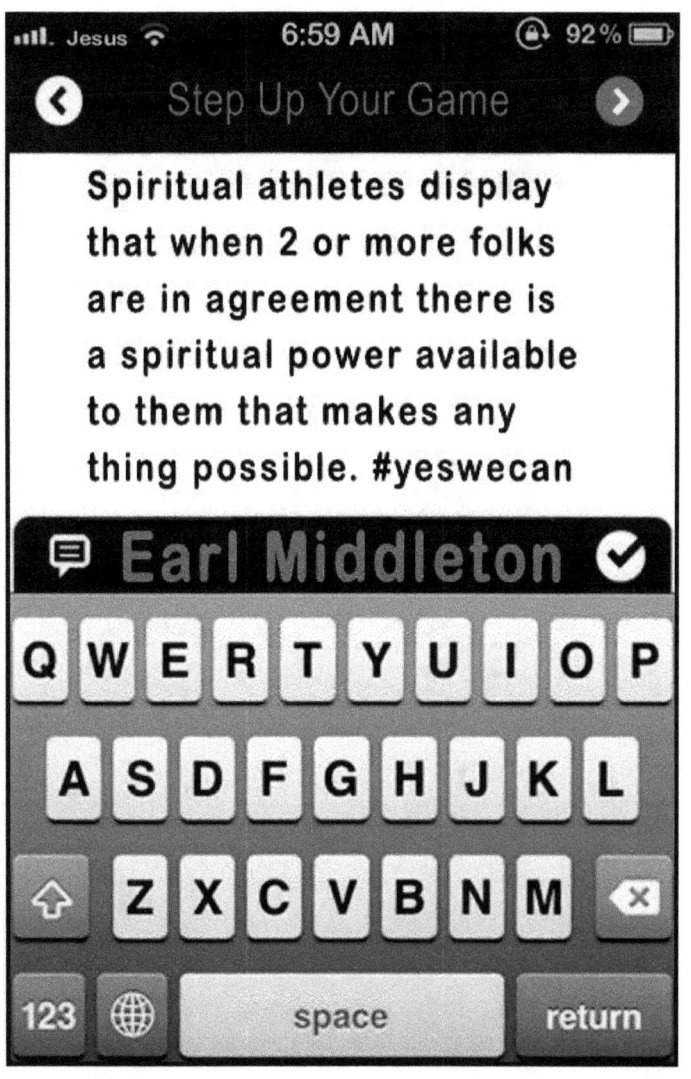

# December 21

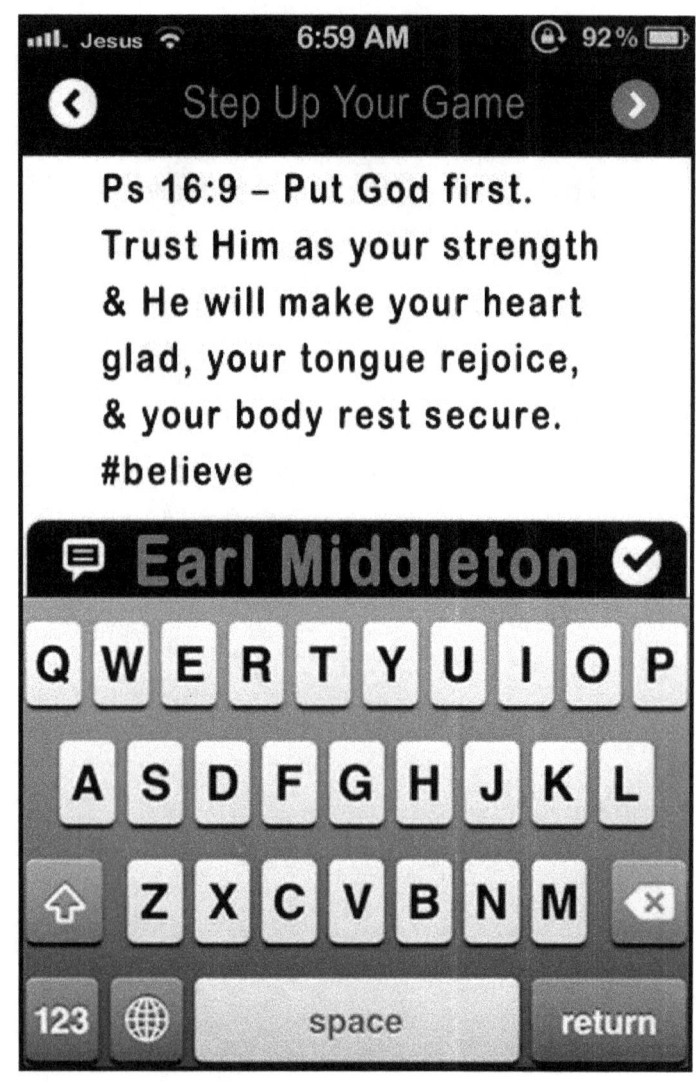

# December 22

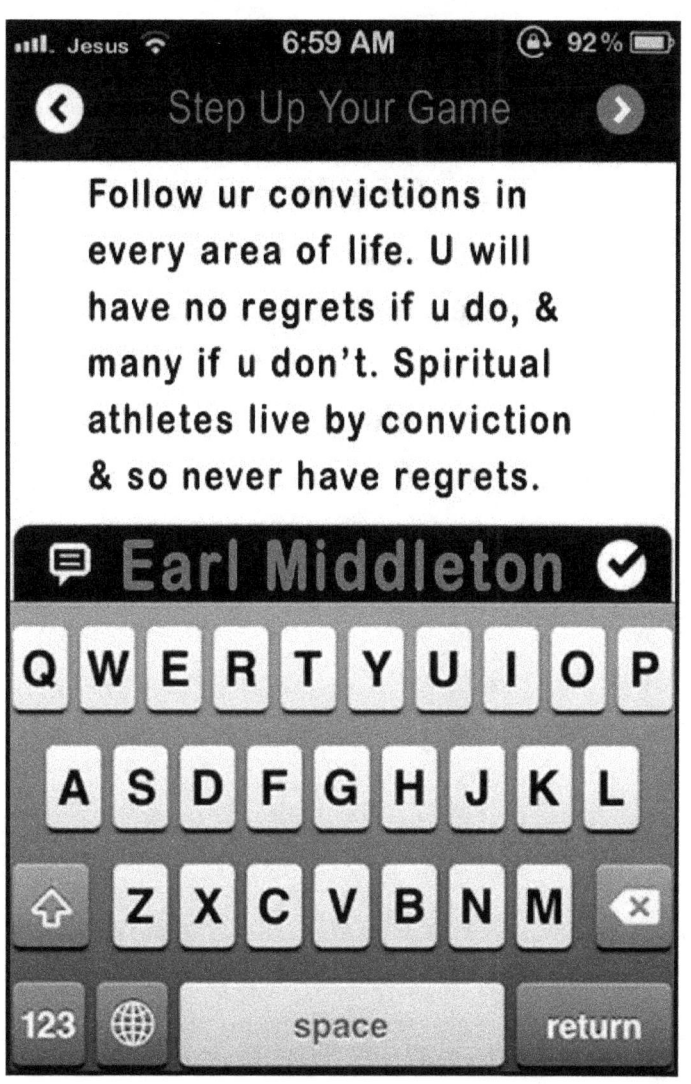

## Step Up Your Game

Follow ur convictions in every area of life. U will have no regrets if u do, & many if u don't. Spiritual athletes live by conviction & so never have regrets.

**Earl Middleton**

# December 23

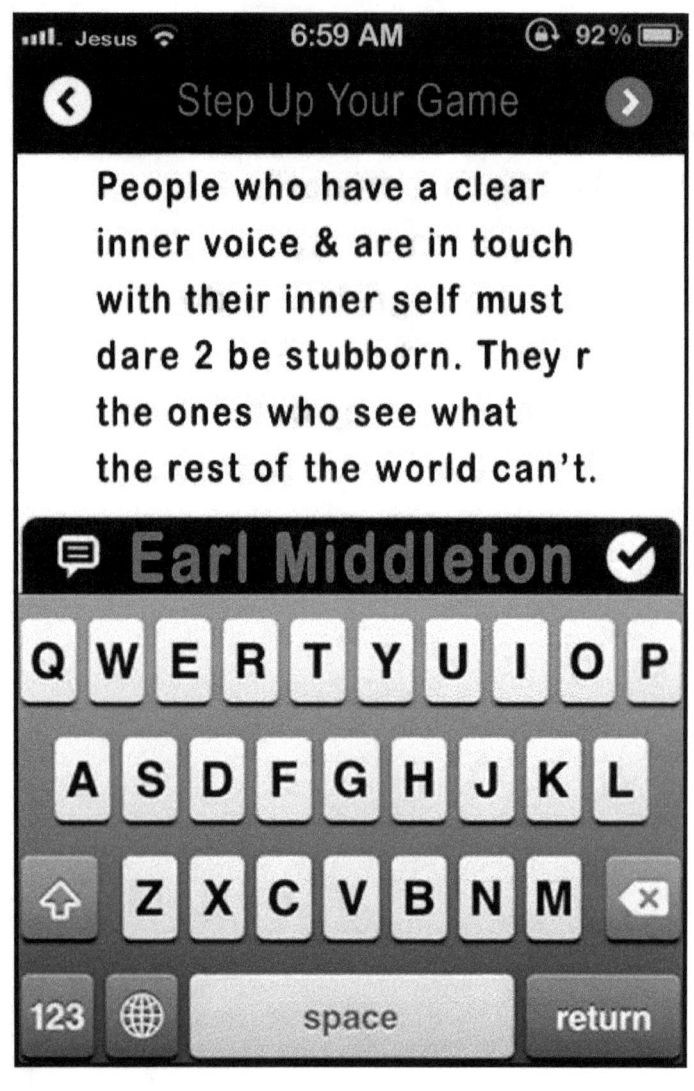

# December 24

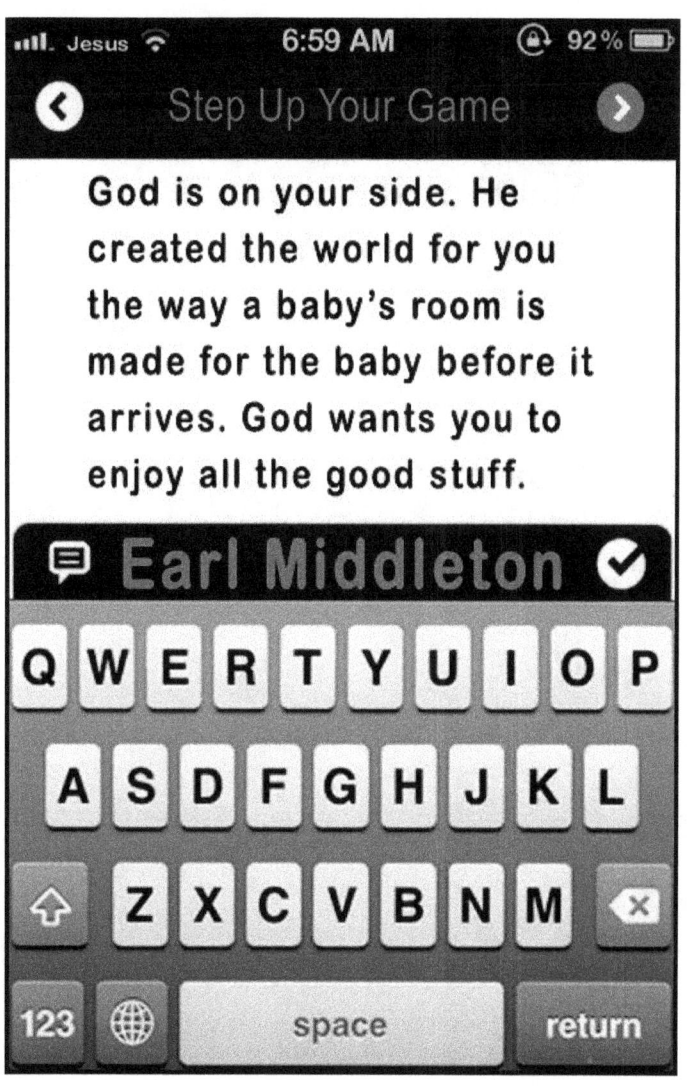

# December 25

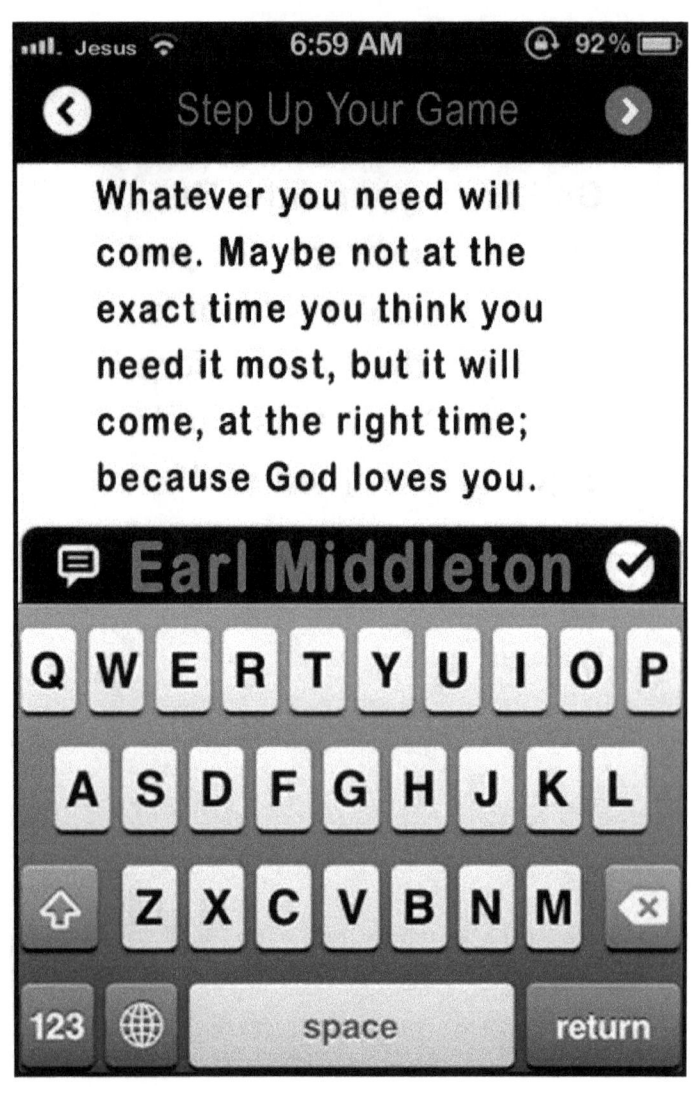

# December 26

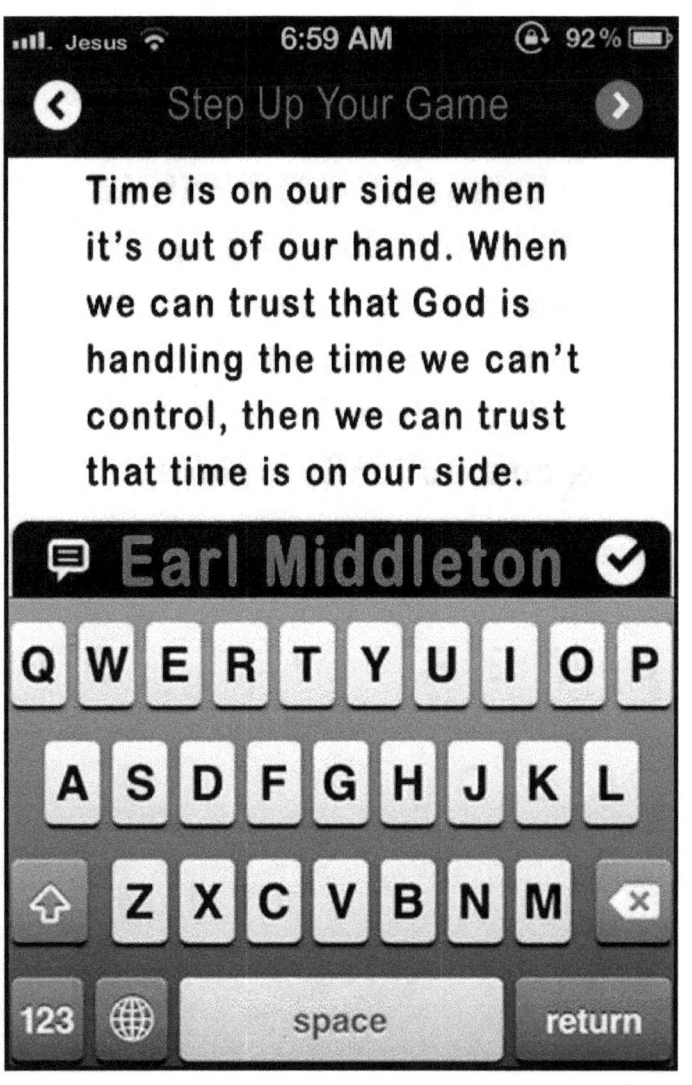

# December 27

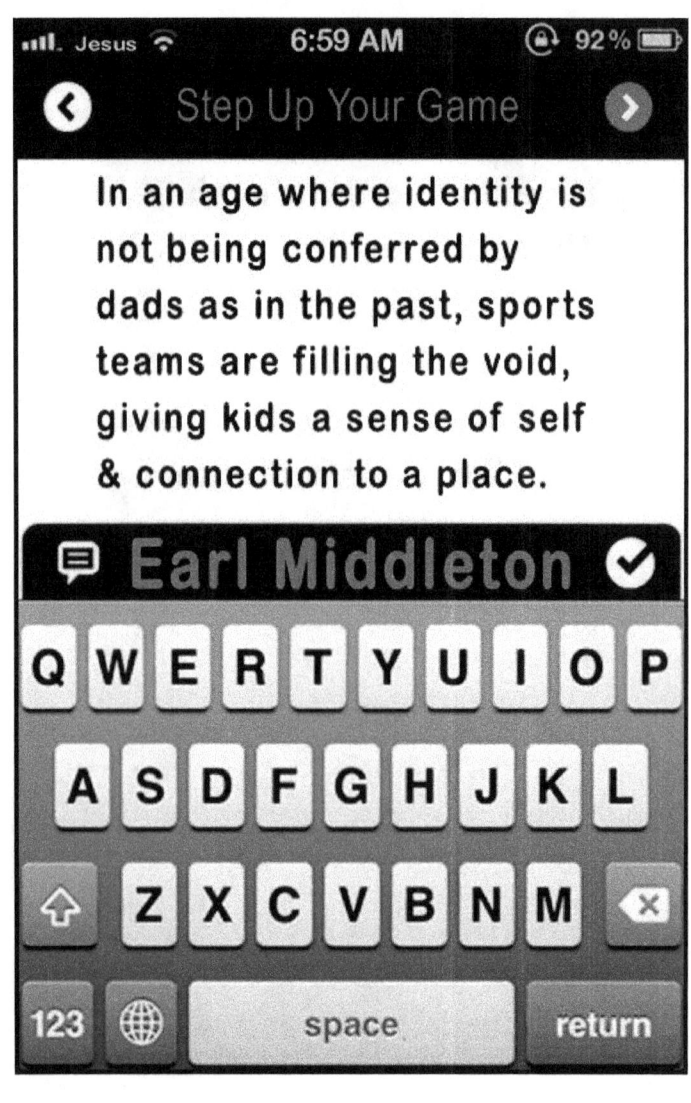

**Step Up Your Game**

In an age where identity is not being conferred by dads as in the past, sports teams are filling the void, giving kids a sense of self & connection to a place.

— Earl Middleton

## December 28

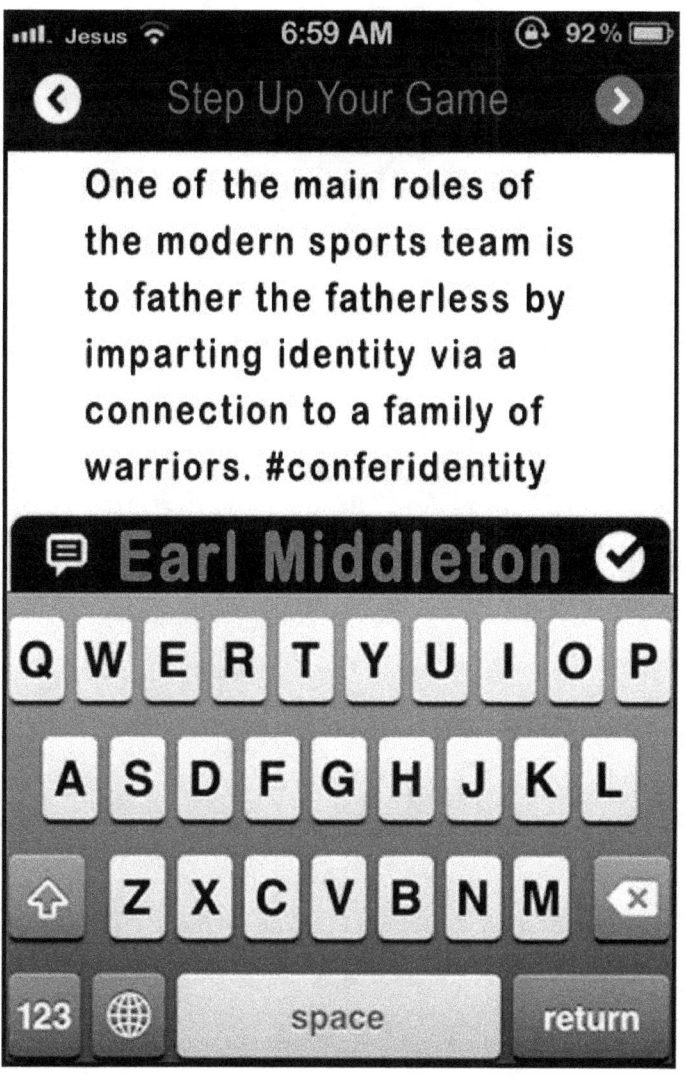

One of the main roles of the modern sports team is to father the fatherless by imparting identity via a connection to a family of warriors. #conferidentity

# December 29

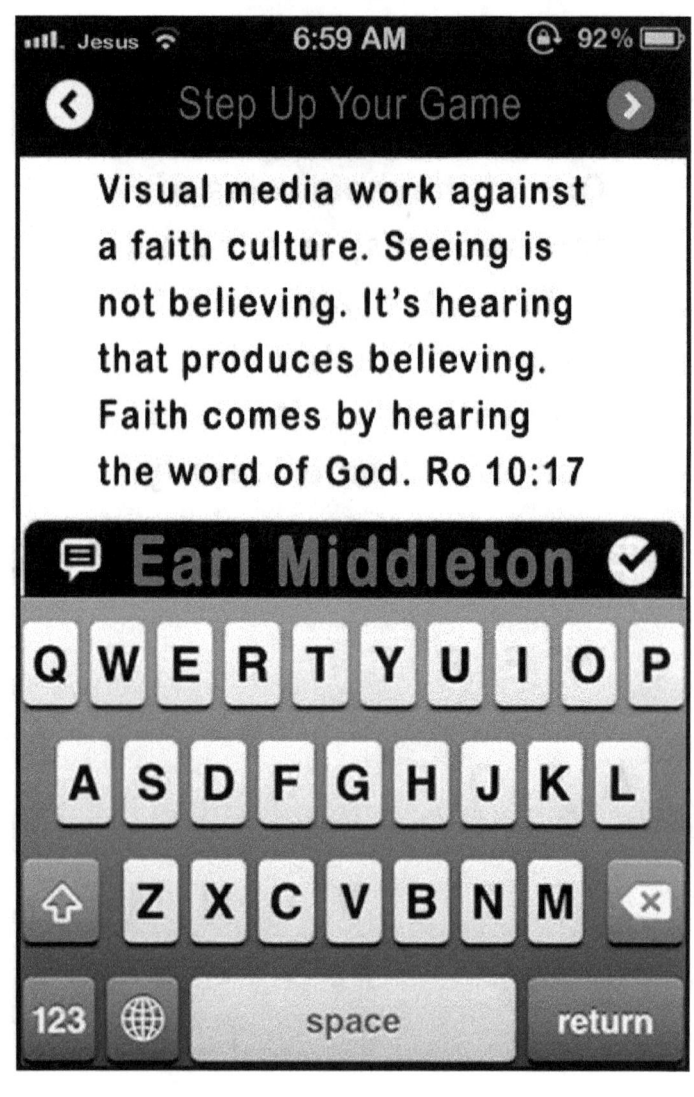

**Step Up Your Game**

Visual media work against a faith culture. Seeing is not believing. It's hearing that produces believing. Faith comes by hearing the word of God. Ro 10:17

Earl Middleton

# December 30

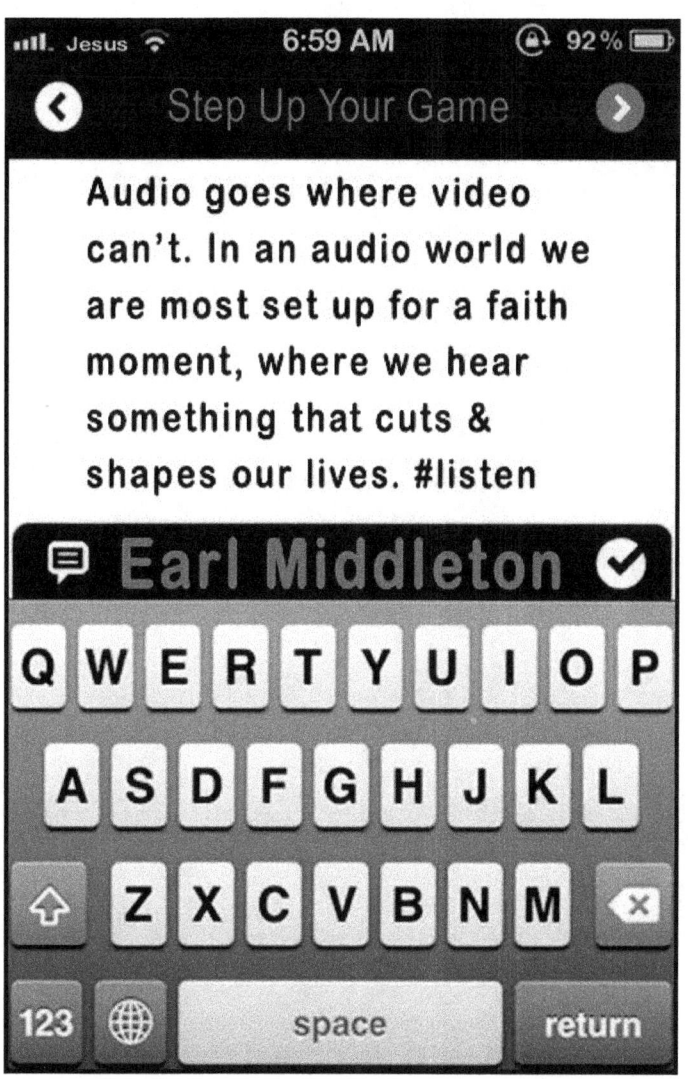

# December 31

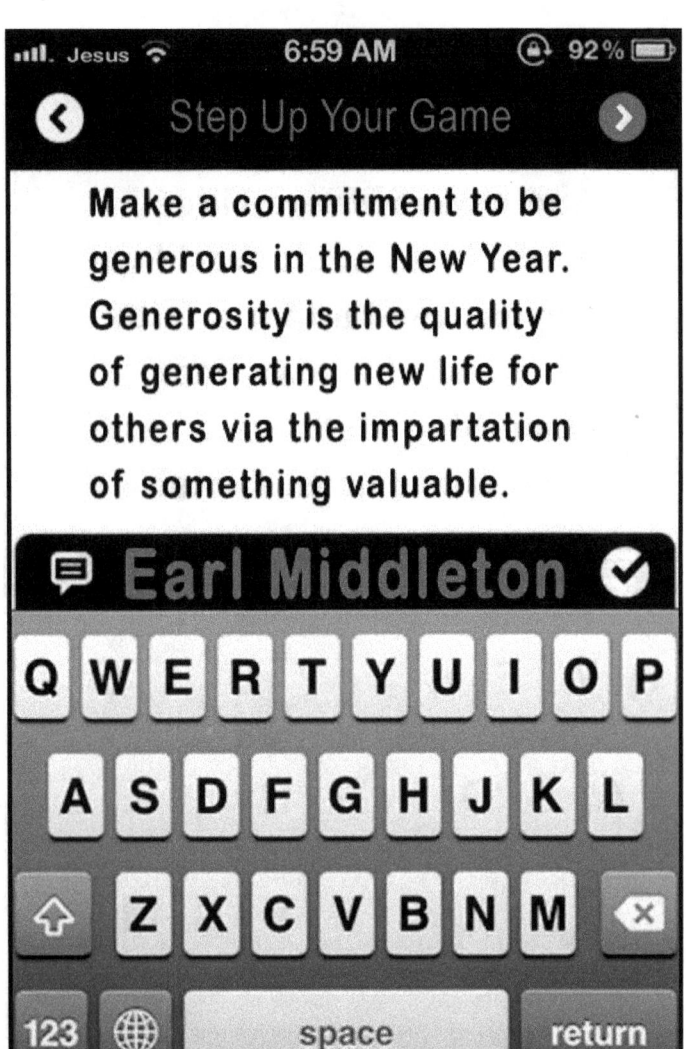

**Step Up Your Game**

Make a commitment to be generous in the New Year. Generosity is the quality of generating new life for others via the impartation of something valuable.

Earl Middleton

# About the Author

**I often felt awkward in a church setting so I quit the pastorate after 22 years. I'm done with religion. But not with God.** After earning a M.Div. degree from Princeton Theological Seminary I was voted out of two pastorates because I've never gotten along with stuffy parishioners and trampled over their traditions at every opportunity. I'm an outgoing, charismatic orator who inspires confidence and conviction in my audiences, but I love being alone in crowds. That's where I was, in my minivan on a crowded street, when I heard the audible voice of God tell me to WRITE! Today I'm the author of a growing catalog of fiction and non-fiction titles, many of them illustrating the power of God's G.R.A.C.E. to heal and restore souls damaged by any form of parental rejection, abandonment, abuse, or neglect. Connect with me at:

- ❖ earl@spiritualathletes.com (e-mail me)
- ❖ @spiritualathlet (you should follow me)
- ❖ spiritualathletes.com (visit my site)

# Other books by Earl Middleton

*In a heart stopping romp through the streets of New York City, **The AntiChrist Was Conceived in Queens** manages to carve out a new genre, the BUFF novel (biblical urban faith fantasy), while following the transformation of Rain Reynolds, a New York City public school legend with real angel's blood in his veins, and Lisa Vickers, a former D.C. anchorwoman turned pastor with a secret, from immortal basketball icon and crack news investigator to enlightened spiritual emissaries and perhaps their kind's last real hope to find a place in heaven. And as usual the way to enlightenment goes straight through the dark.

***Yo, Pastor!*** is a spiritual media solution providing bible-based edutainment designed to both feed your faith and satisfy your soul. Move over Ann Landers, Yo, Pastor! is in the house.

This book delivers 70 thorny questions about current life dilemmas from people just like yourself, and their controversial biblical answers, for your enjoyment and spiritual edification.

**\*F**ather Dowling meets Shaft in the tony Newark suburb of Belton, NJ, in this quirky, unique murder mystery. Rev. Dr. Tony Hook loves preaching, but hates pastoring. Now an old flame is trying to pin a murder on him. Can he get himself ***Off the Hook***?

*A quick, engaging read. Hook makes a terrific main character—as both a pastor and as an amateur detective.*
~ Diane Reverand, former Senior Vice President, *HarperCollins*

www.ingramcontent.com/pod-product-compliance
Lightning Source LLC
Chambersburg PA
CBHW070551100426
42744CB00006B/257